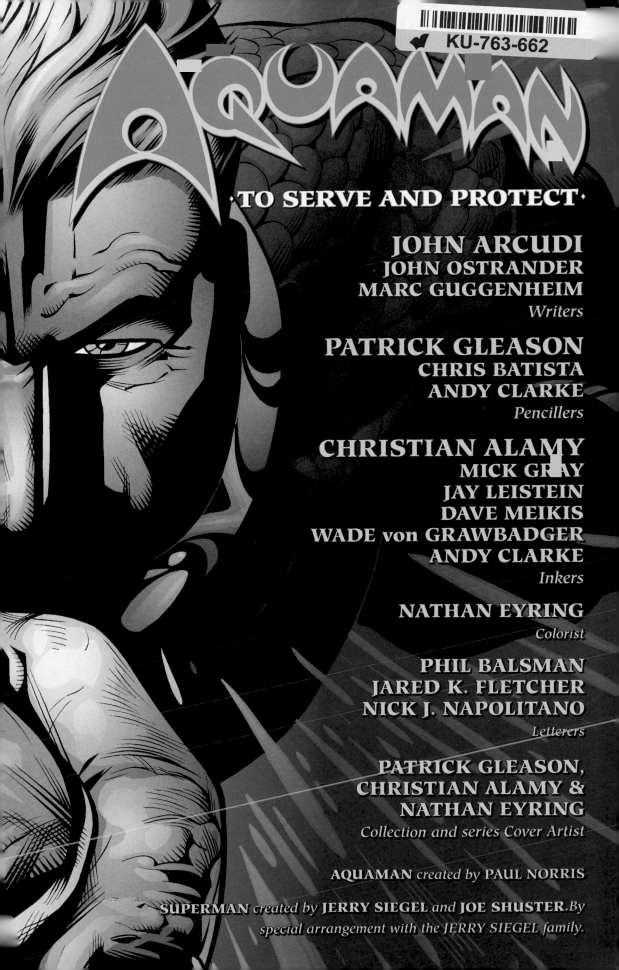

AQUAMAN

·TO SERVE AND PROTECT·

JOHN ARCUDI
JOHN OSTRANDER
MARC GUGGENHEIM
Writers

PATRICK GLEASON
CHRIS BATISTA
ANDY CLARKE
Pencillers

CHRISTIAN ALAMY
MICK GRAY
JAY LEISTEIN
DAVE MEIKIS
WADE von GRAWBADGER
ANDY CLARKE
Inkers

NATHAN EYRING
Colorist

PHIL BALSMAN
JARED K. FLETCHER
NICK J. NAPOLITANO
Letterers

PATRICK GLEASON,
CHRISTIAN ALAMY &
NATHAN EYRING
Collection and series Cover Artist

AQUAMAN *created by* PAUL NORRIS

SUPERMAN *created by* **JERRY SIEGEL** *and* **JOE SHUSTER.***By special arrangement with the JERRY SIEGEL family.*

PETER J. TOMASI Editor – Original Series
HARVEY RICHARDS Assistant Editor – Original Series
JEB WOODARD Group Editor – Collected Editions
STEVE COOK Design Director – Books
CURTIS KING JR. Publication Design

BOB HARRAS Senior VP – Editor-in-Chief, DC Comics

DIANE NELSON President
DAN DIDIO AND JIM LEE Co-Publishers
GEOFF JOHNS Chief Creative Officer
AMIT DESAI Senior VP – Marketing & Global Franchise Management
NAIRI GARDINER Senior VP – Finance
SAM ADES VP – Digital Marketing
BOBBIE CHASE VP – Talent Development
MARK CHIARELLO Senior VP – Art, Design & Collected Editions
JOHN CUNNINGHAM VP – Content Strategy
ANNE DEPIES VP – Strategy Planning & Reporting
DON FALLETTI VP – Manufacturing Operations
LAWRENCE GANEM VP – Editorial Administration & Talent Relations
ALISON GILL Senior VP – Manufacturing & Operations
HANK KANALZ Senior VP – Editorial Strategy & Administration
JAY KOGAN VP – Legal Affairs
DEREK MADDALENA Senior VP – Sales & Business Development
JACK MAHAN VP – Business Affairs

DAN MIRON VP – Sales Planning & Trade Development
NICK NAPOLITANO VP – Manufacturing Administration
CAROL ROEDER VP – Marketing
EDDIE SCANNELL VP – Mass Account & Digital Sales
COURTNEY SIMMONS Senior VP – Publicity & Communications
JIM (SKI) SOKOLOWSKI VP – Comic Book Specialty & Newsstand Sales
SANDY YI Senior VP – Global Franchise Management

AQUAMAN: TO SERVE AND PROTECT

Published by DC Comics. Compilation and all new material Copyright © 2016
DC Comics. All Rights Reserved. Originally published in single magazine form
in AQUAMAN 23-31. Copyright © 2004, 2005 DC Comics. All Rights Reserved.
All characters, their distinctive likenesses and related elements featured in this
publication are trademarks of DC Comics. The stories, characters and incidents
featured in this publication are entirely fictional. DC Comics does not read or
accept unsolicited submissions of ideas, stories or artwork.

DC Comics, 2900 West Alameda Ave., Burbank, CA 91505
Printed by RR Donnelley, Owensville, MO, USA. 6/10/16. First Printing.
ISBN: 978-1-4012-6382-9

Library of Congress Cataloging-in-Publication Data is available.

PEFC Certified
Printed on paper from
sustainably managed
forests and controlled
sources
PEFC/29-31-75   www.pefc.org

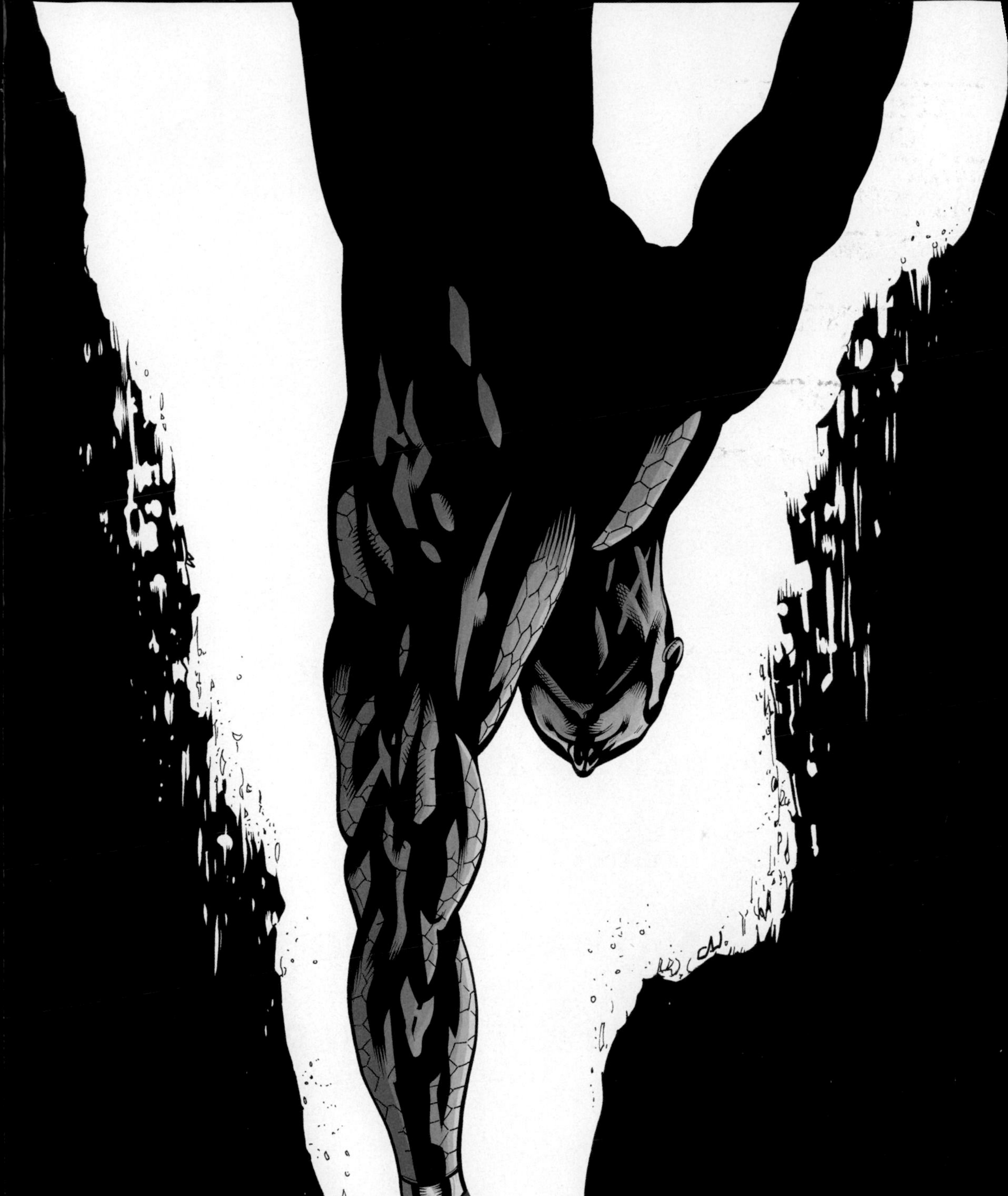

LOOT

JOHN OSTRANDER
Writer

CHRIS BATISTA
Penciller

DAVE MEIKIS
Inker

NATHAN EYRING
Colorist

JARED K. FLETCHER
Letterer

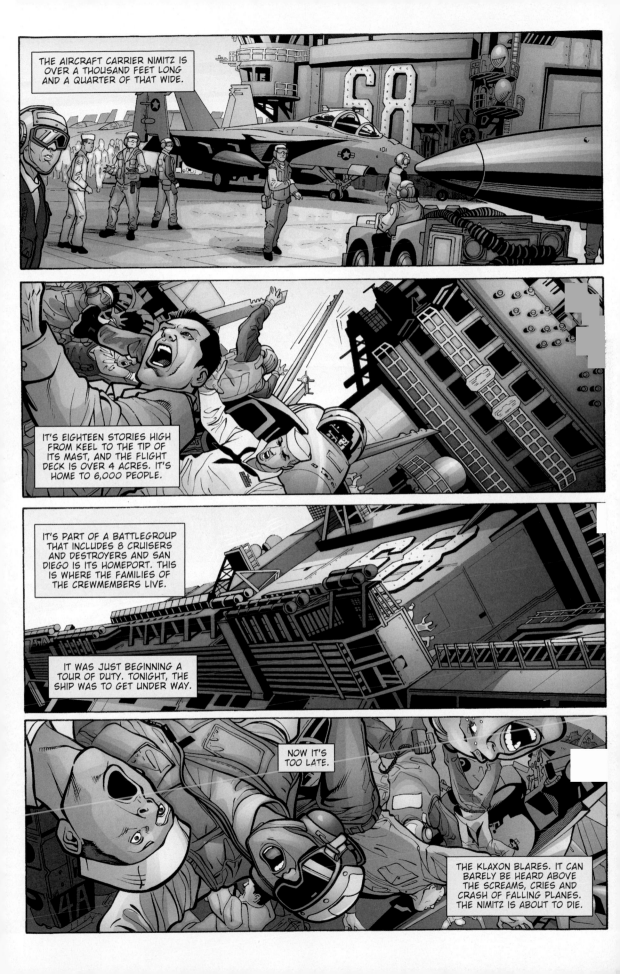

THE AIRCRAFT CARRIER NIMITZ IS OVER A THOUSAND FEET LONG AND A QUARTER OF THAT WIDE.

IT'S EIGHTEEN STORIES HIGH FROM KEEL TO THE TIP OF ITS MAST, AND THE FLIGHT DECK IS OVER 4 ACRES. IT'S HOME TO 6,000 PEOPLE.

IT'S PART OF A BATTLEGROUP THAT INCLUDES 8 CRUISERS AND DESTROYERS AND SAN DIEGO IS ITS HOMEPORT. THIS IS WHERE THE FAMILIES OF THE CREWMEMBERS LIVE.

IT WAS JUST BEGINNING A TOUR OF DUTY. TONIGHT, THE SHIP WAS TO GET UNDER WAY.

NOW IT'S TOO LATE.

THE KLAXON BLARES. IT CAN BARELY BE HEARD ABOVE THE SCREAMS, CRIES AND CRASH OF FALLING PLANES. THE NIMITZ IS ABOUT TO DIE.

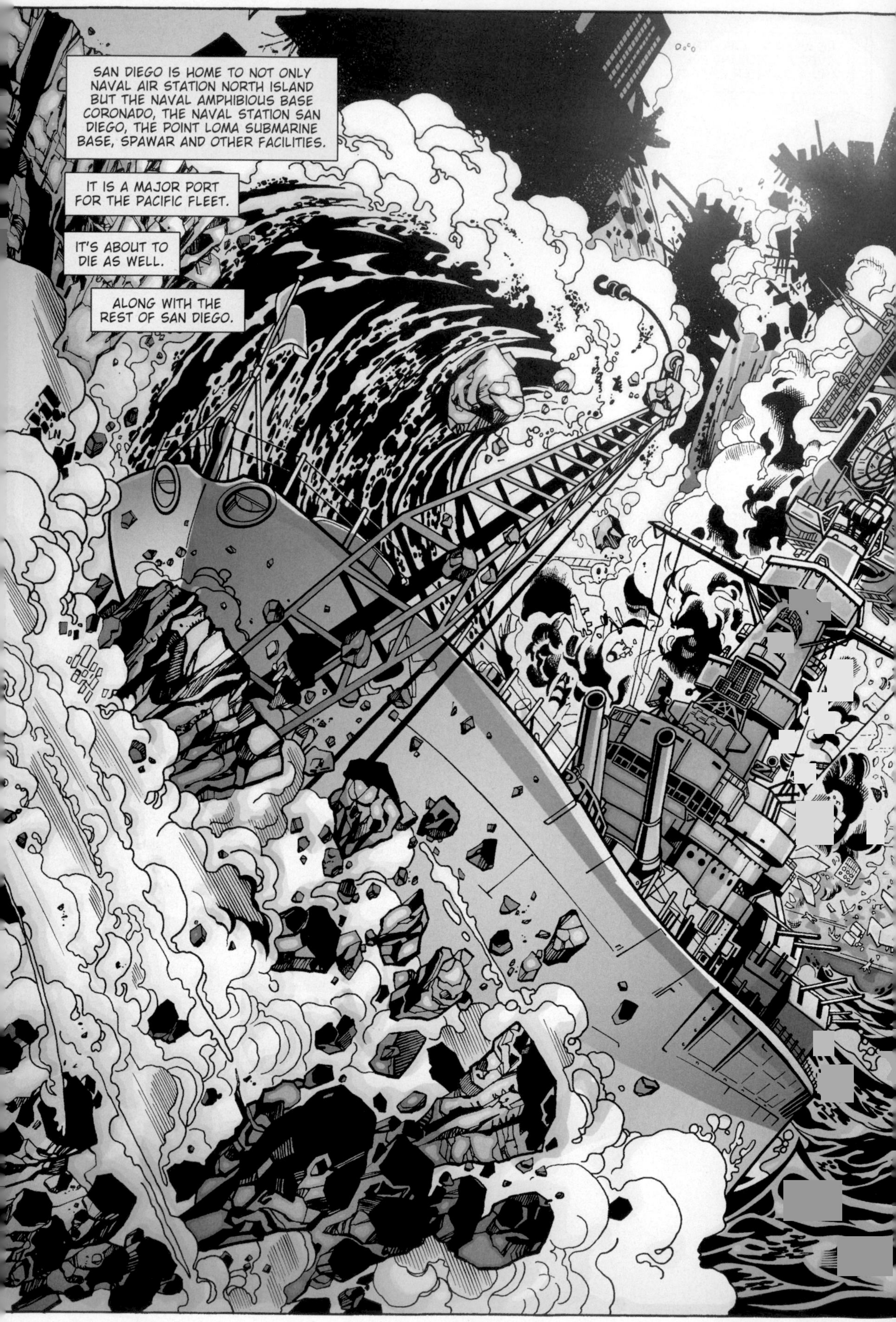
SAN DIEGO IS HOME TO NOT ONLY NAVAL AIR STATION NORTH ISLAND BUT THE NAVAL AMPHIBIOUS BASE CORONADO, THE NAVAL STATION SAN DIEGO, THE POINT LOMA SUBMARINE BASE, SPAWAR AND OTHER FACILITIES.
IT IS A MAJOR PORT FOR THE PACIFIC FLEET.
IT'S ABOUT TO DIE AS WELL.
ALONG WITH THE REST OF SAN DIEGO.

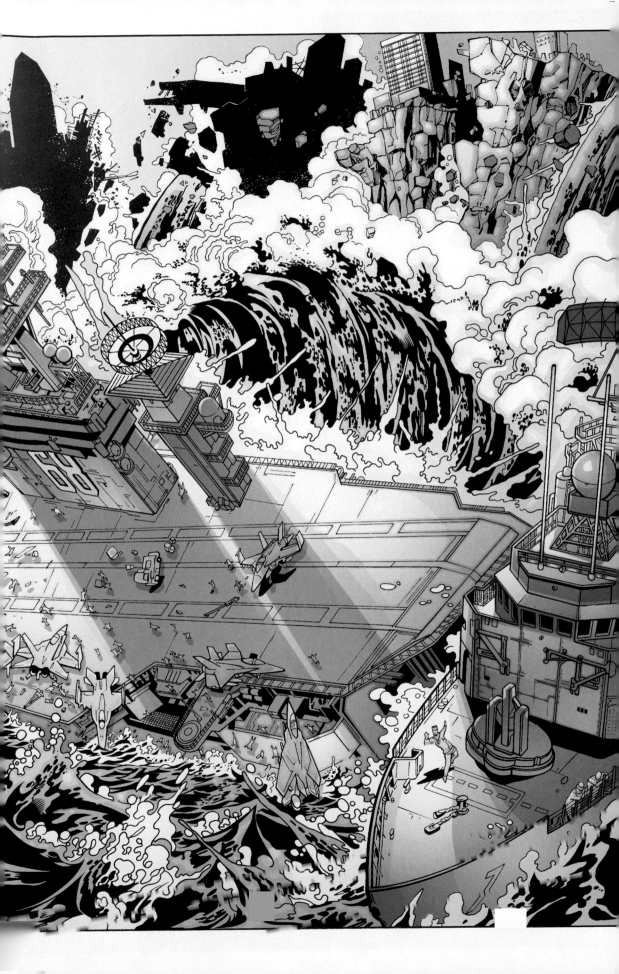

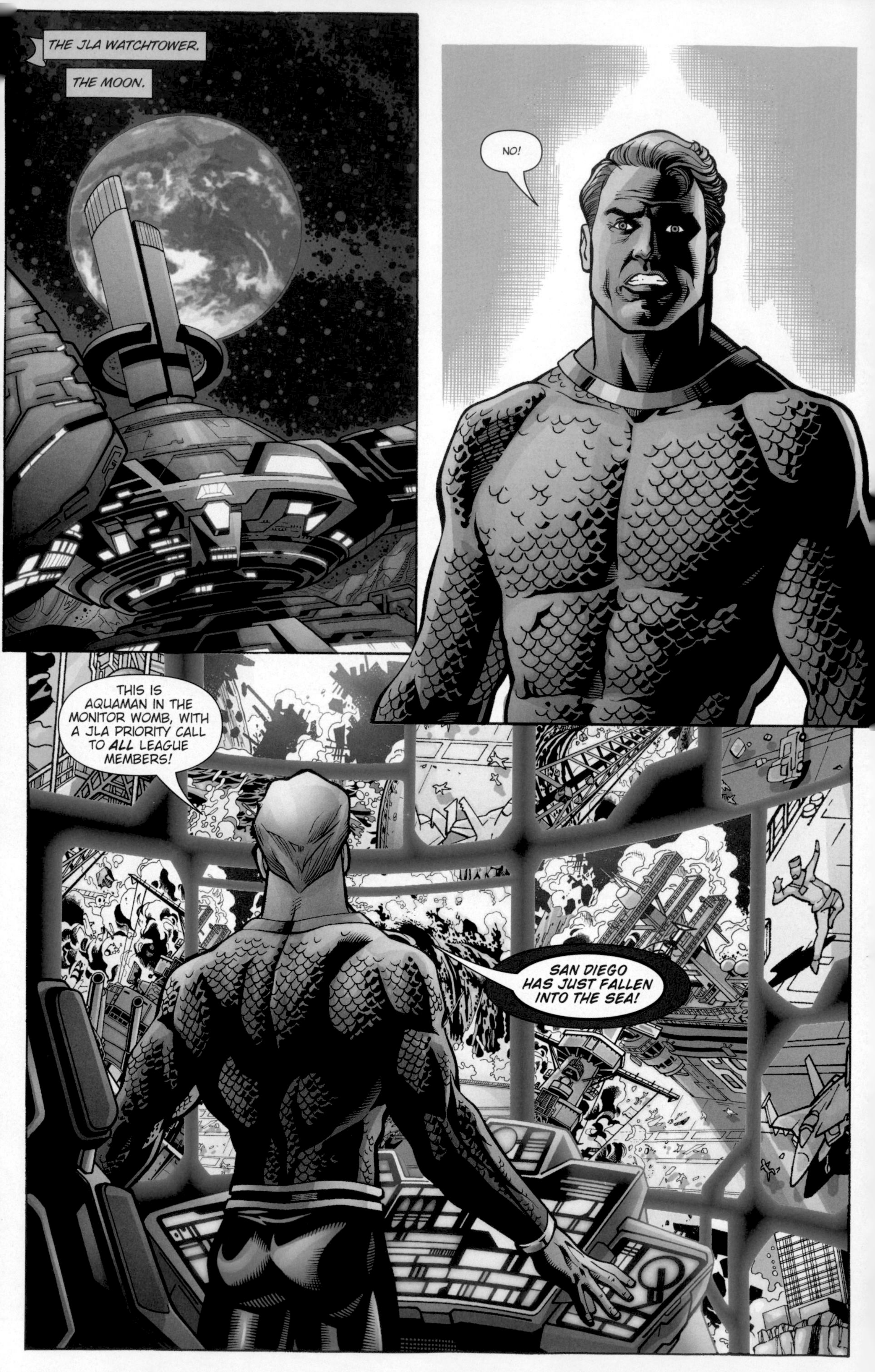
THE JLA WATCHTOWER.
THE MOON.
NO!
THIS IS AQUAMAN IN THE MONITOR WOMB, WITH A JLA PRIORITY CALL TO ALL LEAGUE MEMBERS!
SAN DIEGO HAS JUST FALLEN INTO THE SEA!

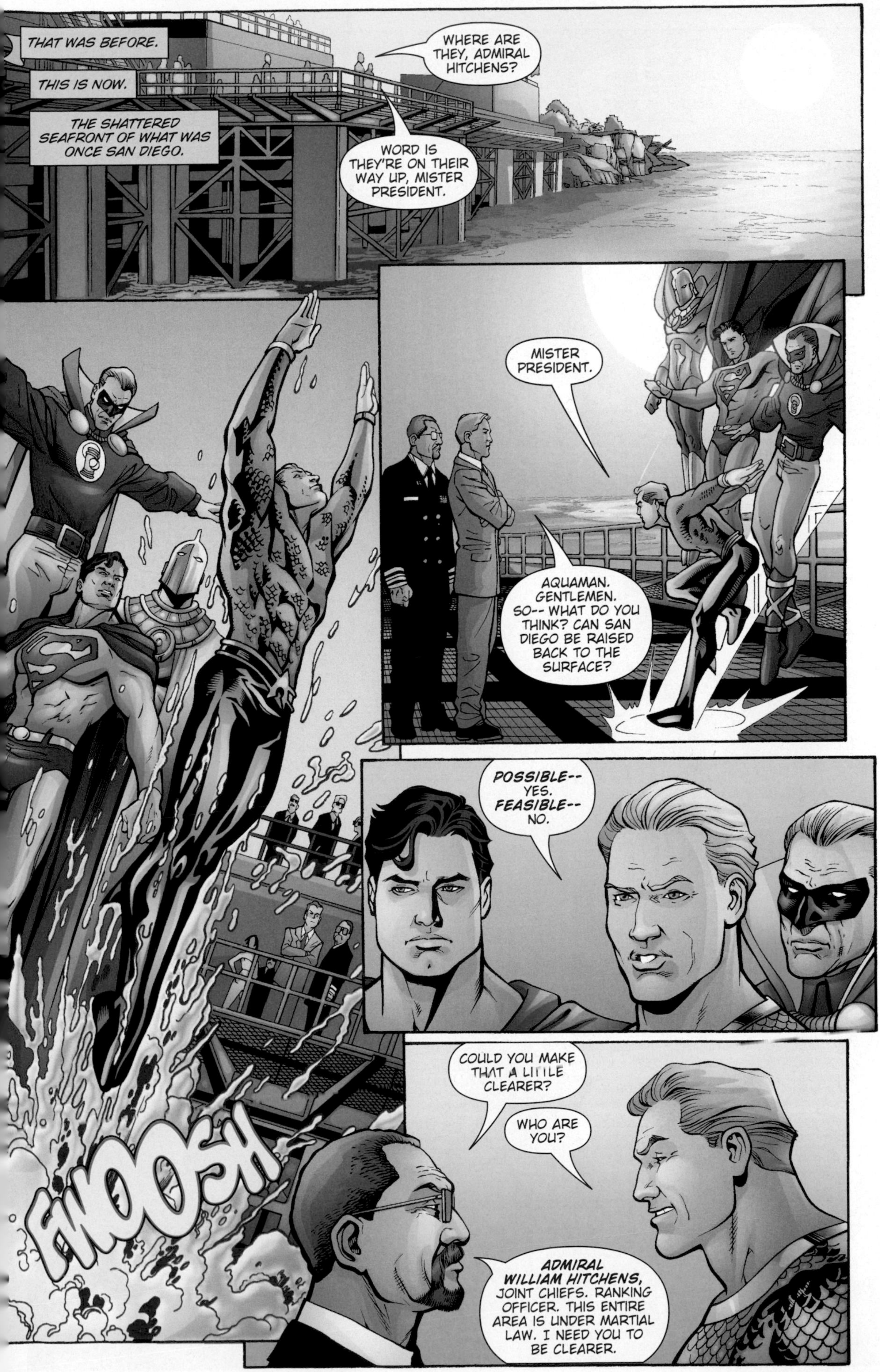
THAT WAS BEFORE.
THIS IS NOW.
THE SHATTERED SEAFRONT OF WHAT WAS ONCE SAN DIEGO.
WHERE ARE THEY, ADMIRAL HITCHENS?
WORD IS THEY'RE ON THEIR WAY UP, MISTER PRESIDENT.
FWOOSH
MISTER PRESIDENT.
AQUAMAN. GENTLEMEN. SO-- WHAT DO YOU THINK? CAN SAN DIEGO BE RAISED BACK TO THE SURFACE?
POSSIBLE-- YES. FEASIBLE-- NO.
COULD YOU MAKE THAT A LITTLE CLEARER?
WHO ARE YOU?
ADMIRAL WILLIAM HITCHENS, JOINT CHIEFS. RANKING OFFICER. THIS ENTIRE AREA IS UNDER MARTIAL LAW. I NEED YOU TO BE CLEARER.

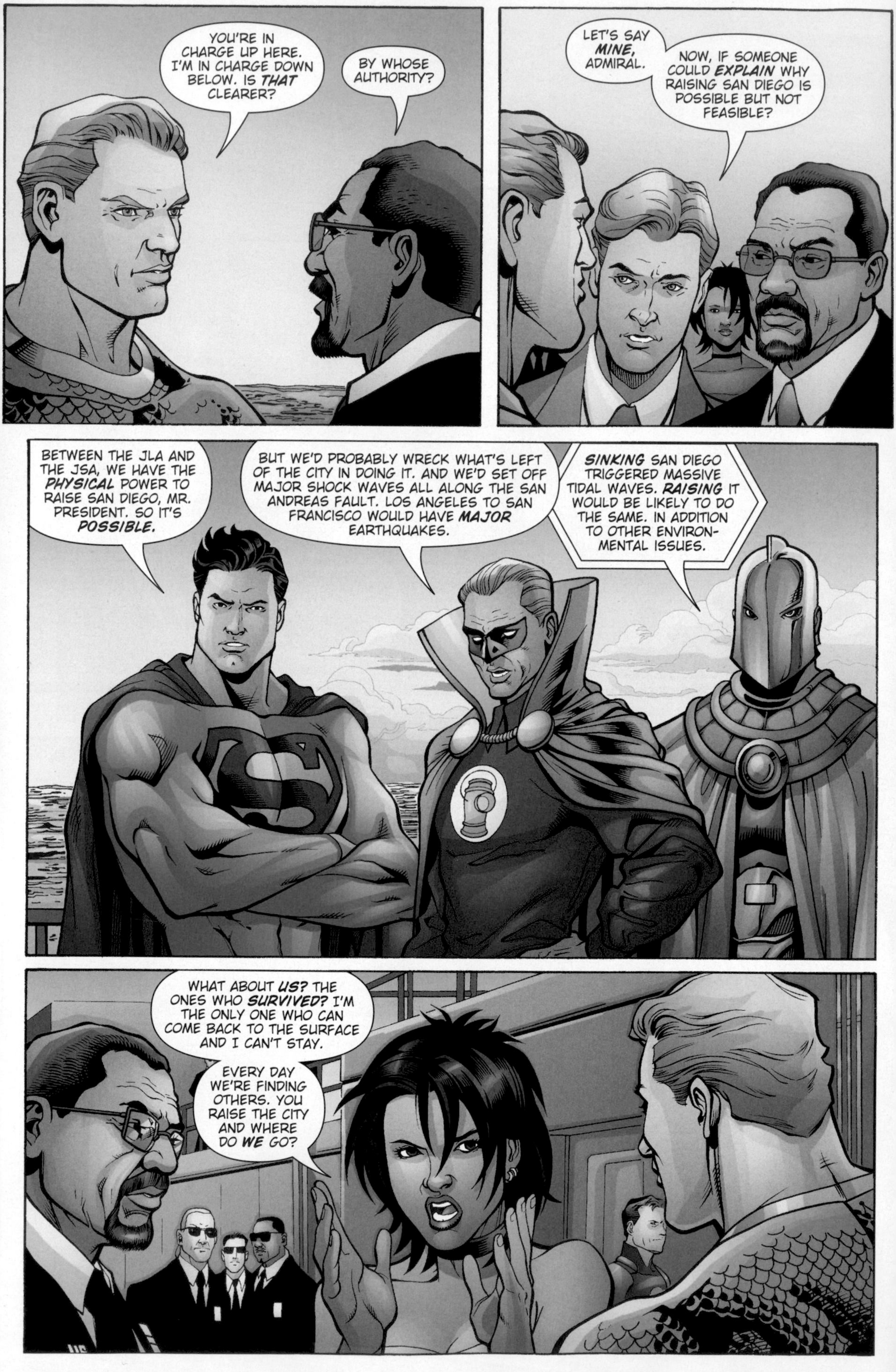
YOU'RE IN CHARGE UP HERE. I'M IN CHARGE DOWN BELOW. IS THAT CLEARER?
BY WHOSE AUTHORITY?
LET'S SAY MINE, ADMIRAL.
NOW, IF SOMEONE COULD EXPLAIN WHY RAISING SAN DIEGO IS POSSIBLE BUT NOT FEASIBLE?
BETWEEN THE JLA AND THE JSA, WE HAVE THE PHYSICAL POWER TO RAISE SAN DIEGO, MR. PRESIDENT. SO IT'S POSSIBLE.
BUT WE'D PROBABLY WRECK WHAT'S LEFT OF THE CITY IN DOING IT. AND WE'D SET OFF MAJOR SHOCK WAVES ALL ALONG THE SAN ANDREAS FAULT. LOS ANGELES TO SAN FRANCISCO WOULD HAVE MAJOR EARTHQUAKES.
SINKING SAN DIEGO TRIGGERED MASSIVE TIDAL WAVES. RAISING IT WOULD BE LIKELY TO DO THE SAME. IN ADDITION TO OTHER ENVIRONMENTAL ISSUES.
WHAT ABOUT US? THE ONES WHO SURVIVED? I'M THE ONLY ONE WHO CAN COME BACK TO THE SURFACE AND I CAN'T STAY.
EVERY DAY WE'RE FINDING OTHERS. YOU RAISE THE CITY AND WHERE DO WE GO?

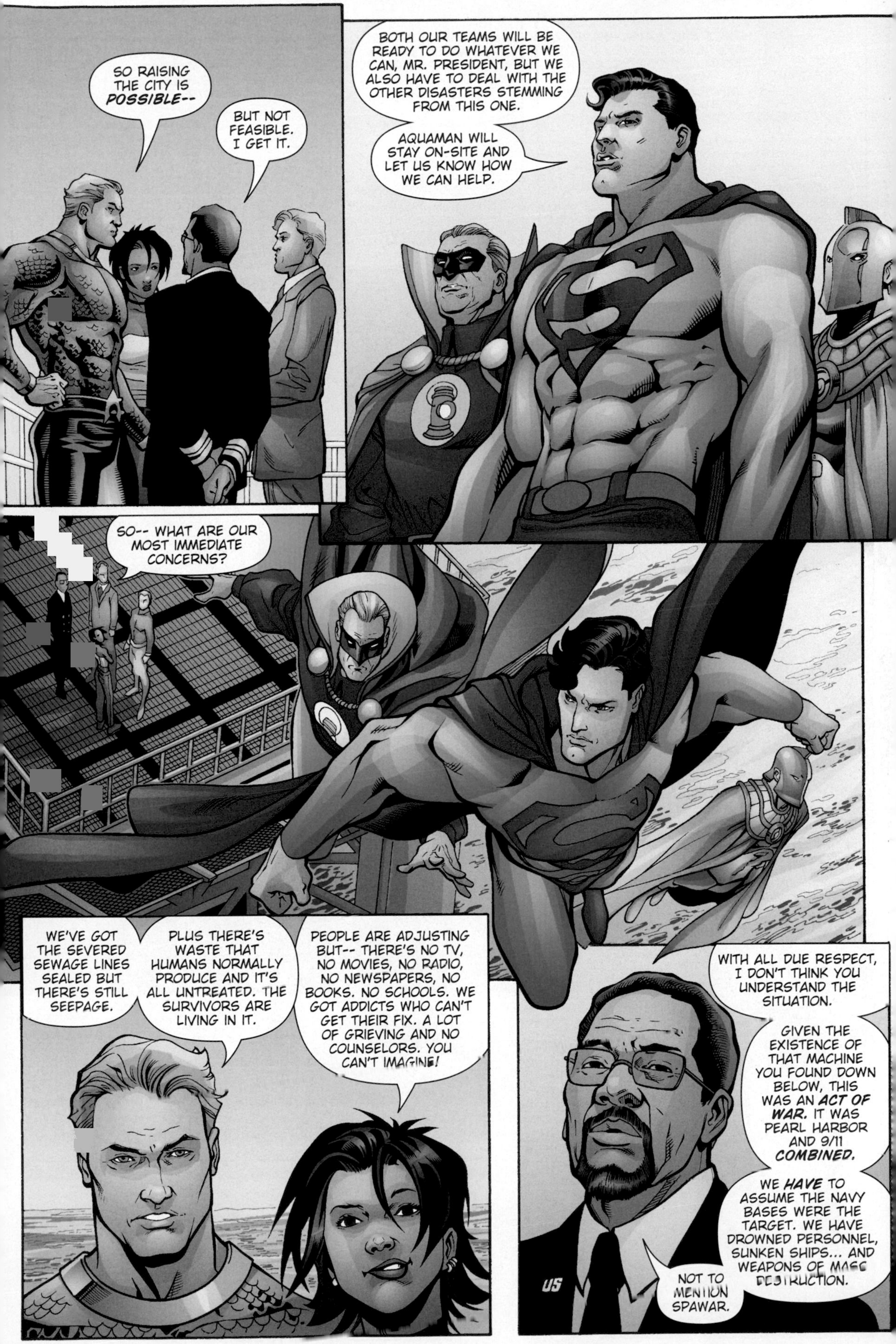
SO RAISING THE CITY IS POSSIBLE--
BUT NOT FEASIBLE. I GET IT.
BOTH OUR TEAMS WILL BE READY TO DO WHATEVER WE CAN, MR. PRESIDENT, BUT WE ALSO HAVE TO DEAL WITH THE OTHER DISASTERS STEMMING FROM THIS ONE.
AQUAMAN WILL STAY ON-SITE AND LET US KNOW HOW WE CAN HELP.
SO-- WHAT ARE OUR MOST IMMEDIATE CONCERNS?
WE'VE GOT THE SEVERED SEWAGE LINES SEALED BUT THERE'S STILL SEEPAGE.
PLUS THERE'S WASTE THAT HUMANS NORMALLY PRODUCE AND IT'S ALL UNTREATED. THE SURVIVORS ARE LIVING IN IT.
PEOPLE ARE ADJUSTING BUT-- THERE'S NO TV, NO MOVIES, NO RADIO, NO NEWSPAPERS, NO BOOKS. NO SCHOOLS. WE GOT ADDICTS WHO CAN'T GET THEIR FIX. A LOT OF GRIEVING AND NO COUNSELORS. YOU CAN'T IMAGINE!
WITH ALL DUE RESPECT, I DON'T THINK YOU UNDERSTAND THE SITUATION.
GIVEN THE EXISTENCE OF THAT MACHINE YOU FOUND DOWN BELOW, THIS WAS AN ACT OF WAR. IT WAS PEARL HARBOR AND 9/11 COMBINED.
WE HAVE TO ASSUME THE NAVY BASES WERE THE TARGET. WE HAVE DROWNED PERSONNEL, SUNKEN SHIPS... AND WEAPONS OF MASS DESTRUCTION.
NOT TO MENTION SPAWAR.

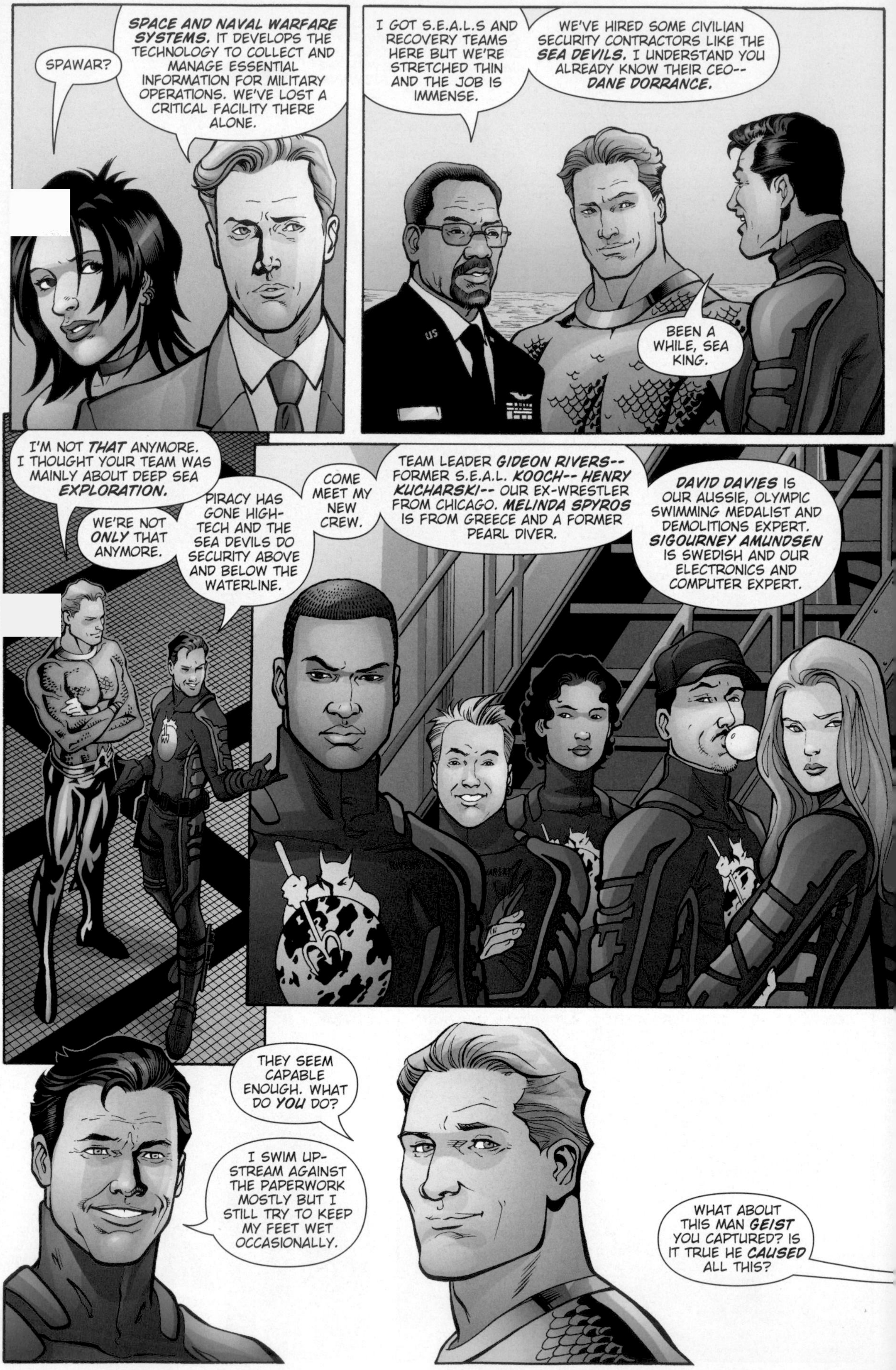
SPAWAR?
SPACE AND NAVAL WARFARE SYSTEMS. IT DEVELOPS THE TECHNOLOGY TO COLLECT AND MANAGE ESSENTIAL INFORMATION FOR MILITARY OPERATIONS. WE'VE LOST A CRITICAL FACILITY THERE ALONE.
I GOT S.E.A.L.S AND RECOVERY TEAMS HERE BUT WE'RE STRETCHED THIN AND THE JOB IS IMMENSE.
WE'VE HIRED SOME CIVILIAN SECURITY CONTRACTORS LIKE THE SEA DEVILS. I UNDERSTAND YOU ALREADY KNOW THEIR CEO-- DANE DORRANCE.
BEEN A WHILE, SEA KING.
I'M NOT THAT ANYMORE. I THOUGHT YOUR TEAM WAS MAINLY ABOUT DEEP SEA EXPLORATION.
WE'RE NOT ONLY THAT ANYMORE.
PIRACY HAS GONE HIGH-TECH AND THE SEA DEVILS DO SECURITY ABOVE AND BELOW THE WATERLINE.
COME MEET MY NEW CREW.
TEAM LEADER GIDEON RIVERS-- FORMER S.E.A.L. KOOCH-- HENRY KUCHARSKI-- OUR EX-WRESTLER FROM CHICAGO. MELINDA SPYROS IS FROM GREECE AND A FORMER PEARL DIVER.
DAVID DAVIES IS OUR AUSSIE, OLYMPIC SWIMMING MEDALIST AND DEMOLITIONS EXPERT. SIGOURNEY AMUNDSEN IS SWEDISH AND OUR ELECTRONICS AND COMPUTER EXPERT.
THEY SEEM CAPABLE ENOUGH. WHAT DO YOU DO?
I SWIM UP-STREAM AGAINST THE PAPERWORK MOSTLY BUT I STILL TRY TO KEEP MY FEET WET OCCASIONALLY.
WHAT ABOUT THIS MAN GEIST YOU CAPTURED? IS IT TRUE HE CAUSED ALL THIS?

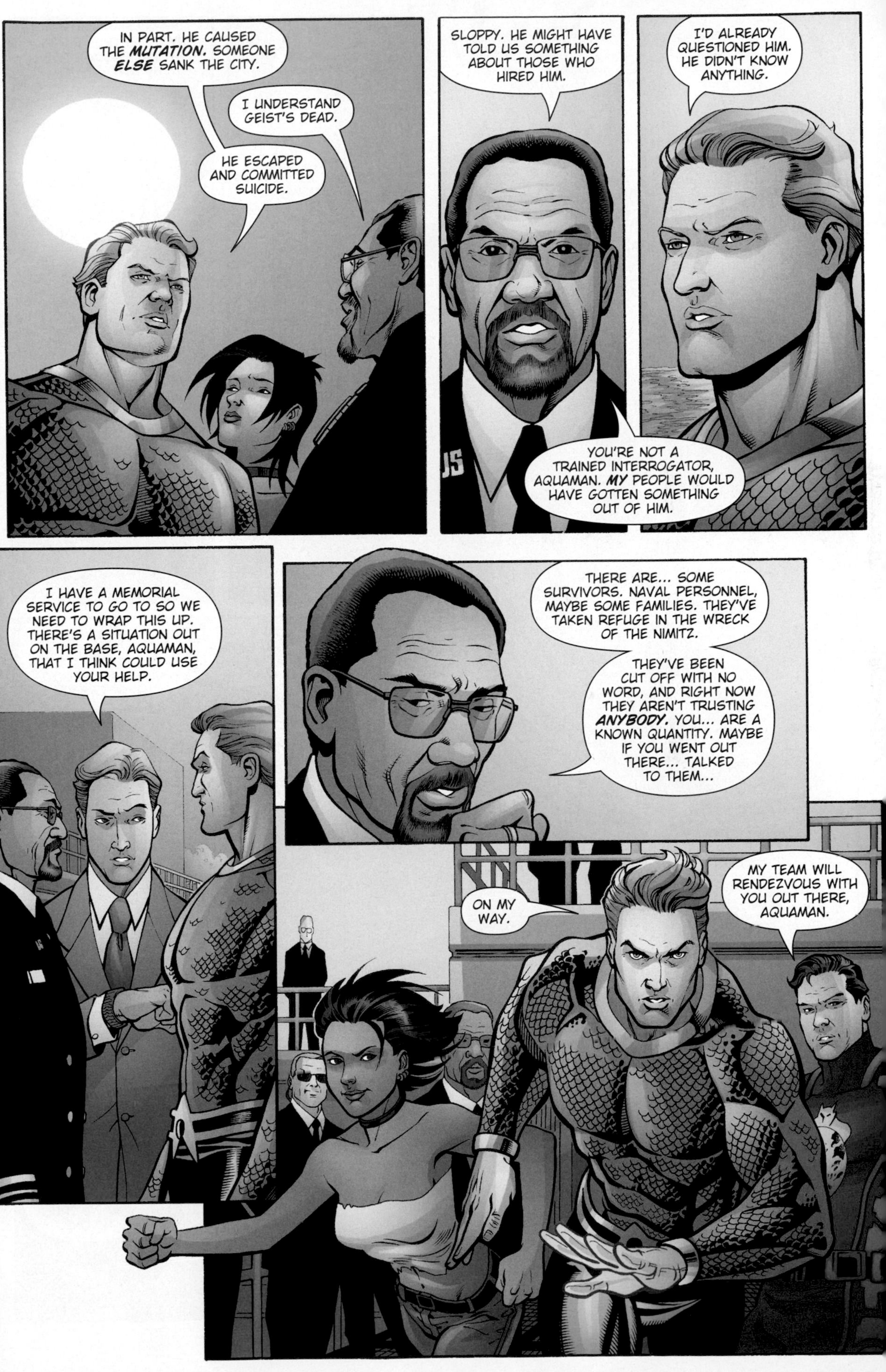
IN PART. HE CAUSED THE **MUTATION.** SOMEONE **ELSE** SANK THE CITY.
I UNDERSTAND GEIST'S DEAD.
HE ESCAPED AND COMMITTED SUICIDE.
SLOPPY. HE MIGHT HAVE TOLD US SOMETHING ABOUT THOSE WHO HIRED HIM.
I'D ALREADY QUESTIONED HIM. HE DIDN'T KNOW ANYTHING.
YOU'RE NOT A TRAINED INTERROGATOR, AQUAMAN. **MY** PEOPLE WOULD HAVE GOTTEN SOMETHING OUT OF HIM.
I HAVE A MEMORIAL SERVICE TO GO TO SO WE NEED TO WRAP THIS UP. THERE'S A SITUATION OUT ON THE BASE, AQUAMAN, THAT I THINK COULD USE YOUR HELP.
THERE ARE... SOME SURVIVORS. NAVAL PERSONNEL, MAYBE SOME FAMILIES. THEY'VE TAKEN REFUGE IN THE WRECK OF THE NIMITZ.
THEY'VE BEEN CUT OFF WITH NO WORD, AND RIGHT NOW THEY AREN'T TRUSTING **ANYBODY.** YOU... ARE A KNOWN QUANTITY. MAYBE IF YOU WENT OUT THERE... TALKED TO THEM...
ON MY WAY.
MY TEAM WILL RENDEZVOUS WITH YOU OUT THERE, AQUAMAN.

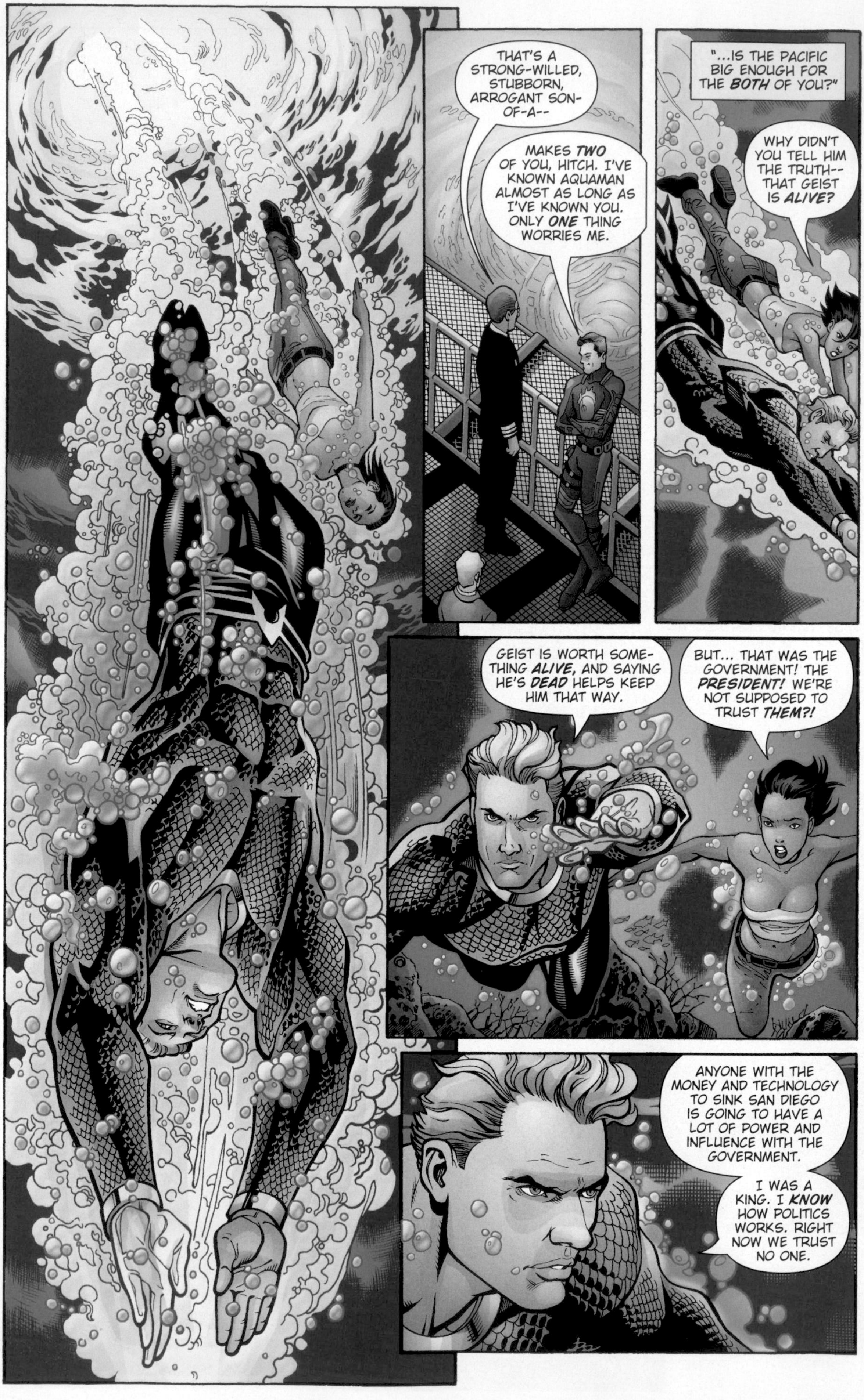

THAT'S A STRONG-WILLED, STUBBORN, ARROGANT SON-OF-A--
MAKES *TWO* OF YOU, HITCH. I'VE KNOWN AQUAMAN ALMOST AS LONG AS I'VE KNOWN YOU. ONLY *ONE* THING WORRIES ME.
"...IS THE PACIFIC BIG ENOUGH FOR THE *BOTH* OF YOU?"
WHY DIDN'T YOU TELL HIM THE TRUTH-- THAT GEIST IS *ALIVE?*
GEIST IS WORTH SOMETHING *ALIVE,* AND SAYING HE'S *DEAD* HELPS KEEP HIM THAT WAY.
BUT... THAT WAS THE GOVERNMENT! THE *PRESIDENT!* WE'RE NOT SUPPOSED TO TRUST *THEM?!*
ANYONE WITH THE MONEY AND TECHNOLOGY TO SINK SAN DIEGO IS GOING TO HAVE A LOT OF POWER AND INFLUENCE WITH THE GOVERNMENT.
I WAS A KING. I *KNOW* HOW POLITICS WORKS. RIGHT NOW WE TRUST NO ONE.

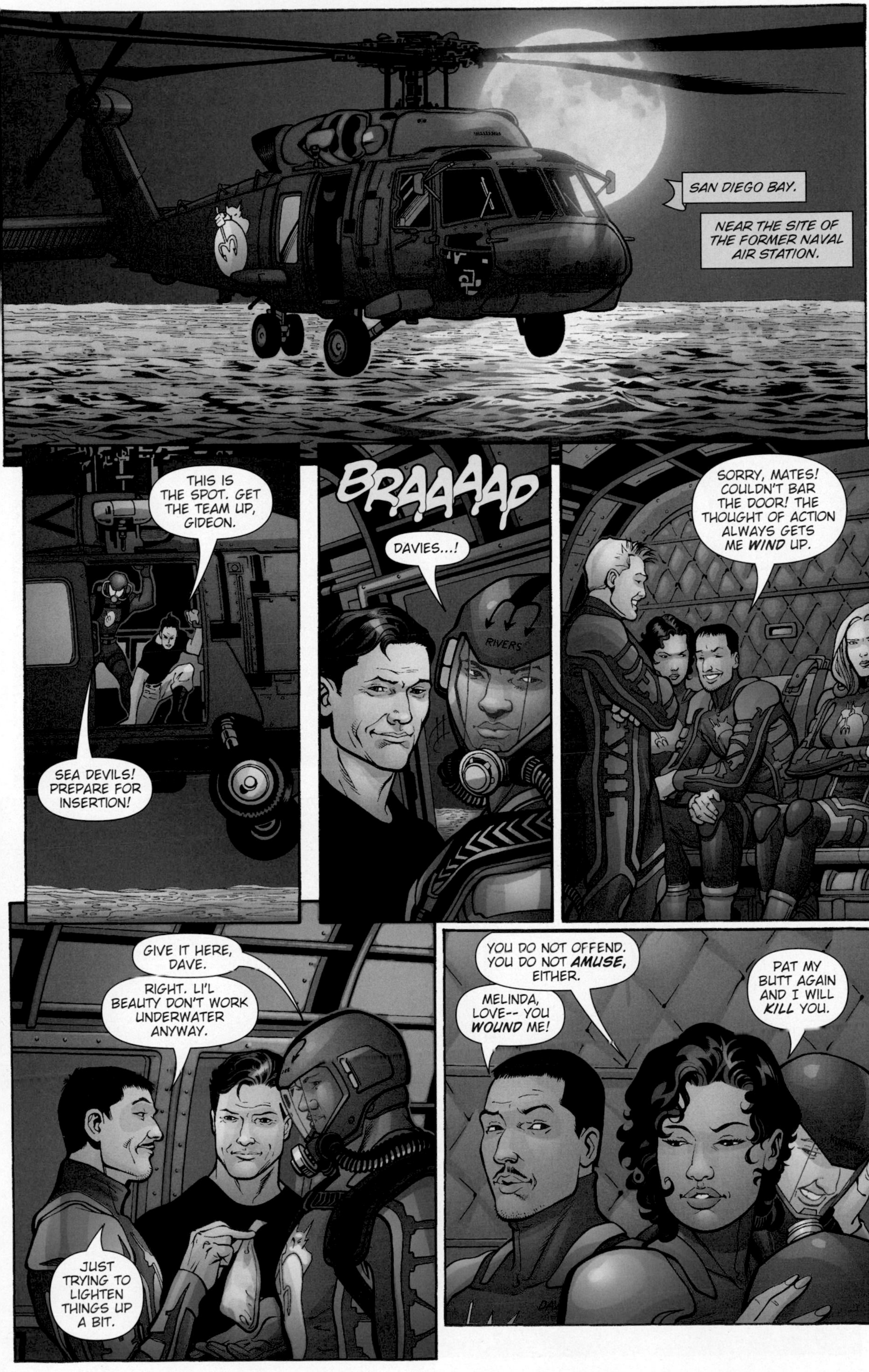
SAN DIEGO BAY.
NEAR THE SITE OF THE FORMER NAVAL AIR STATION.
THIS IS THE SPOT. GET THE TEAM UP, GIDEON.
SEA DEVILS! PREPARE FOR INSERTION!
BRAAAAP
DAVIES...!
SORRY, MATES! COULDN'T BAR THE DOOR! THE THOUGHT OF ACTION ALWAYS GETS ME WIND UP.
GIVE IT HERE, DAVE.
RIGHT. LI'L BEAUTY DON'T WORK UNDERWATER ANYWAY.
JUST TRYING TO LIGHTEN THINGS UP A BIT.
YOU DO NOT OFFEND. YOU DO NOT AMUSE, EITHER.
MELINDA, LOVE-- YOU WOUND ME!
PAT MY BUTT AGAIN AND I WILL KILL YOU.

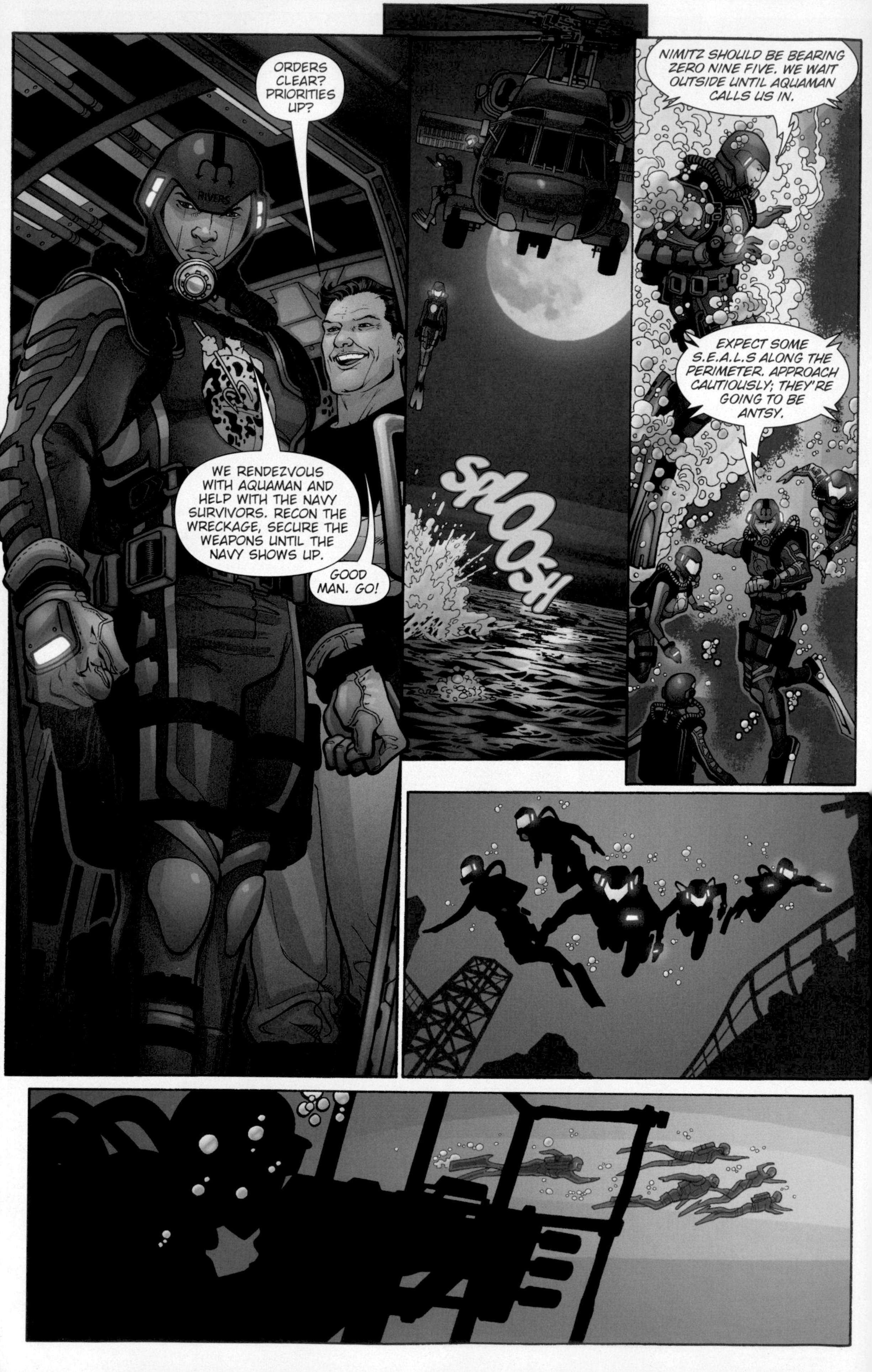
ORDERS CLEAR? PRIORITIES UP?
RIVERS
WE RENDEZVOUS WITH AQUAMAN AND HELP WITH THE NAVY SURVIVORS. RECON THE WRECKAGE, SECURE THE WEAPONS UNTIL THE NAVY SHOWS UP.
GOOD MAN. GO!
SPLOOSH
NIMITZ SHOULD BE BEARING ZERO NINE FIVE. WE WAIT OUTSIDE UNTIL AQUAMAN CALLS US IN.
EXPECT SOME S.E.A.L.S ALONG THE PERIMETER. APPROACH CAUTIOUSLY; THEY'RE GOING TO BE ANTSY.

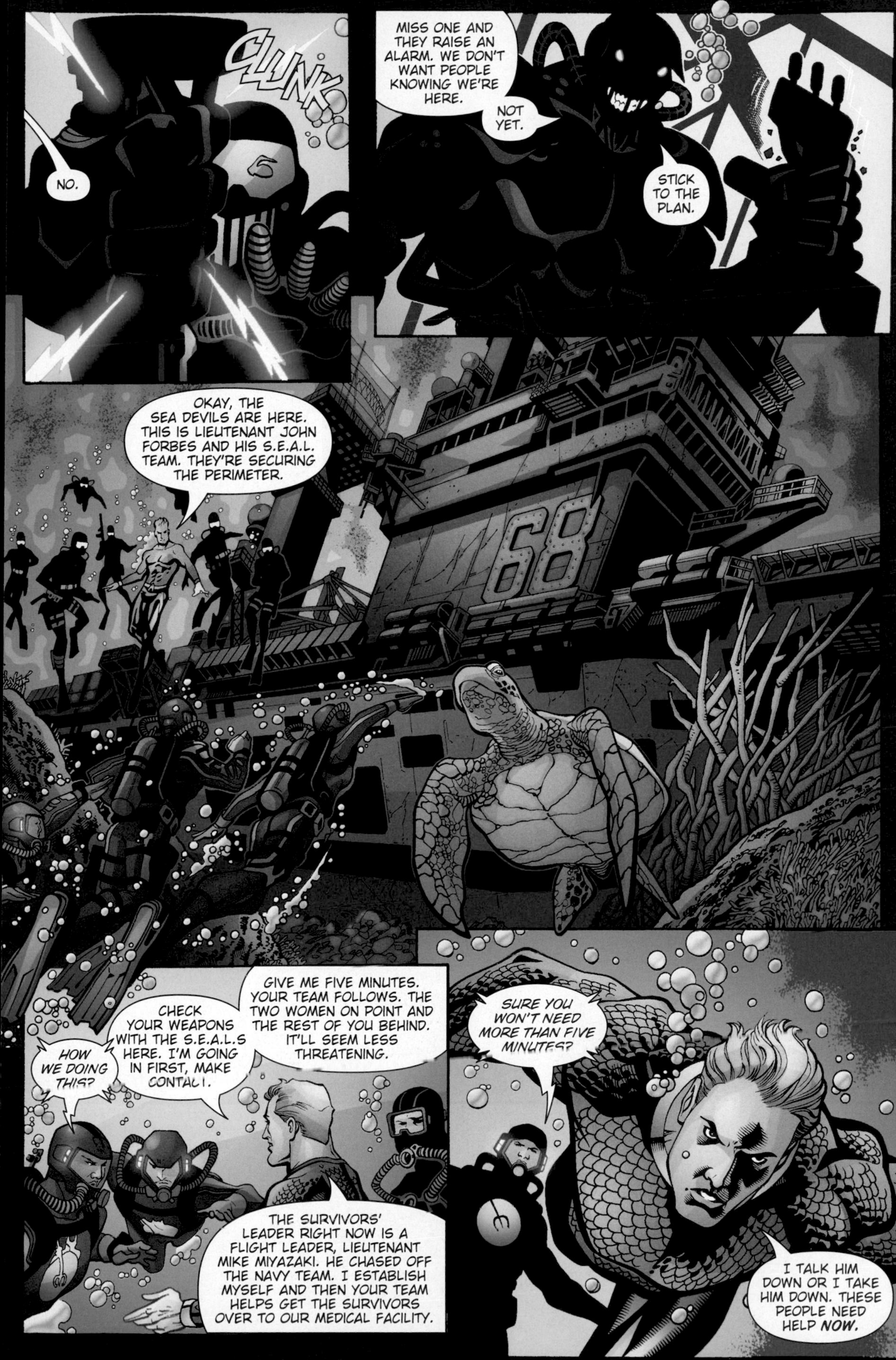
CLUNK
NO.
MISS ONE AND THEY RAISE AN ALARM. WE DON'T WANT PEOPLE KNOWING WE'RE HERE.
NOT YET.
STICK TO THE PLAN.
OKAY, THE SEA DEVILS ARE HERE. THIS IS LIEUTENANT JOHN FORBES AND HIS S.E.A.L. TEAM. THEY'RE SECURING THE PERIMETER.
68
HOW WE DOING THIS?
CHECK YOUR WEAPONS WITH THE S.E.A.L.S HERE. I'M GOING IN FIRST, MAKE CONTACT.
GIVE ME FIVE MINUTES. YOUR TEAM FOLLOWS. THE TWO WOMEN ON POINT AND THE REST OF YOU BEHIND. IT'LL SEEM LESS THREATENING.
THE SURVIVORS' LEADER RIGHT NOW IS A FLIGHT LEADER, LIEUTENANT MIKE MIYAZAKI. HE CHASED OFF THE NAVY TEAM. I ESTABLISH MYSELF AND THEN YOUR TEAM HELPS GET THE SURVIVORS OVER TO OUR MEDICAL FACILITY.
SURE YOU WON'T NEED MORE THAN FIVE MINUTES?
I TALK HIM DOWN OR I TAKE HIM DOWN. THESE PEOPLE NEED HELP NOW.

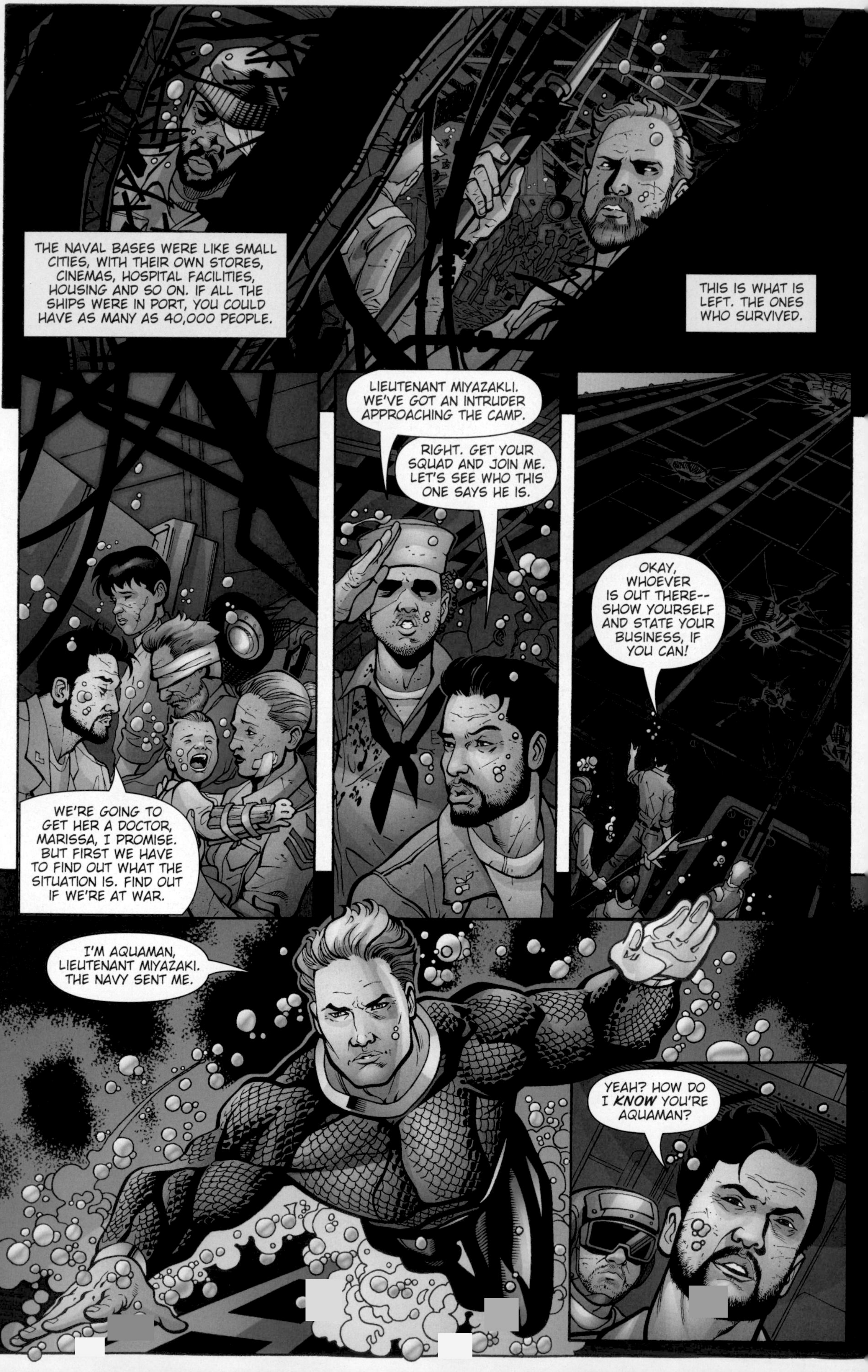
THE NAVAL BASES WERE LIKE SMALL CITIES, WITH THEIR OWN STORES, CINEMAS, HOSPITAL FACILITIES, HOUSING AND SO ON. IF ALL THE SHIPS WERE IN PORT, YOU COULD HAVE AS MANY AS 40,000 PEOPLE.
THIS IS WHAT IS LEFT. THE ONES WHO SURVIVED.
WE'RE GOING TO GET HER A DOCTOR, MARISSA, I PROMISE. BUT FIRST WE HAVE TO FIND OUT WHAT THE SITUATION IS. FIND OUT IF WE'RE AT WAR.
LIEUTENANT MIYAZAKLI. WE'VE GOT AN INTRUDER APPROACHING THE CAMP.
RIGHT. GET YOUR SQUAD AND JOIN ME. LET'S SEE WHO THIS ONE SAYS HE IS.
OKAY, WHOEVER IS OUT THERE-- SHOW YOURSELF AND STATE YOUR BUSINESS, IF YOU CAN!
I'M AQUAMAN, LIEUTENANT MIYAZAKI. THE NAVY SENT ME.
YEAH? HOW DO I KNOW YOU'RE AQUAMAN?

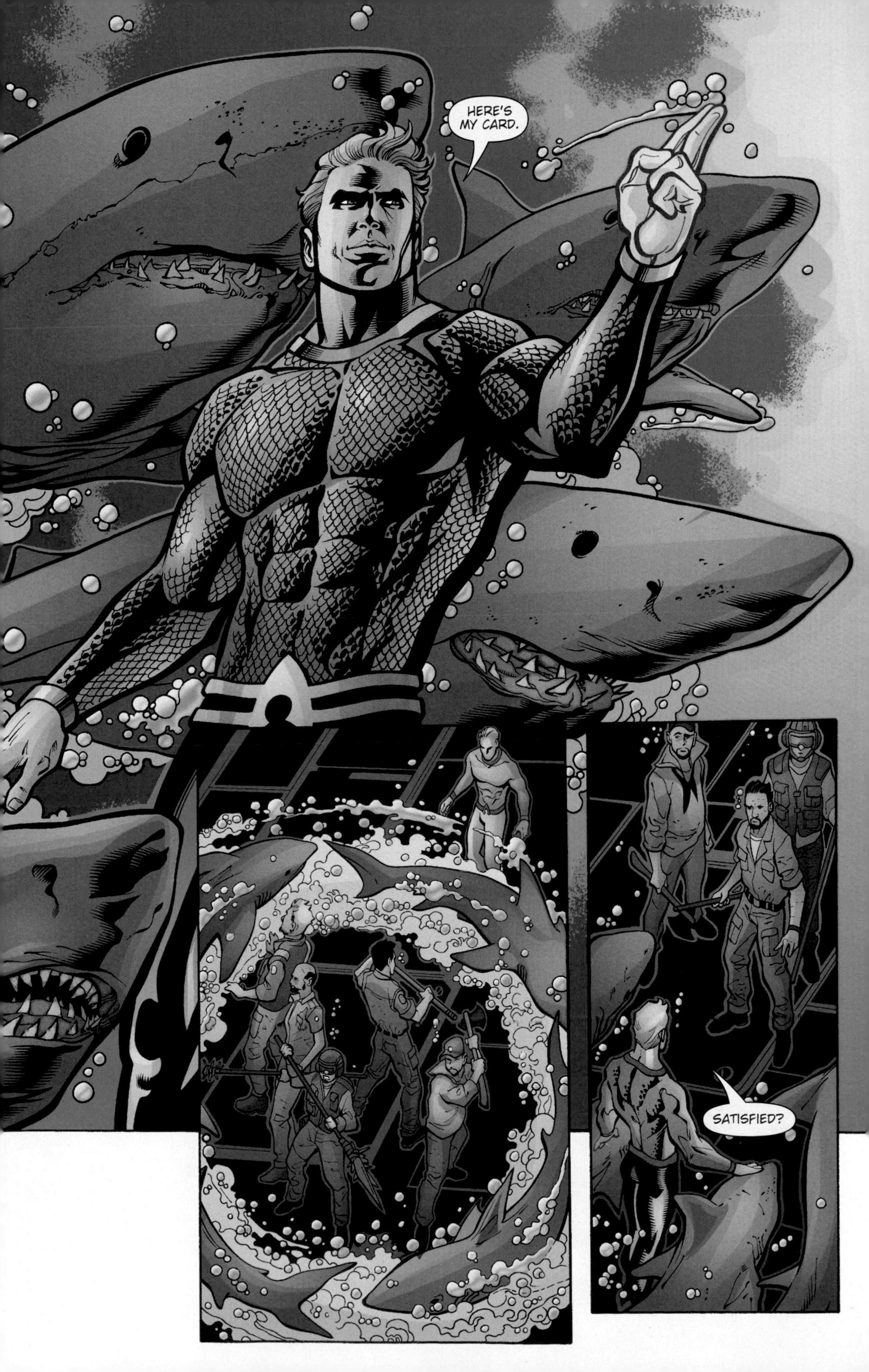
HERE'S MY CARD.
SATISFIED?

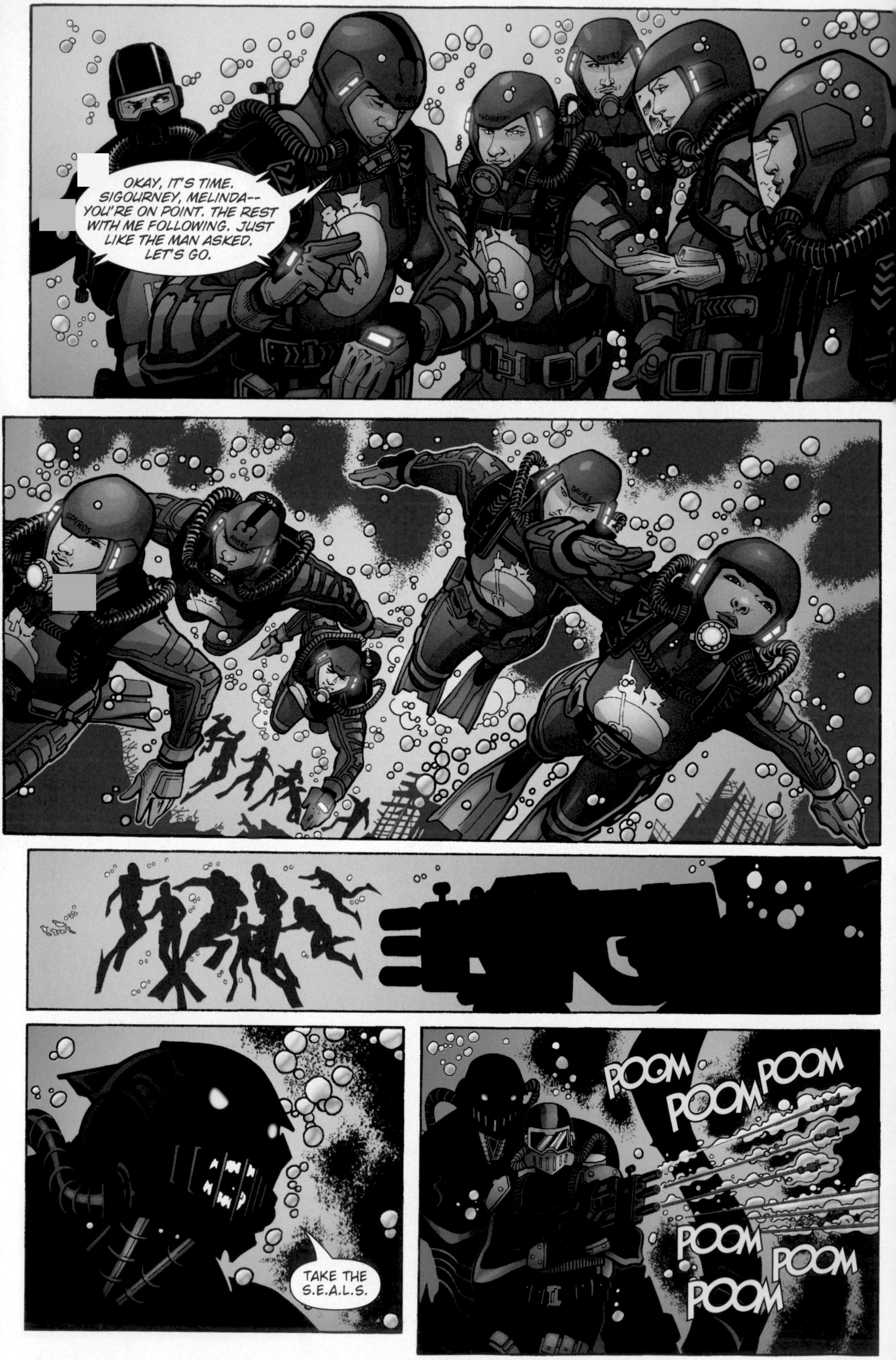

OKAY, IT'S TIME. SIGOURNEY, MELINDA-- YOU'RE ON POINT. THE REST WITH ME FOLLOWING. JUST LIKE THE MAN ASKED. LET'S GO.
TAKE THE S.E.A.L.S.
POOM POOM POOM
POOM POOM POOM

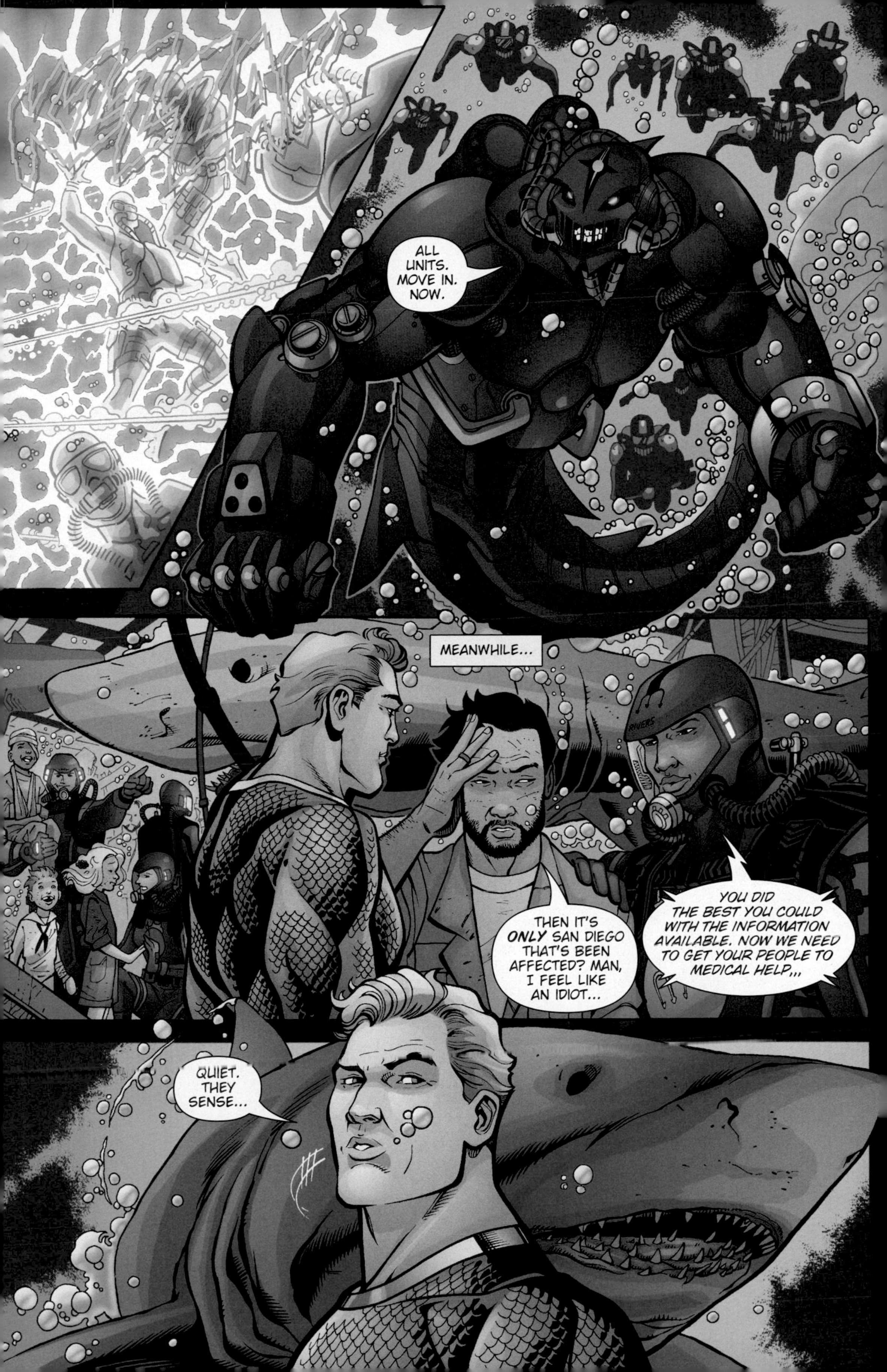
ALL UNITS. MOVE IN. NOW.
MEANWHILE...
THEN IT'S ONLY SAN DIEGO THAT'S BEEN AFFECTED? MAN, I FEEL LIKE AN IDIOT...
YOU DID THE BEST YOU COULD WITH THE INFORMATION AVAILABLE. NOW WE NEED TO GET YOUR PEOPLE TO MEDICAL HELP,,,
QUIET. THEY SENSE...

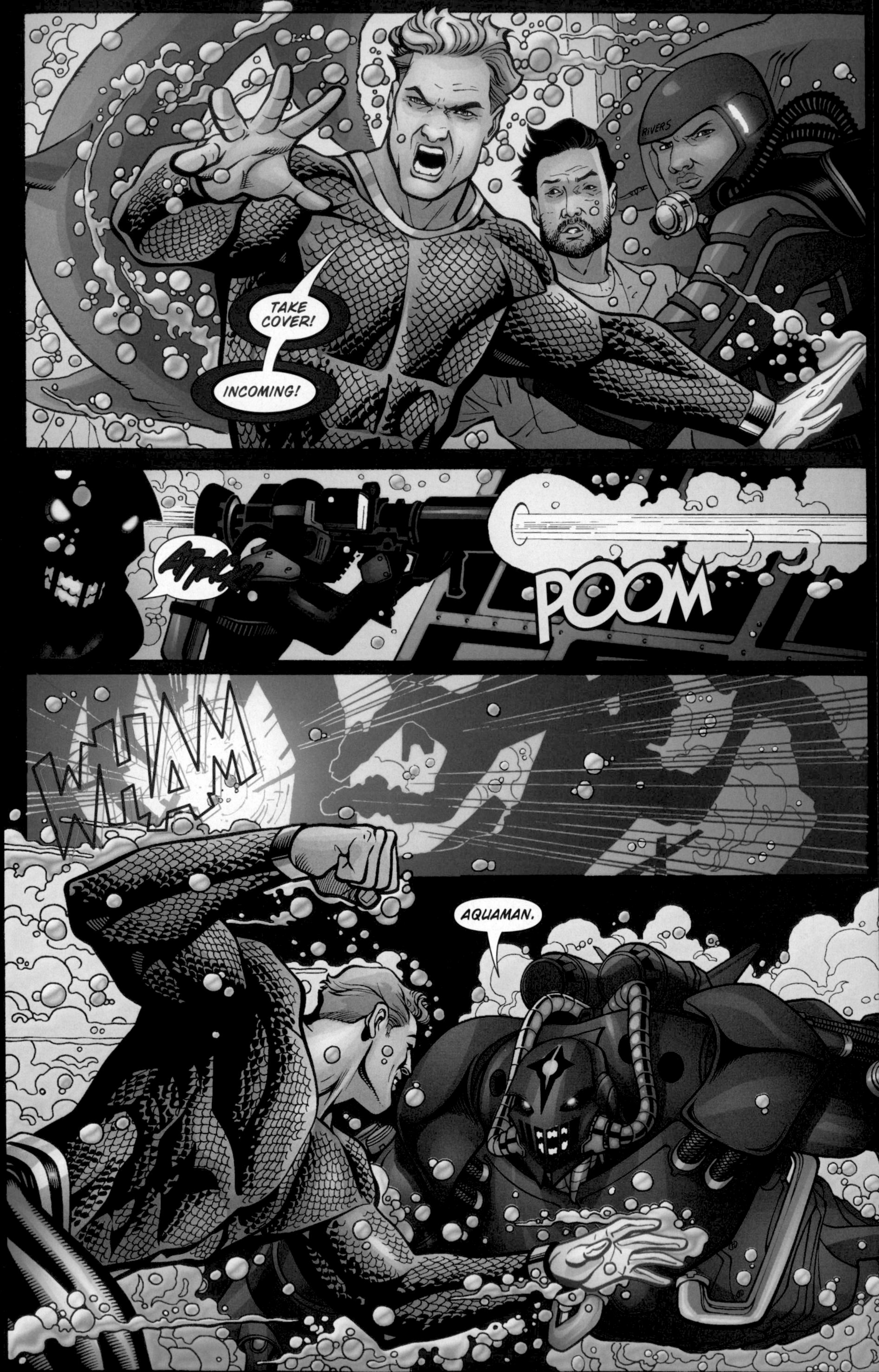
RIVERS
TAKE COVER!
INCOMING!
POOM
WHAM
AQUAMAN.

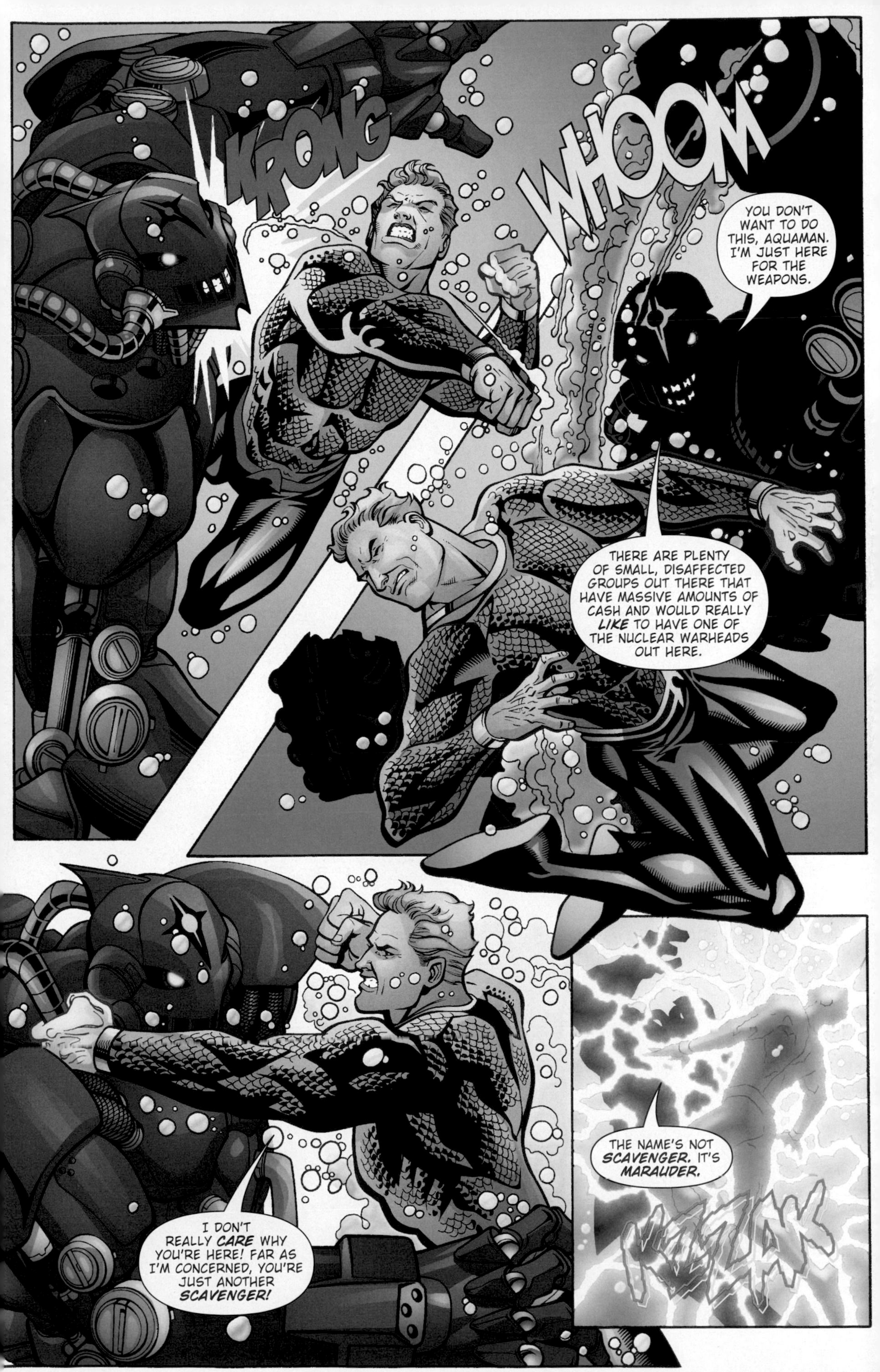
KRONG
WHOOM
YOU DON'T WANT TO DO THIS, AQUAMAN. I'M JUST HERE FOR THE WEAPONS.
THERE ARE PLENTY OF SMALL, DISAFFECTED GROUPS OUT THERE THAT HAVE MASSIVE AMOUNTS OF CASH AND WOULD REALLY *LIKE* TO HAVE ONE OF THE NUCLEAR WARHEADS OUT HERE.
I DON'T REALLY *CARE* WHY YOU'RE HERE! FAR AS I'M CONCERNED, YOU'RE JUST ANOTHER *SCAVENGER!*
THE NAME'S NOT *SCAVENGER.* IT'S *MARAUDER.*

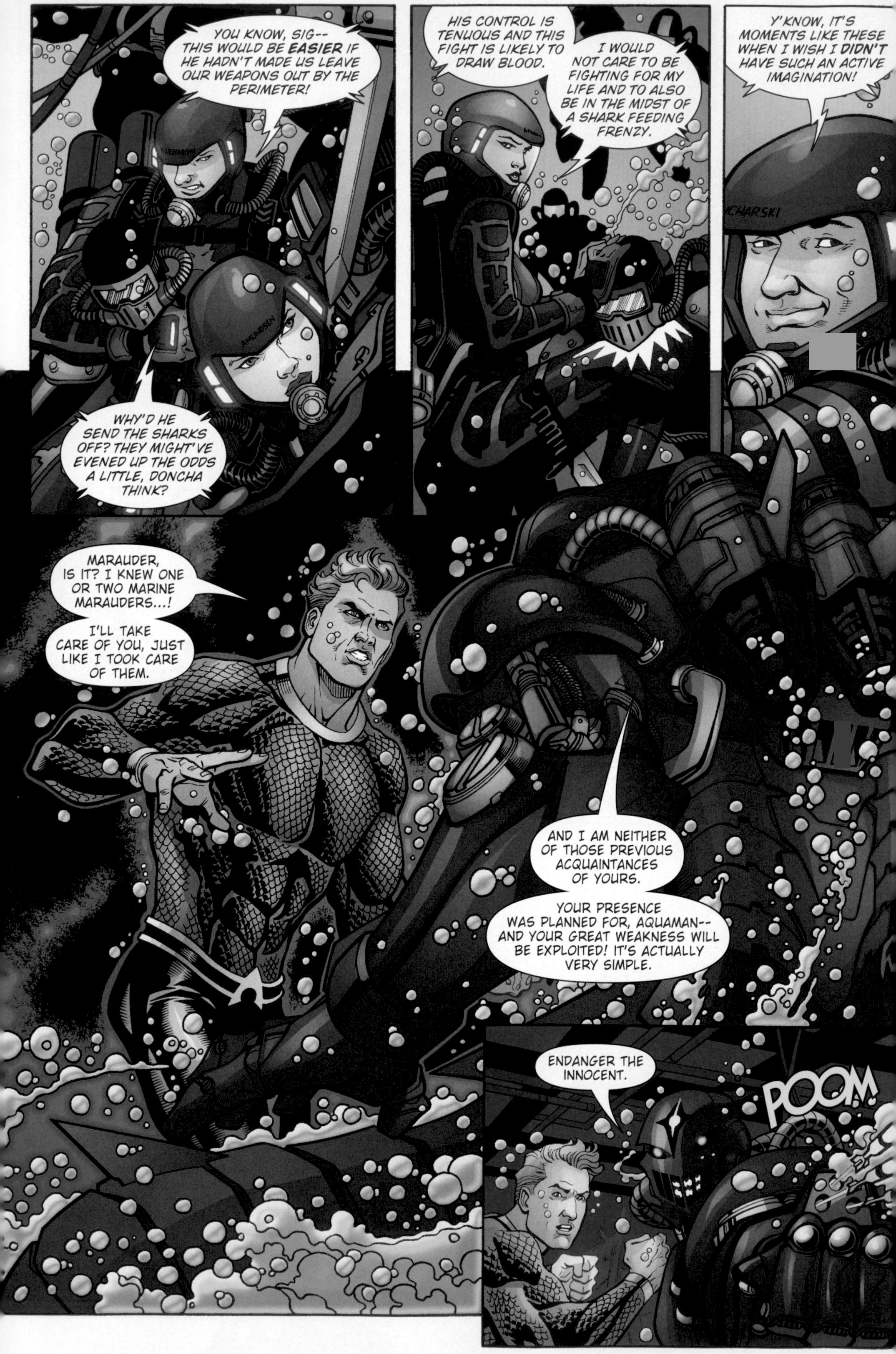
YOU KNOW, SIG-- THIS WOULD BE **EASIER** IF HE HADN'T MADE US LEAVE OUR WEAPONS OUT BY THE PERIMETER!
WHY'D HE SEND THE SHARKS OFF? THEY MIGHT'VE EVENED UP THE ODDS A LITTLE, DONCHA THINK?
HIS CONTROL IS TENUOUS AND THIS FIGHT IS LIKELY TO DRAW BLOOD.
I WOULD NOT CARE TO BE FIGHTING FOR MY LIFE AND TO ALSO BE IN THE MIDST OF A SHARK FEEDING FRENZY.
Y'KNOW, IT'S MOMENTS LIKE THESE WHEN I WISH I **DIDN'T** HAVE SUCH AN ACTIVE IMAGINATION!
MARAUDER, IS IT? I KNEW ONE OR TWO MARINE MARAUDERS...!
I'LL TAKE CARE OF YOU, JUST LIKE I TOOK CARE OF THEM.
AND I AM NEITHER OF THOSE PREVIOUS ACQUAINTANCES OF YOURS.
YOUR PRESENCE WAS PLANNED FOR, AQUAMAN-- AND YOUR GREAT WEAKNESS WILL BE EXPLOITED! IT'S ACTUALLY VERY SIMPLE.
ENDANGER THE INNOCENT.
POOM

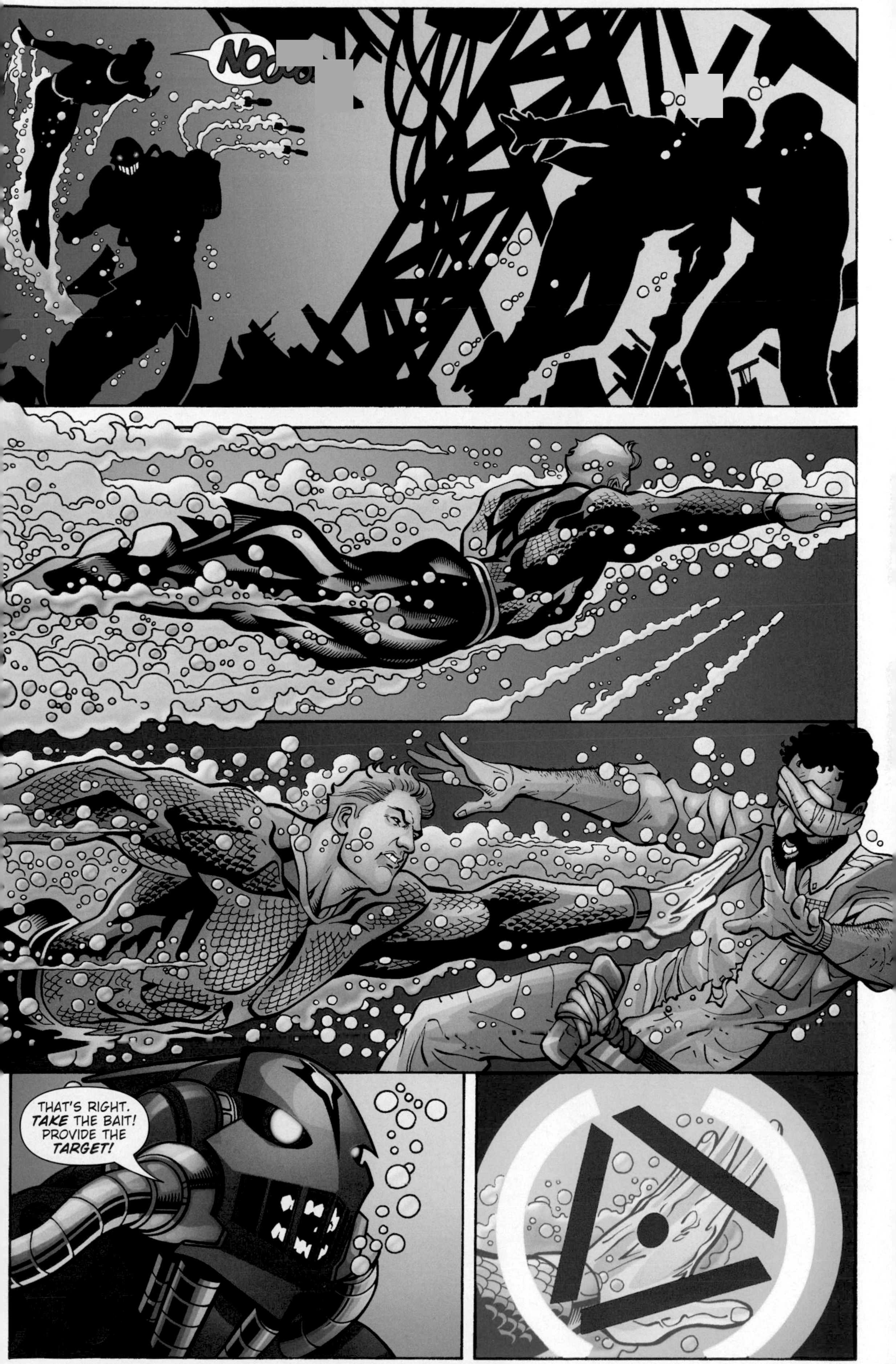
NOO
THAT'S RIGHT. TAKE THE BAIT! PROVIDE THE TARGET!

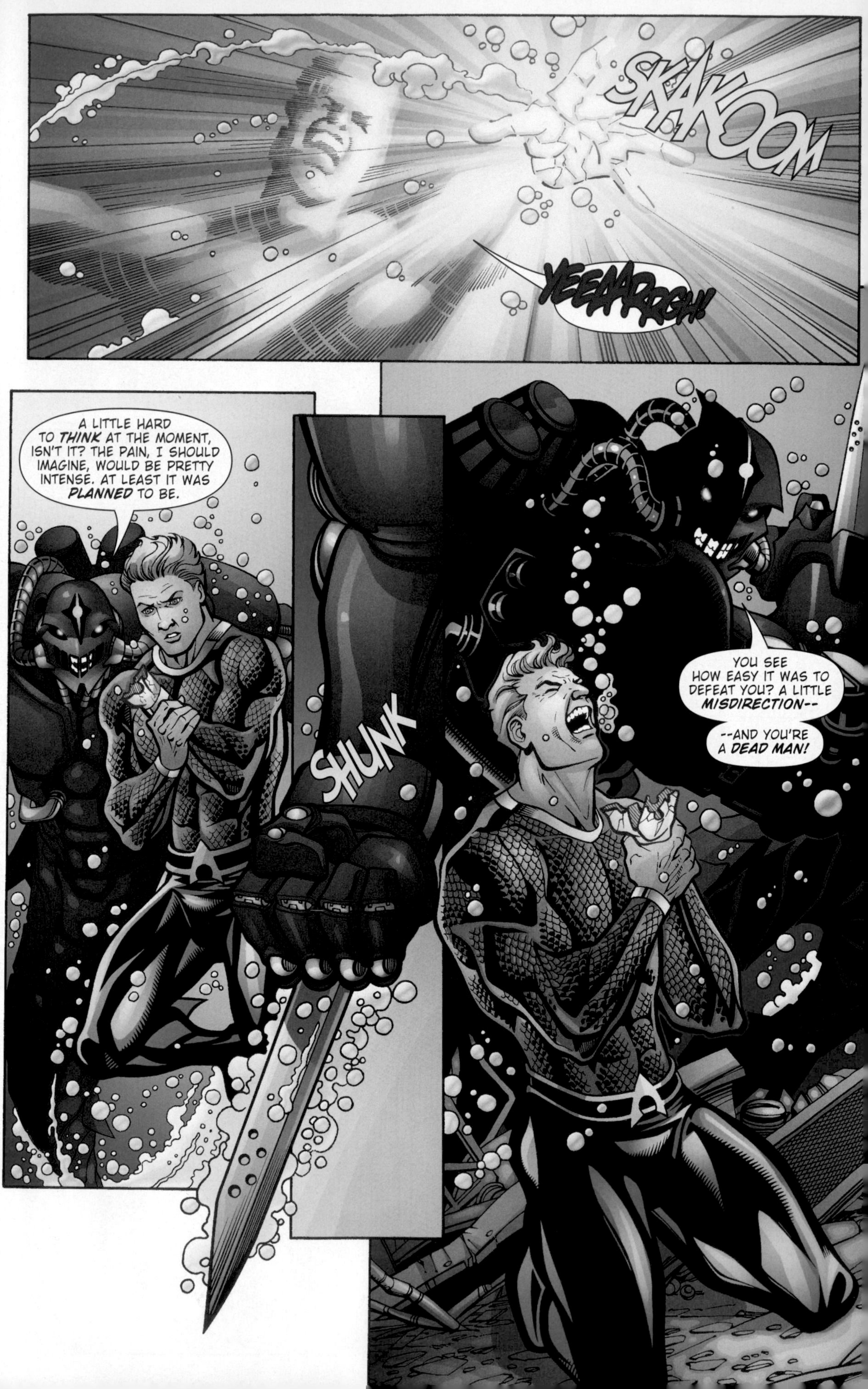
SKAKOOM
YEEAAARRGH!
A LITTLE HARD TO THINK AT THE MOMENT, ISN'T IT? THE PAIN, I SHOULD IMAGINE, WOULD BE PRETTY INTENSE. AT LEAST IT WAS PLANNED TO BE.
SHUNK
YOU SEE HOW EASY IT WAS TO DEFEAT YOU? A LITTLE MISDIRECTION--
--AND YOU'RE A DEAD MAN!

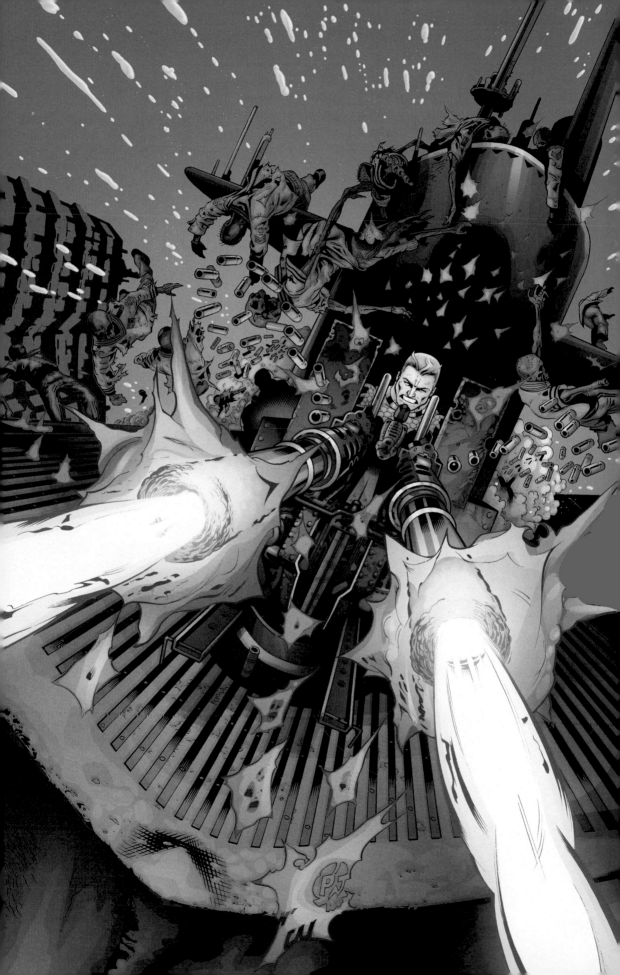

PLUNDER

JOHN OSTRANDER
Writer

CHRIS BATISTA
Penciller

DAVE MEIKIS
MIKE GRAY
JAY LEISTEIN
WADE von GRAWBADGER
Inkers

NATHAN EYRING
Colorist

JARED K. FLETCHER
Letterer

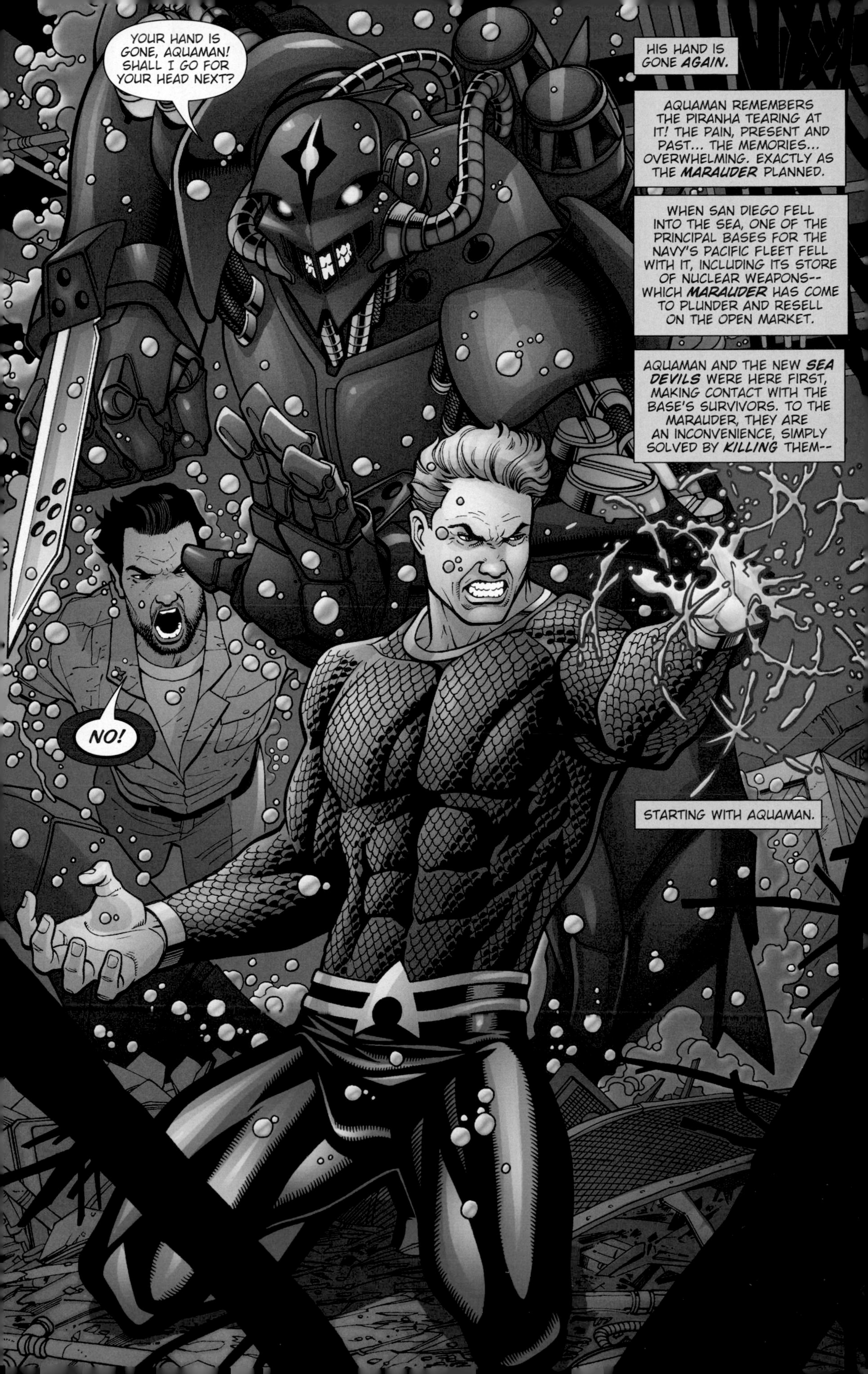
YOUR HAND IS GONE, AQUAMAN! SHALL I GO FOR YOUR HEAD NEXT?
HIS HAND IS GONE AGAIN.
AQUAMAN REMEMBERS THE PIRANHA TEARING AT IT! THE PAIN, PRESENT AND PAST... THE MEMORIES... OVERWHELMING. EXACTLY AS THE MARAUDER PLANNED.
WHEN SAN DIEGO FELL INTO THE SEA, ONE OF THE PRINCIPAL BASES FOR THE NAVY'S PACIFIC FLEET FELL WITH IT, INCLUDING ITS STORE OF NUCLEAR WEAPONS-- WHICH MARAUDER HAS COME TO PLUNDER AND RESELL ON THE OPEN MARKET.
AQUAMAN AND THE NEW SEA DEVILS WERE HERE FIRST, MAKING CONTACT WITH THE BASE'S SURVIVORS. TO THE MARAUDER, THEY ARE AN INCONVENIENCE, SIMPLY SOLVED BY KILLING THEM--
NO!
STARTING WITH AQUAMAN.

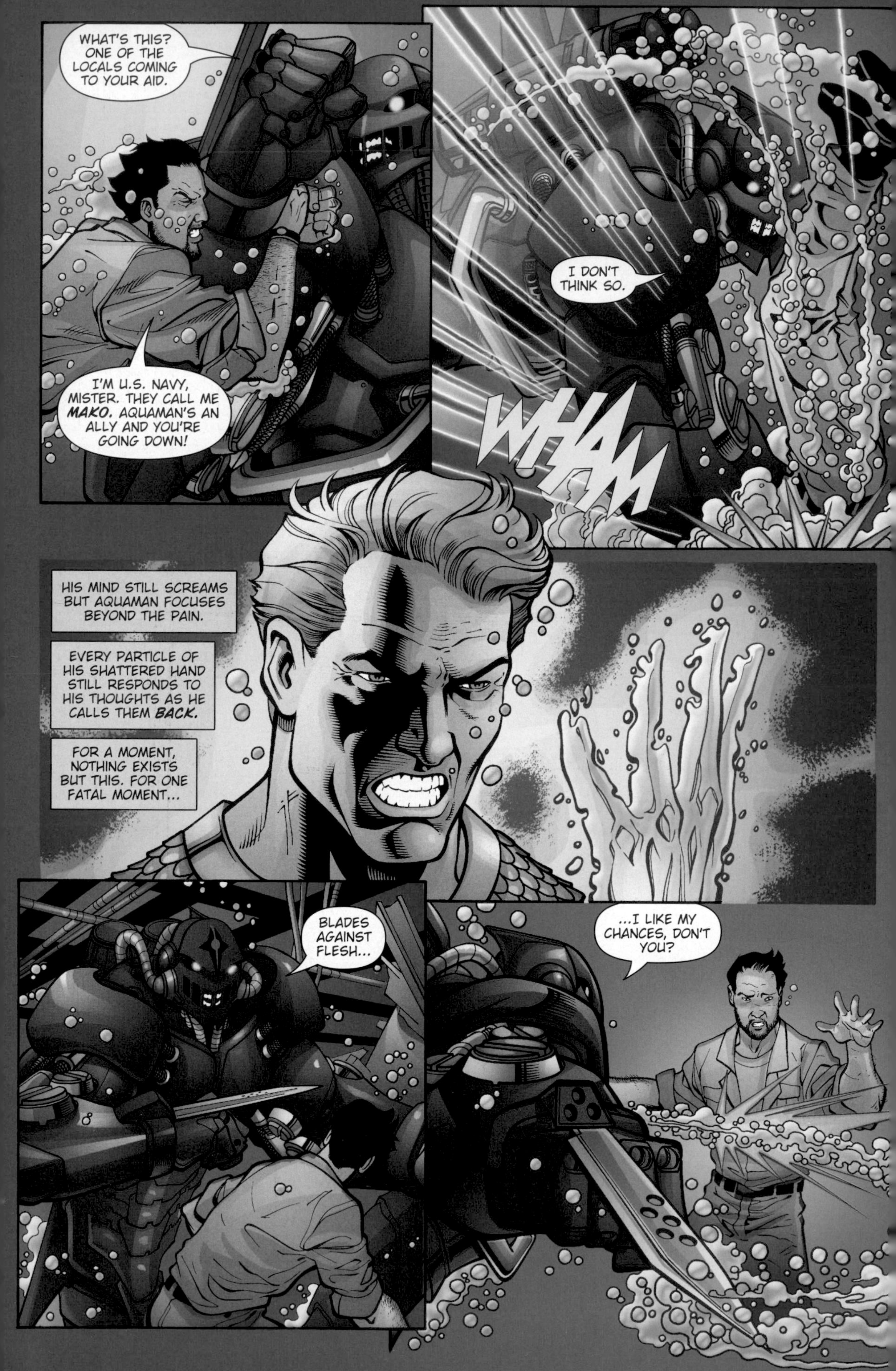
WHAT'S THIS? ONE OF THE LOCALS COMING TO YOUR AID.
I'M U.S. NAVY, MISTER. THEY CALL ME MAKO. AQUAMAN'S AN ALLY AND YOU'RE GOING DOWN!
I DON'T THINK SO.
WHAM
HIS MIND STILL SCREAMS BUT AQUAMAN FOCUSES BEYOND THE PAIN.
EVERY PARTICLE OF HIS SHATTERED HAND STILL RESPONDS TO HIS THOUGHTS AS HE CALLS THEM BACK.
FOR A MOMENT, NOTHING EXISTS BUT THIS. FOR ONE FATAL MOMENT...
BLADES AGAINST FLESH...
...I LIKE MY CHANCES, DON'T YOU?

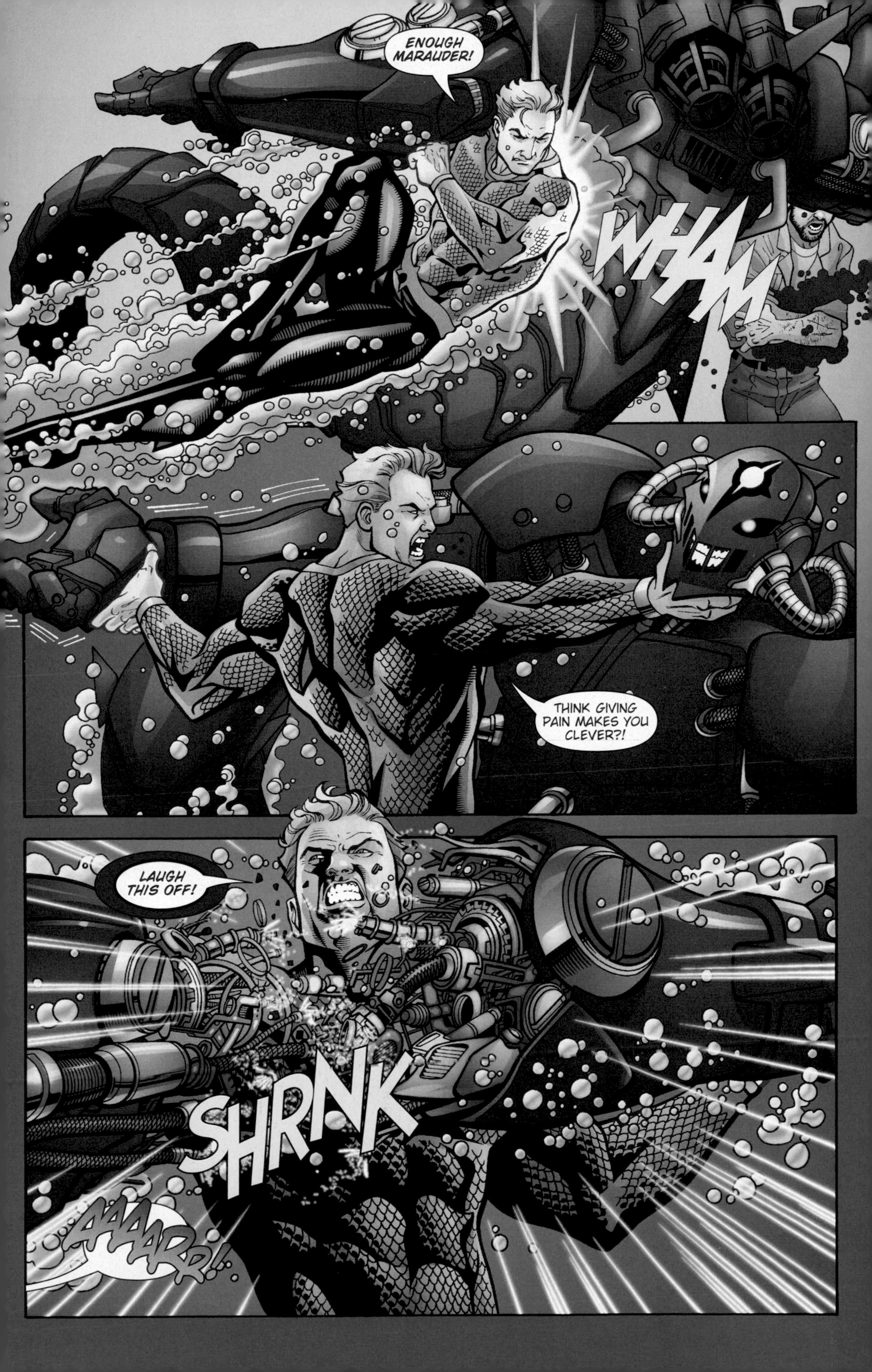
ENOUGH MARAUDER!
WHAM
THINK GIVING PAIN MAKES YOU CLEVER?!
LAUGH THIS OFF!
SHRNK
AAAARRR!

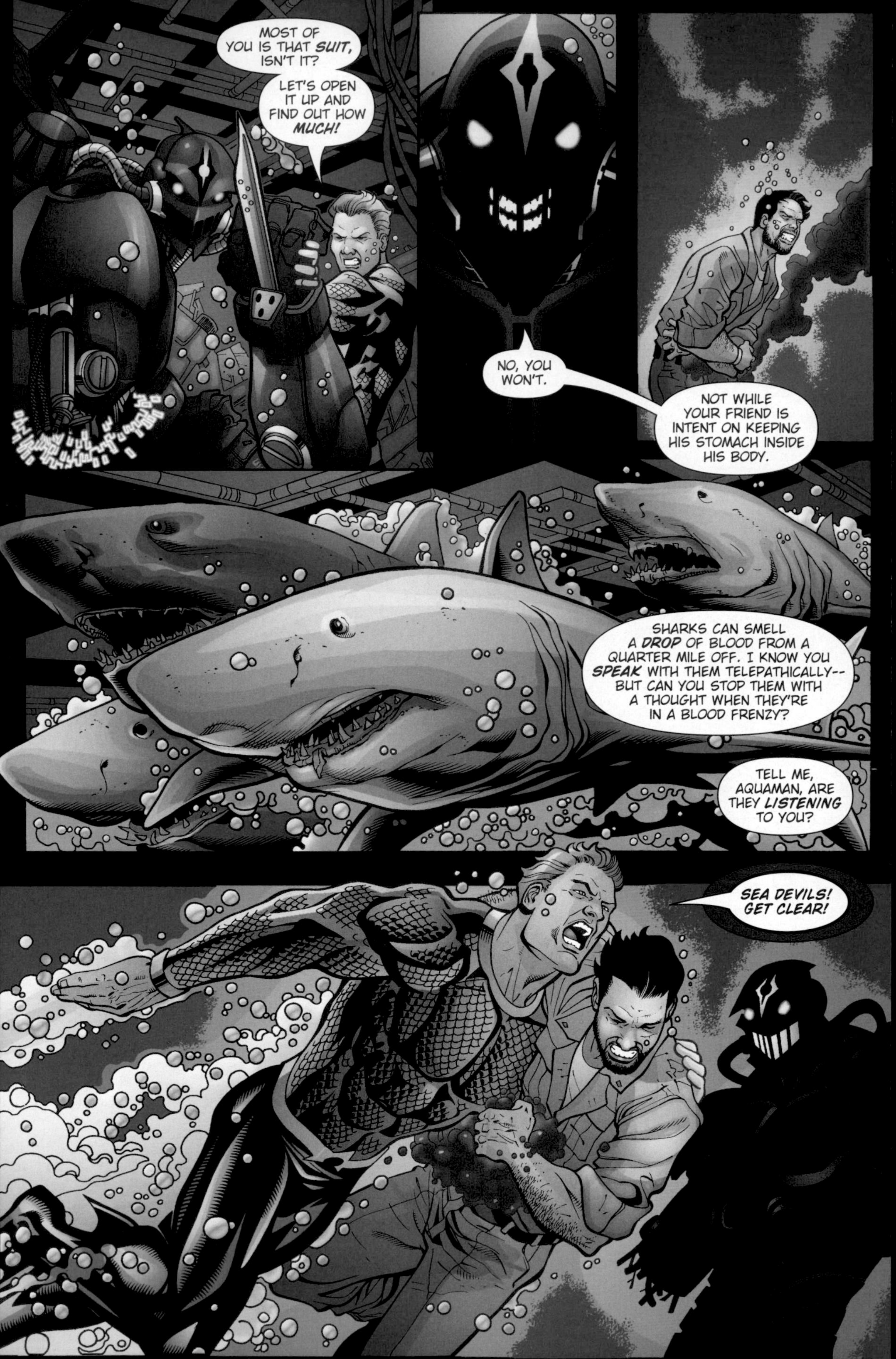
MOST OF YOU IS THAT SUIT, ISN'T IT?
LET'S OPEN IT UP AND FIND OUT HOW MUCH!
NO, YOU WON'T.
NOT WHILE YOUR FRIEND IS INTENT ON KEEPING HIS STOMACH INSIDE HIS BODY.
SHARKS CAN SMELL A DROP OF BLOOD FROM A QUARTER MILE OFF. I KNOW YOU SPEAK WITH THEM TELEPATHICALLY-- BUT CAN YOU STOP THEM WITH A THOUGHT WHEN THEY'RE IN A BLOOD FRENZY?
TELL ME, AQUAMAN, ARE THEY LISTENING TO YOU?
SEA DEVILS! GET CLEAR!

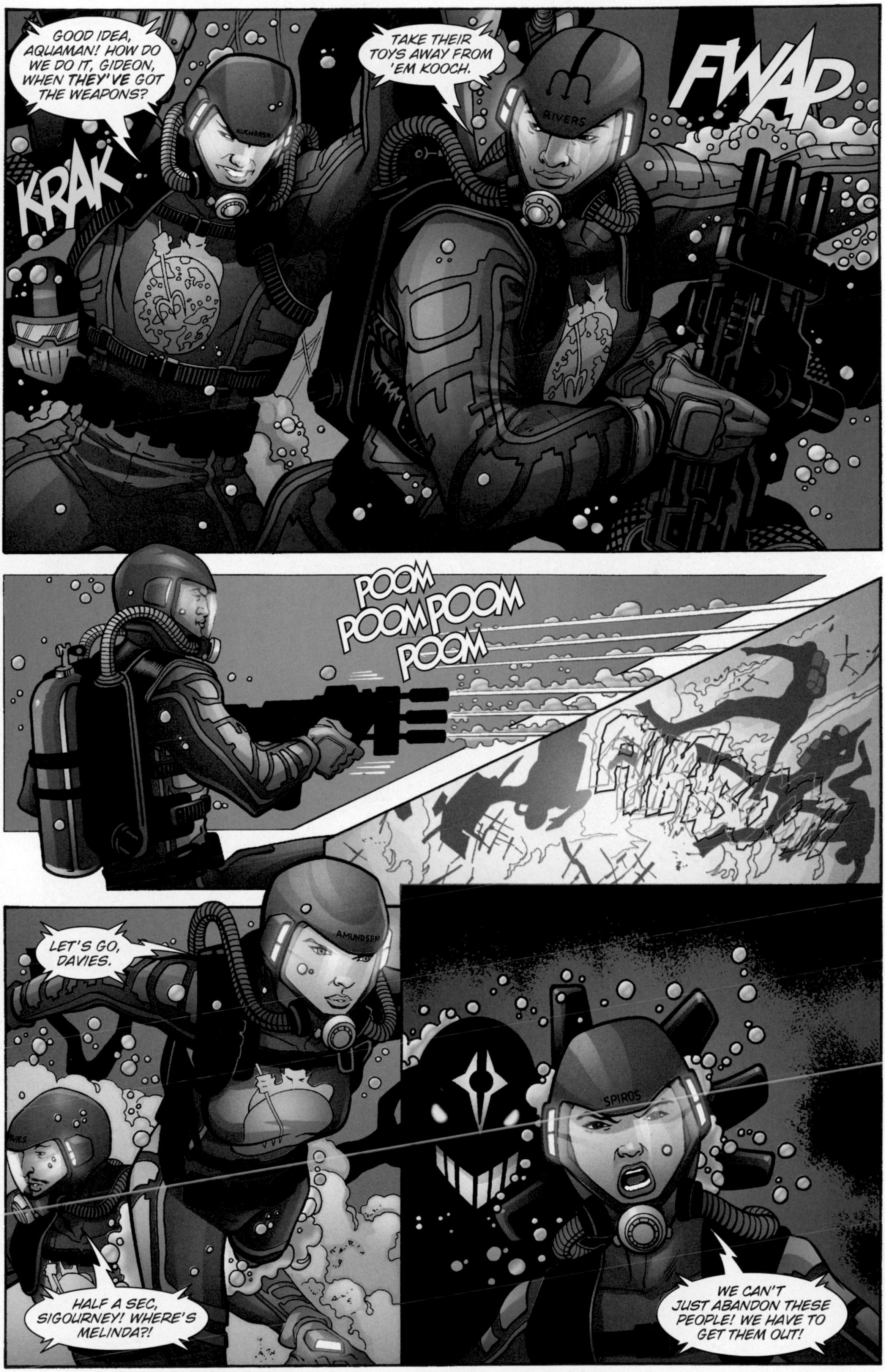
GOOD IDEA, AQUAMAN! HOW DO WE DO IT, GIDEON, WHEN THEY'VE GOT THE WEAPONS?
KRAK
TAKE THEIR TOYS AWAY FROM 'EM KOOCH.
FWAP
POOM POOM POOM POOM
LET'S GO, DAVIES.
HALF A SEC, SIGOURNEY! WHERE'S MELINDA?!
WE CAN'T JUST ABANDON THESE PEOPLE! WE HAVE TO GET THEM OUT!

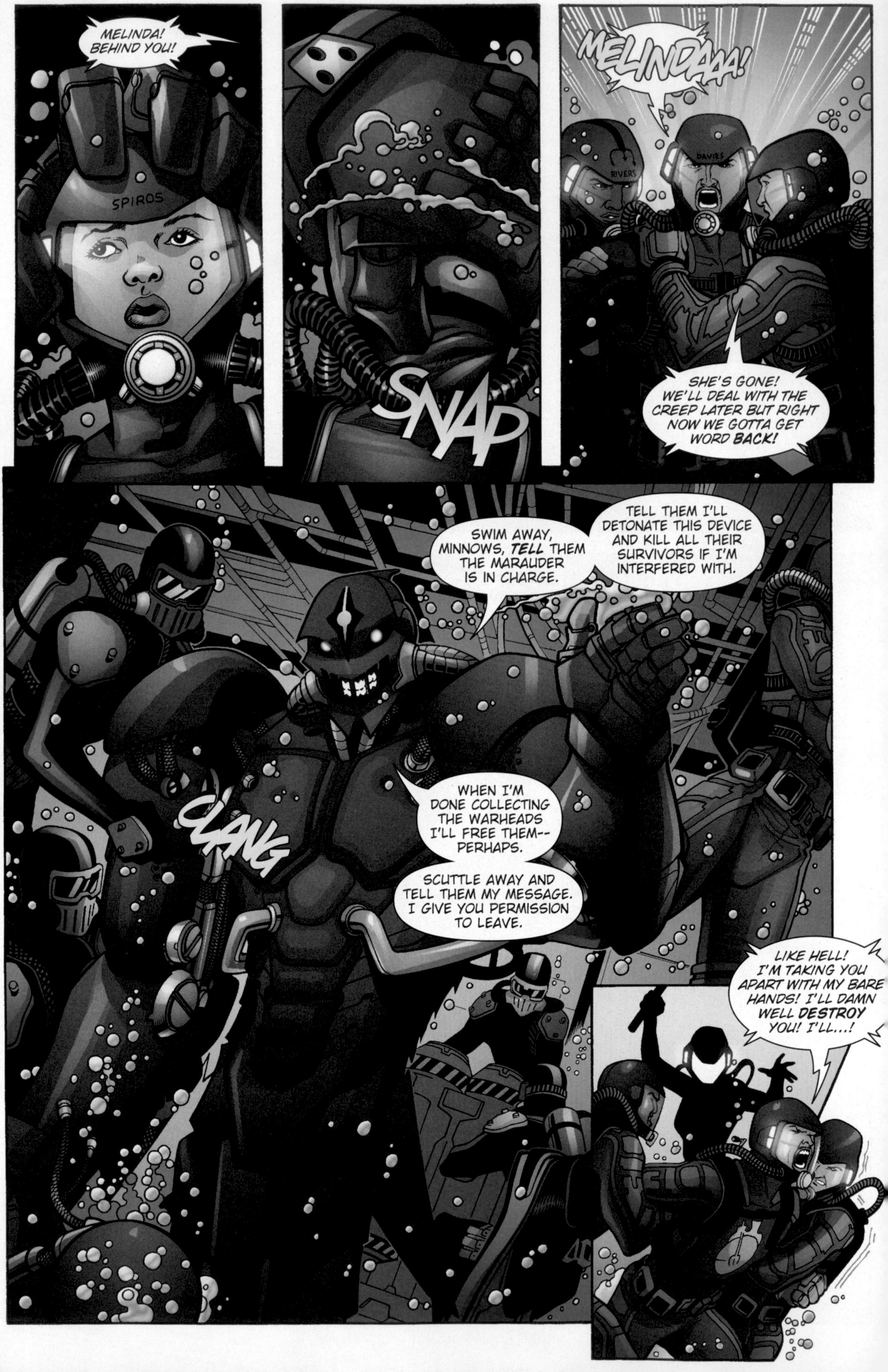
MELINDA! BEHIND YOU!
SNAP
MELINDAAA!
SHE'S GONE! WE'LL DEAL WITH THE CREEP LATER BUT RIGHT NOW WE GOTTA GET WORD BACK!
SWIM AWAY, MINNOWS, TELL THEM THE MARAUDER IS IN CHARGE.
TELL THEM I'LL DETONATE THIS DEVICE AND KILL ALL THEIR SURVIVORS IF I'M INTERFERED WITH.
CLANG
WHEN I'M DONE COLLECTING THE WARHEADS I'LL FREE THEM--PERHAPS.
SCUTTLE AWAY AND TELL THEM MY MESSAGE. I GIVE YOU PERMISSION TO LEAVE.
LIKE HELL! I'M TAKING YOU APART WITH MY BARE HANDS! I'LL DAMN WELL DESTROY YOU! I'LL...!

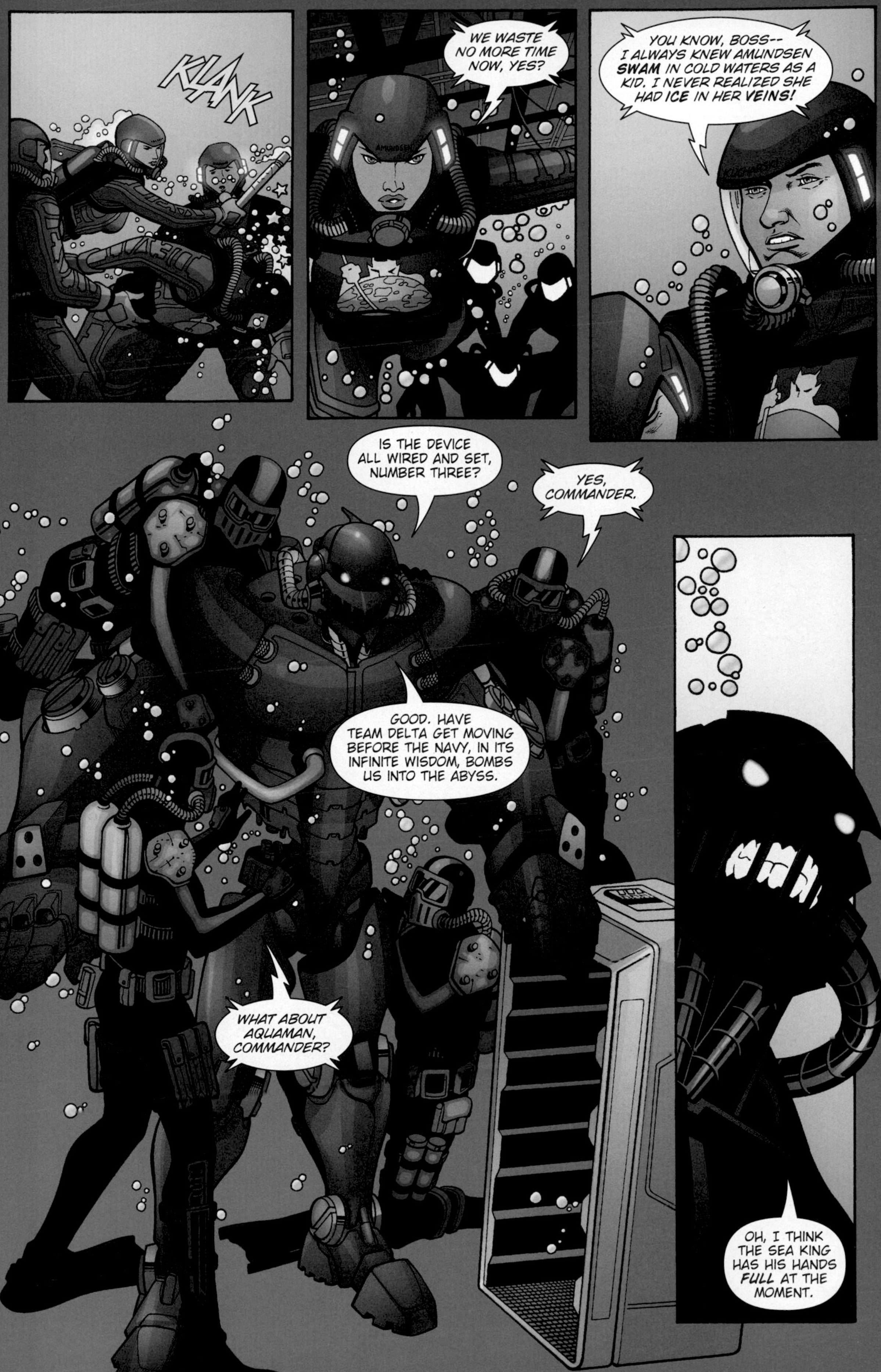
KLANK
WE WASTE NO MORE TIME NOW, YES?
YOU KNOW, BOSS-- I ALWAYS KNEW AMUNDSEN **SWAM** IN COLD WATERS AS A KID. I NEVER REALIZED SHE HAD **ICE** IN HER **VEINS!**
IS THE DEVICE ALL WIRED AND SET, NUMBER THREE?
YES, COMMANDER.
GOOD. HAVE TEAM DELTA GET MOVING BEFORE THE NAVY, IN ITS INFINITE WISDOM, BOMBS US INTO THE ABYSS.
WHAT ABOUT AQUAMAN, COMMANDER?
OH, I THINK THE SEA KING HAS HIS HANDS *FULL* AT THE MOMENT.

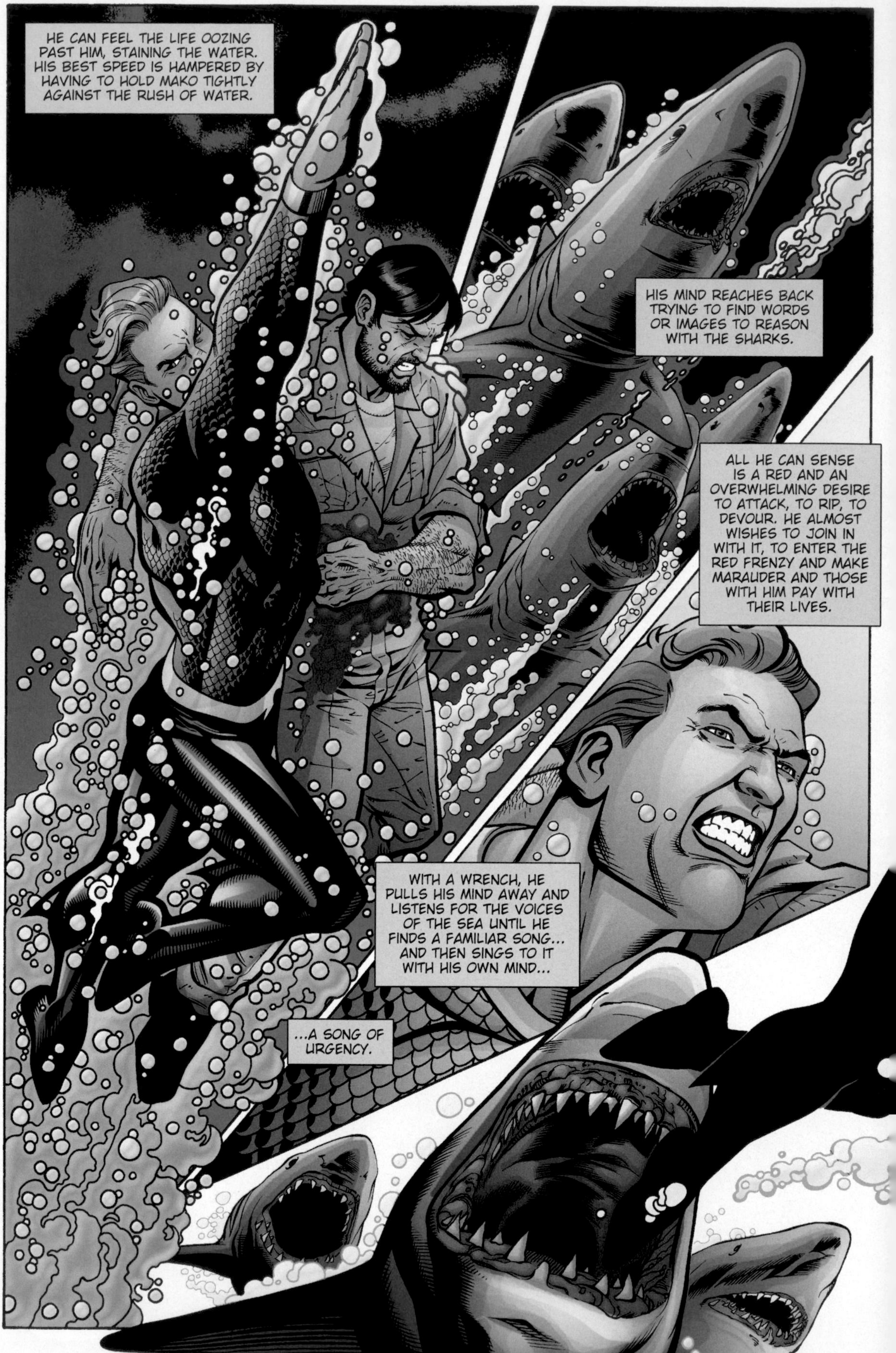
HE CAN FEEL THE LIFE OOZING PAST HIM, STAINING THE WATER. HIS BEST SPEED IS HAMPERED BY HAVING TO HOLD MAKO TIGHTLY AGAINST THE RUSH OF WATER.
HIS MIND REACHES BACK TRYING TO FIND WORDS OR IMAGES TO REASON WITH THE SHARKS.
ALL HE CAN SENSE IS A RED AND AN OVERWHELMING DESIRE TO ATTACK, TO RIP, TO DEVOUR. HE ALMOST WISHES TO JOIN IN WITH IT, TO ENTER THE RED FRENZY AND MAKE MARAUDER AND THOSE WITH HIM PAY WITH THEIR LIVES.
WITH A WRENCH, HE PULLS HIS MIND AWAY AND LISTENS FOR THE VOICES OF THE SEA UNTIL HE FINDS A FAMILIAR SONG... AND THEN SINGS TO IT WITH HIS OWN MIND...
...A SONG OF URGENCY.

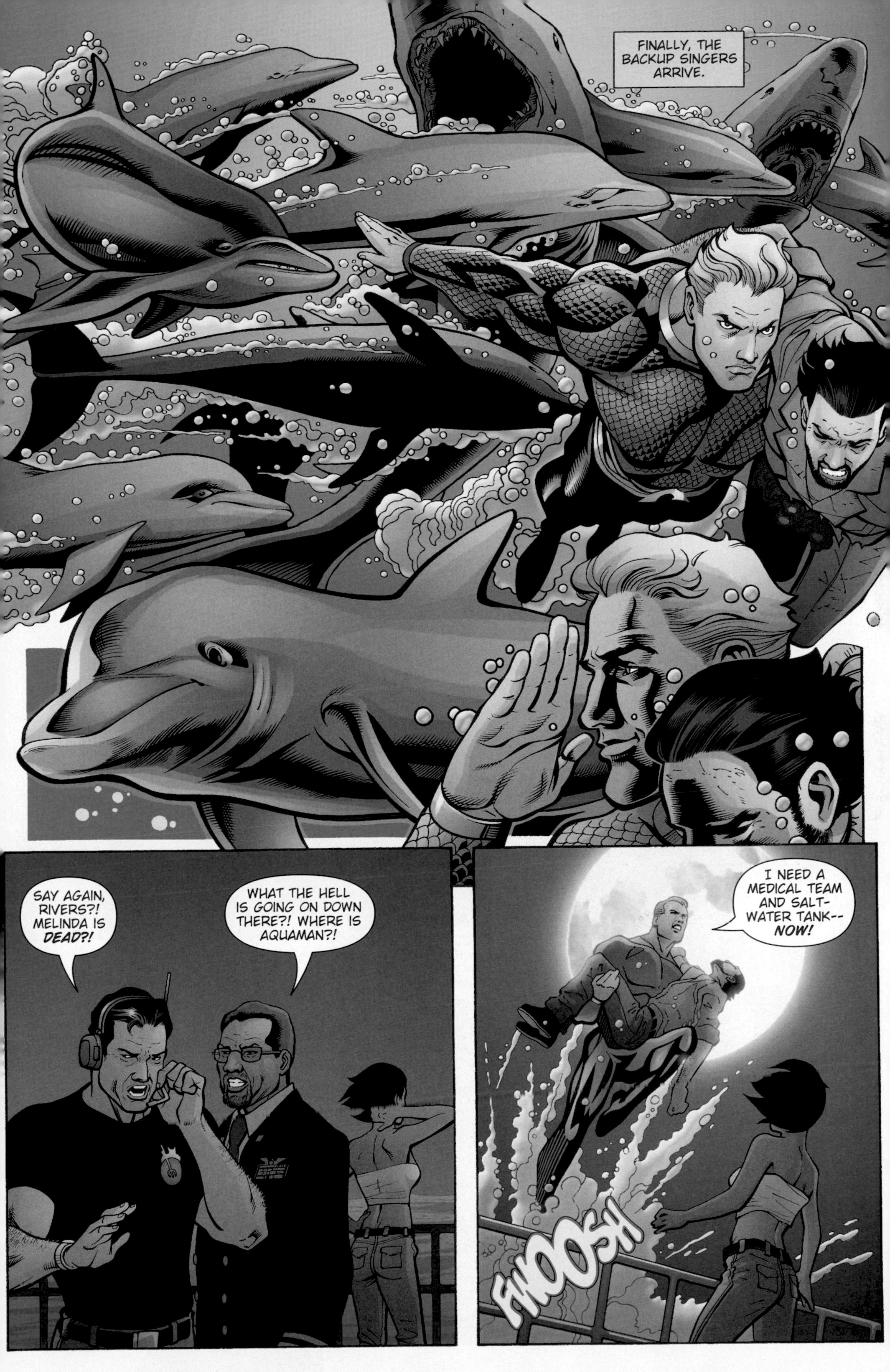
FINALLY, THE BACKUP SINGERS ARRIVE.
SAY AGAIN, RIVERS?! MELINDA IS DEAD?!
WHAT THE HELL IS GOING ON DOWN THERE?! WHERE IS AQUAMAN?!
I NEED A MEDICAL TEAM AND SALT-WATER TANK-- NOW!
FWOOSH

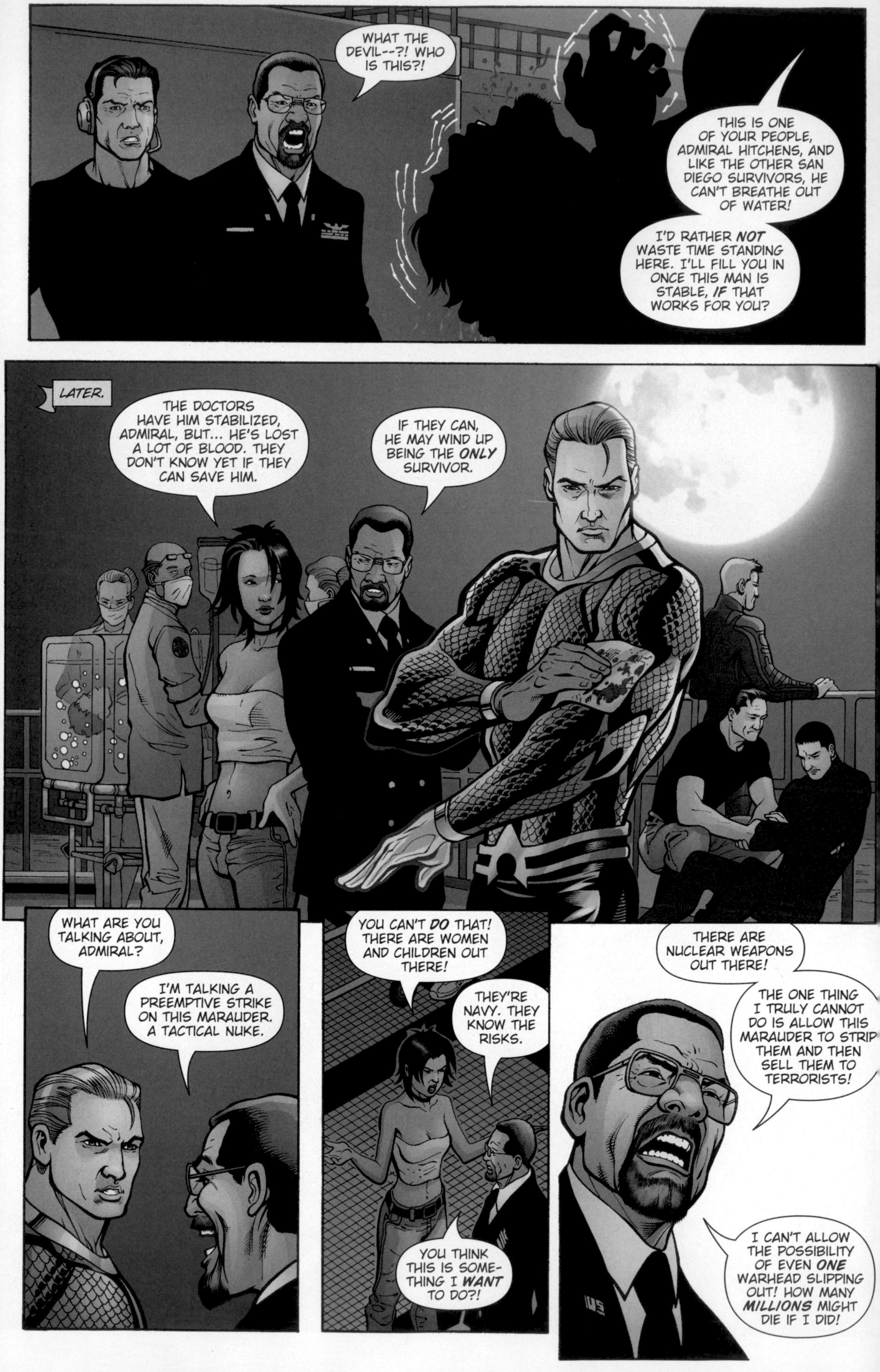
WHAT THE DEVIL--?! WHO IS THIS?!
THIS IS ONE OF YOUR PEOPLE, ADMIRAL HITCHENS, AND LIKE THE OTHER SAN DIEGO SURVIVORS, HE CAN'T BREATHE OUT OF WATER!
I'D RATHER NOT WASTE TIME STANDING HERE. I'LL FILL YOU IN ONCE THIS MAN IS STABLE, IF THAT WORKS FOR YOU?
LATER.
THE DOCTORS HAVE HIM STABILIZED, ADMIRAL, BUT... HE'S LOST A LOT OF BLOOD. THEY DON'T KNOW YET IF THEY CAN SAVE HIM.
IF THEY CAN, HE MAY WIND UP BEING THE ONLY SURVIVOR.
WHAT ARE YOU TALKING ABOUT, ADMIRAL?
I'M TALKING A PREEMPTIVE STRIKE ON THIS MARAUDER. A TACTICAL NUKE.
YOU CAN'T DO THAT! THERE ARE WOMEN AND CHILDREN OUT THERE!
THEY'RE NAVY. THEY KNOW THE RISKS.
YOU THINK THIS IS SOMETHING I WANT TO DO?!
THERE ARE NUCLEAR WEAPONS OUT THERE!
THE ONE THING I TRULY CANNOT DO IS ALLOW THIS MARAUDER TO STRIP THEM AND THEN SELL THEM TO TERRORISTS!
I CAN'T ALLOW THE POSSIBILITY OF EVEN ONE WARHEAD SLIPPING OUT! HOW MANY MILLIONS MIGHT DIE IF I DID!

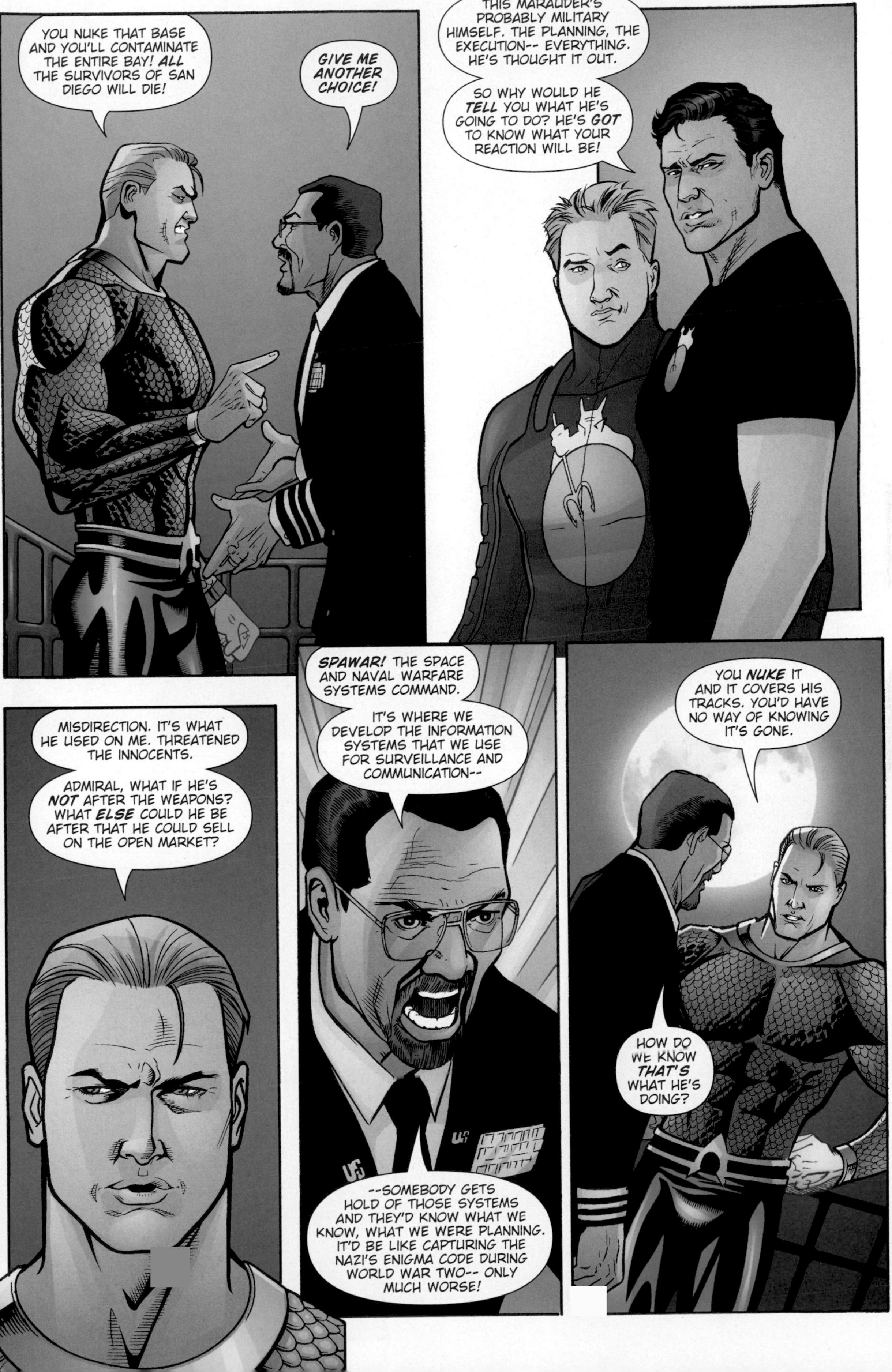
YOU NUKE THAT BASE AND YOU'LL CONTAMINATE THE ENTIRE BAY! ALL THE SURVIVORS OF SAN DIEGO WILL DIE!
GIVE ME ANOTHER CHOICE!
THIS MARAUDER'S PROBABLY MILITARY HIMSELF. THE PLANNING, THE EXECUTION-- EVERYTHING. HE'S THOUGHT IT OUT.
SO WHY WOULD HE TELL YOU WHAT HE'S GOING TO DO? HE'S GOT TO KNOW WHAT YOUR REACTION WILL BE!
MISDIRECTION. IT'S WHAT HE USED ON ME. THREATENED THE INNOCENTS.
ADMIRAL, WHAT IF HE'S NOT AFTER THE WEAPONS? WHAT ELSE COULD HE BE AFTER THAT HE COULD SELL ON THE OPEN MARKET?
SPAWAR! THE SPACE AND NAVAL WARFARE SYSTEMS COMMAND.
IT'S WHERE WE DEVELOP THE INFORMATION SYSTEMS THAT WE USE FOR SURVEILLANCE AND COMMUNICATION--
--SOMEBODY GETS HOLD OF THOSE SYSTEMS AND THEY'D KNOW WHAT WE KNOW, WHAT WE WERE PLANNING. IT'D BE LIKE CAPTURING THE NAZI'S ENIGMA CODE DURING WORLD WAR TWO-- ONLY MUCH WORSE!
YOU NUKE IT AND IT COVERS HIS TRACKS. YOU'D HAVE NO WAY OF KNOWING IT'S GONE.
HOW DO WE KNOW THAT'S WHAT HE'S DOING?

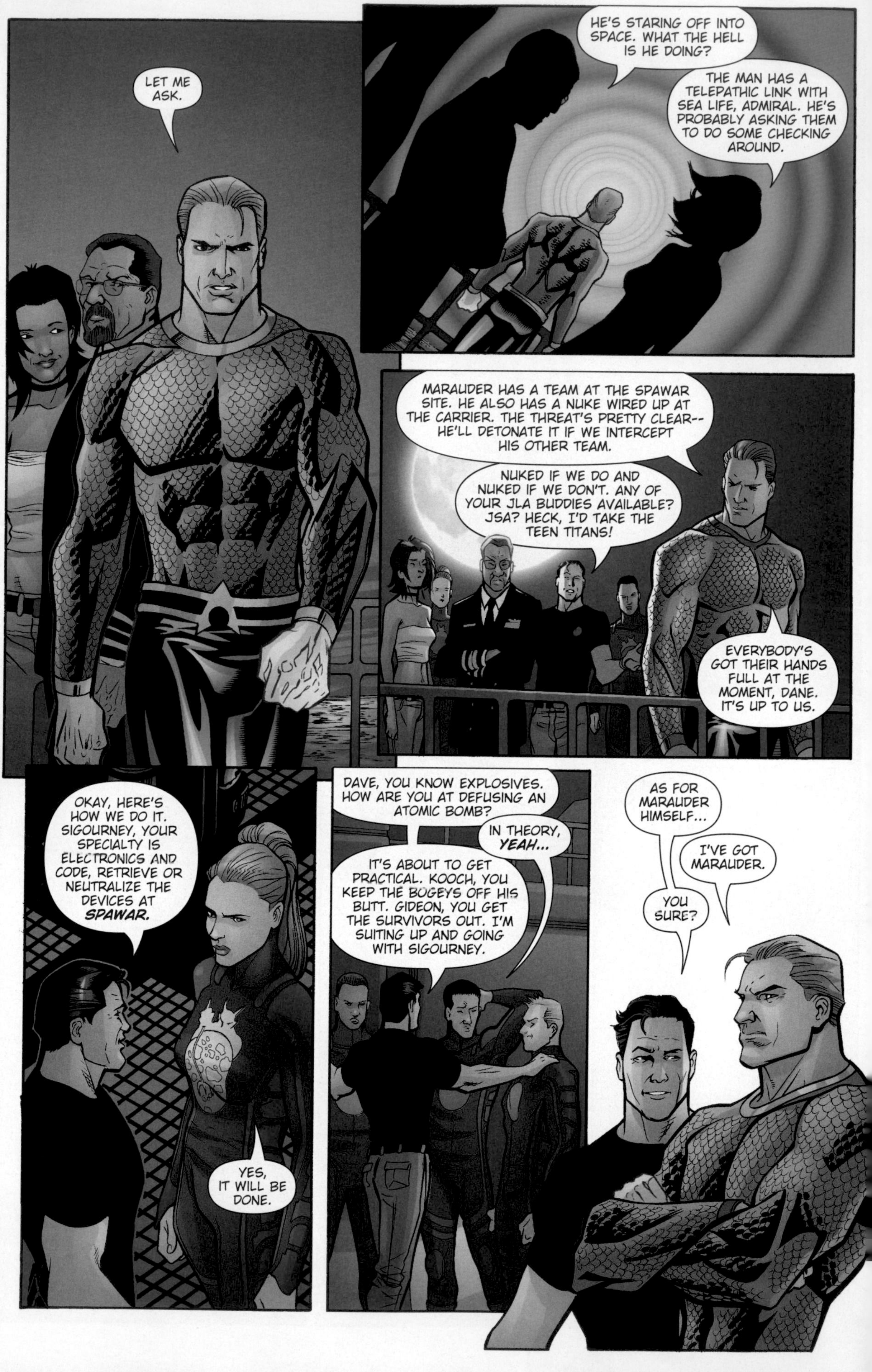
LET ME ASK.
HE'S STARING OFF INTO SPACE. WHAT THE HELL IS HE DOING?
THE MAN HAS A TELEPATHIC LINK WITH SEA LIFE, ADMIRAL. HE'S PROBABLY ASKING THEM TO DO SOME CHECKING AROUND.
MARAUDER HAS A TEAM AT THE SPAWAR SITE. HE ALSO HAS A NUKE WIRED UP AT THE CARRIER. THE THREAT'S PRETTY CLEAR-- HE'LL DETONATE IT IF WE INTERCEPT HIS OTHER TEAM.
NUKED IF WE DO AND NUKED IF WE DON'T. ANY OF YOUR JLA BUDDIES AVAILABLE? JSA? HECK, I'D TAKE THE TEEN TITANS!
EVERYBODY'S GOT THEIR HANDS FULL AT THE MOMENT, DANE. IT'S UP TO US.
OKAY, HERE'S HOW WE DO IT. SIGOURNEY, YOUR SPECIALTY IS ELECTRONICS AND CODE, RETRIEVE OR NEUTRALIZE THE DEVICES AT SPAWAR.
YES, IT WILL BE DONE.
DAVE, YOU KNOW EXPLOSIVES. HOW ARE YOU AT DEFUSING AN ATOMIC BOMB?
IN THEORY, YEAH...
IT'S ABOUT TO GET PRACTICAL. KOOCH, YOU KEEP THE BOGEYS OFF HIS BUTT. GIDEON, YOU GET THE SURVIVORS OUT. I'M SUITING UP AND GOING WITH SIGOURNEY.
AS FOR MARAUDER HIMSELF...
I'VE GOT MARAUDER.
YOU SURE?

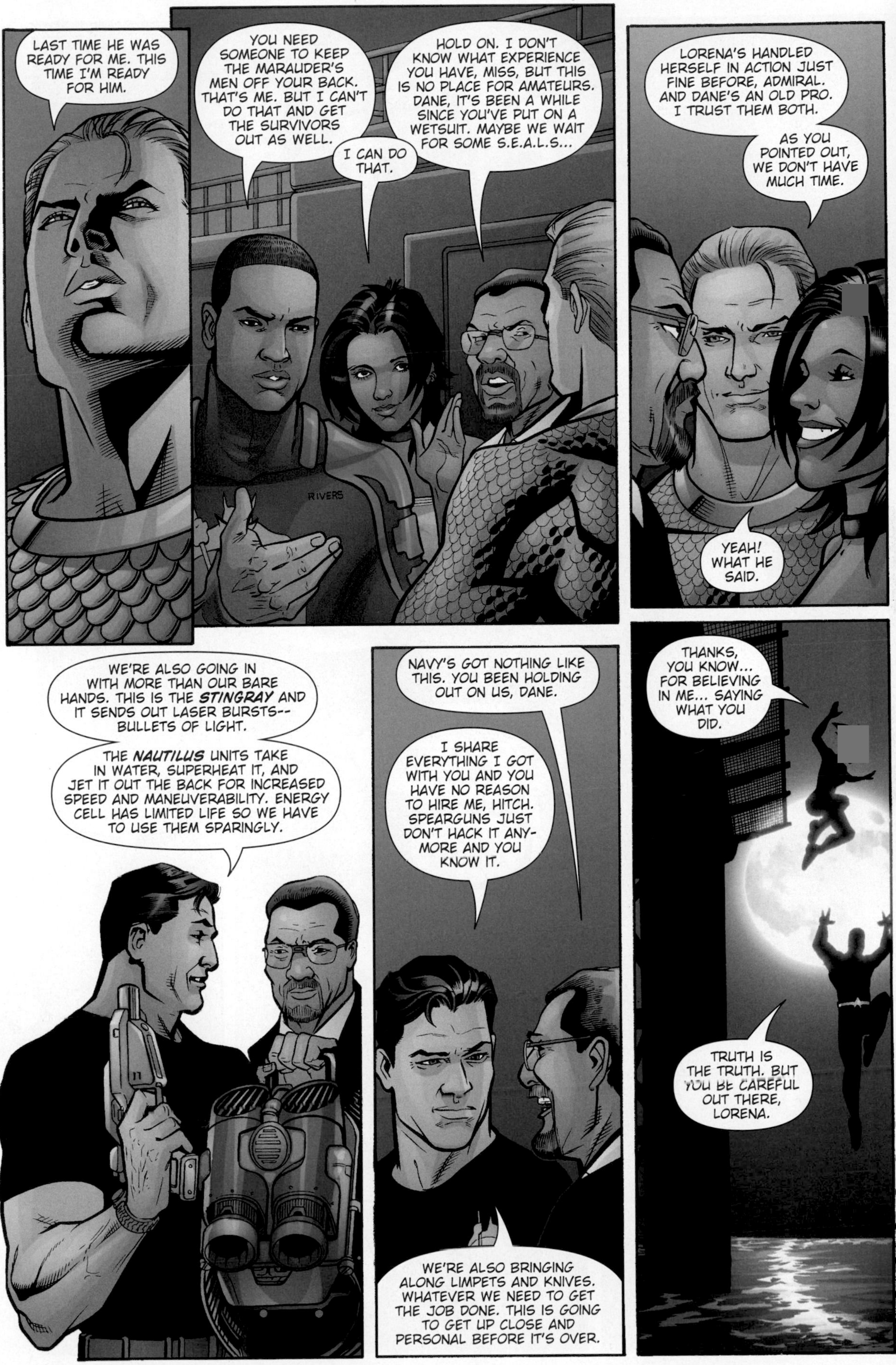
LAST TIME HE WAS READY FOR ME. THIS TIME I'M READY FOR HIM.
YOU NEED SOMEONE TO KEEP THE MARAUDER'S MEN OFF YOUR BACK. THAT'S ME. BUT I CAN'T DO THAT AND GET THE SURVIVORS OUT AS WELL.
I CAN DO THAT.
HOLD ON. I DON'T KNOW WHAT EXPERIENCE YOU HAVE, MISS, BUT THIS IS NO PLACE FOR AMATEURS. DANE, IT'S BEEN A WHILE SINCE YOU'VE PUT ON A WETSUIT. MAYBE WE WAIT FOR SOME S.E.A.L.S...
RIVERS
LORENA'S HANDLED HERSELF IN ACTION JUST FINE BEFORE, ADMIRAL. AND DANE'S AN OLD PRO. I TRUST THEM BOTH.
AS YOU POINTED OUT, WE DON'T HAVE MUCH TIME.
YEAH! WHAT HE SAID.
WE'RE ALSO GOING IN WITH MORE THAN OUR BARE HANDS. THIS IS THE *STINGRAY* AND IT SENDS OUT LASER BURSTS--BULLETS OF LIGHT.
THE *NAUTILUS* UNITS TAKE IN WATER, SUPERHEAT IT, AND JET IT OUT THE BACK FOR INCREASED SPEED AND MANEUVERABILITY. ENERGY CELL HAS LIMITED LIFE SO WE HAVE TO USE THEM SPARINGLY.
NAVY'S GOT NOTHING LIKE THIS. YOU BEEN HOLDING OUT ON US, DANE.
I SHARE EVERYTHING I GOT WITH YOU AND YOU HAVE NO REASON TO HIRE ME, HITCH. SPEARGUNS JUST DON'T HACK IT ANYMORE AND YOU KNOW IT.
WE'RE ALSO BRINGING ALONG LIMPETS AND KNIVES. WHATEVER WE NEED TO GET THE JOB DONE. THIS IS GOING TO GET UP CLOSE AND PERSONAL BEFORE IT'S OVER.
THANKS, YOU KNOW... FOR BELIEVING IN ME... SAYING WHAT YOU DID.
TRUTH IS THE TRUTH. BUT YOU BE CAREFUL OUT THERE, LORENA.

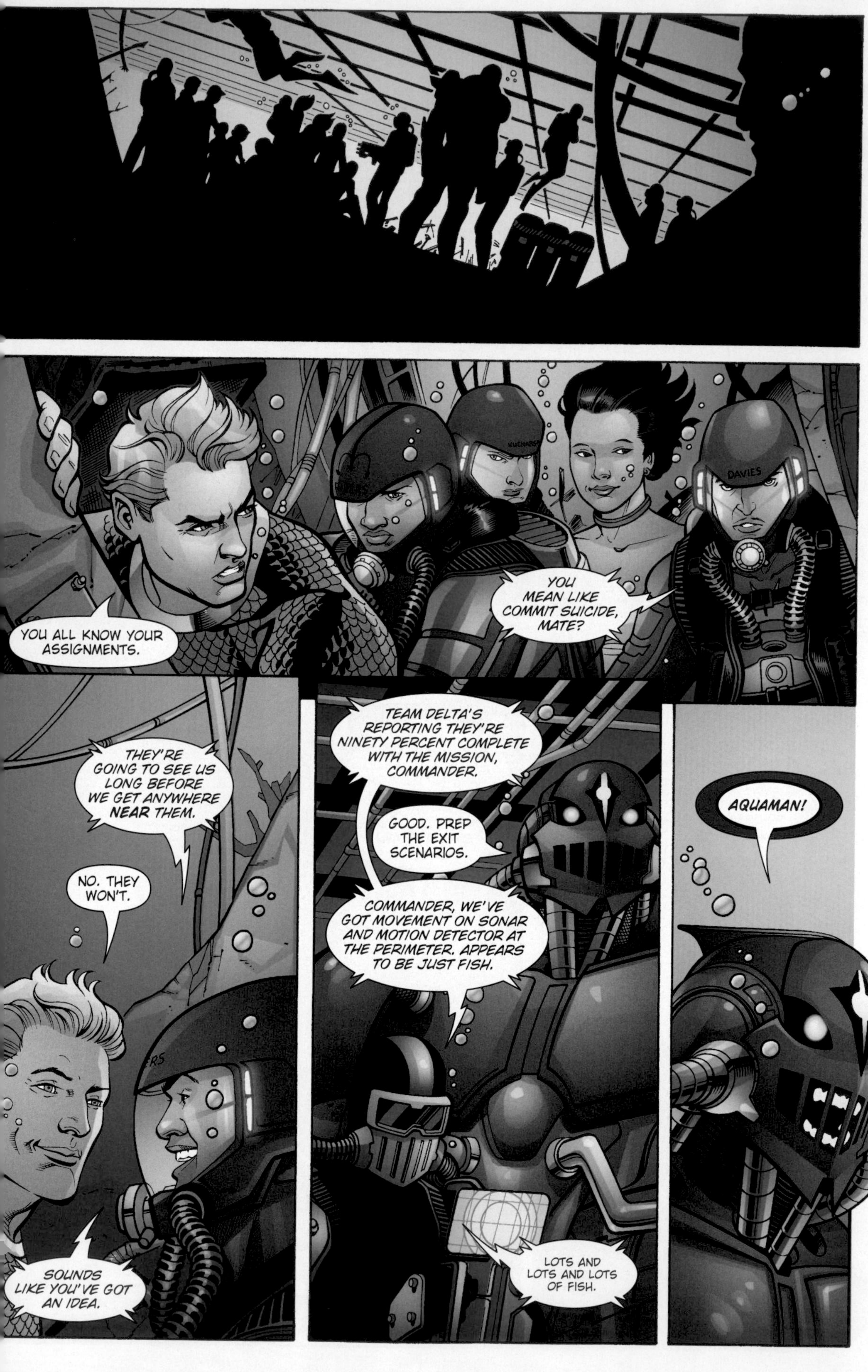
YOU ALL KNOW YOUR ASSIGNMENTS.
YOU MEAN LIKE COMMIT SUICIDE, MATE?
THEY'RE GOING TO SEE US LONG BEFORE WE GET ANYWHERE NEAR THEM.
NO. THEY WON'T.
SOUNDS LIKE YOU'VE GOT AN IDEA.
TEAM DELTA'S REPORTING THEY'RE NINETY PERCENT COMPLETE WITH THE MISSION, COMMANDER.
GOOD. PREP THE EXIT SCENARIOS.
COMMANDER, WE'VE GOT MOVEMENT ON SONAR AND MOTION DETECTOR AT THE PERIMETER. APPEARS TO BE JUST FISH.
LOTS AND LOTS AND LOTS OF FISH.
AQUAMAN!

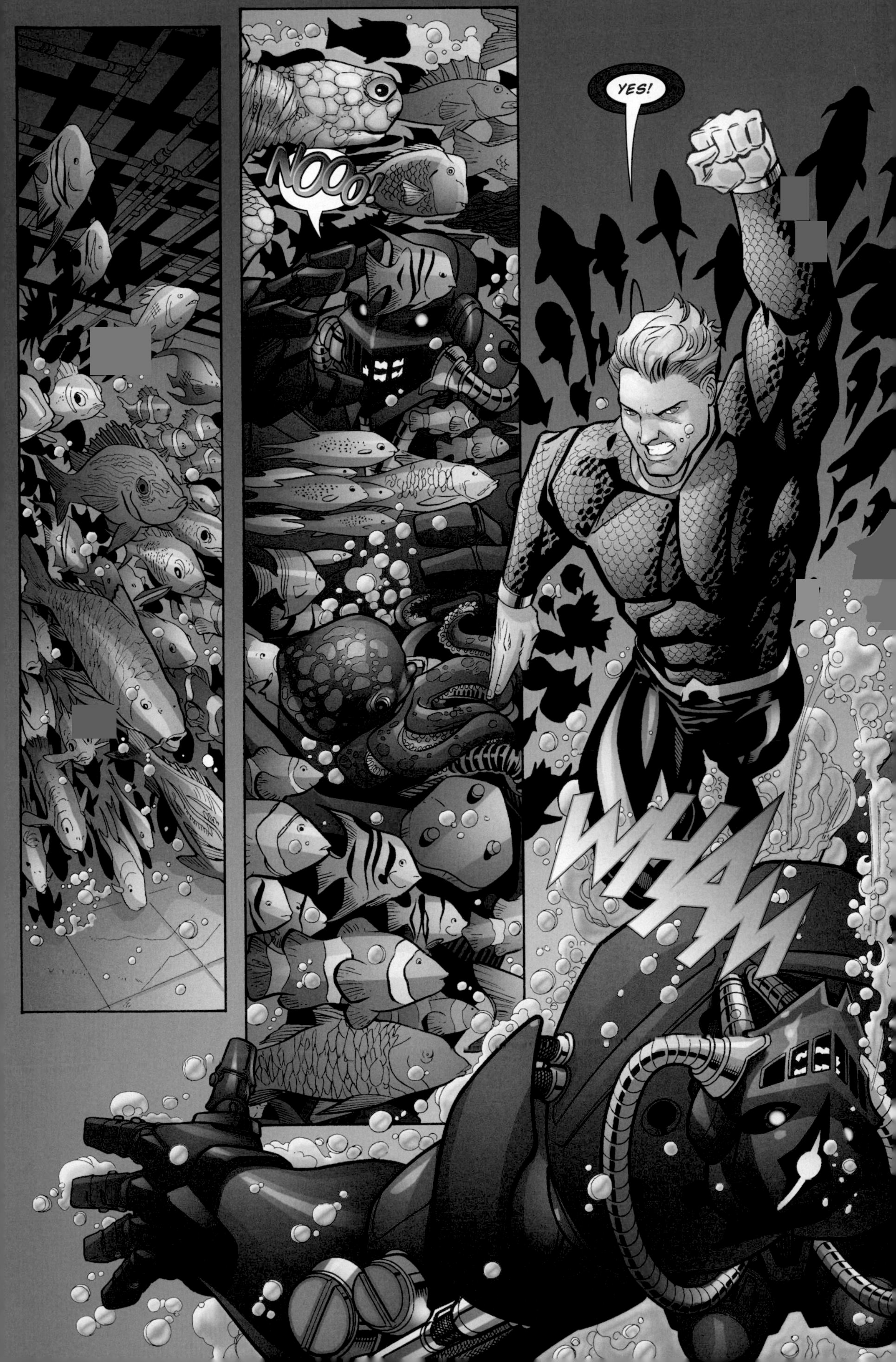
NOOO!
YES!
WHAM

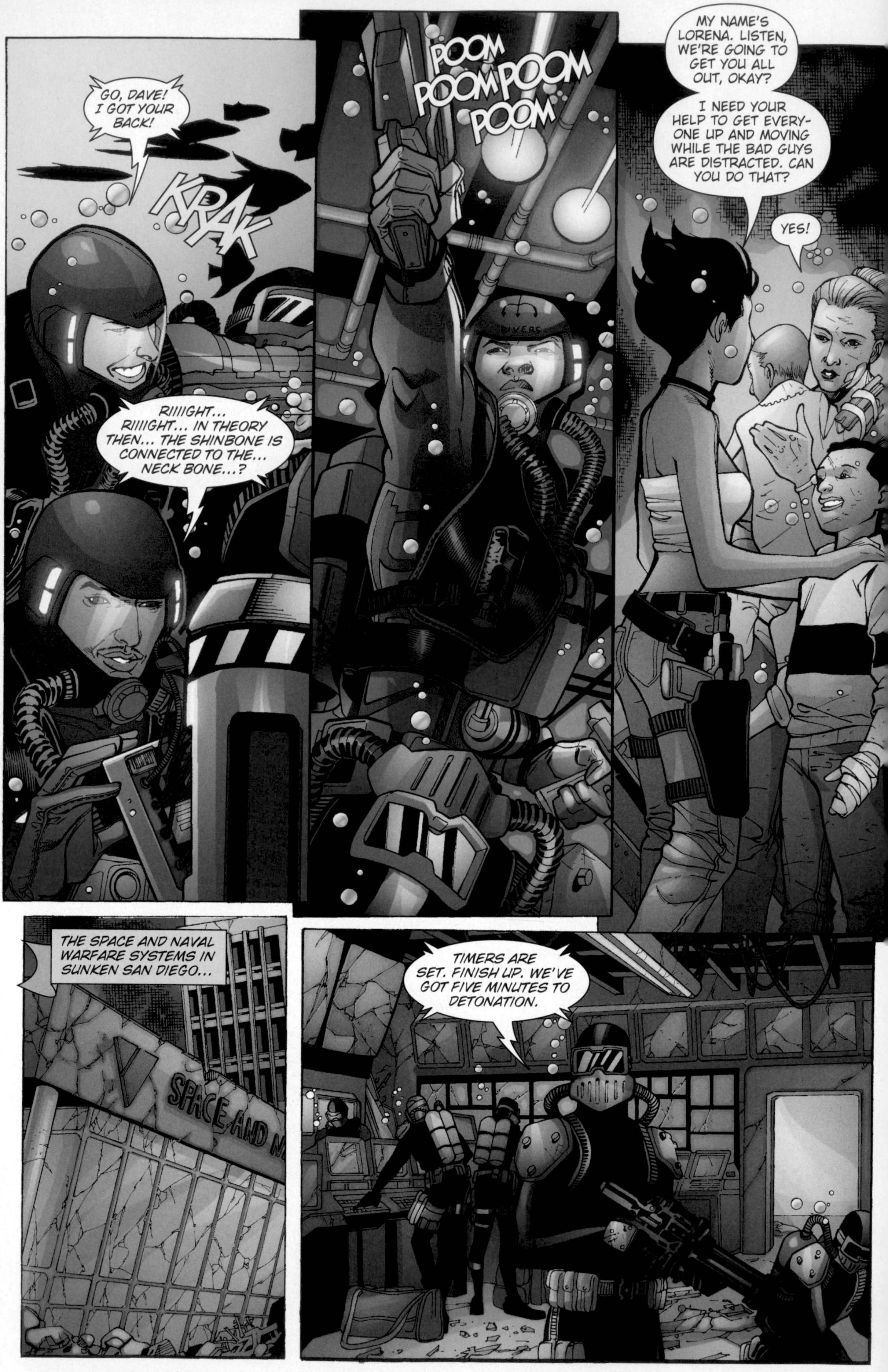
GO, DAVE! I GOT YOUR BACK!
KRAK
RIIIIGHT... RIIIIGHT... IN THEORY THEN... THE SHINBONE IS CONNECTED TO THE... NECK BONE...?
POOM POOM POOM POOM
MY NAME'S LORENA. LISTEN, WE'RE GOING TO GET YOU ALL OUT, OKAY?
I NEED YOUR HELP TO GET EVERY-ONE UP AND MOVING WHILE THE BAD GUYS ARE DISTRACTED. CAN YOU DO THAT?
YES!
THE SPACE AND NAVAL WARFARE SYSTEMS IN SUNKEN SAN DIEGO...
SPACE AND N
TIMERS ARE SET. FINISH UP. WE'VE GOT FIVE MINUTES TO DETONATION.

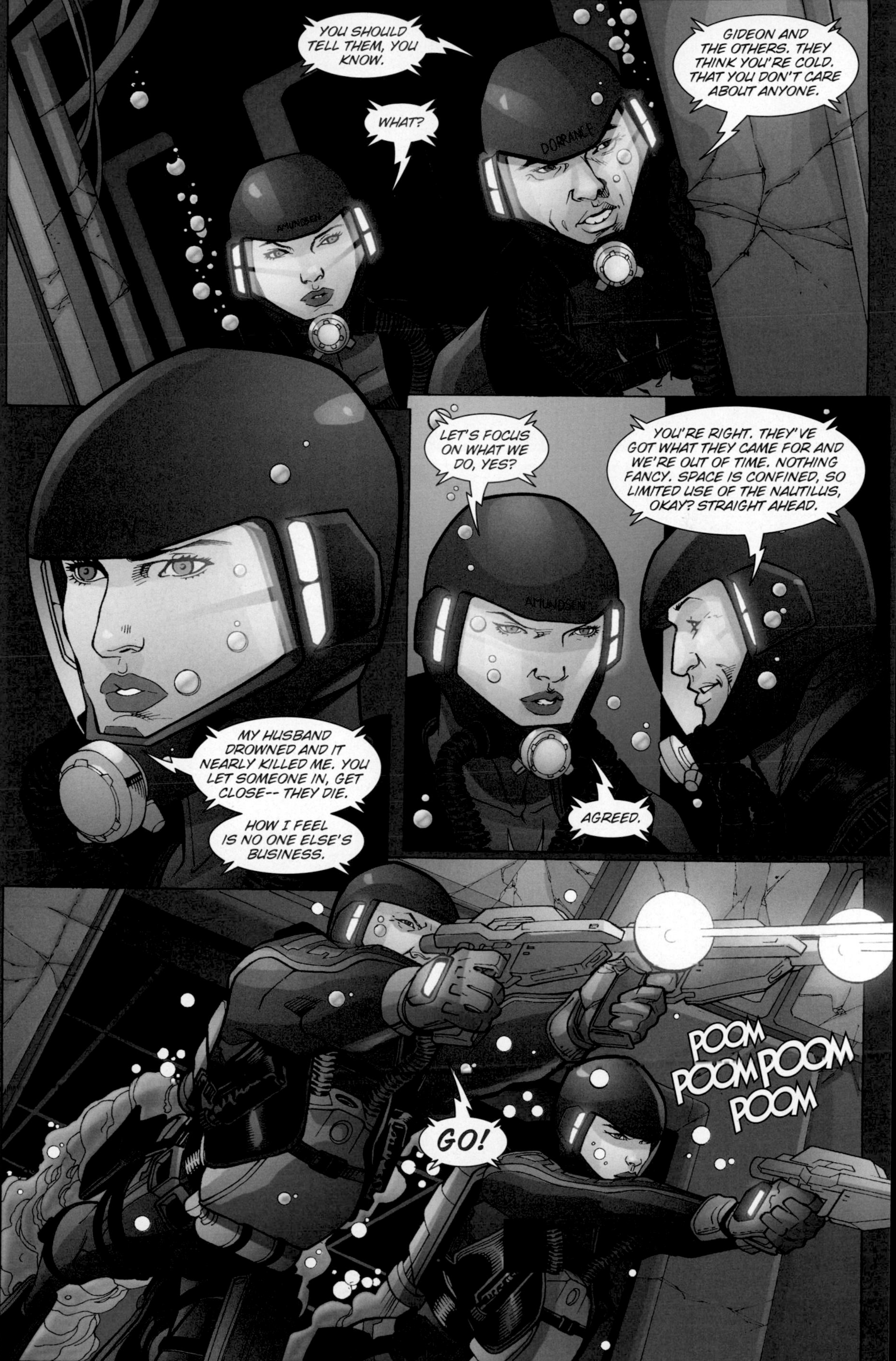
YOU SHOULD TELL THEM, YOU KNOW.
WHAT?
GIDEON AND THE OTHERS. THEY THINK YOU'RE COLD. THAT YOU DON'T CARE ABOUT ANYONE.
DORRANCE
AMUNDSEN
MY HUSBAND DROWNED AND IT NEARLY KILLED ME. YOU LET SOMEONE IN, GET CLOSE-- THEY DIE.
HOW I FEEL IS NO ONE ELSE'S BUSINESS.
LET'S FOCUS ON WHAT WE DO, YES?
YOU'RE RIGHT. THEY'VE GOT WHAT THEY CAME FOR AND WE'RE OUT OF TIME. NOTHING FANCY. SPACE IS CONFINED, SO LIMITED USE OF THE NAUTILUS, OKAY? STRAIGHT AHEAD.
AMUNDSEN
AGREED.
POOM POOM POOM POOM
GO!

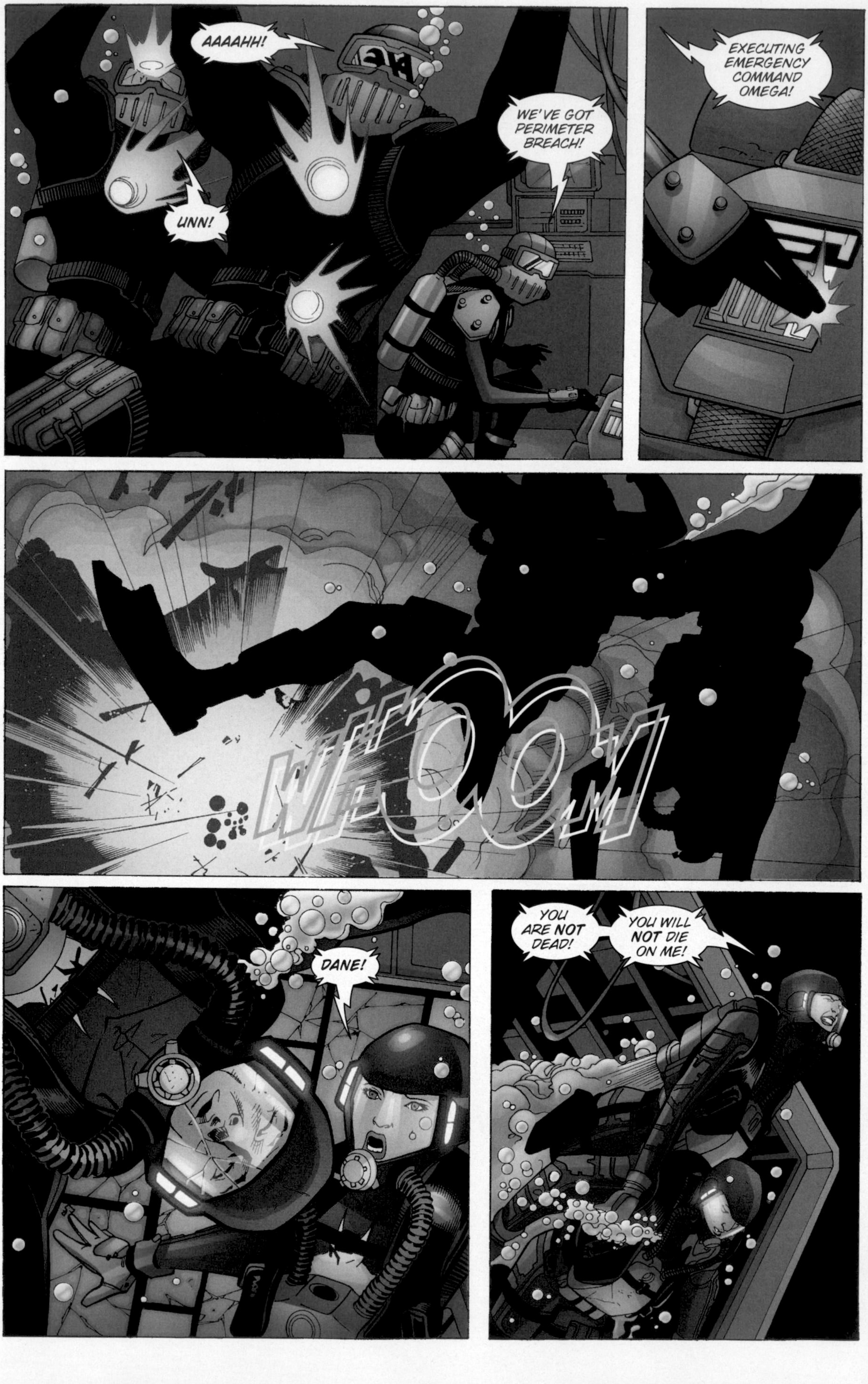
AAAAHH!
UNN!
WE'VE GOT PERIMETER BREACH!
EXECUTING EMERGENCY COMMAND OMEGA!
DANE!
YOU ARE NOT DEAD!
YOU WILL NOT DIE ON ME!

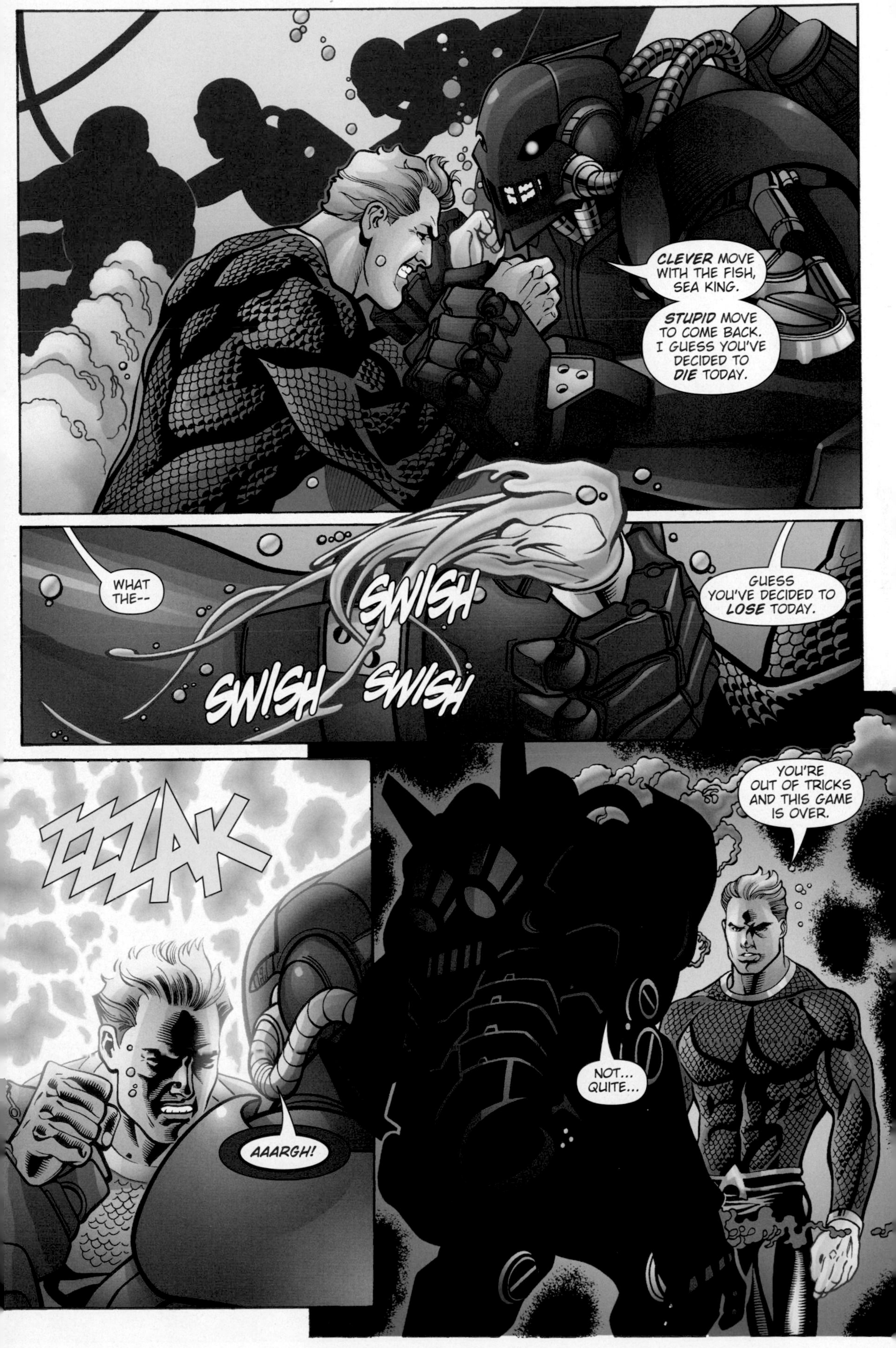
CLEVER MOVE WITH THE FISH, SEA KING.
STUPID MOVE TO COME BACK. I GUESS YOU'VE DECIDED TO DIE TODAY.
WHAT THE--
SWISH
SWISH
SWISH
GUESS YOU'VE DECIDED TO LOSE TODAY.
ZZZZAK
AAARGH!
YOU'RE OUT OF TRICKS AND THIS GAME IS OVER.
NOT... QUITE...

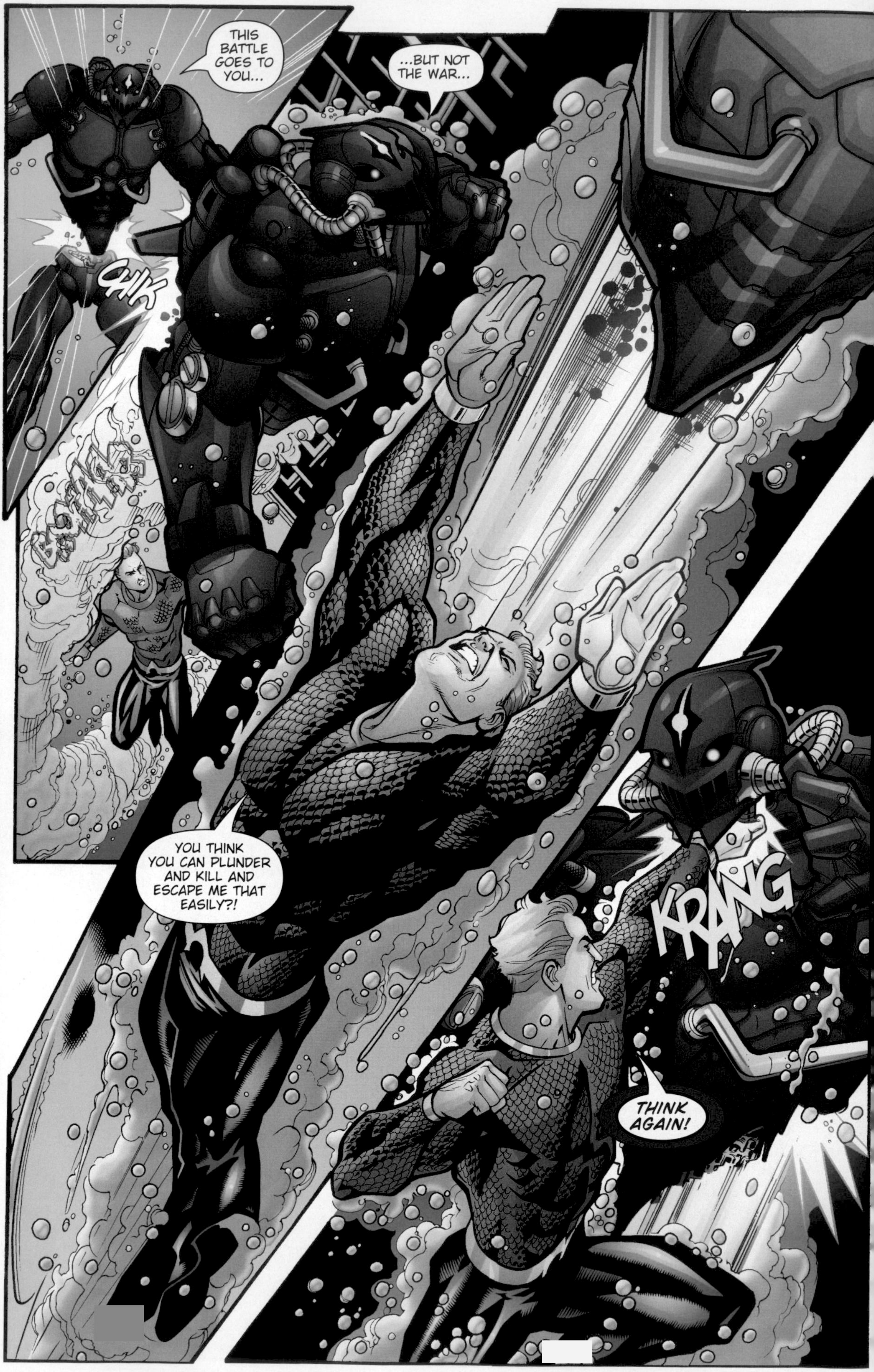
THIS BATTLE GOES TO YOU...
...BUT NOT THE WAR...
CHIK
YOU THINK YOU CAN PLUNDER AND KILL AND ESCAPE ME THAT EASILY?!
KRANG
THINK AGAIN!

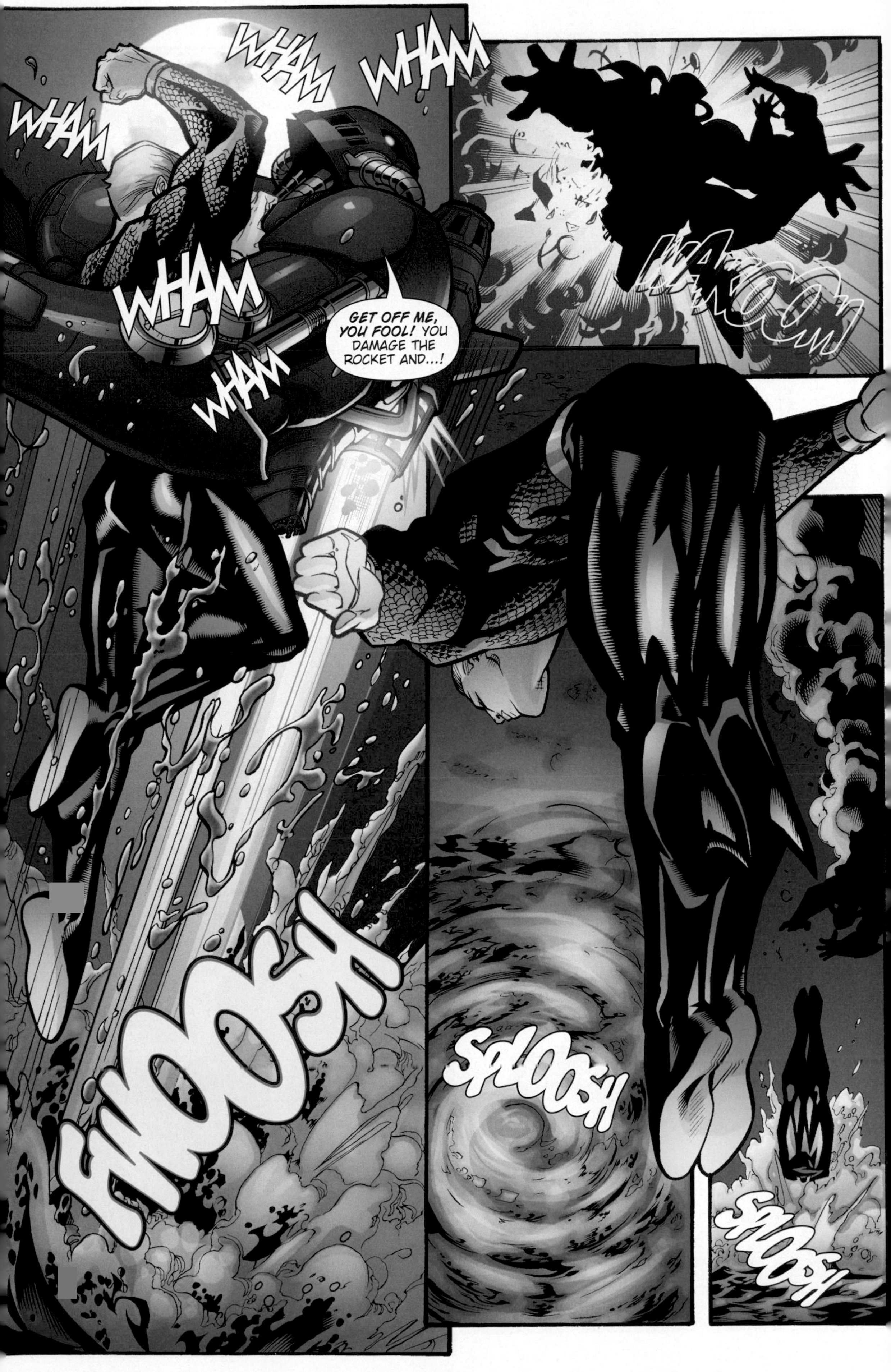
WHAM
WHAM
WHAM
WHAM
WHAM
GET OFF ME, YOU FOOL! YOU DAMAGE THE ROCKET AND...!
FWOOSH
SPLOOSH
SPLOOSH

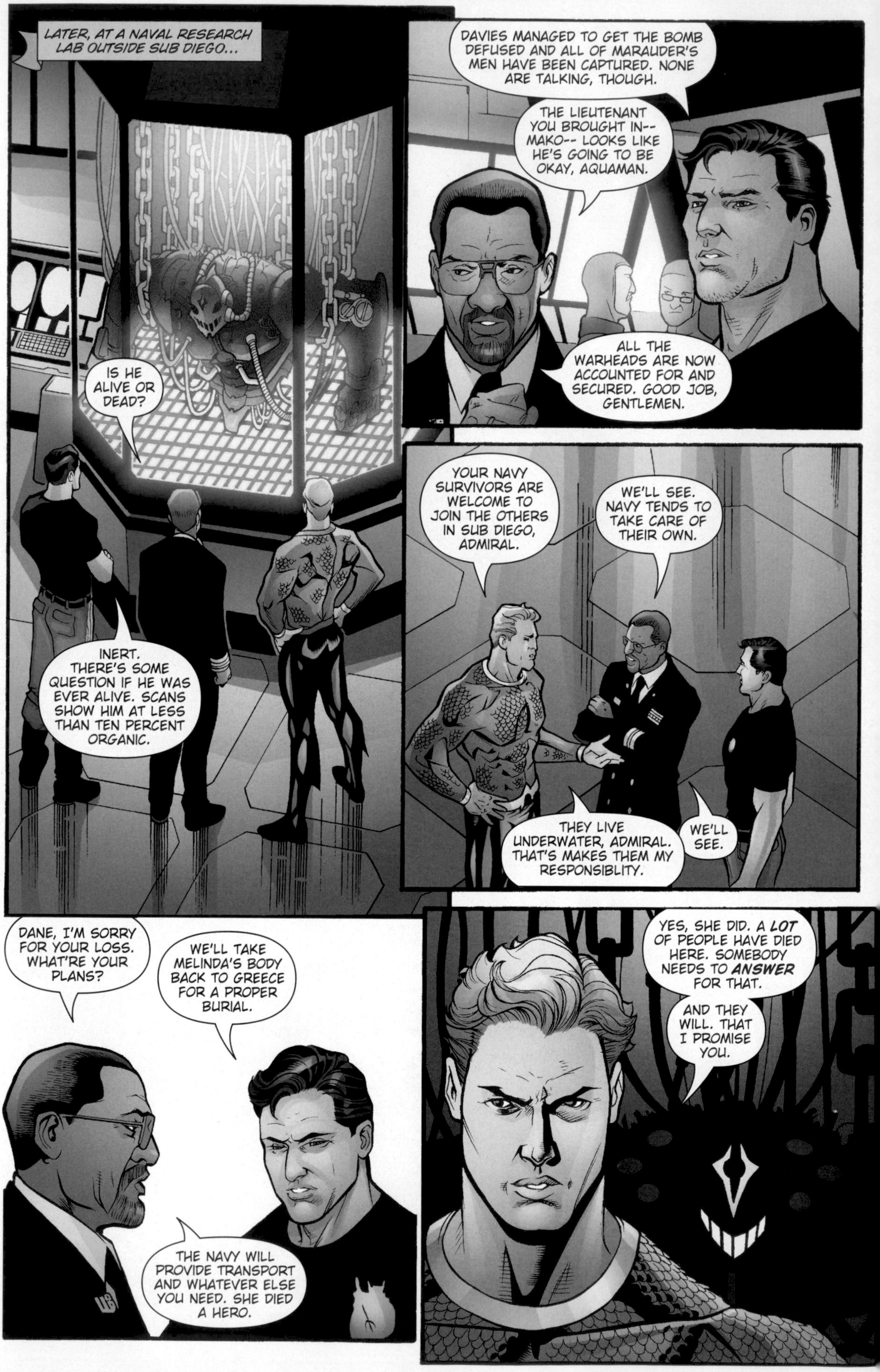
LATER, AT A NAVAL RESEARCH LAB OUTSIDE SUB DIEGO...
IS HE ALIVE OR DEAD?
INERT. THERE'S SOME QUESTION IF HE WAS EVER ALIVE. SCANS SHOW HIM AT LESS THAN TEN PERCENT ORGANIC.
DAVIES MANAGED TO GET THE BOMB DEFUSED AND ALL OF MARAUDER'S MEN HAVE BEEN CAPTURED. NONE ARE TALKING, THOUGH.
THE LIEUTENANT YOU BROUGHT IN-- MAKO-- LOOKS LIKE HE'S GOING TO BE OKAY, AQUAMAN.
ALL THE WARHEADS ARE NOW ACCOUNTED FOR AND SECURED. GOOD JOB, GENTLEMEN.
YOUR NAVY SURVIVORS ARE WELCOME TO JOIN THE OTHERS IN SUB DIEGO, ADMIRAL.
WE'LL SEE. NAVY TENDS TO TAKE CARE OF THEIR OWN.
THEY LIVE UNDERWATER, ADMIRAL. THAT'S MAKES THEM MY RESPONSIBLITY.
WE'LL SEE.
DANE, I'M SORRY FOR YOUR LOSS. WHAT'RE YOUR PLANS?
WE'LL TAKE MELINDA'S BODY BACK TO GREECE FOR A PROPER BURIAL.
THE NAVY WILL PROVIDE TRANSPORT AND WHATEVER ELSE YOU NEED. SHE DIED A HERO.
YES, SHE DID. A LOT OF PEOPLE HAVE DIED HERE. SOMEBODY NEEDS TO ANSWER FOR THAT.
AND THEY WILL. THAT I PROMISE YOU.

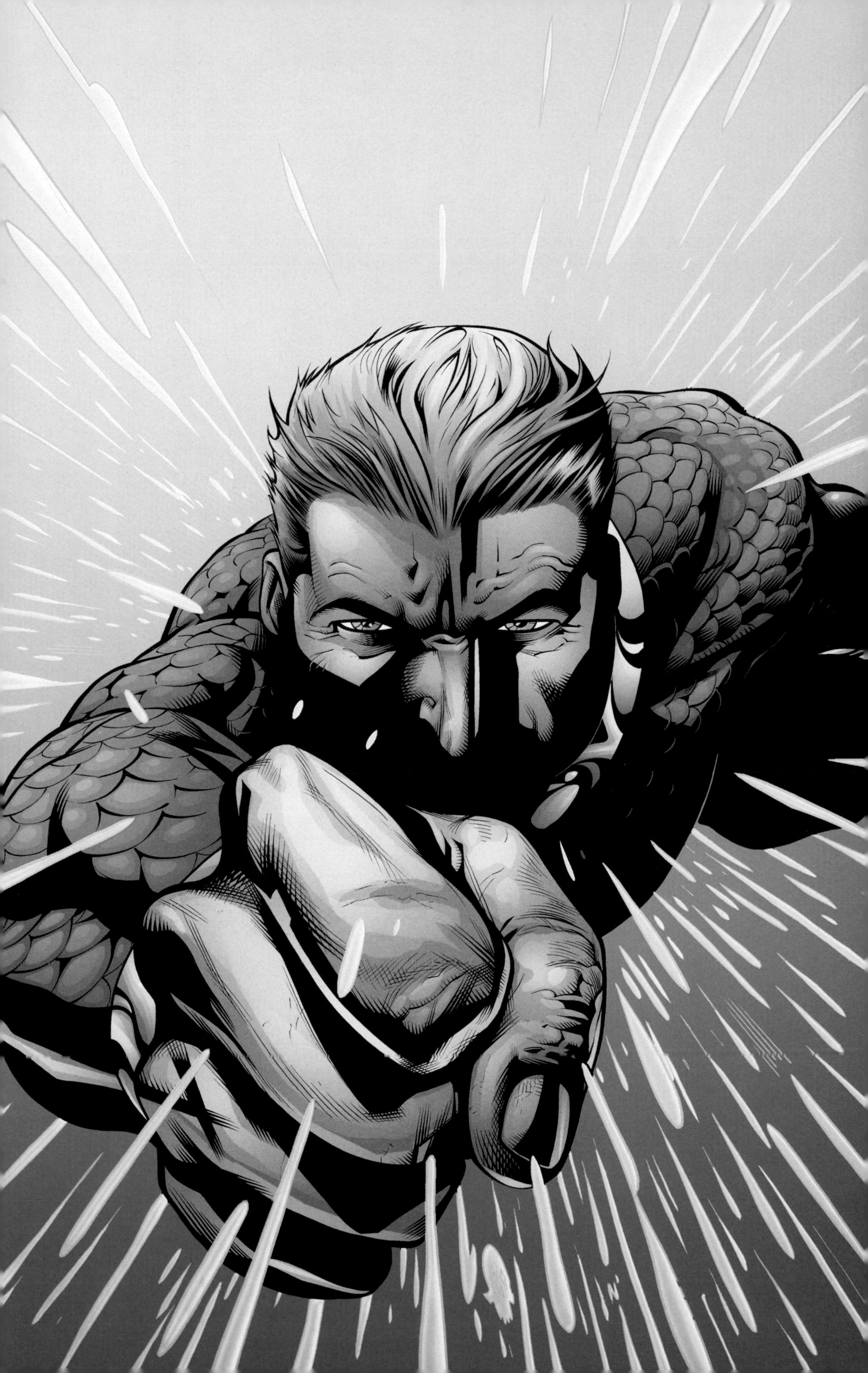

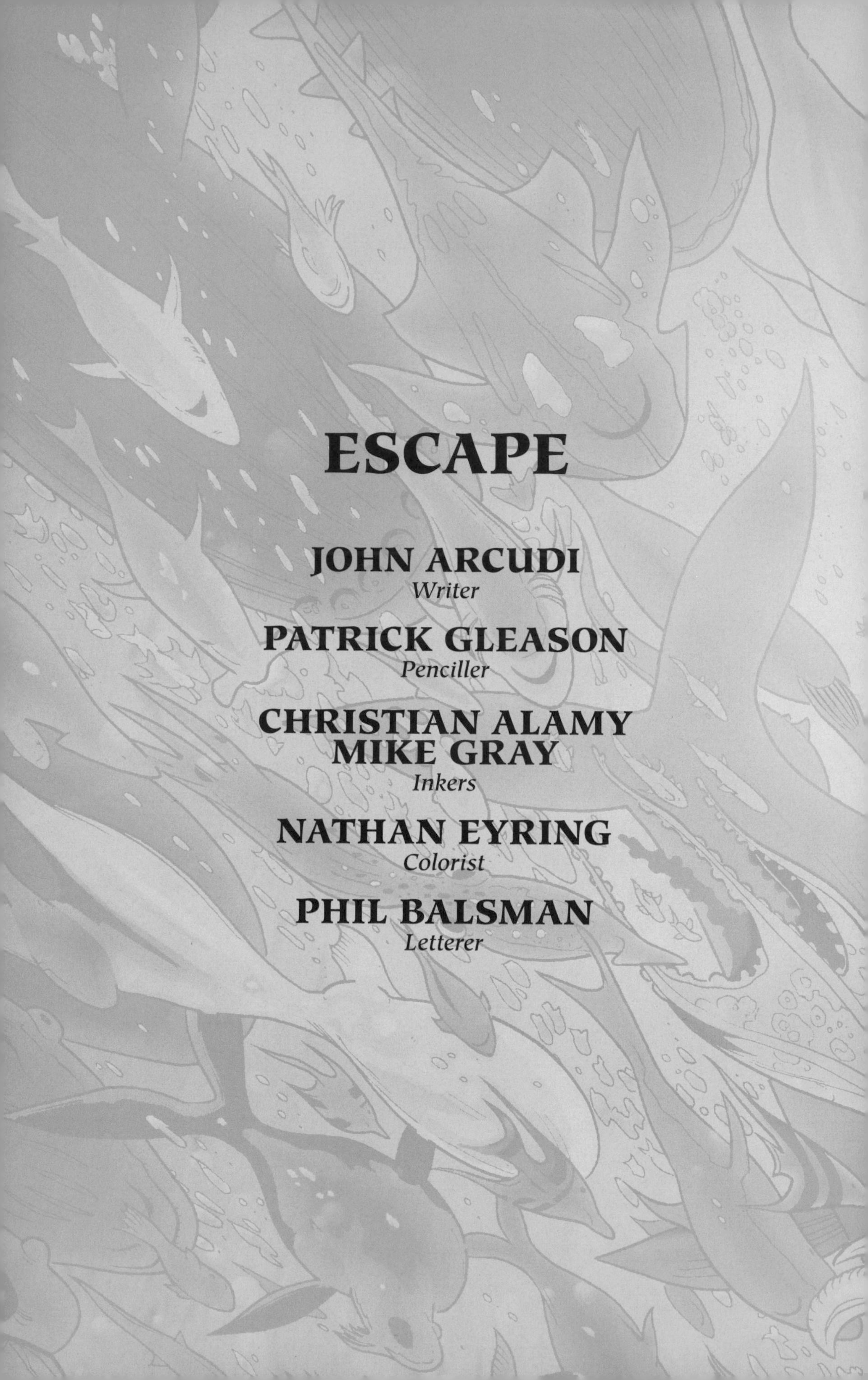

ESCAPE

JOHN ARCUDI
Writer

PATRICK GLEASON
Penciller

CHRISTIAN ALAMY
MIKE GRAY
Inkers

NATHAN EYRING
Colorist

PHIL BALSMAN
Letterer

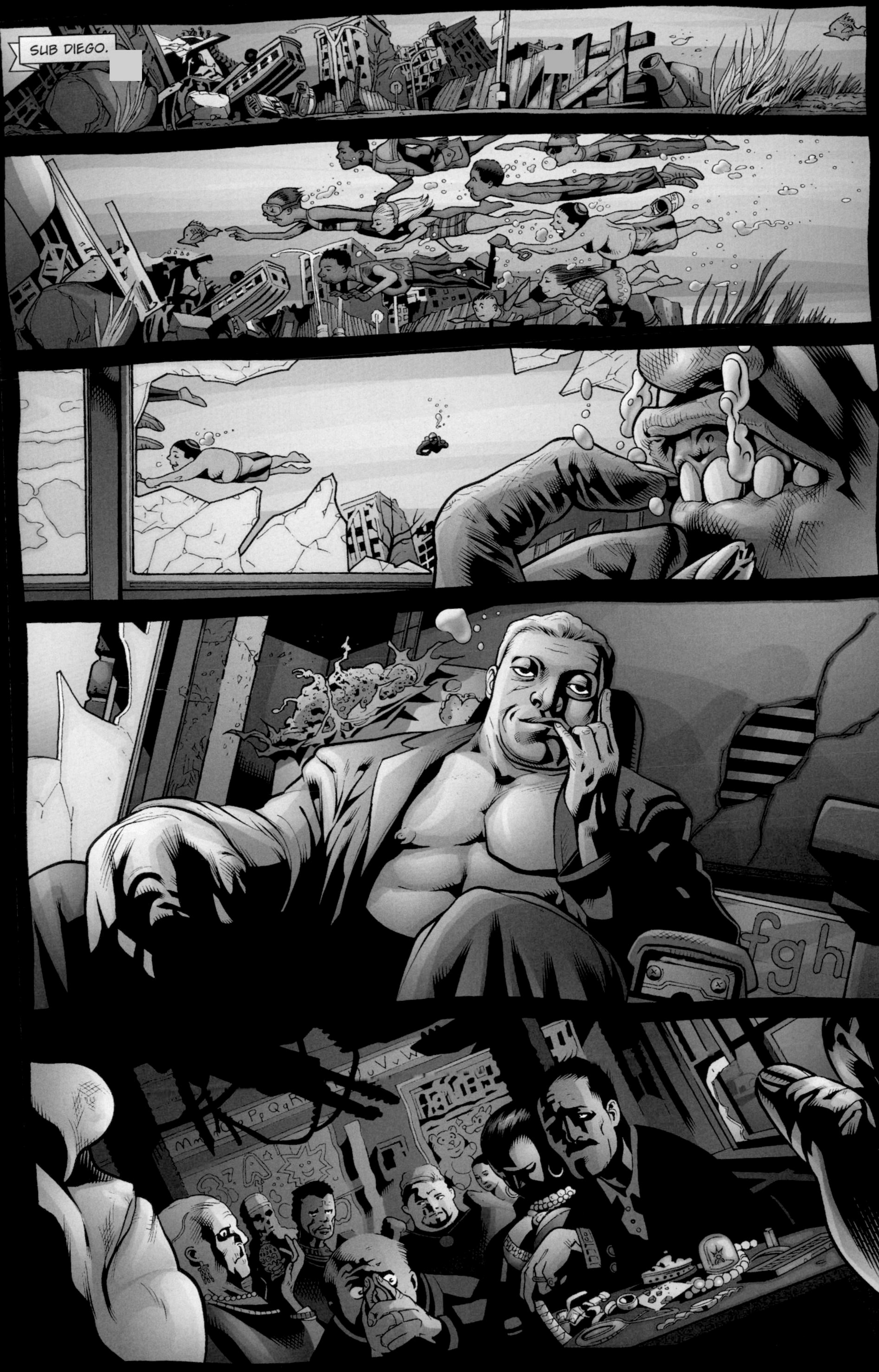
SUB DIEGO.
fgh

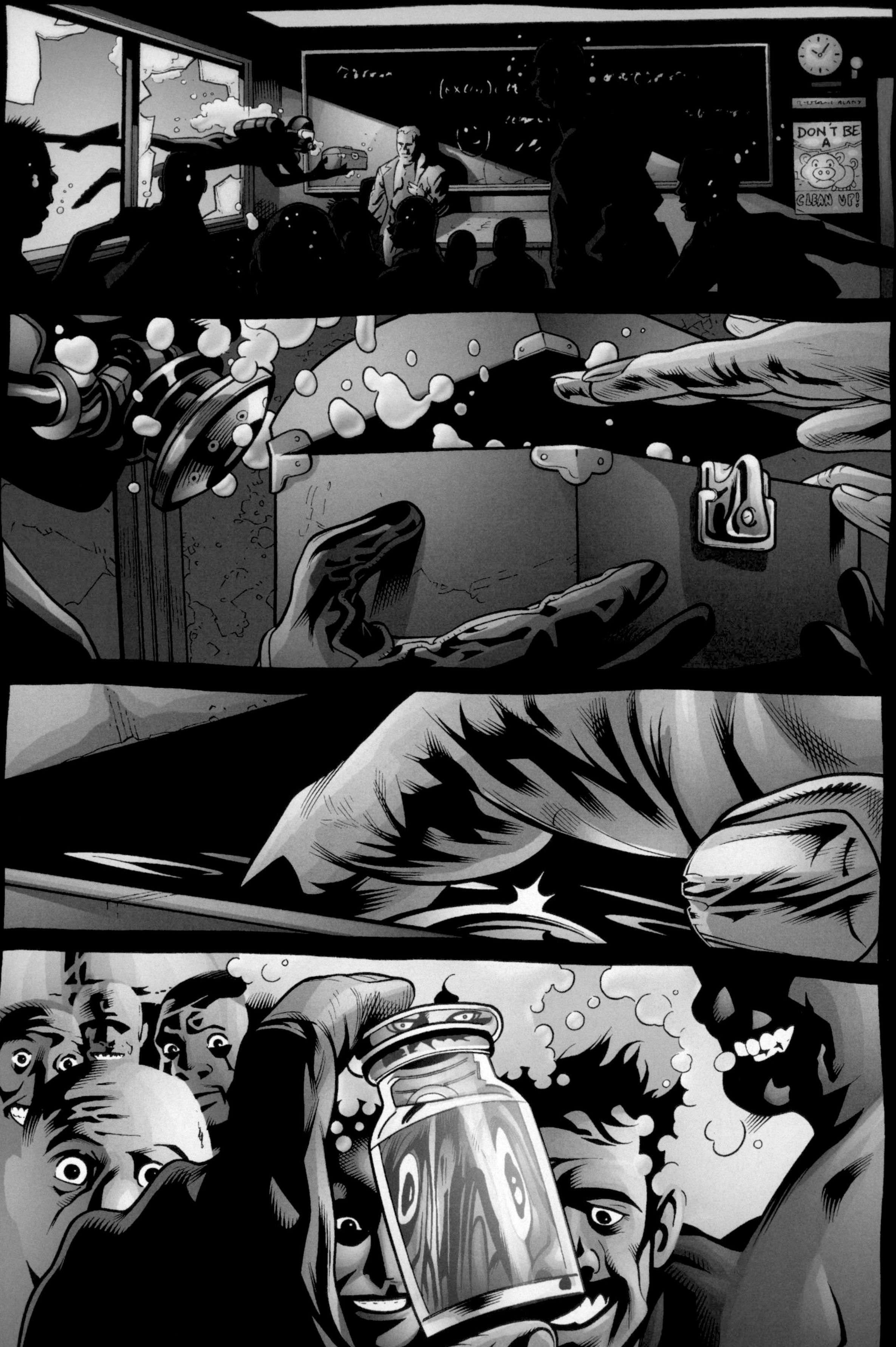
DON'T BE A
CLEAN UP!

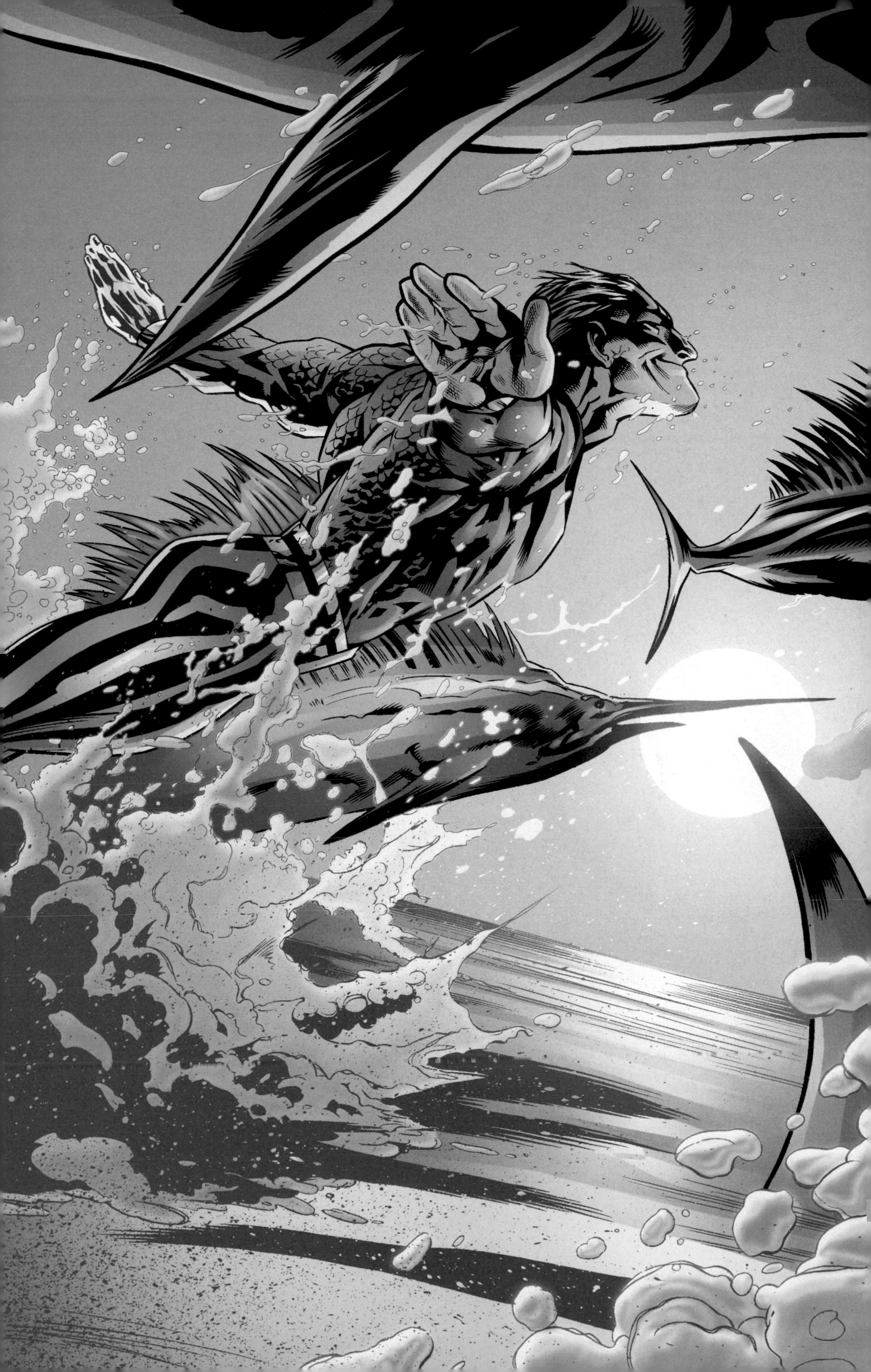

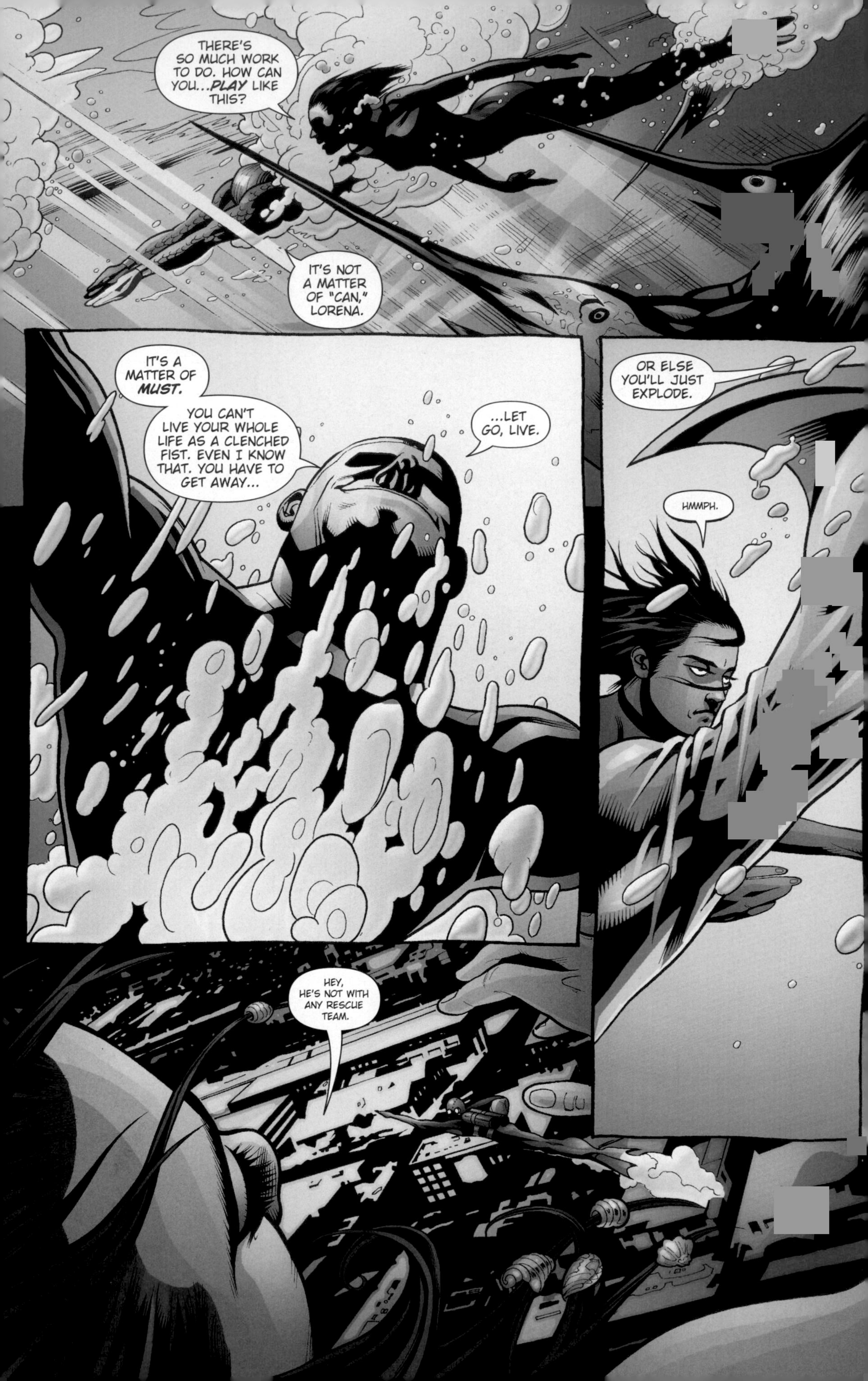
THERE'S SO MUCH WORK TO DO. HOW CAN YOU...PLAY LIKE THIS?
IT'S NOT A MATTER OF "CAN," LORENA.
IT'S A MATTER OF MUST.
YOU CAN'T LIVE YOUR WHOLE LIFE AS A CLENCHED FIST. EVEN I KNOW THAT. YOU HAVE TO GET AWAY...
...LET GO, LIVE.
OR ELSE YOU'LL JUST EXPLODE.
HMMPH.
HEY, HE'S NOT WITH ANY RESCUE TEAM.

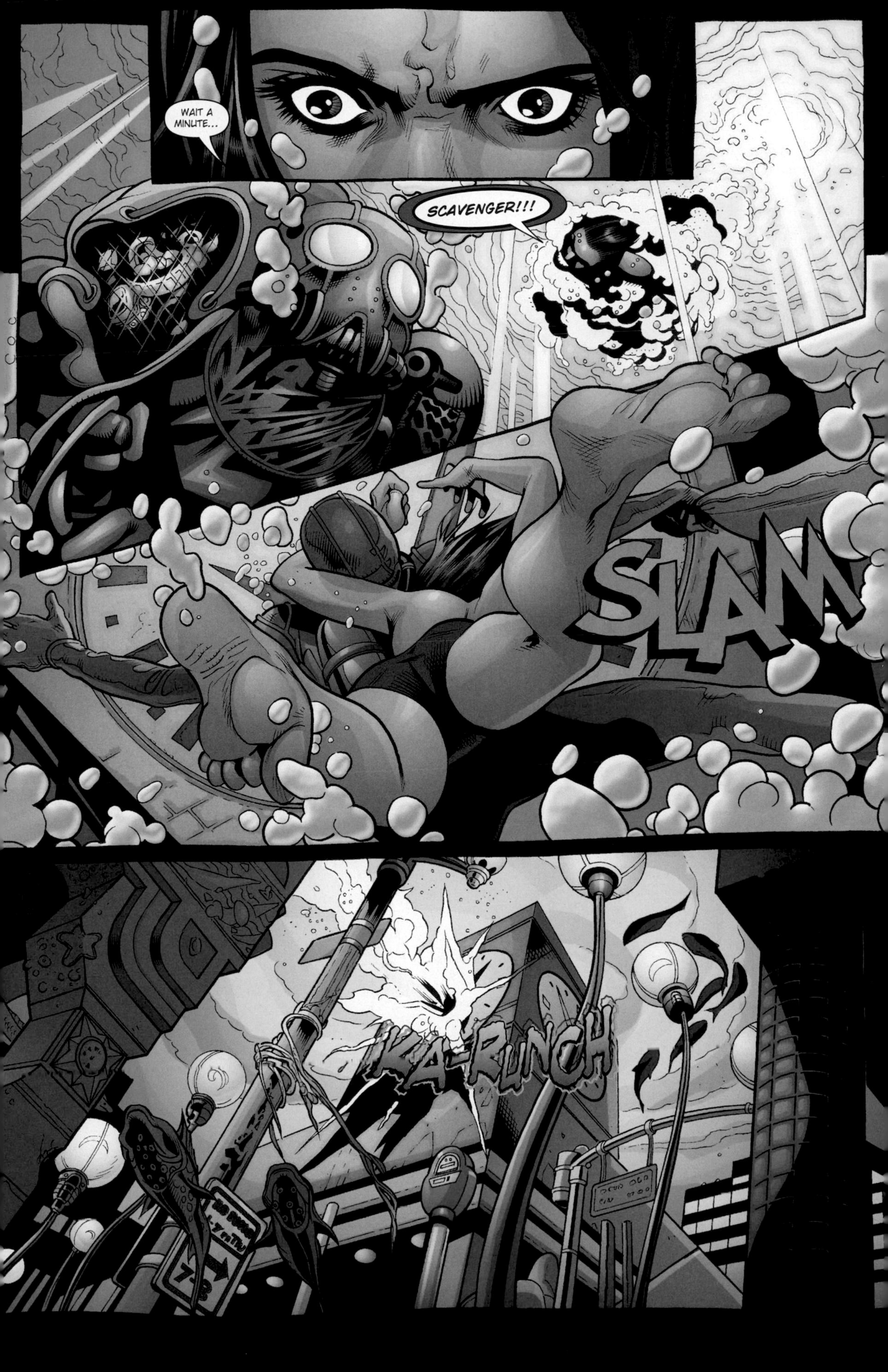
WAIT A MINUTE...
SCAVENGER!!!
SLAM
KA-RUNCH

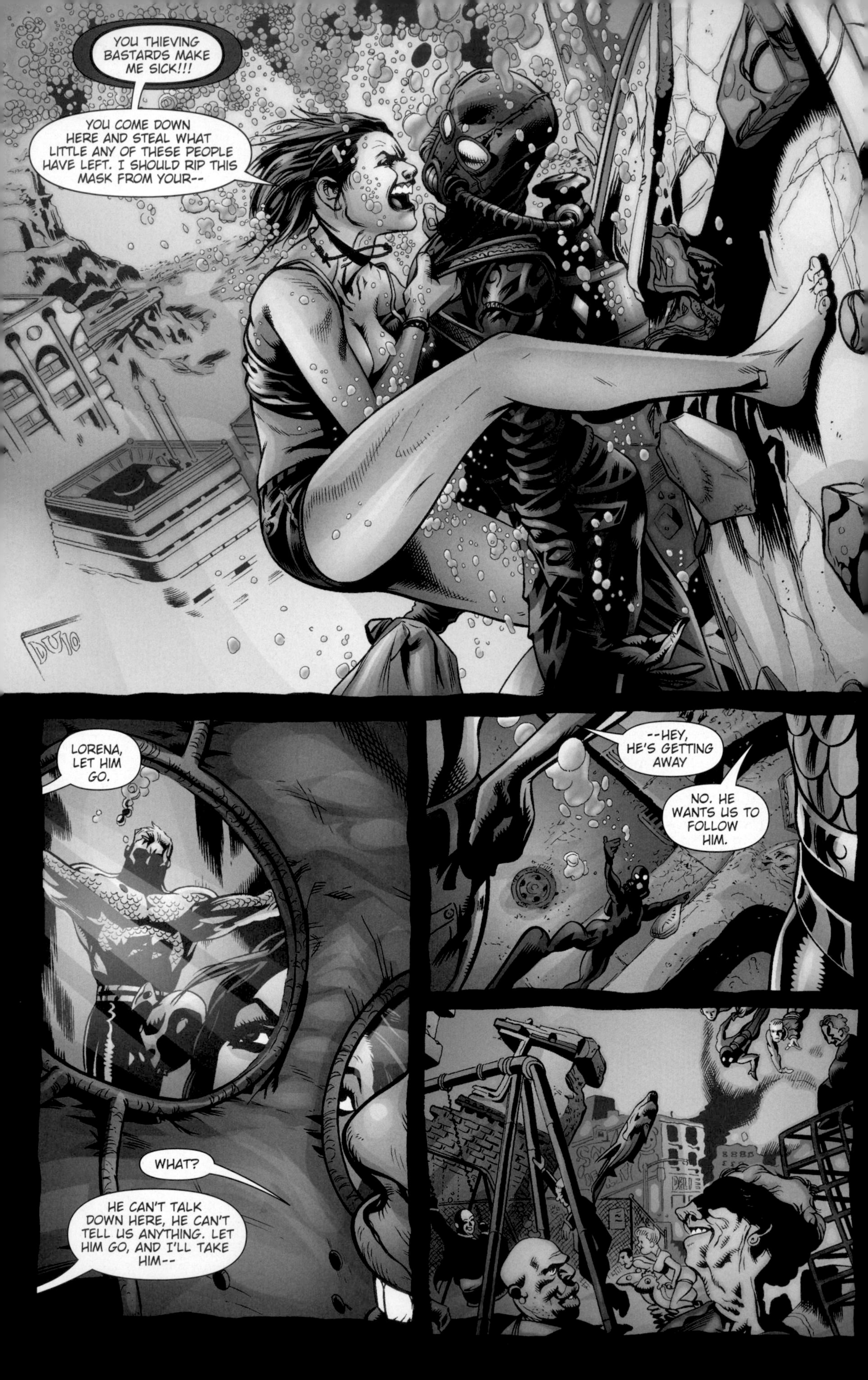
YOU THIEVING BASTARDS MAKE ME SICK!!!
YOU COME DOWN HERE AND STEAL WHAT LITTLE ANY OF THESE PEOPLE HAVE LEFT. I SHOULD RIP THIS MASK FROM YOUR--
LORENA, LET HIM GO.
WHAT?
HE CAN'T TALK DOWN HERE, HE CAN'T TELL US ANYTHING. LET HIM GO, AND I'LL TAKE HIM--
--HEY, HE'S GETTING AWAY
NO. HE WANTS US TO FOLLOW HIM.

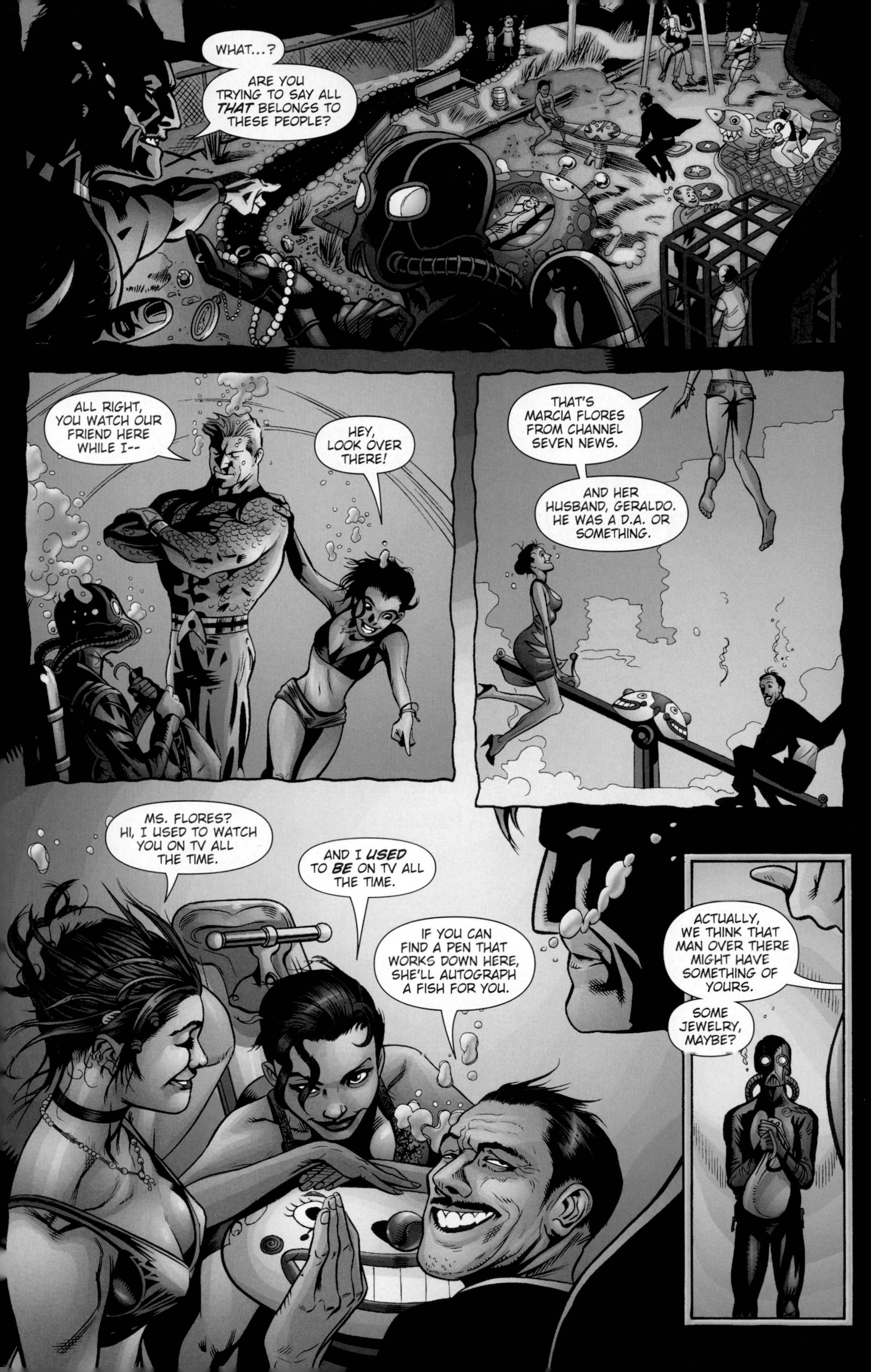
WHAT...?
ARE YOU TRYING TO SAY ALL *THAT* BELONGS TO THESE PEOPLE?
ALL RIGHT, YOU WATCH OUR FRIEND HERE WHILE I--
HEY, LOOK OVER THERE!
THAT'S MARCIA FLORES FROM CHANNEL SEVEN NEWS.
AND HER HUSBAND, GERALDO. HE WAS A D.A. OR SOMETHING.
MS. FLORES? HI, I USED TO WATCH YOU ON TV ALL THE TIME.
AND I *USED* TO *BE* ON TV ALL THE TIME.
IF YOU CAN FIND A PEN THAT WORKS DOWN HERE, SHE'LL AUTOGRAPH A FISH FOR YOU.
ACTUALLY, WE THINK THAT MAN OVER THERE MIGHT HAVE SOMETHING OF YOURS.
SOME JEWELRY, MAYBE?

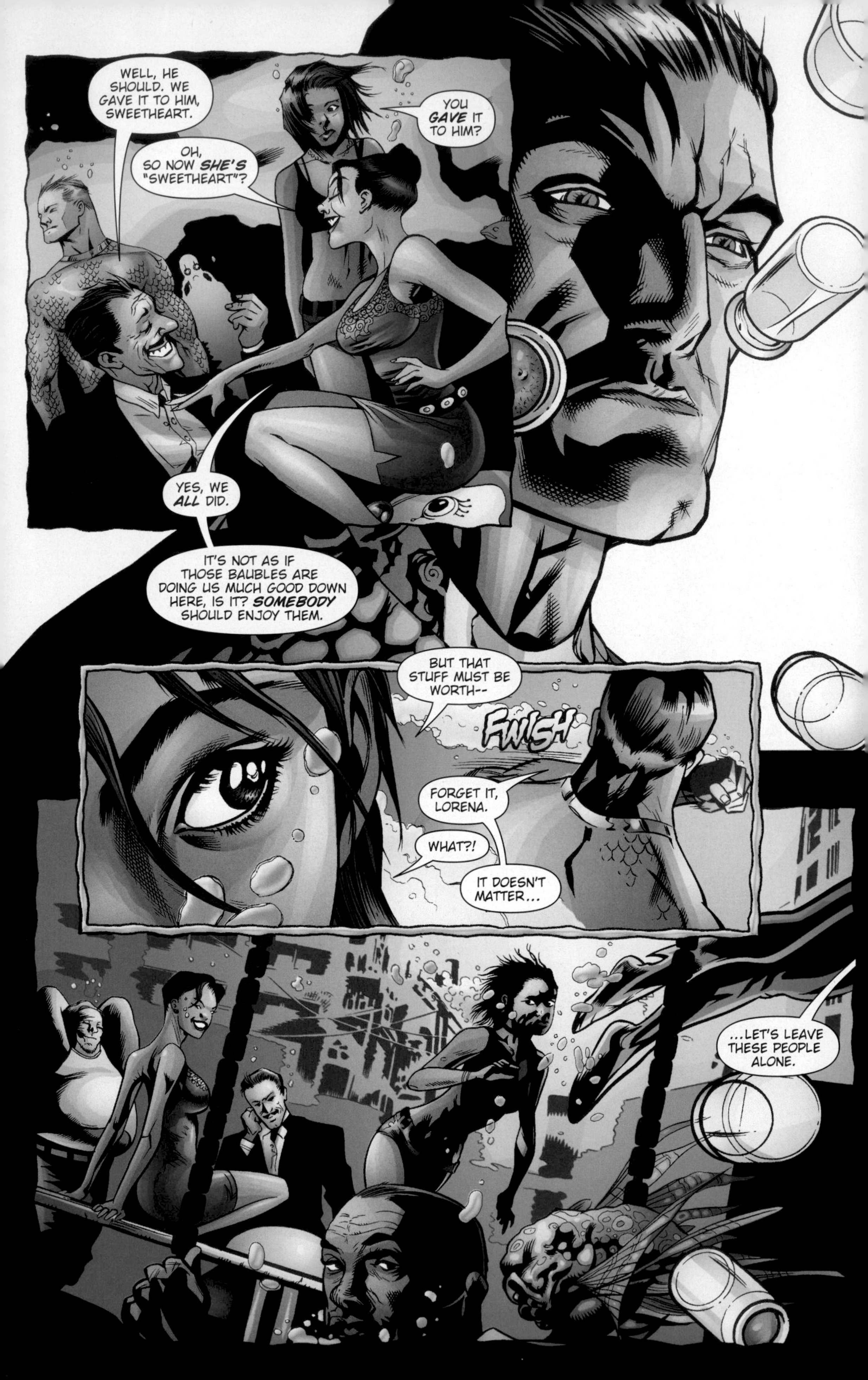

WELL, HE SHOULD. WE GAVE IT TO HIM, SWEETHEART.
YOU GAVE IT TO HIM?
OH, SO NOW SHE'S "SWEETHEART"?
YES, WE ALL DID.
IT'S NOT AS IF THOSE BAUBLES ARE DOING US MUCH GOOD DOWN HERE, IS IT? SOMEBODY SHOULD ENJOY THEM.
BUT THAT STUFF MUST BE WORTH--
FWISH
FORGET IT, LORENA.
WHAT?!
IT DOESN'T MATTER...
...LET'S LEAVE THESE PEOPLE ALONE.

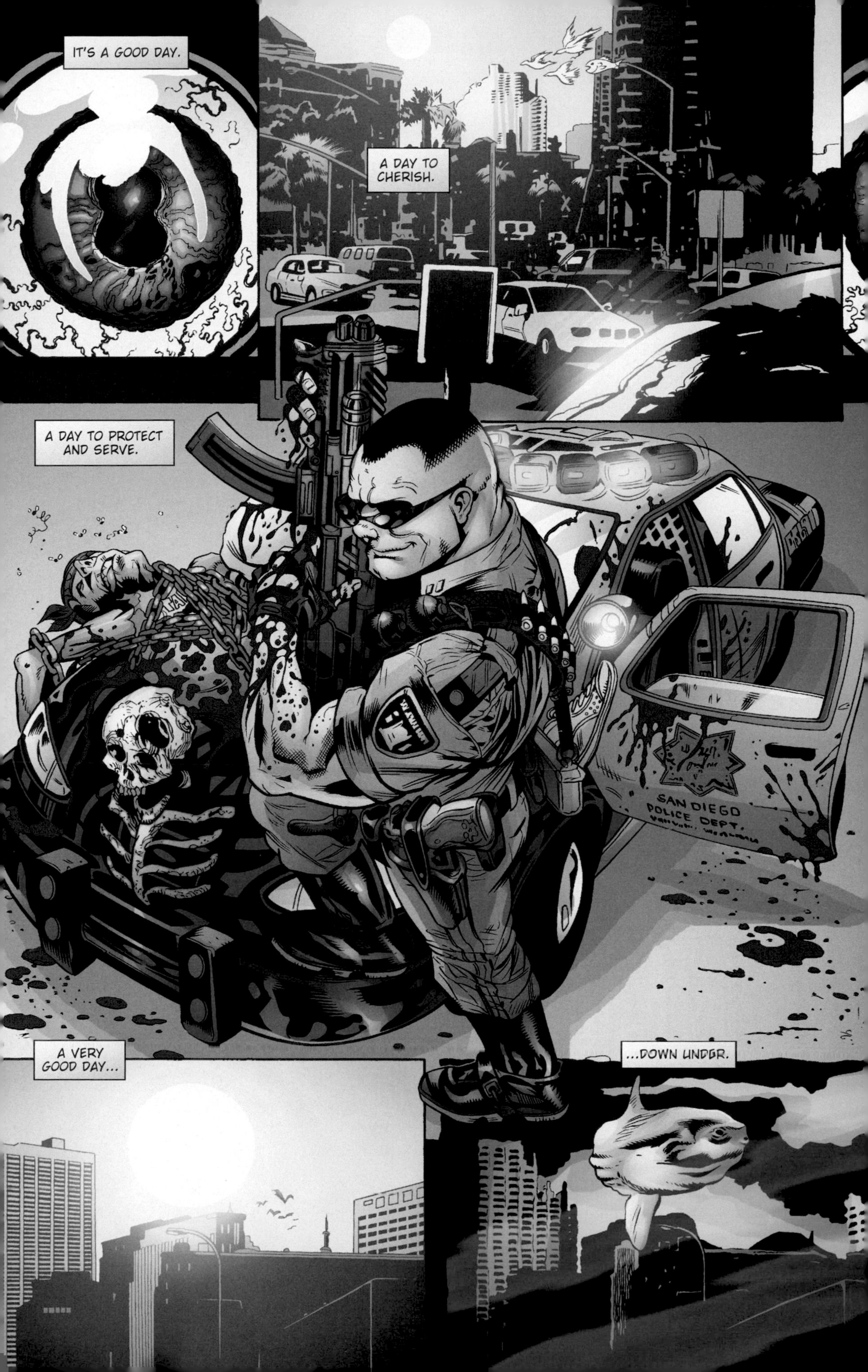
IT'S A GOOD DAY.
A DAY TO CHERISH.
A DAY TO PROTECT AND SERVE.
SAN DIEGO POLICE DEPT.
A VERY GOOD DAY...
...DOWN UNDER.

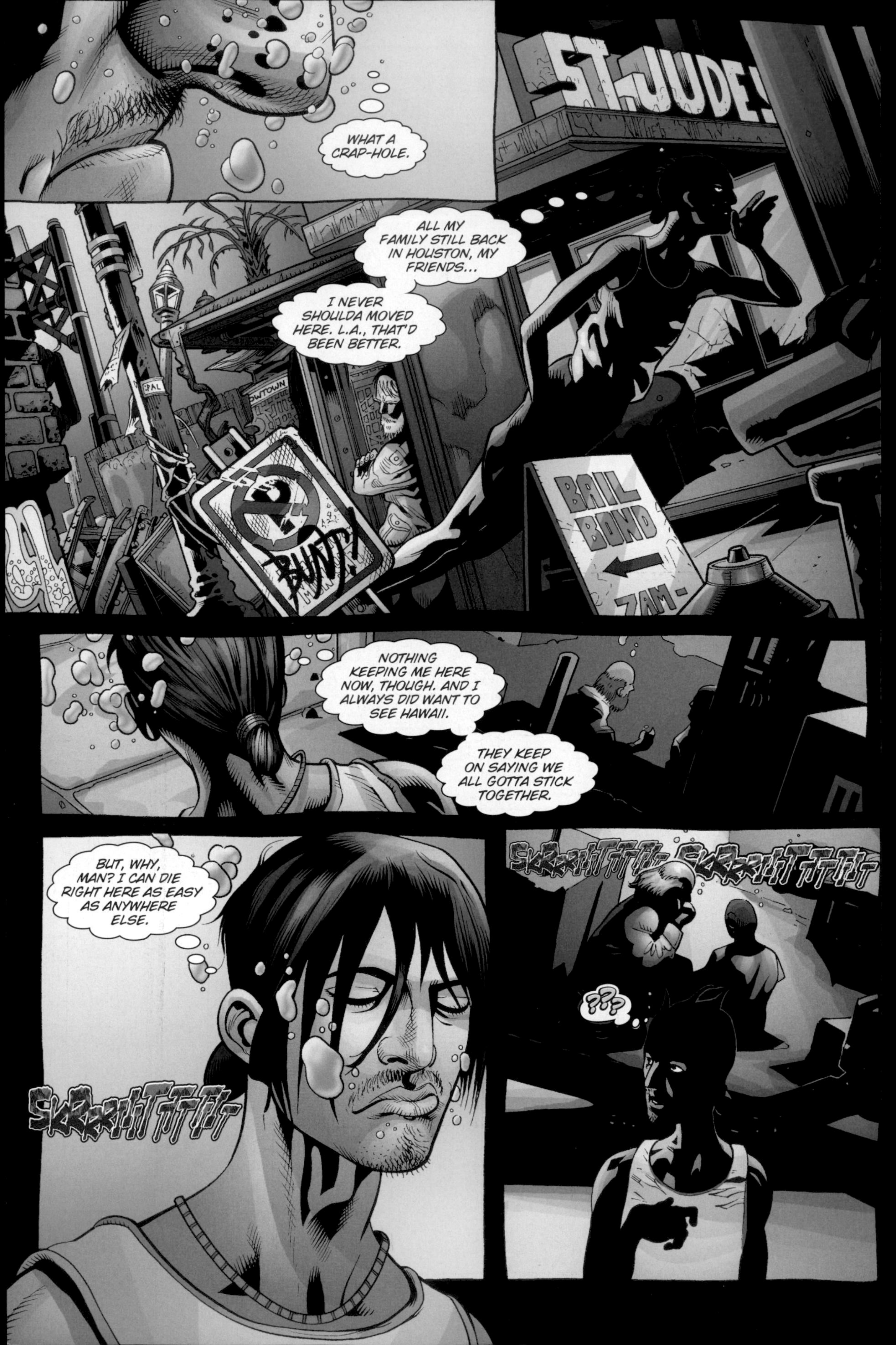
ST. JUDE!
WHAT A CRAP-HOLE.
ALL MY FAMILY STILL BACK IN HOUSTON, MY FRIENDS...
I NEVER SHOULDA MOVED HERE. L.A., THAT'D BEEN BETTER.
BAIL BOND
NOTHING KEEPING ME HERE NOW, THOUGH. AND I ALWAYS DID WANT TO SEE HAWAII.
THEY KEEP ON SAYING WE ALL GOTTA STICK TOGETHER.
BUT, WHY, MAN? I CAN DIE RIGHT HERE AS EASY AS ANYWHERE ELSE.
???

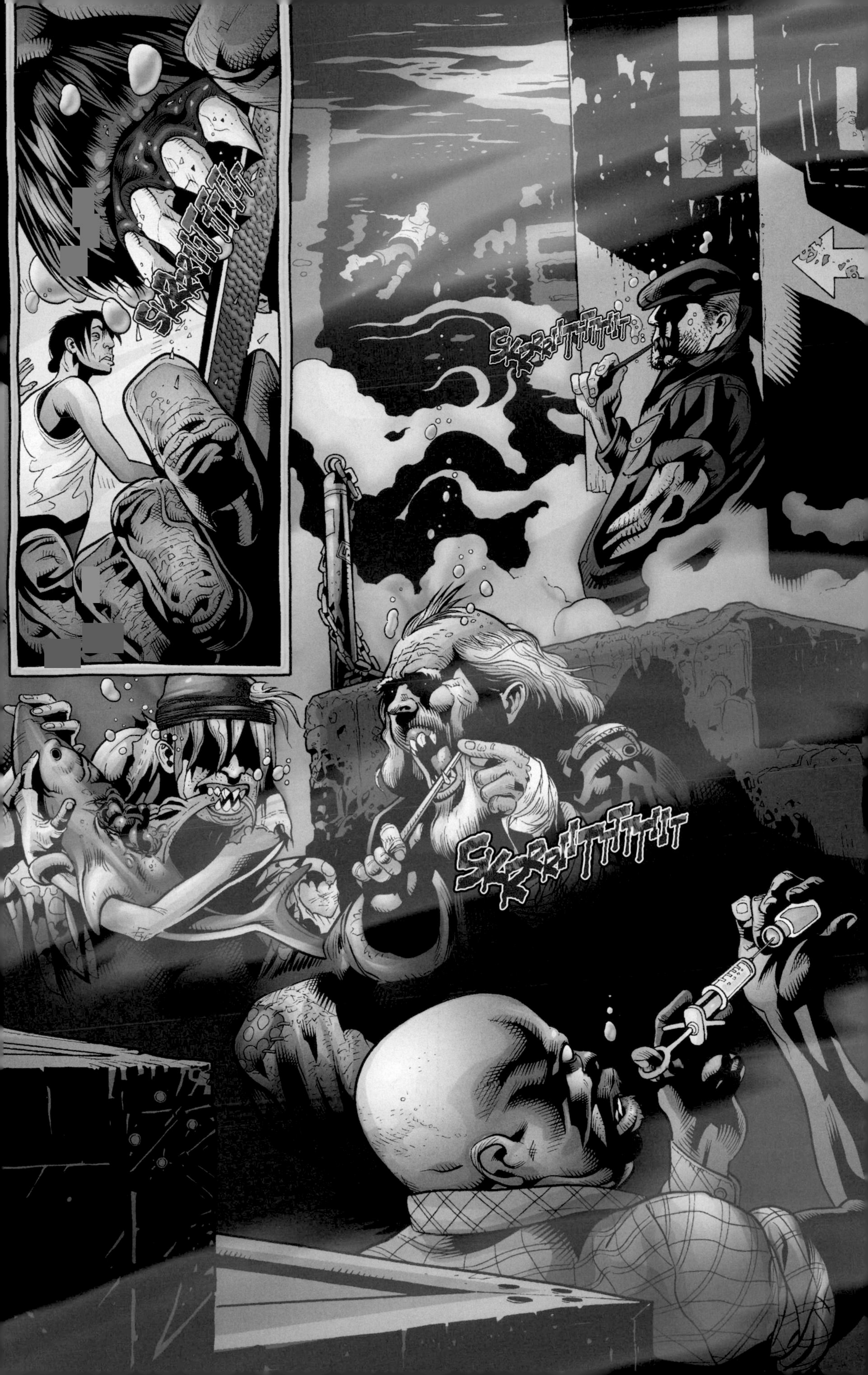

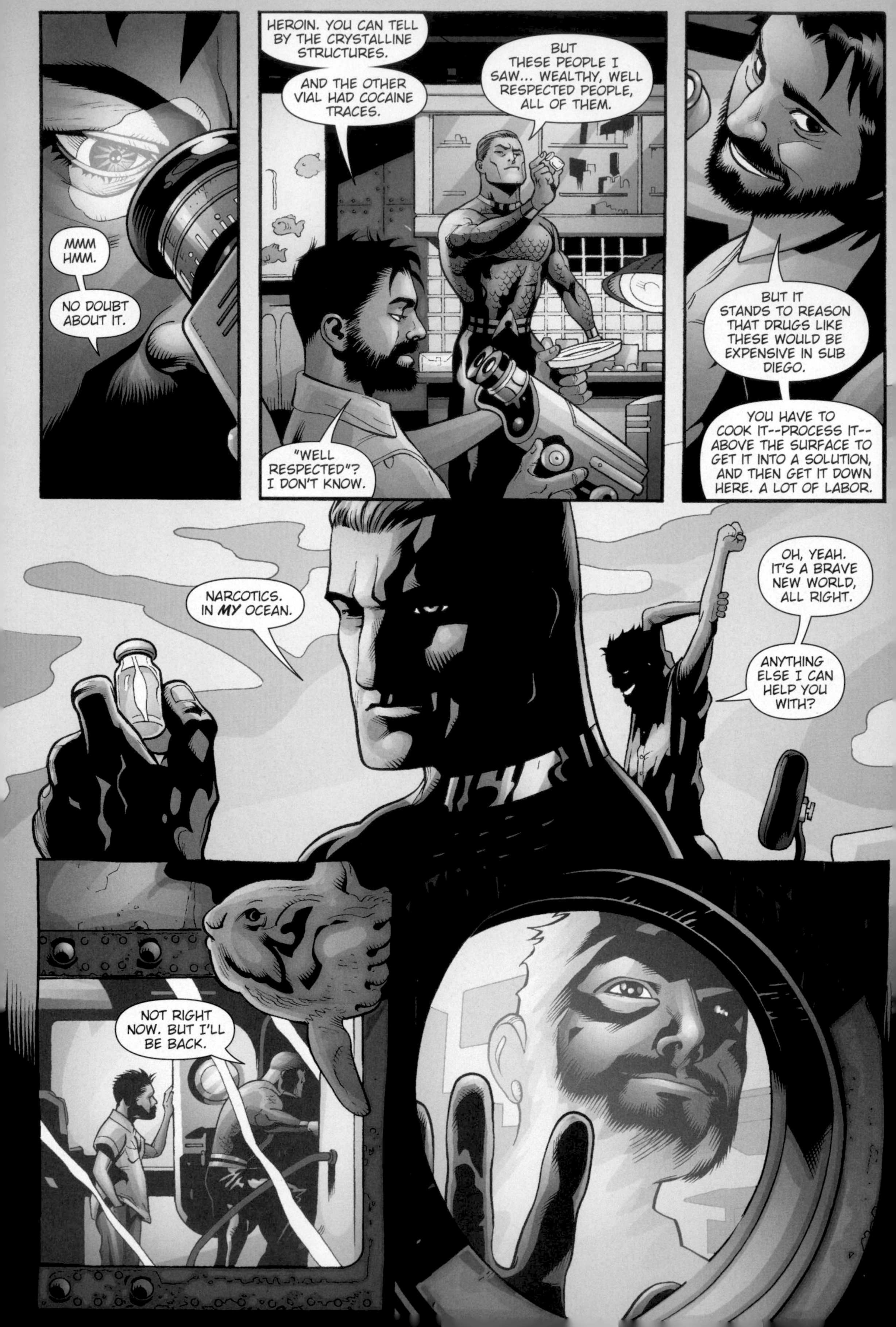
MMM HMM.
NO DOUBT ABOUT IT.
HEROIN. YOU CAN TELL BY THE CRYSTALLINE STRUCTURES.
AND THE OTHER VIAL HAD COCAINE TRACES.
BUT THESE PEOPLE I SAW... WEALTHY, WELL RESPECTED PEOPLE, ALL OF THEM.
"WELL RESPECTED"? I DON'T KNOW.
BUT IT STANDS TO REASON THAT DRUGS LIKE THESE WOULD BE EXPENSIVE IN SUB DIEGO.
YOU HAVE TO COOK IT--PROCESS IT--ABOVE THE SURFACE TO GET IT INTO A SOLUTION, AND THEN GET IT DOWN HERE. A LOT OF LABOR.
NARCOTICS. IN *MY* OCEAN.
OH, YEAH. IT'S A BRAVE NEW WORLD, ALL RIGHT.
ANYTHING ELSE I CAN HELP YOU WITH?
NOT RIGHT NOW. BUT I'LL BE BACK.

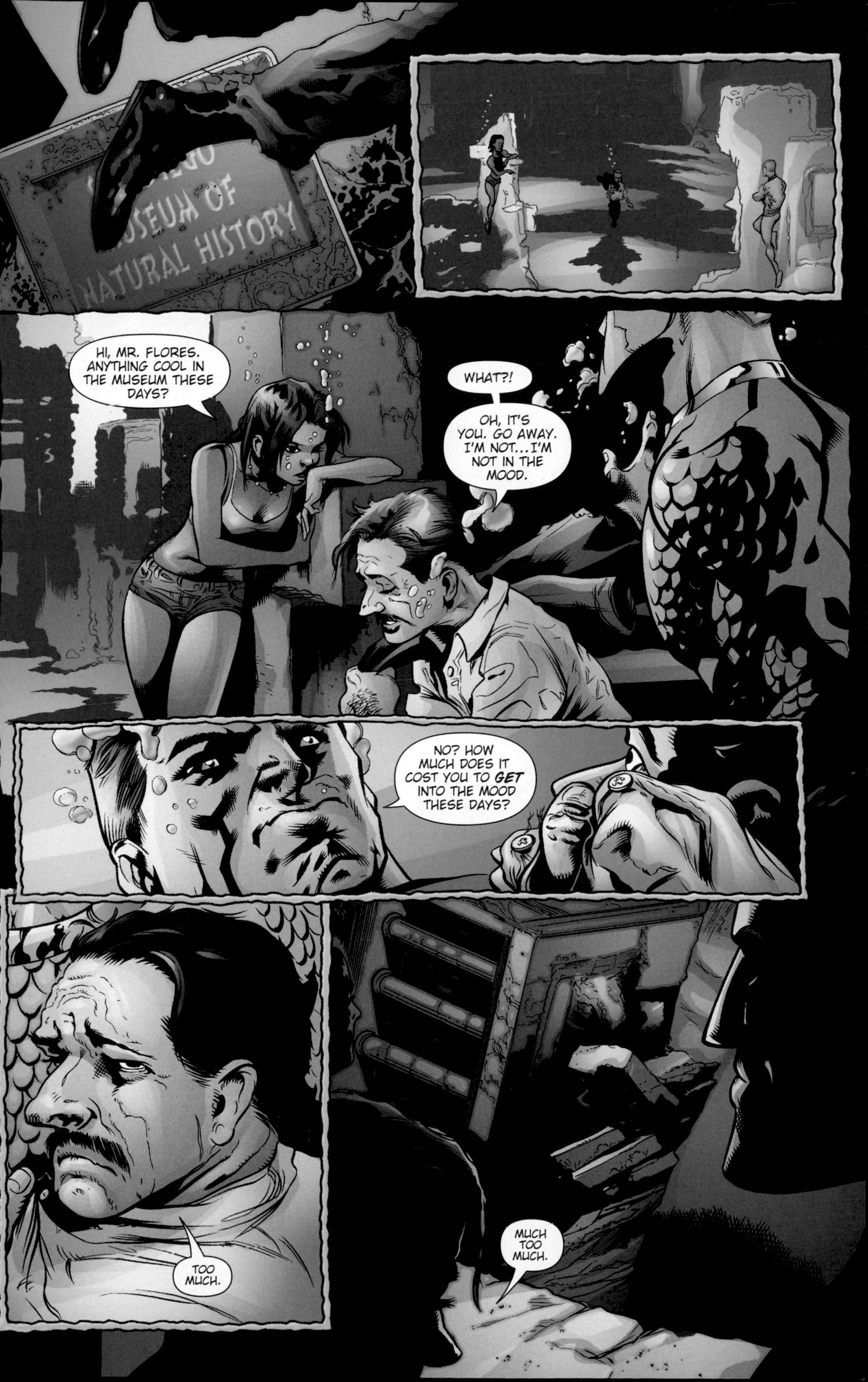

MUSEUM OF
NATURAL HISTORY
HI, MR. FLORES. ANYTHING COOL IN THE MUSEUM THESE DAYS?
WHAT?!
OH, IT'S YOU. GO AWAY. I'M NOT...I'M NOT IN THE MOOD.
NO? HOW MUCH DOES IT COST YOU TO **GET** INTO THE MOOD THESE DAYS?
TOO MUCH.
MUCH TOO MUCH.

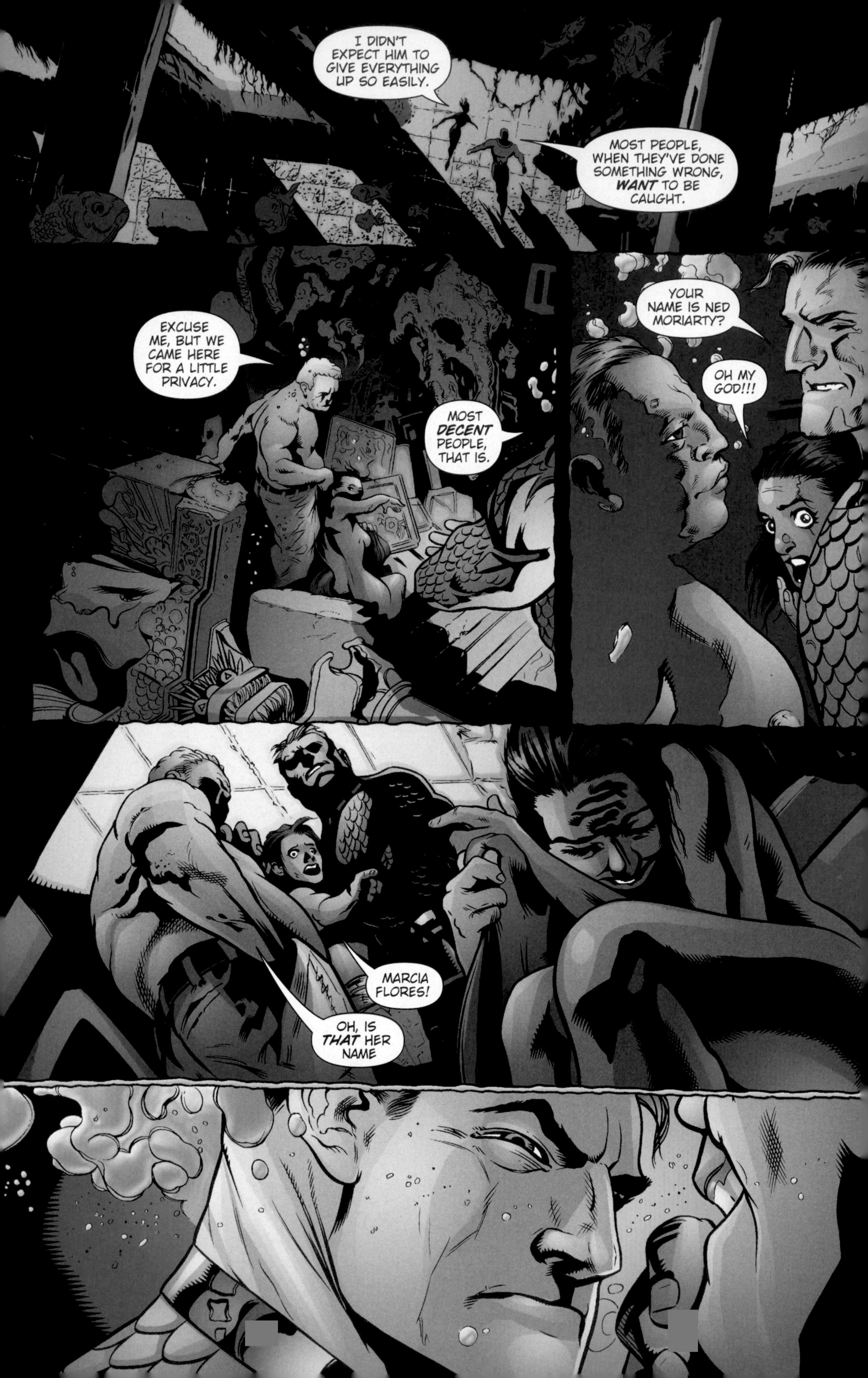

I DIDN'T EXPECT HIM TO GIVE EVERYTHING UP SO EASILY.
MOST PEOPLE, WHEN THEY'VE DONE SOMETHING WRONG, ***WANT*** TO BE CAUGHT.
EXCUSE ME, BUT WE CAME HERE FOR A LITTLE PRIVACY.
MOST ***DECENT*** PEOPLE, THAT IS.
YOUR NAME IS NED MORIARTY?
OH MY GOD!!!
MARCIA FLORES!
OH, IS ***THAT*** HER NAME

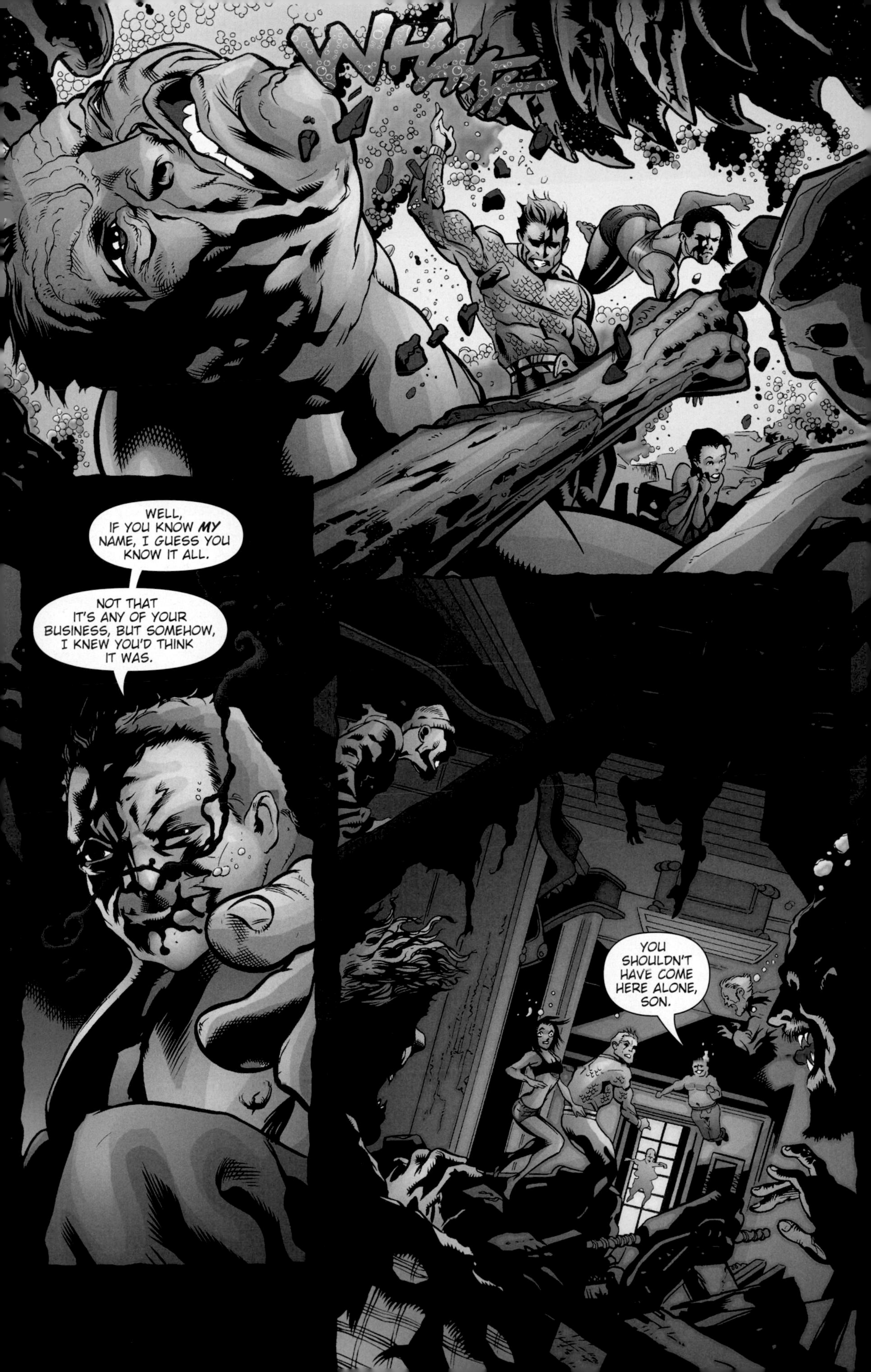
WHAK
WELL, IF YOU KNOW *MY* NAME, I GUESS YOU KNOW IT ALL.
NOT THAT IT'S ANY OF YOUR BUSINESS, BUT SOMEHOW, I KNEW YOU'D THINK IT WAS.
YOU SHOULDN'T HAVE COME HERE ALONE, SON.

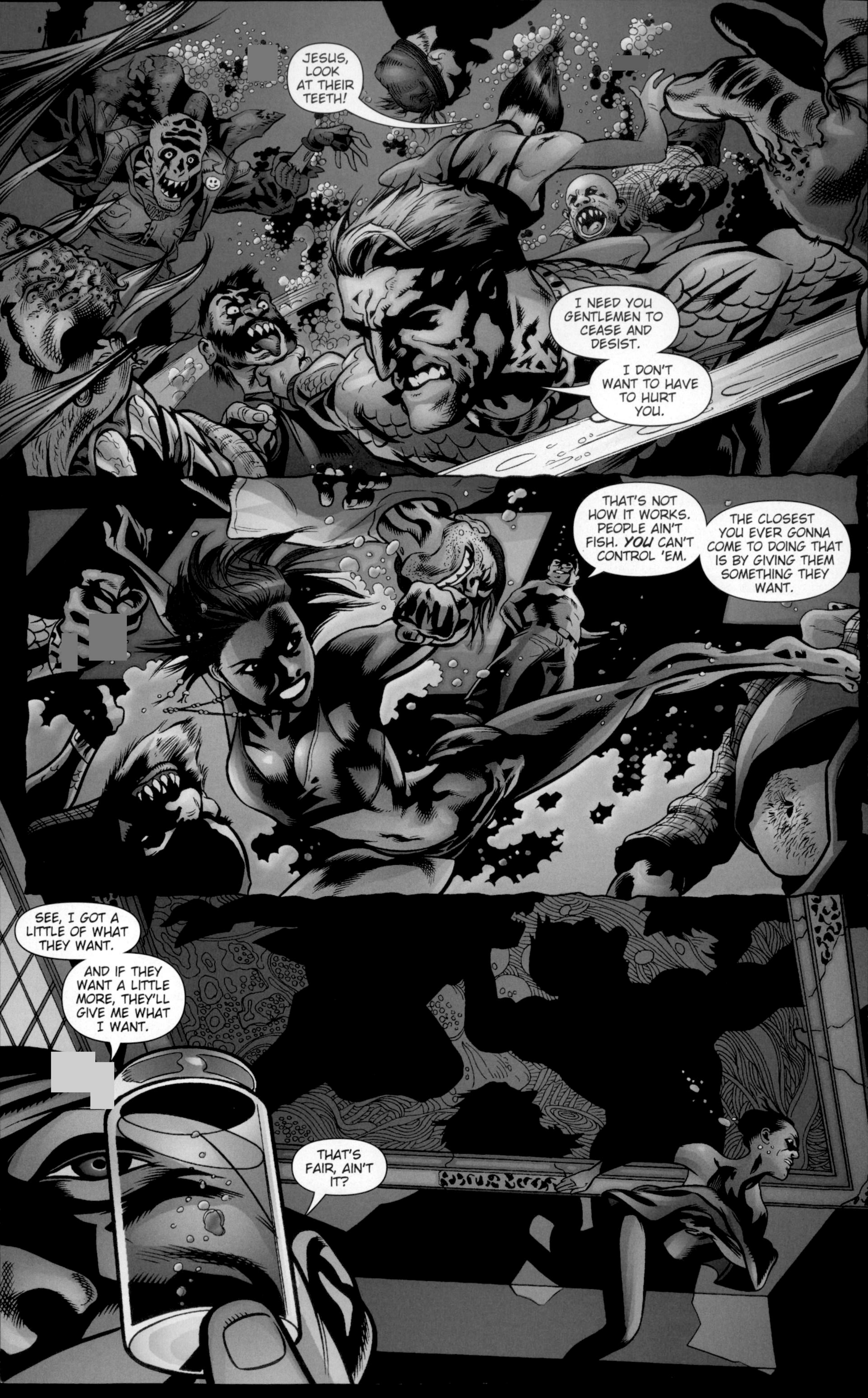
JESUS, LOOK AT THEIR TEETH!
I NEED YOU GENTLEMEN TO CEASE AND DESIST.
I DON'T WANT TO HAVE TO HURT YOU.
THAT'S NOT HOW IT WORKS. PEOPLE AIN'T FISH. *YOU* CAN'T CONTROL 'EM.
THE CLOSEST YOU EVER GONNA COME TO DOING THAT IS BY GIVING THEM SOMETHING THEY WANT.
SEE, I GOT A LITTLE OF WHAT THEY WANT.
AND IF THEY WANT A LITTLE MORE, THEY'LL GIVE ME WHAT I WANT.
THAT'S FAIR, AIN'T IT?

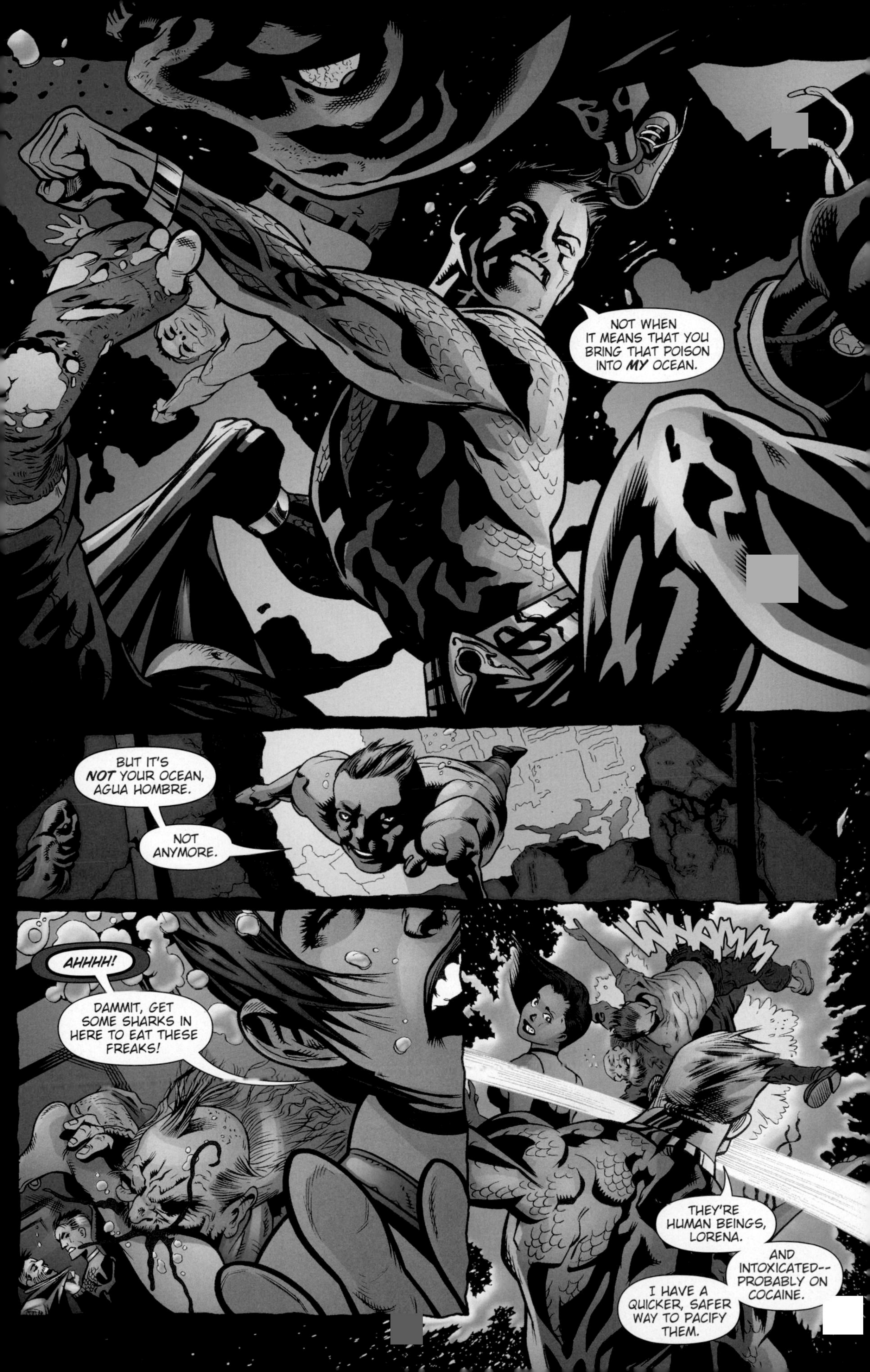
NOT WHEN IT MEANS THAT YOU BRING THAT POISON INTO MY OCEAN.
BUT IT'S NOT YOUR OCEAN, AGUA HOMBRE.
NOT ANYMORE.
AHHHH!
DAMMIT, GET SOME SHARKS IN HERE TO EAT THESE FREAKS!
WHAMM
THEY'RE HUMAN BEINGS, LORENA.
AND INTOXICATED-- PROBABLY ON COCAINE.
I HAVE A QUICKER, SAFER WAY TO PACIFY THEM.

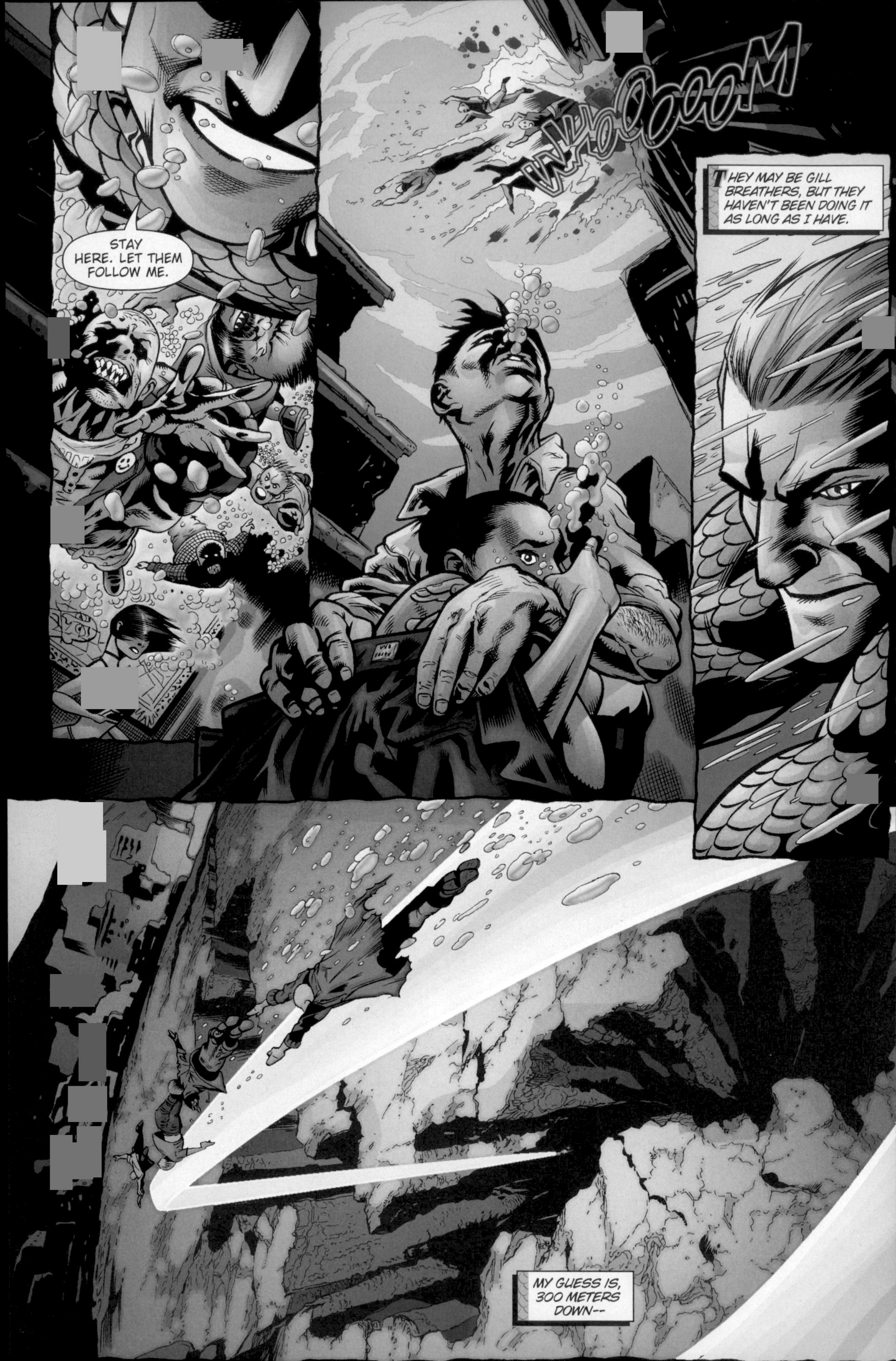
STAY HERE. LET THEM FOLLOW ME.
WHOOOOOOOM
THEY MAY BE GILL BREATHERS, BUT THEY HAVEN'T BEEN DOING IT AS LONG AS I HAVE.
MY GUESS IS, 300 METERS DOWN--

U**NDER HYPERBARIC CONDITIONS--**

--WHERE THE OXYGEN IS--

--SCARCER.

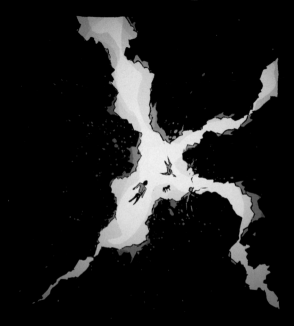

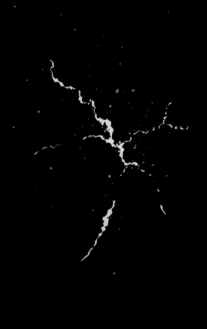

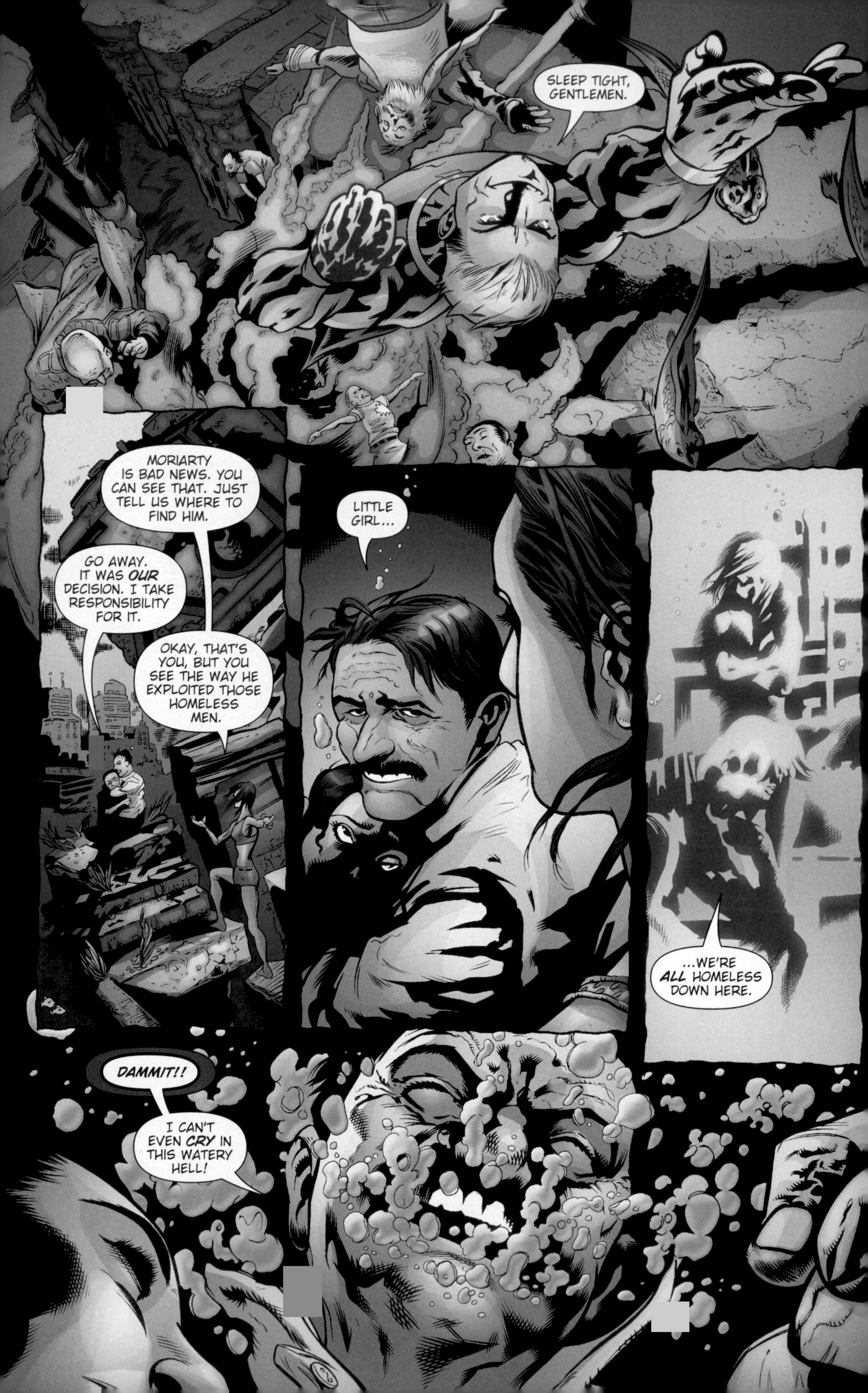
SLEEP TIGHT, GENTLEMEN.
MORIARTY IS BAD NEWS. YOU CAN SEE THAT. JUST TELL US WHERE TO FIND HIM.
GO AWAY. IT WAS *OUR* DECISION. I TAKE RESPONSIBILITY FOR IT.
OKAY, THAT'S YOU, BUT YOU SEE THE WAY HE EXPLOITED THOSE HOMELESS MEN.
LITTLE GIRL...
...WE'RE *ALL* HOMELESS DOWN HERE.
DAMMIT!!
I CAN'T EVEN *CRY* IN THIS WATERY HELL!

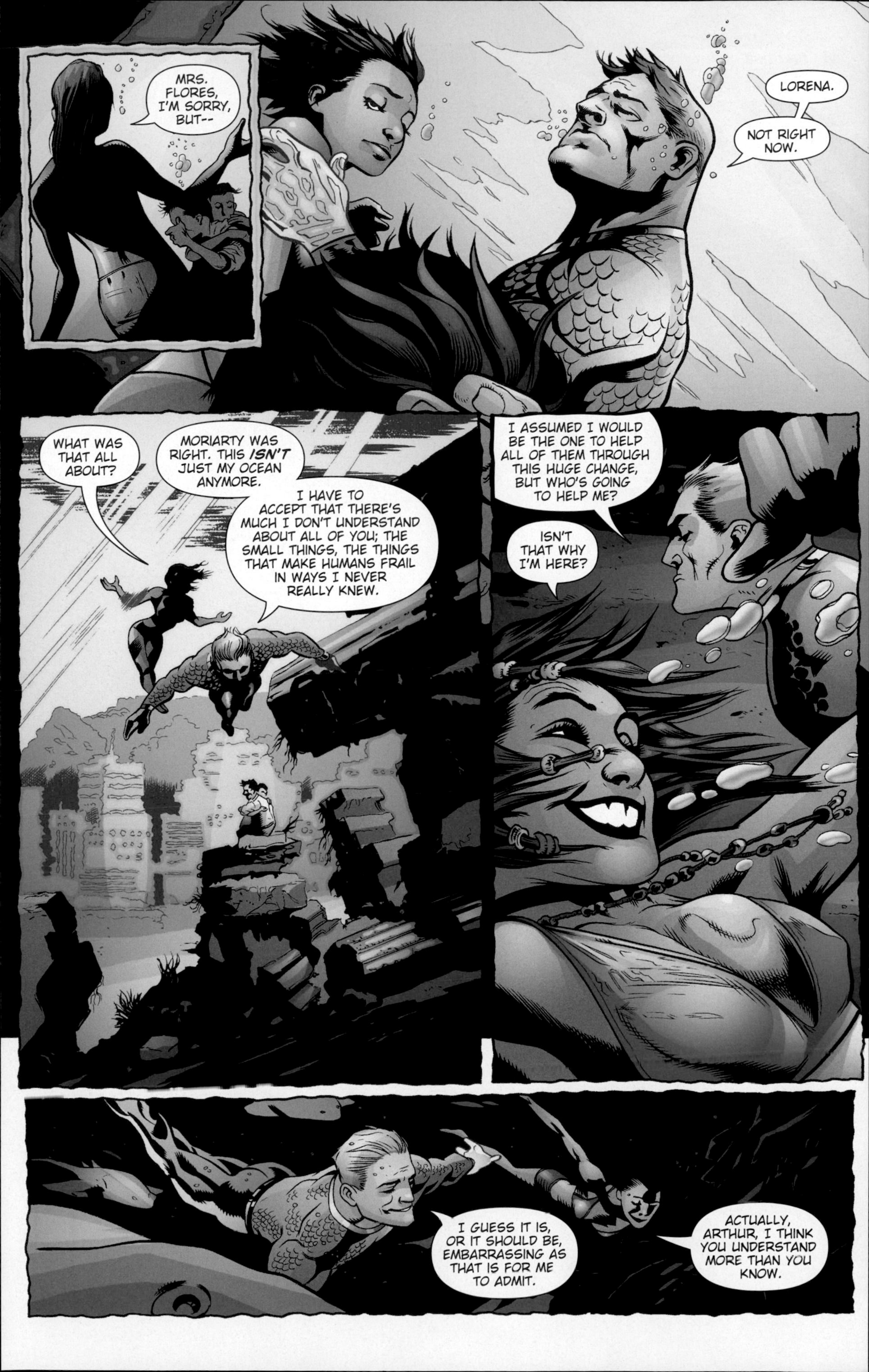
MRS. FLORES, I'M SORRY, BUT--
LORENA.
NOT RIGHT NOW.
WHAT WAS THAT ALL ABOUT?
MORIARTY WAS RIGHT. THIS *ISN'T* JUST MY OCEAN ANYMORE.
I HAVE TO ACCEPT THAT THERE'S MUCH I DON'T UNDERSTAND ABOUT ALL OF YOU; THE SMALL THINGS, THE THINGS THAT MAKE HUMANS FRAIL IN WAYS I NEVER REALLY KNEW.
I ASSUMED I WOULD BE THE ONE TO HELP ALL OF THEM THROUGH THIS HUGE CHANGE, BUT WHO'S GOING TO HELP ME?
ISN'T THAT WHY I'M HERE?
I GUESS IT IS, OR IT SHOULD BE, EMBARRASSING AS THAT IS FOR ME TO ADMIT.
ACTUALLY, ARTHUR, I THINK YOU UNDERSTAND MORE THAN YOU KNOW.

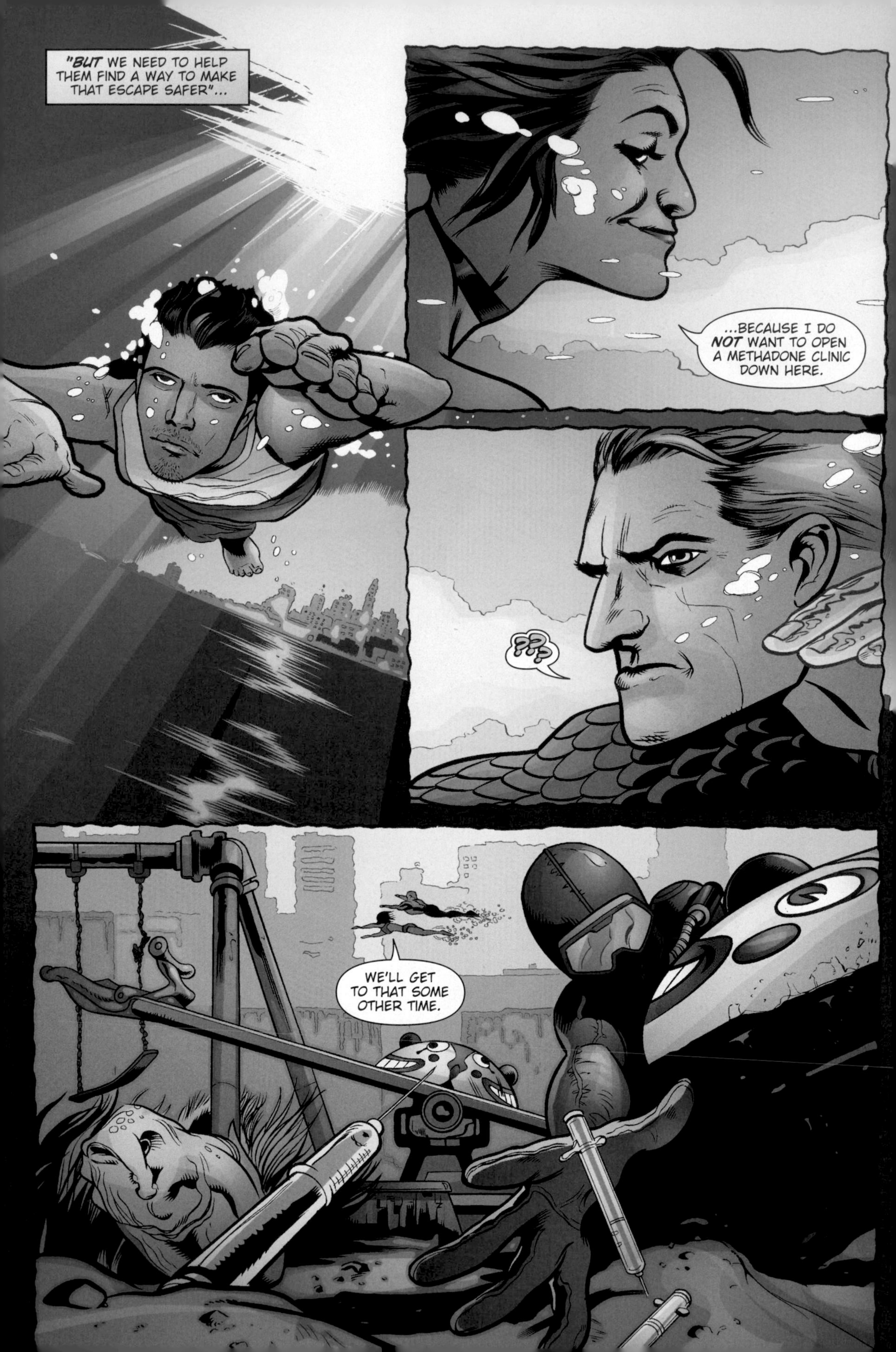
"*BUT* WE NEED TO HELP THEM FIND A WAY TO MAKE THAT ESCAPE SAFER"...
...BECAUSE I DO *NOT* WANT TO OPEN A METHADONE CLINIC DOWN HERE.
???
WE'LL GET TO THAT SOME OTHER TIME.

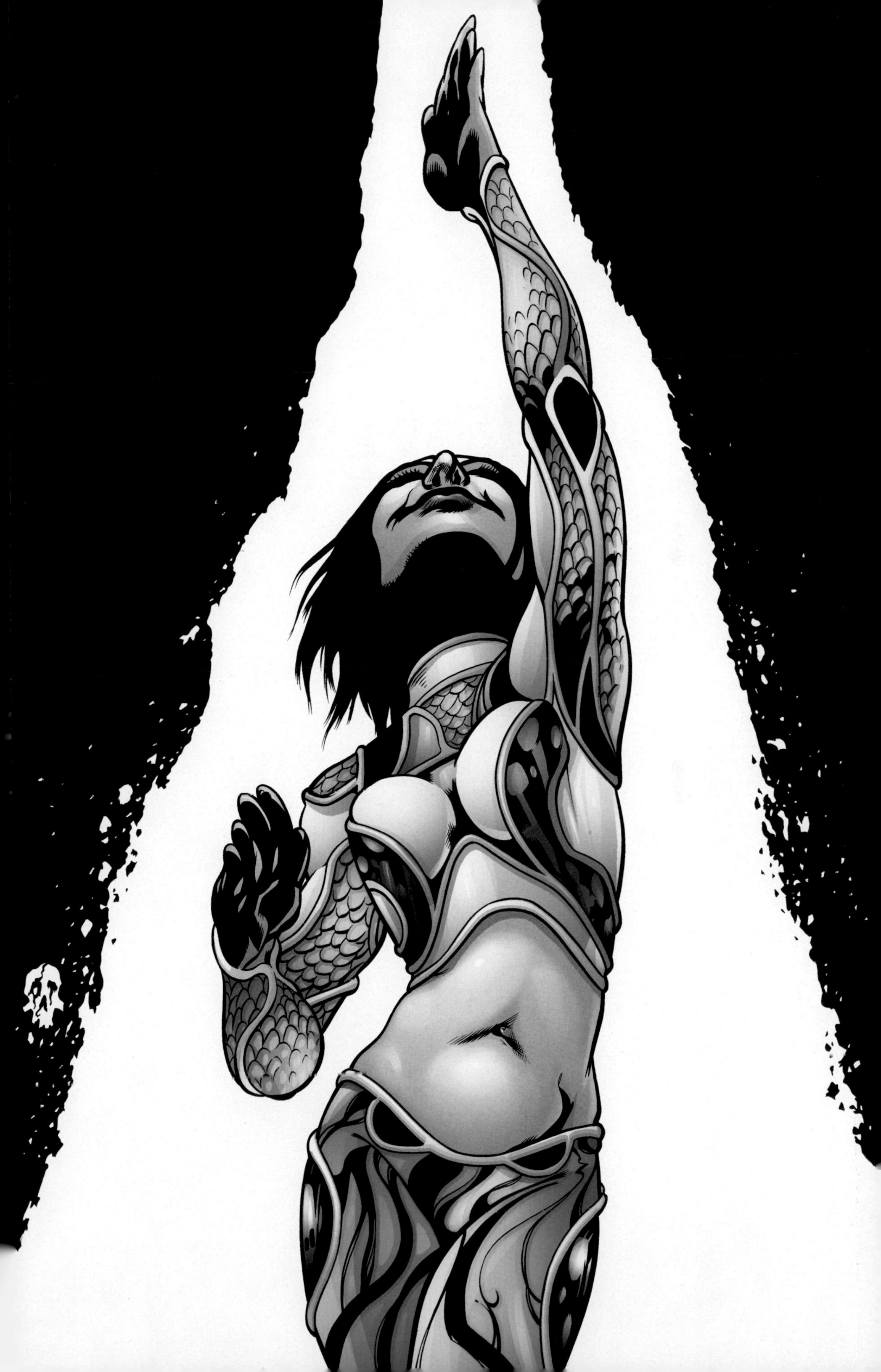

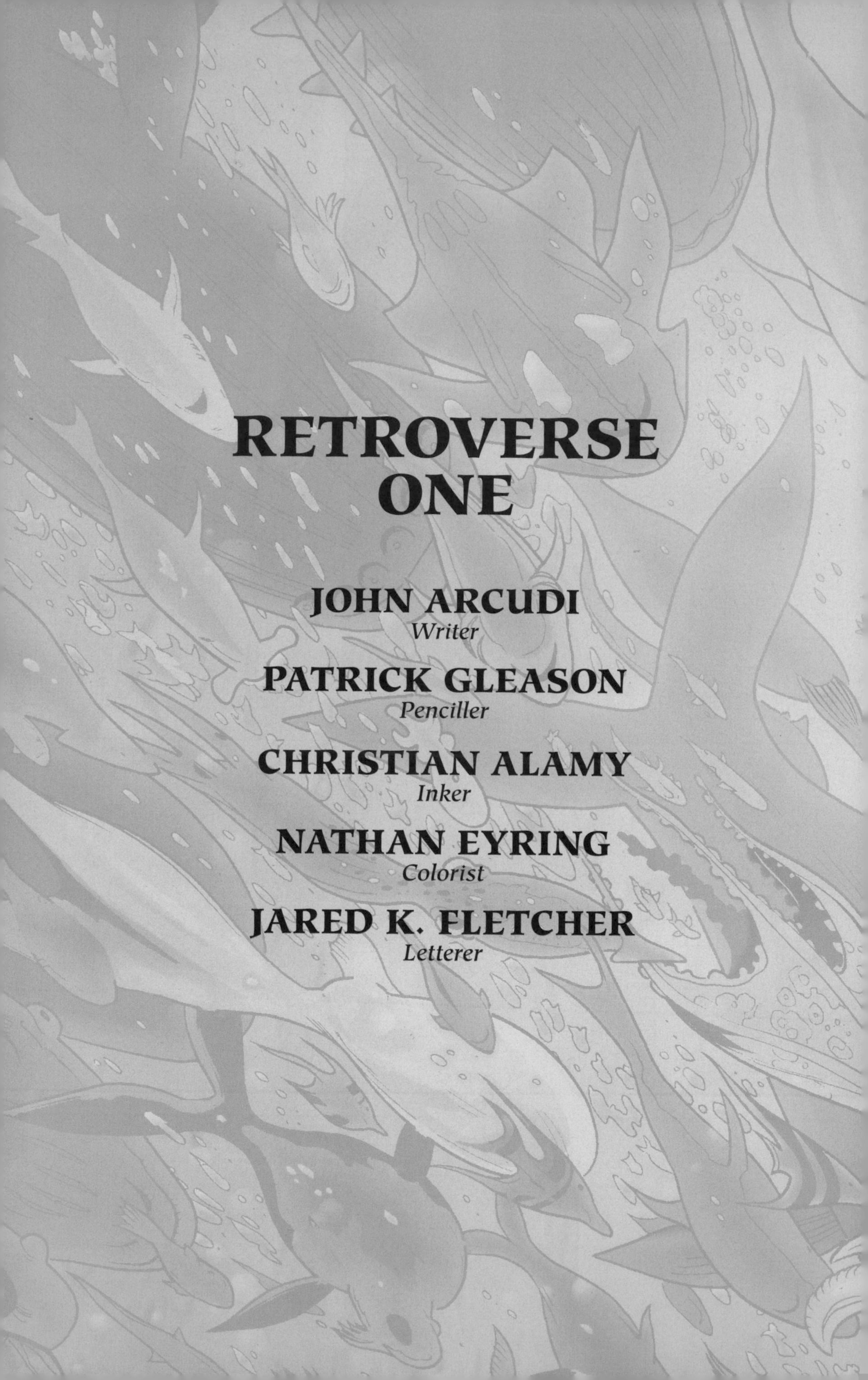

RETROVERSE ONE

JOHN ARCUDI
Writer

PATRICK GLEASON
Penciller

CHRISTIAN ALAMY
Inker

NATHAN EYRING
Colorist

JARED K. FLETCHER
Letterer

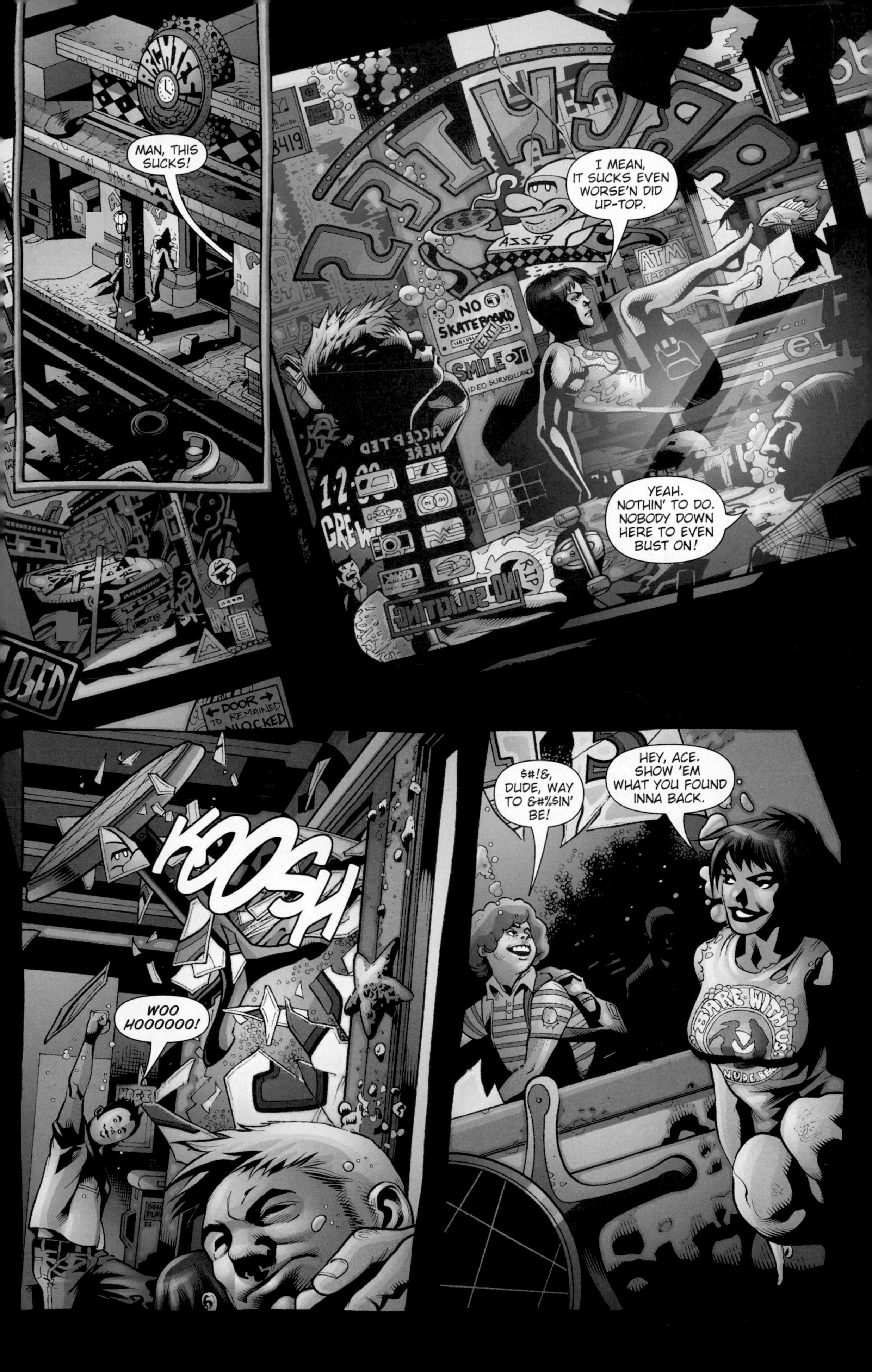
MAN, THIS SUCKS!
I MEAN, IT SUCKS EVEN WORSE'N DID UP-TOP.
YEAH. NOTHIN' TO DO. NOBODY DOWN HERE TO EVEN BUST ON!
KOOSH
WOO HOOOOOO!
$#!&, DUDE, WAY TO &#%$IN' BE!
HEY, ACE. SHOW 'EM WHAT YOU FOUND INNA BACK.

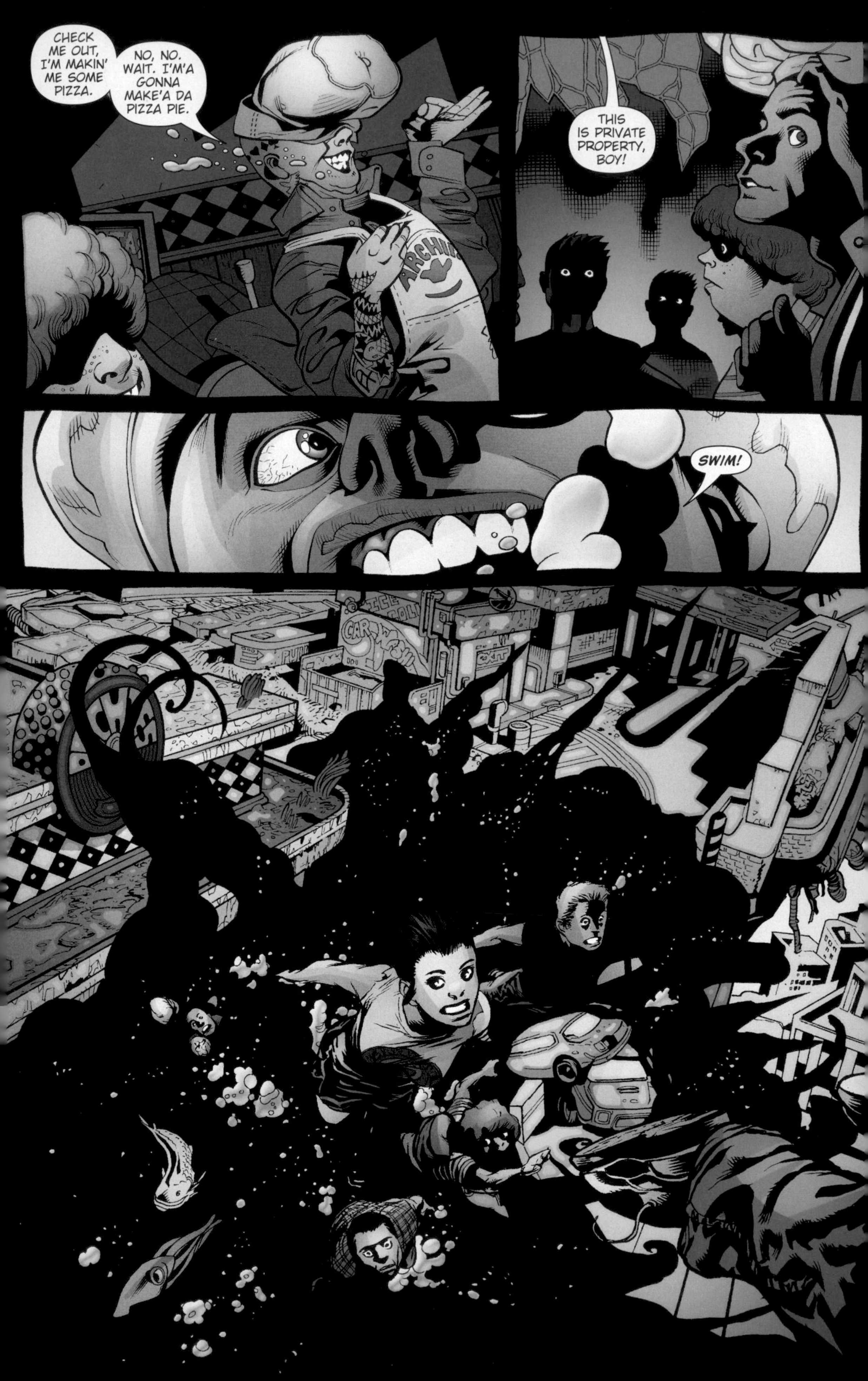
CHECK ME OUT, I'M MAKIN' ME SOME PIZZA.
NO, NO. WAIT. I'M'A GONNA MAKE'A DA PIZZA PIE.
THIS IS PRIVATE PROPERTY, BOY!
SWIM!

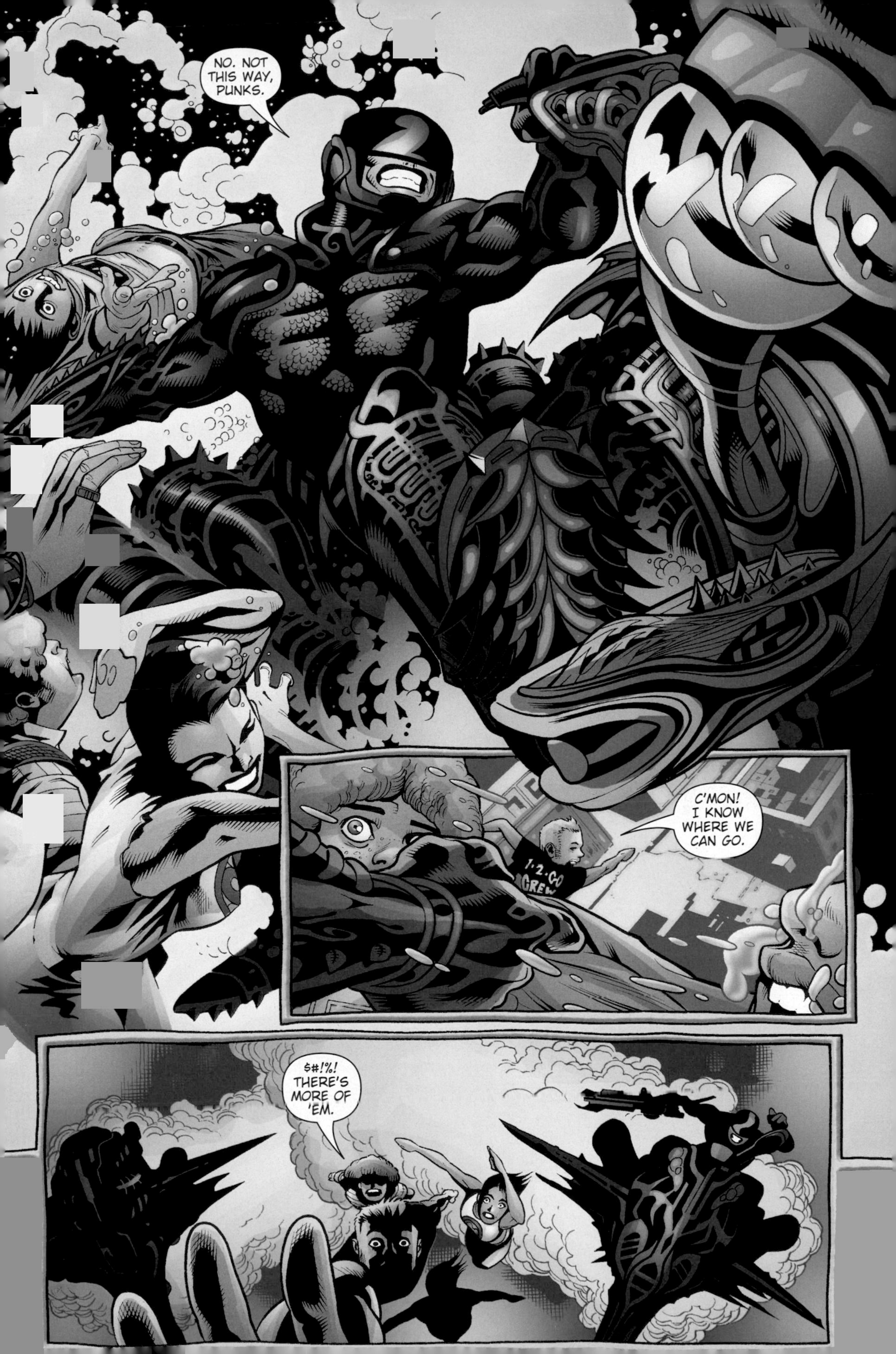
NO. NOT THIS WAY, PUNKS.
C'MON! I KNOW WHERE WE CAN GO.
1-2-GO CREW
$#!%! THERE'S MORE OF 'EM.

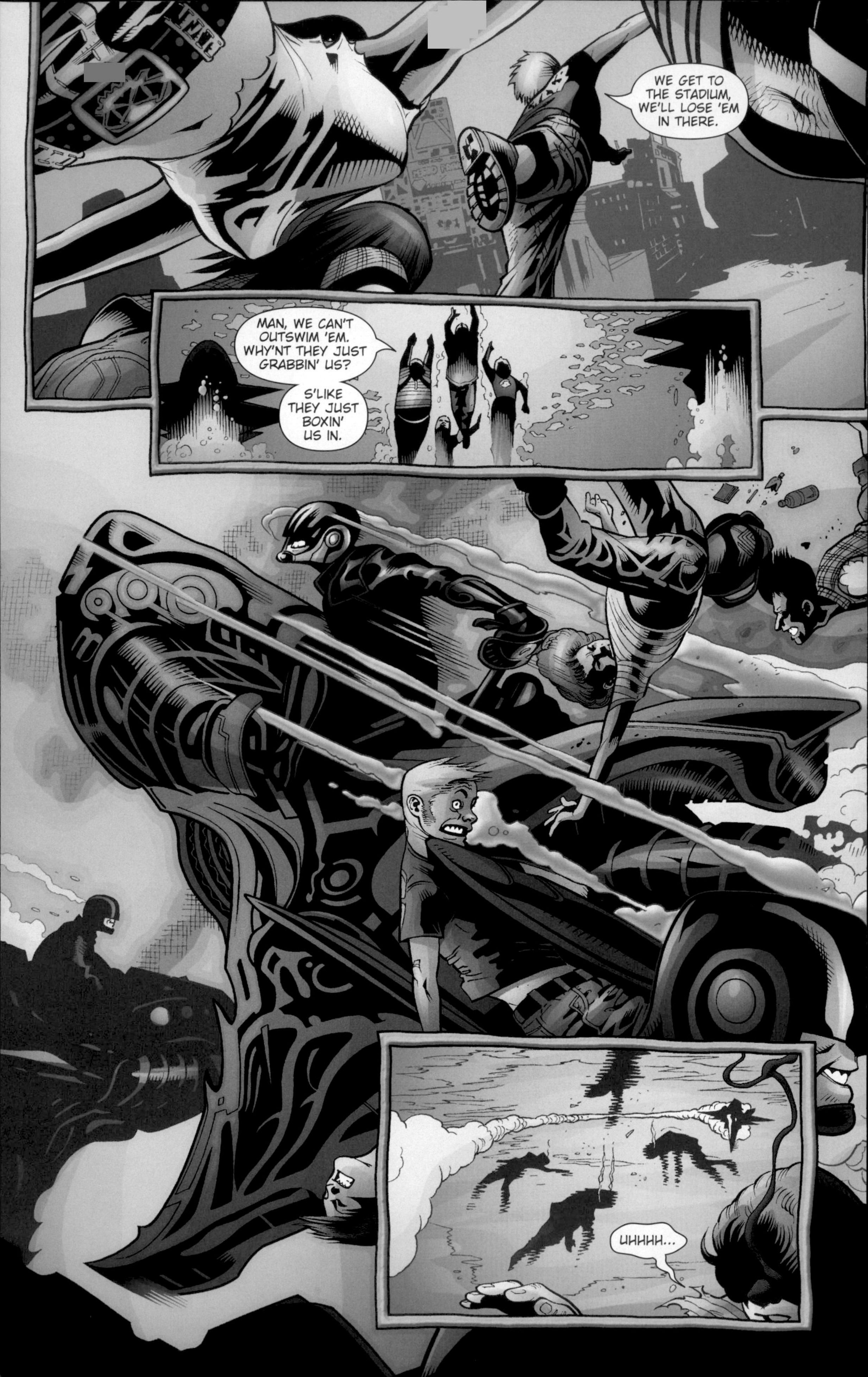
WE GET TO THE STADIUM, WE'LL LOSE 'EM IN THERE.
MAN, WE CAN'T OUTSWIM 'EM. WHY'NT THEY JUST GRABBIN' US?
S'LIKE THEY JUST BOXIN' US IN.
UHHHH...

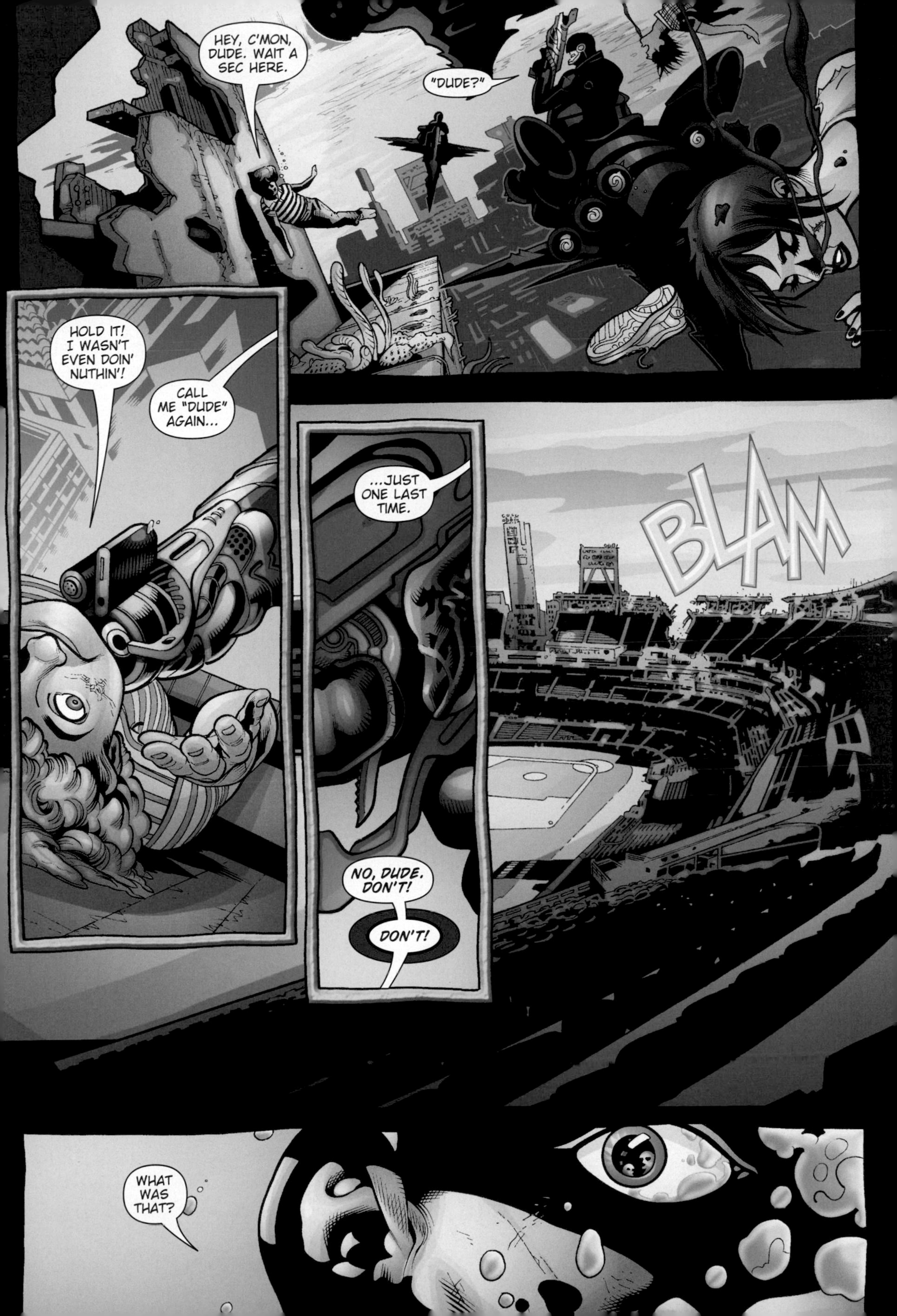
HEY, C'MON, DUDE. WAIT A SEC HERE.
"DUDE?"
HOLD IT! I WASN'T EVEN DOIN' NUTHIN'!
CALL ME "DUDE" AGAIN...
...JUST ONE LAST TIME.
BLAM
NO, DUDE. DON'T!
DON'T!
WHAT WAS THAT?

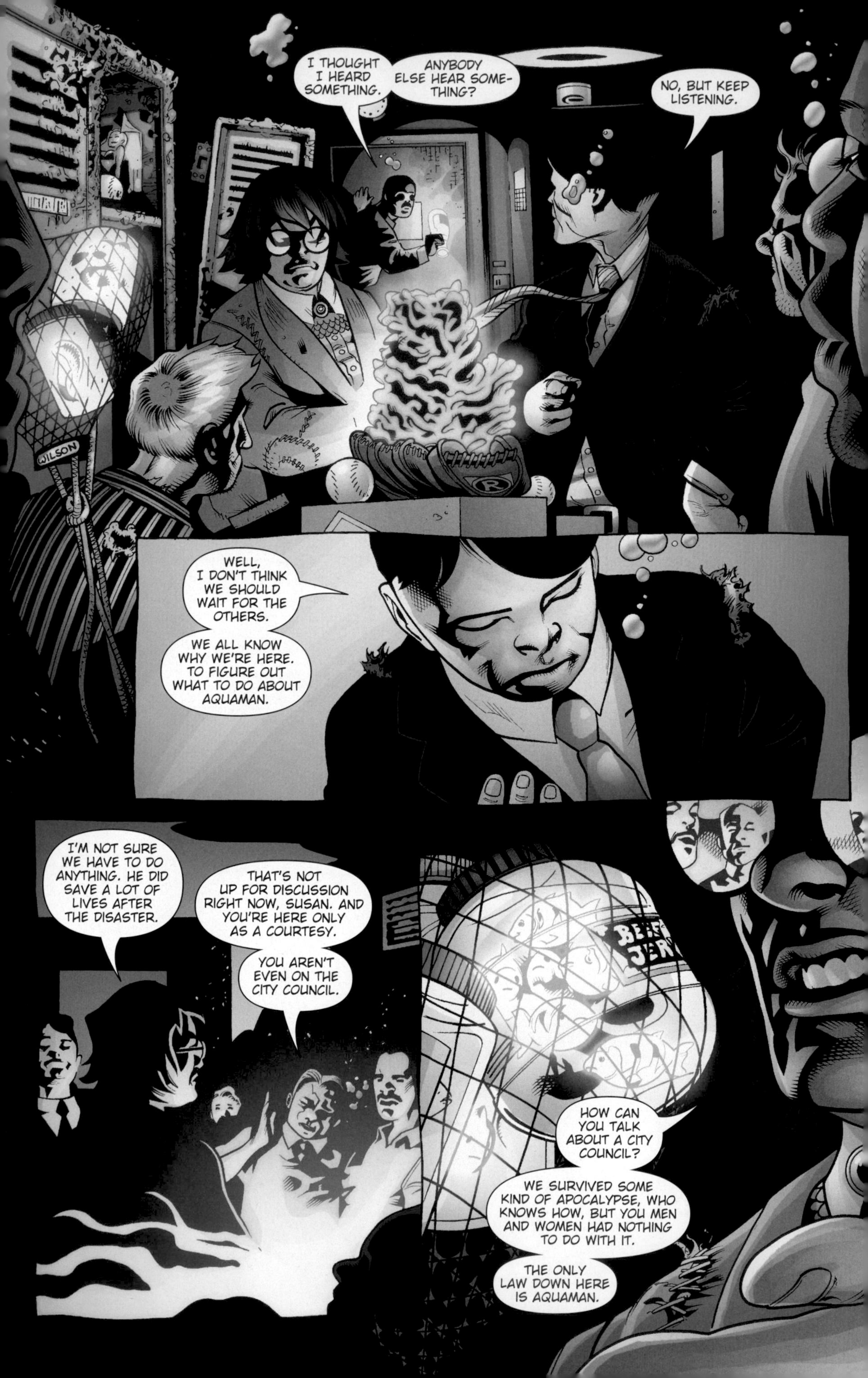
I THOUGHT I HEARD SOMETHING.
ANYBODY ELSE HEAR SOME-THING?
NO, BUT KEEP LISTENING.
WILSON
WELL, I DON'T THINK WE SHOULD WAIT FOR THE OTHERS.
WE ALL KNOW WHY WE'RE HERE. TO FIGURE OUT WHAT TO DO ABOUT AQUAMAN.
I'M NOT SURE WE HAVE TO DO ANYTHING. HE DID SAVE A LOT OF LIVES AFTER THE DISASTER.
THAT'S NOT UP FOR DISCUSSION RIGHT NOW, SUSAN. AND YOU'RE HERE ONLY AS A COURTESY.
YOU AREN'T EVEN ON THE CITY COUNCIL.
HOW CAN YOU TALK ABOUT A CITY COUNCIL?
WE SURVIVED SOME KIND OF APOCALYPSE, WHO KNOWS HOW, BUT YOU MEN AND WOMEN HAD NOTHING TO DO WITH IT.
THE ONLY LAW DOWN HERE IS AQUAMAN.

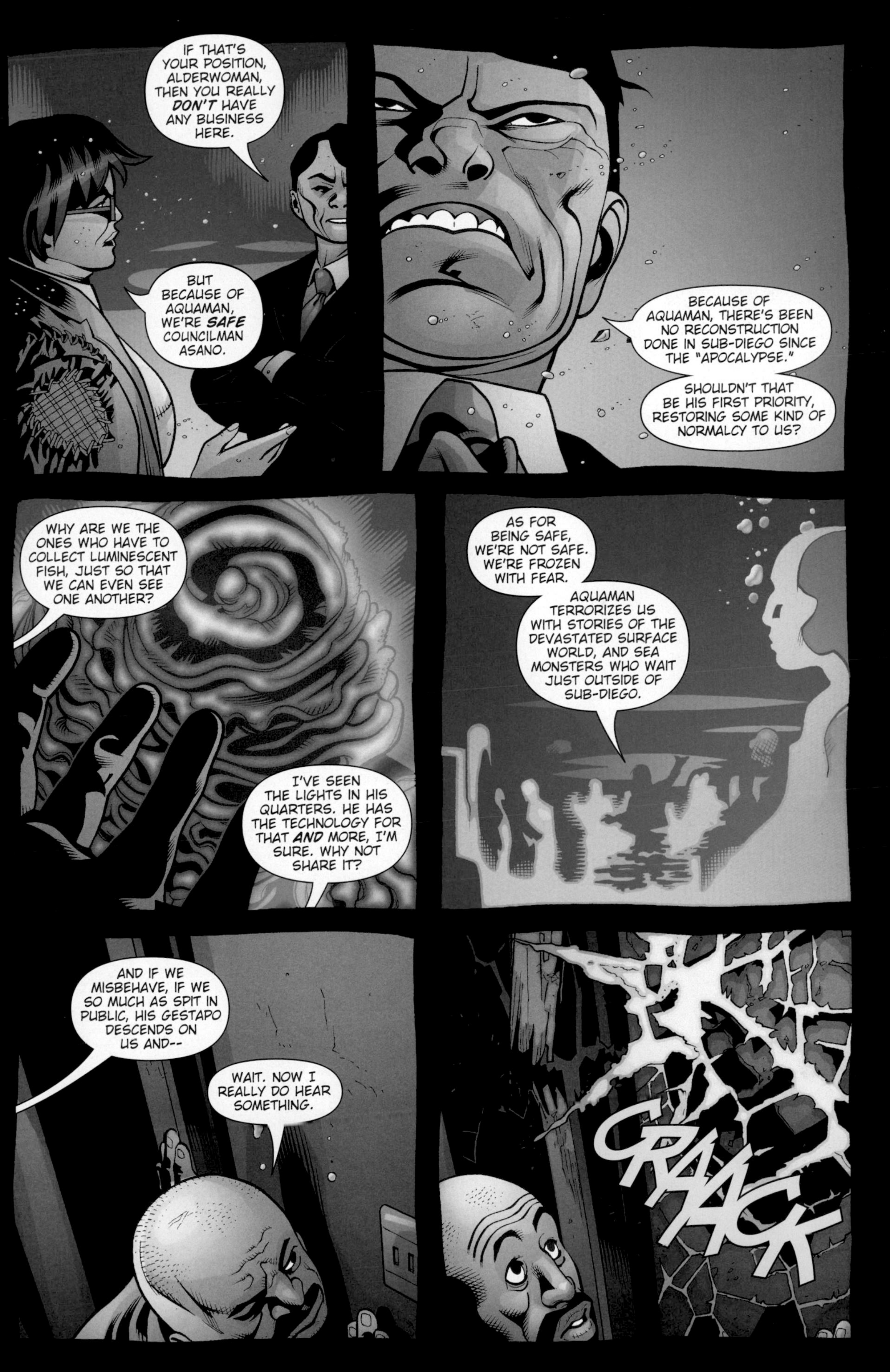
IF THAT'S YOUR POSITION, ALDERWOMAN, THEN YOU REALLY DON'T HAVE ANY BUSINESS HERE.
BUT BECAUSE OF AQUAMAN, WE'RE SAFE COUNCILMAN ASANO.
BECAUSE OF AQUAMAN, THERE'S BEEN NO RECONSTRUCTION DONE IN SUB-DIEGO SINCE THE "APOCALYPSE."
SHOULDN'T THAT BE HIS FIRST PRIORITY, RESTORING SOME KIND OF NORMALCY TO US?
WHY ARE WE THE ONES WHO HAVE TO COLLECT LUMINESCENT FISH, JUST SO THAT WE CAN EVEN SEE ONE ANOTHER?
I'VE SEEN THE LIGHTS IN HIS QUARTERS. HE HAS THE TECHNOLOGY FOR THAT AND MORE, I'M SURE. WHY NOT SHARE IT?
AS FOR BEING SAFE, WE'RE NOT SAFE. WE'RE FROZEN WITH FEAR.
AQUAMAN TERRORIZES US WITH STORIES OF THE DEVASTATED SURFACE WORLD, AND SEA MONSTERS WHO WAIT JUST OUTSIDE OF SUB-DIEGO.
AND IF WE MISBEHAVE, IF WE SO MUCH AS SPIT IN PUBLIC, HIS GESTAPO DESCENDS ON US AND--
WAIT. NOW I REALLY DO HEAR SOMETHING.
CRAACK

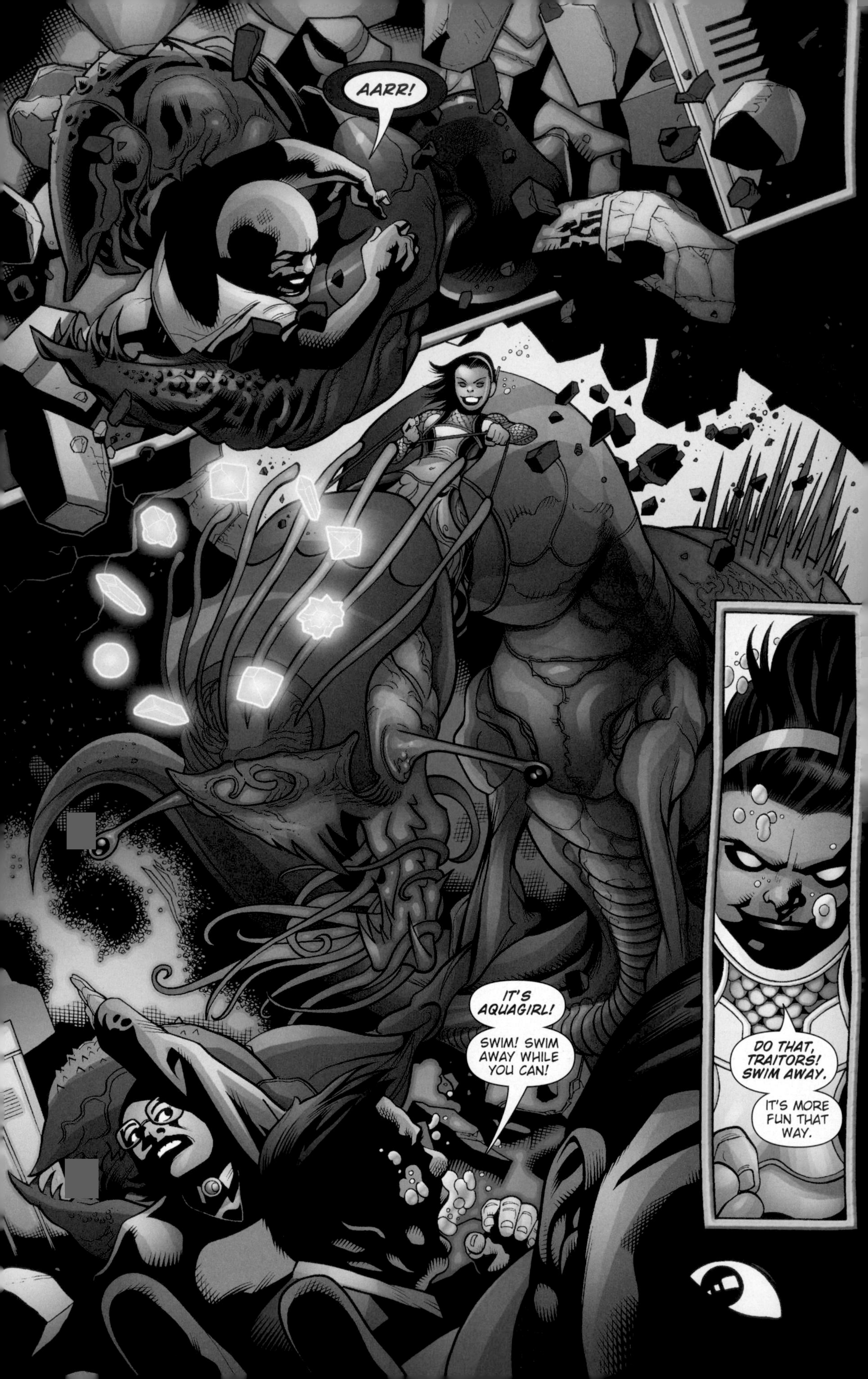
AARR!
IT'S AQUAGIRL!
SWIM! SWIM AWAY WHILE YOU CAN!
DO THAT, TRAITORS! SWIM AWAY.
IT'S MORE FUN THAT WAY.

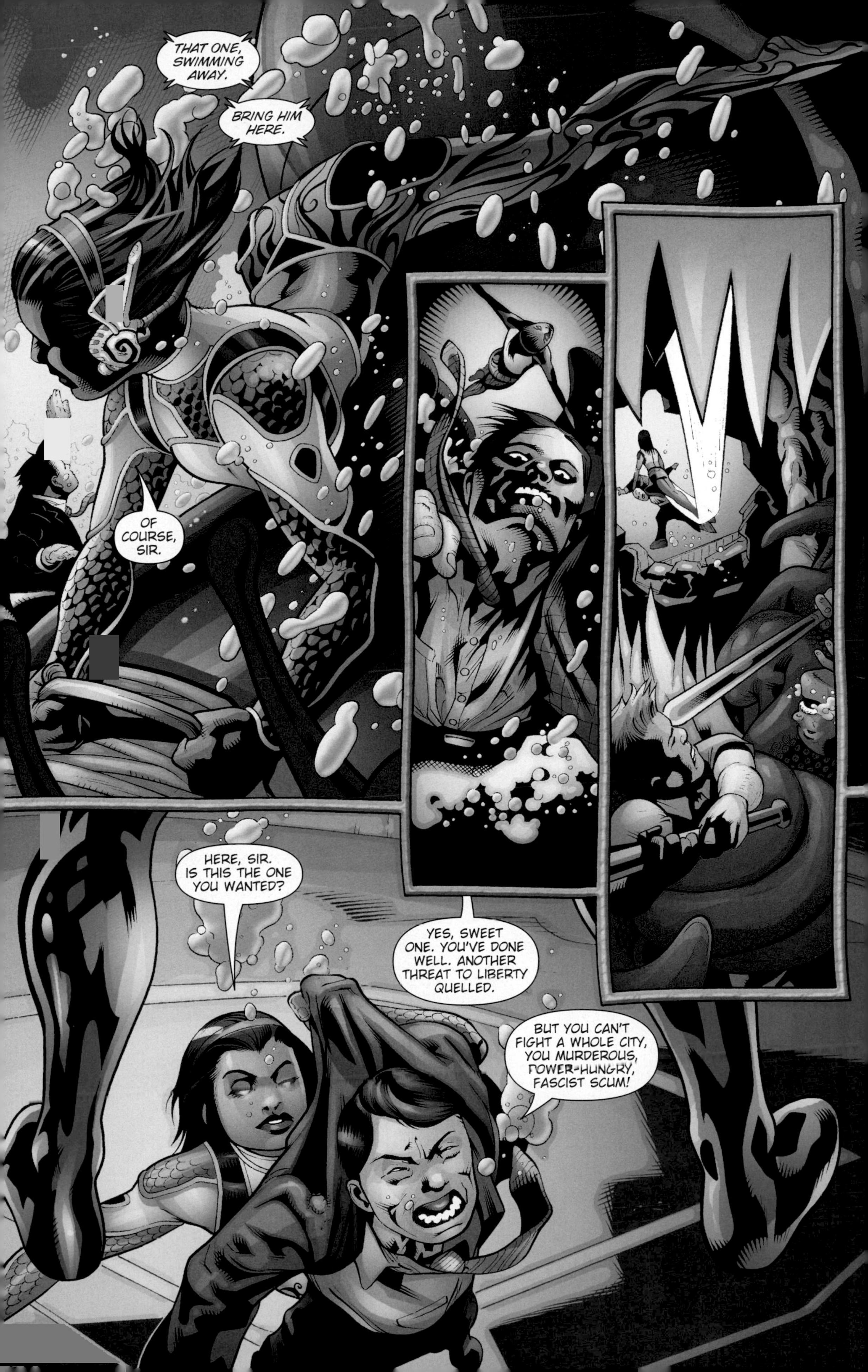
THAT ONE, SWIMMING AWAY.
BRING HIM HERE.
OF COURSE, SIR.
HERE, SIR. IS THIS THE ONE YOU WANTED?
YES, SWEET ONE. YOU'VE DONE WELL. ANOTHER THREAT TO LIBERTY QUELLED.
BUT YOU CAN'T FIGHT A WHOLE CITY, YOU MURDEROUS, POWER-HUNGRY, FASCIST SCUM!

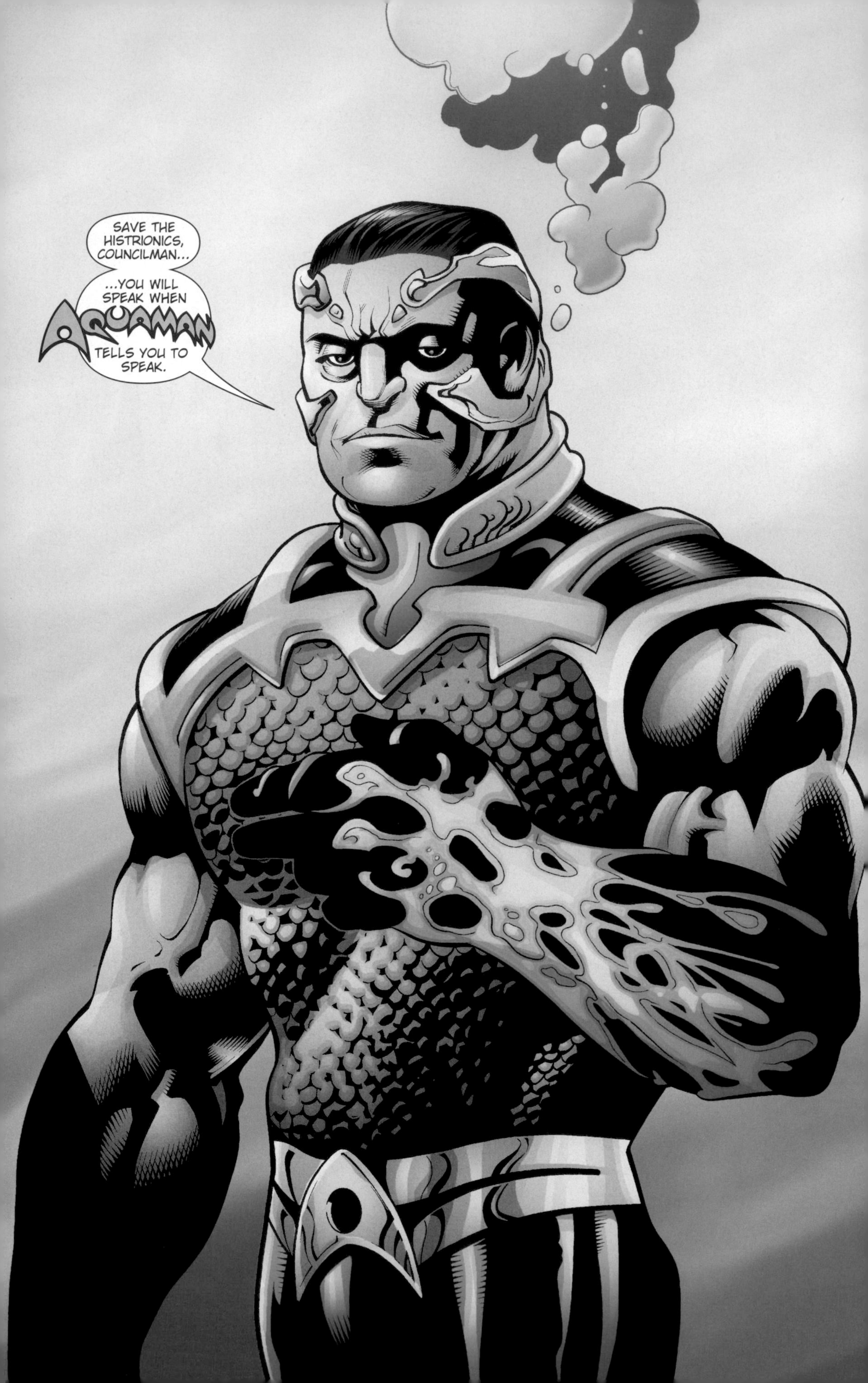
SAVE THE HISTRIONICS, COUNCILMAN...
...YOU WILL SPEAK WHEN AQUAMAN TELLS YOU TO SPEAK.

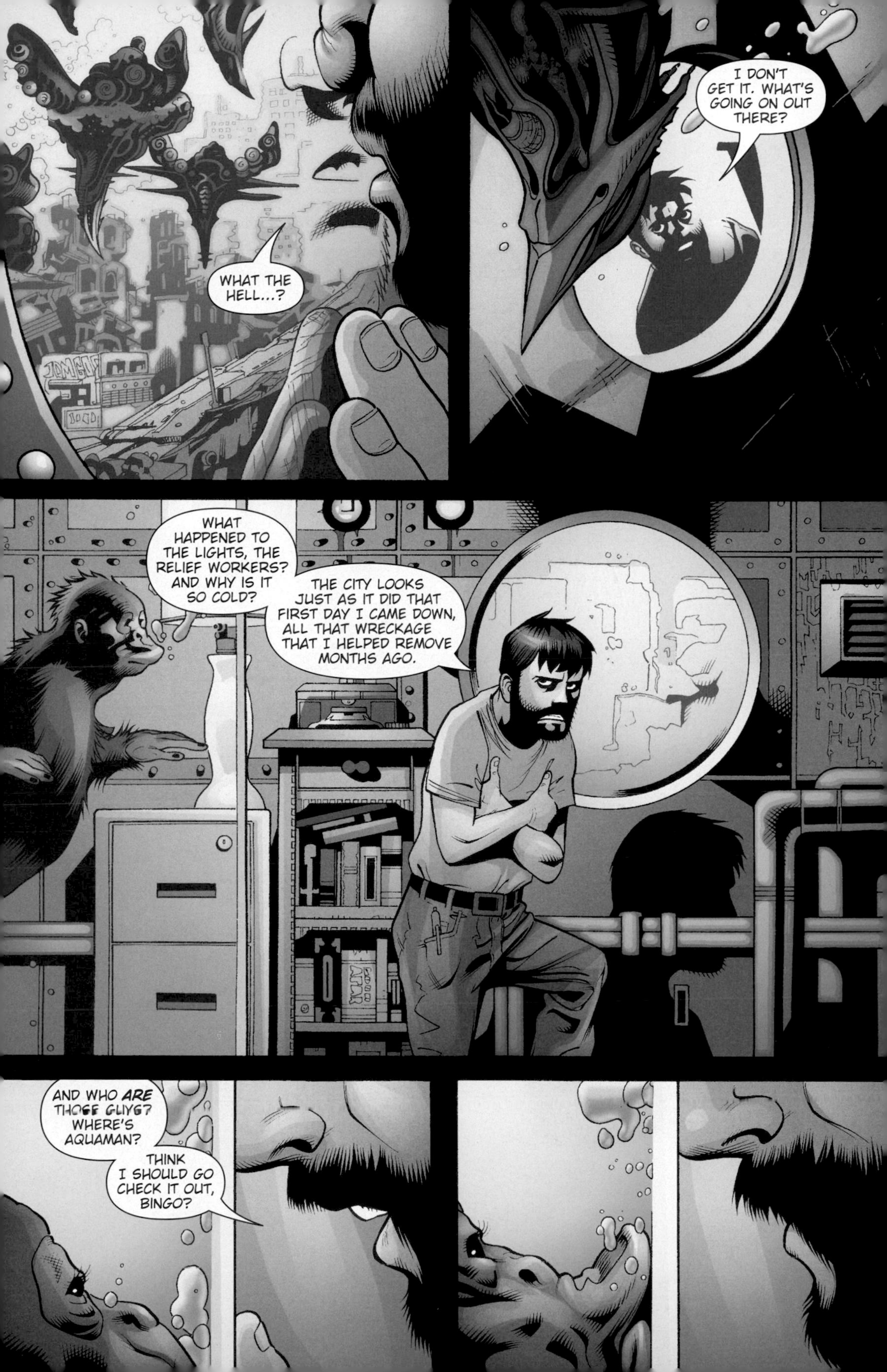
WHAT THE HELL...?
I DON'T GET IT. WHAT'S GOING ON OUT THERE?
WHAT HAPPENED TO THE LIGHTS, THE RELIEF WORKERS? AND WHY IS IT SO COLD?
THE CITY LOOKS JUST AS IT DID THAT FIRST DAY I CAME DOWN, ALL THAT WRECKAGE THAT I HELPED REMOVE MONTHS AGO.
AND WHO ARE THOSE GUYS? WHERE'S AQUAMAN?
THINK I SHOULD GO CHECK IT OUT, BINGO?

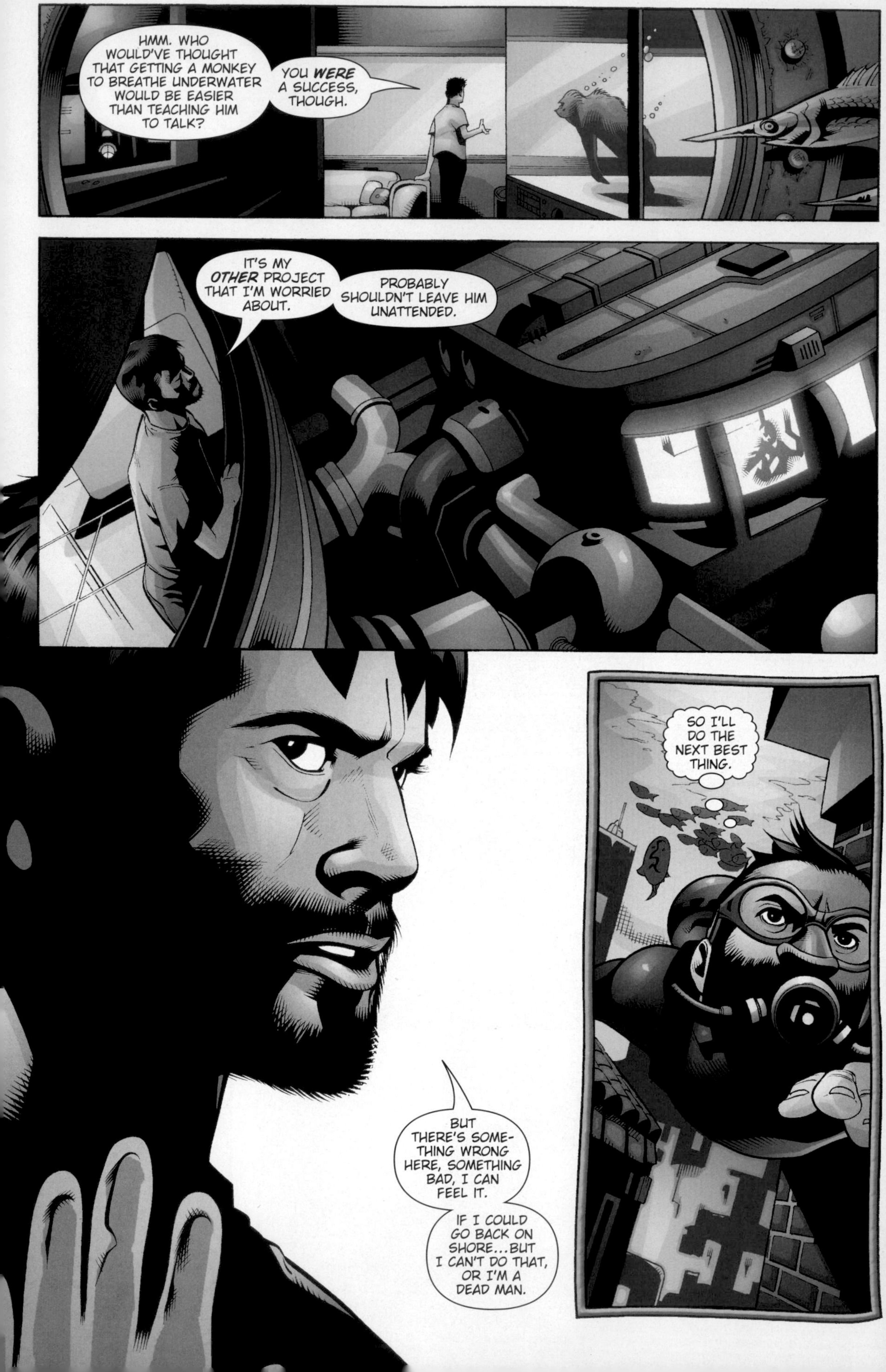
HMM. WHO WOULD'VE THOUGHT THAT GETTING A MONKEY TO BREATHE UNDERWATER WOULD BE EASIER THAN TEACHING HIM TO TALK?
YOU **WERE** A SUCCESS, THOUGH.
IT'S MY **OTHER** PROJECT THAT I'M WORRIED ABOUT.
PROBABLY SHOULDN'T LEAVE HIM UNATTENDED.
SO I'LL DO THE NEXT BEST THING.
BUT THERE'S SOMETHING WRONG HERE, SOMETHING BAD, I CAN FEEL IT.
IF I COULD GO BACK ON SHORE...BUT I CAN'T DO THAT, OR I'M A DEAD MAN.

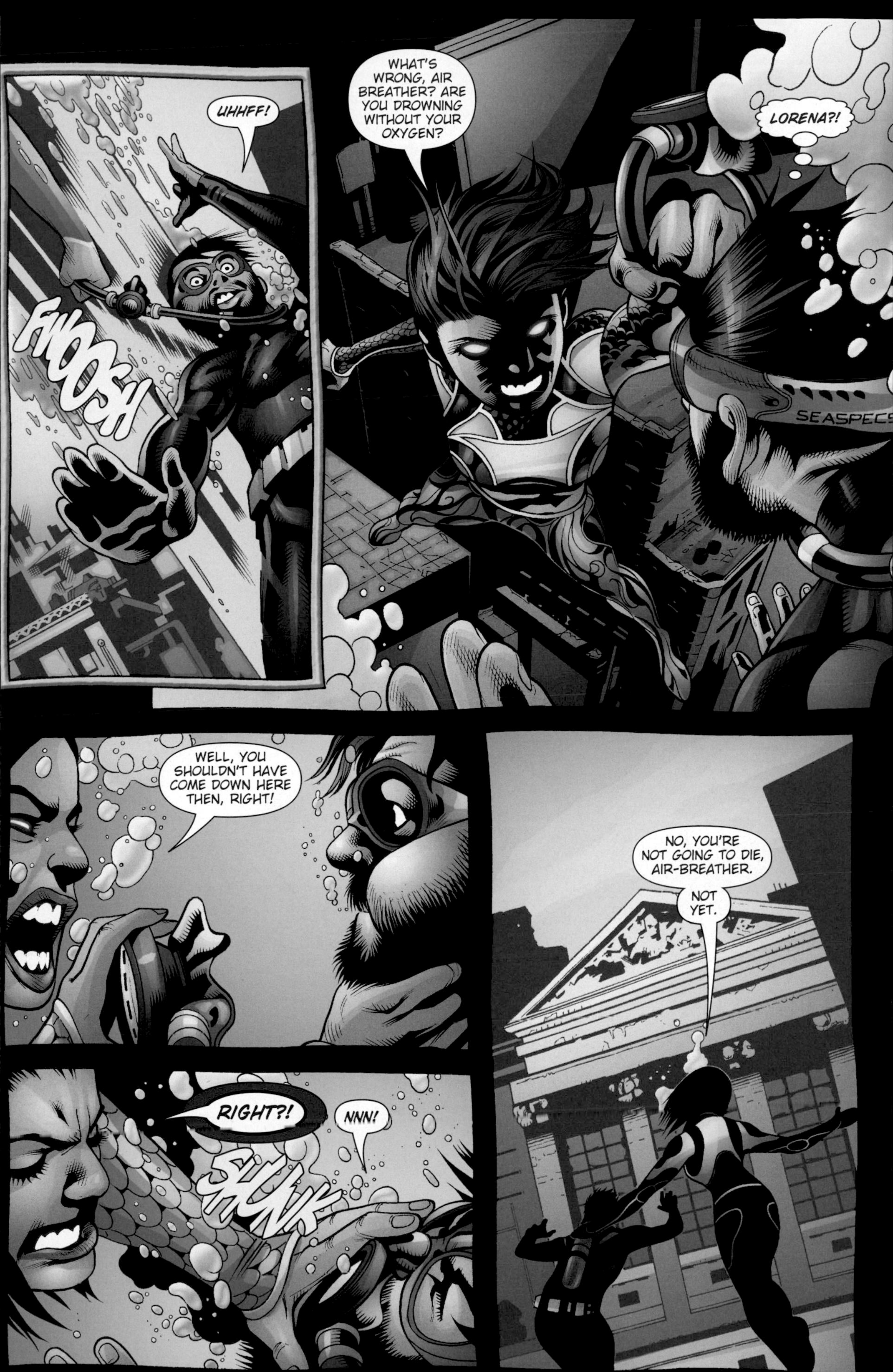
UHHFF!
FWOOSH
WHAT'S WRONG, AIR BREATHER? ARE YOU DROWNING WITHOUT YOUR OXYGEN?
LORENA?!
SEASPECS
WELL, YOU SHOULDN'T HAVE COME DOWN HERE THEN, RIGHT!
RIGHT?!
NNN!
SHUNK
NO, YOU'RE NOT GOING TO DIE, AIR-BREATHER.
NOT YET.

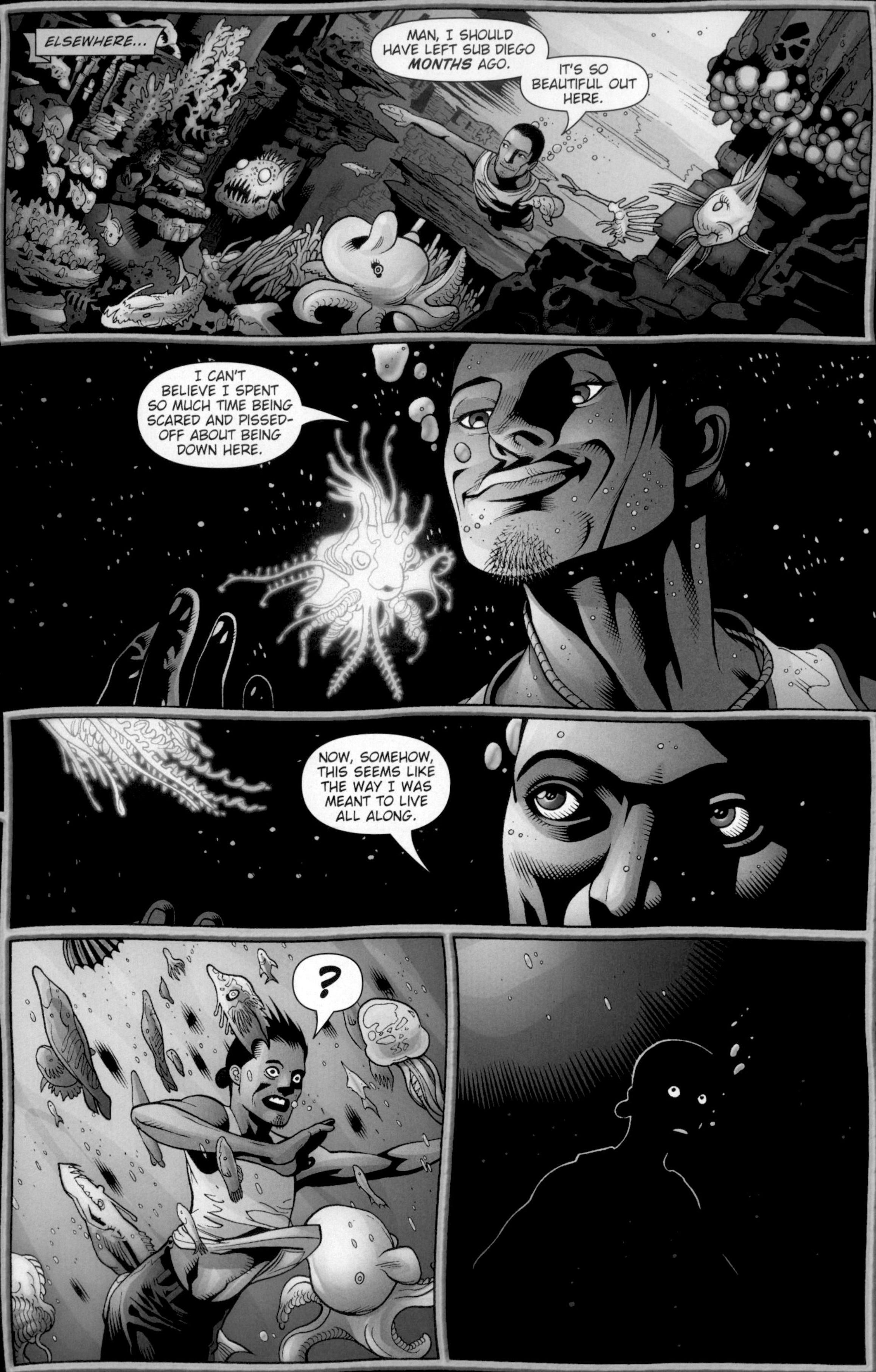
ELSEWHERE...
MAN, I SHOULD HAVE LEFT SUB DIEGO MONTHS AGO.
IT'S SO BEAUTIFUL OUT HERE.
I CAN'T BELIEVE I SPENT SO MUCH TIME BEING SCARED AND PISSED-OFF ABOUT BEING DOWN HERE.
NOW, SOMEHOW, THIS SEEMS LIKE THE WAY I WAS MEANT TO LIVE ALL ALONG.
?

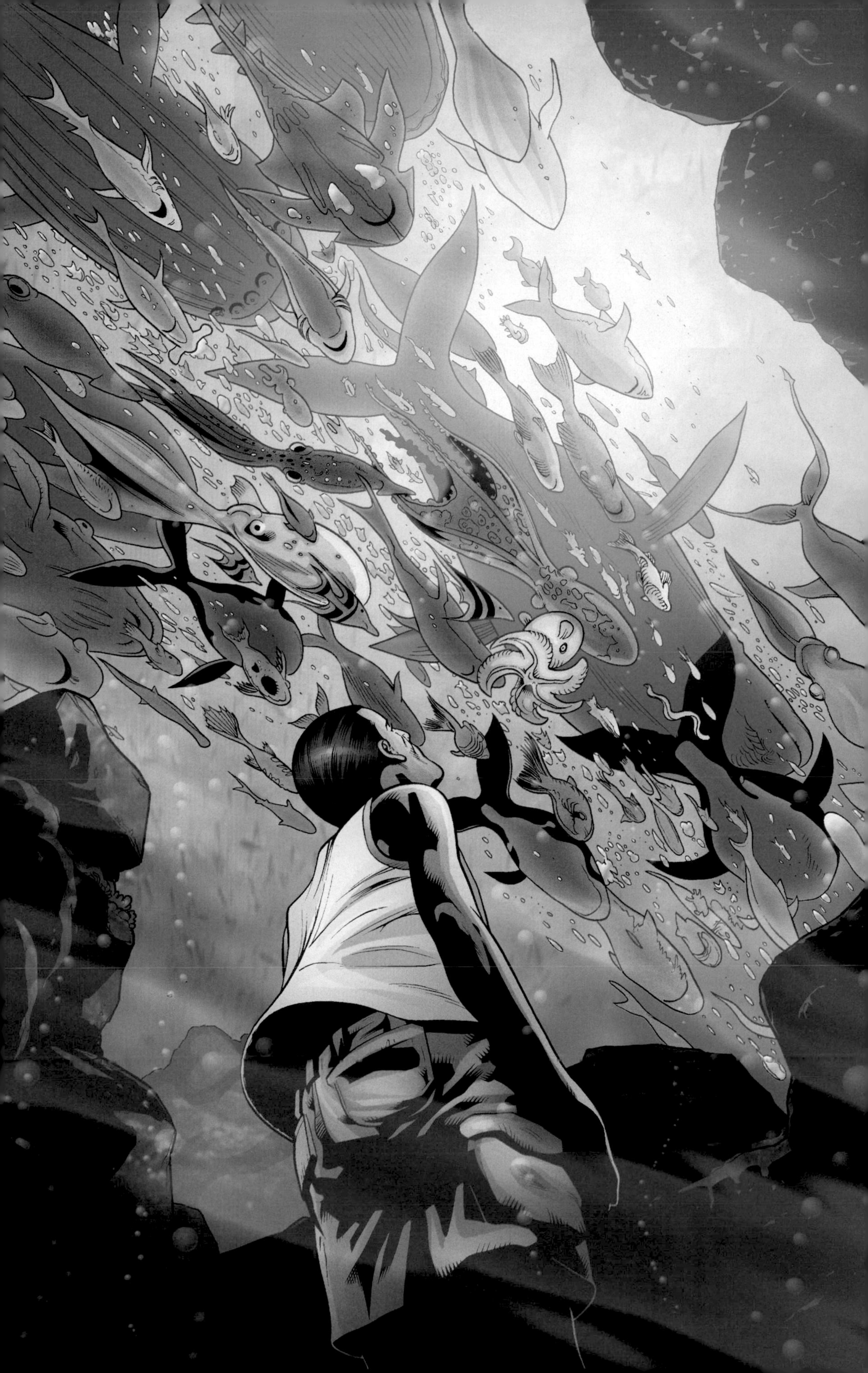

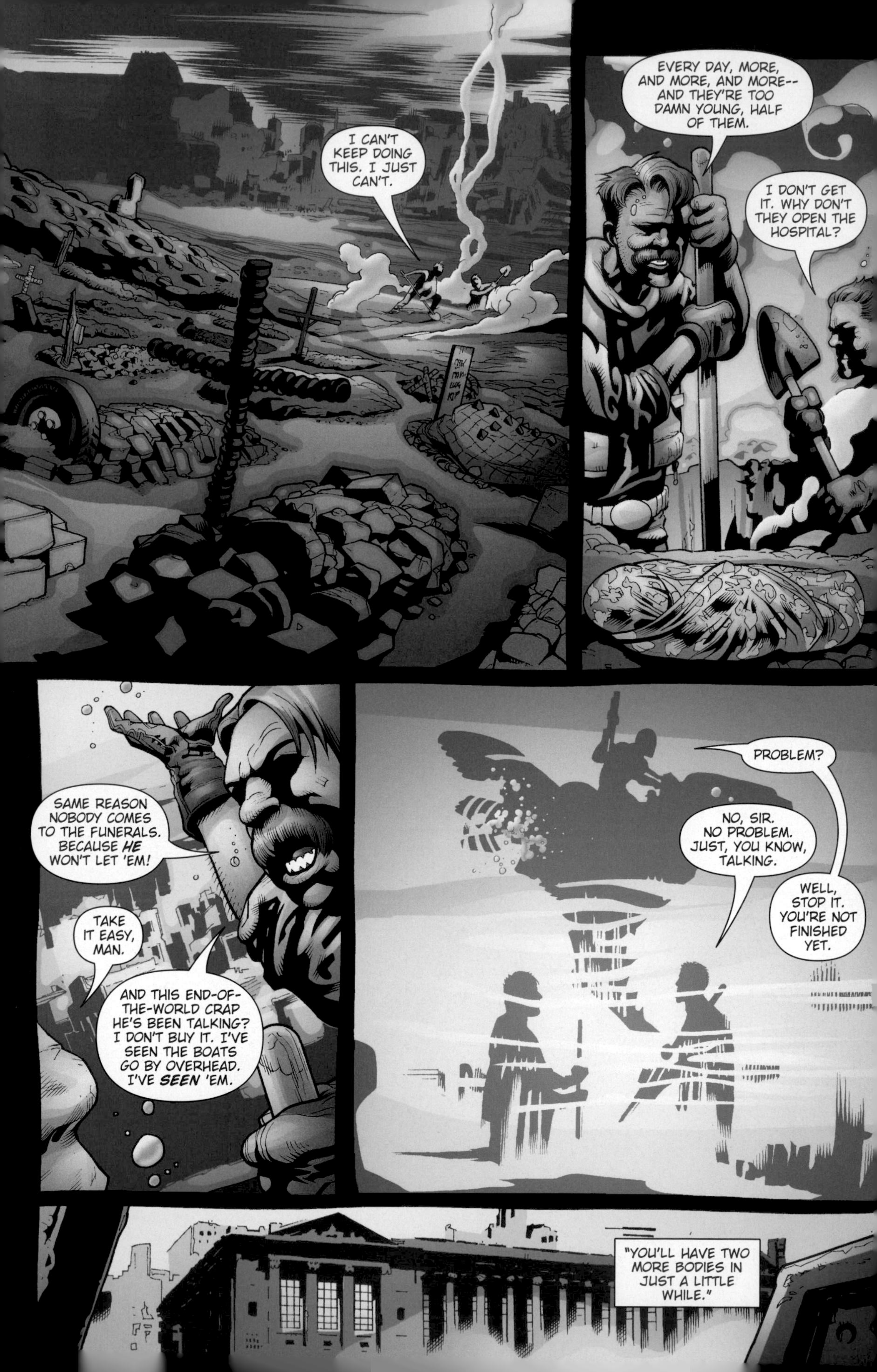
I CAN'T KEEP DOING THIS. I JUST CAN'T.
EVERY DAY, MORE, AND MORE, AND MORE-- AND THEY'RE TOO DAMN YOUNG, HALF OF THEM.
I DON'T GET IT. WHY DON'T THEY OPEN THE HOSPITAL?
SAME REASON NOBODY COMES TO THE FUNERALS. BECAUSE HE WON'T LET 'EM!
TAKE IT EASY, MAN.
AND THIS END-OF-THE-WORLD CRAP HE'S BEEN TALKING? I DON'T BUY IT. I'VE SEEN THE BOATS GO BY OVERHEAD. I'VE SEEN 'EM.
PROBLEM?
NO, SIR. NO PROBLEM. JUST, YOU KNOW, TALKING.
WELL, STOP IT. YOU'RE NOT FINISHED YET.
"YOU'LL HAVE TWO MORE BODIES IN JUST A LITTLE WHILE."

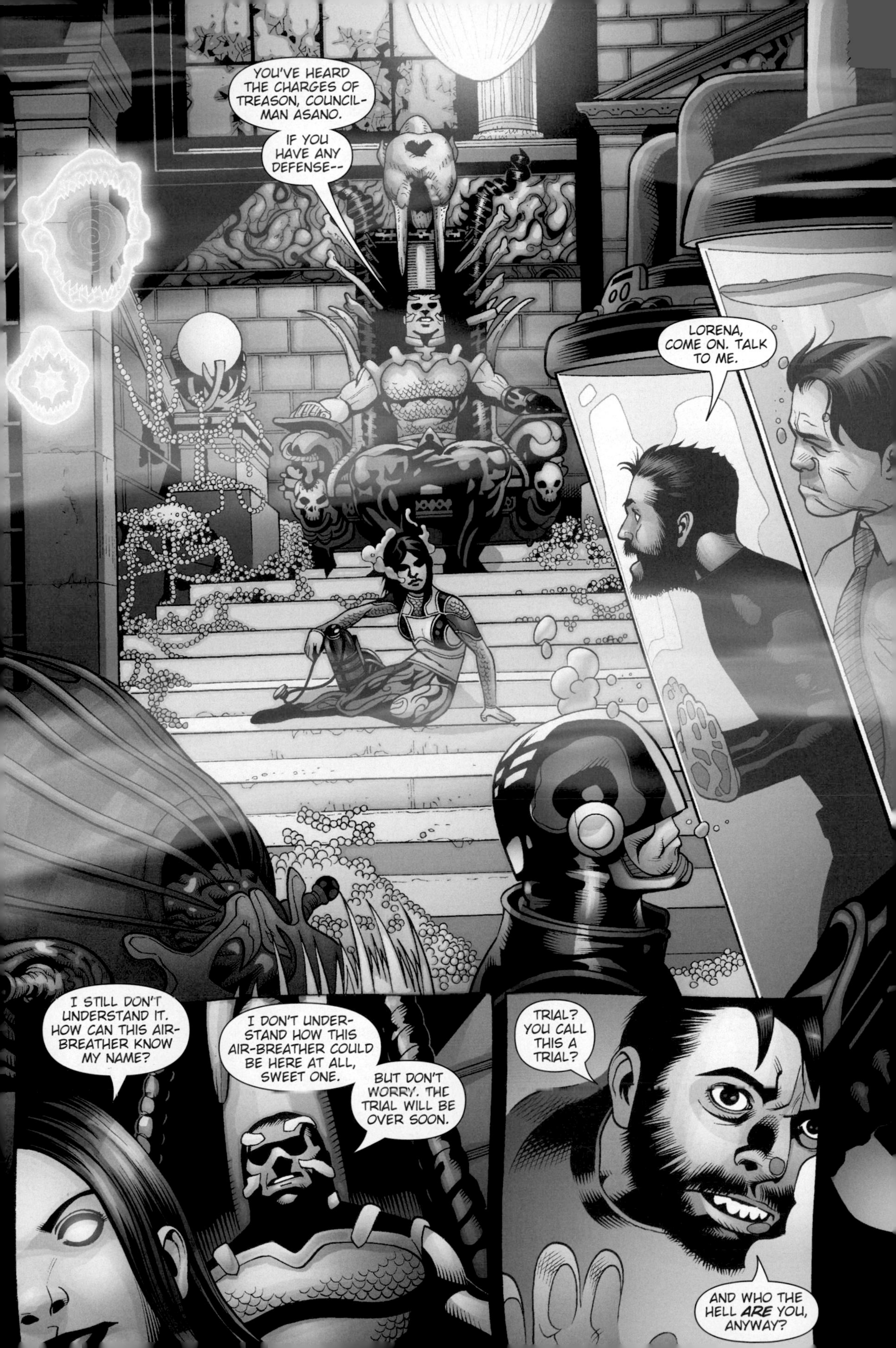
YOU'VE HEARD THE CHARGES OF TREASON, COUNCIL-MAN ASANO.
IF YOU HAVE ANY DEFENSE--
LORENA, COME ON. TALK TO ME.
I STILL DON'T UNDERSTAND IT. HOW CAN THIS AIR-BREATHER KNOW MY NAME?
I DON'T UNDER-STAND HOW THIS AIR-BREATHER COULD BE HERE AT ALL, SWEET ONE.
BUT DON'T WORRY. THE TRIAL WILL BE OVER SOON.
TRIAL? YOU CALL THIS A TRIAL?
AND WHO THE HELL ARE YOU, ANYWAY?

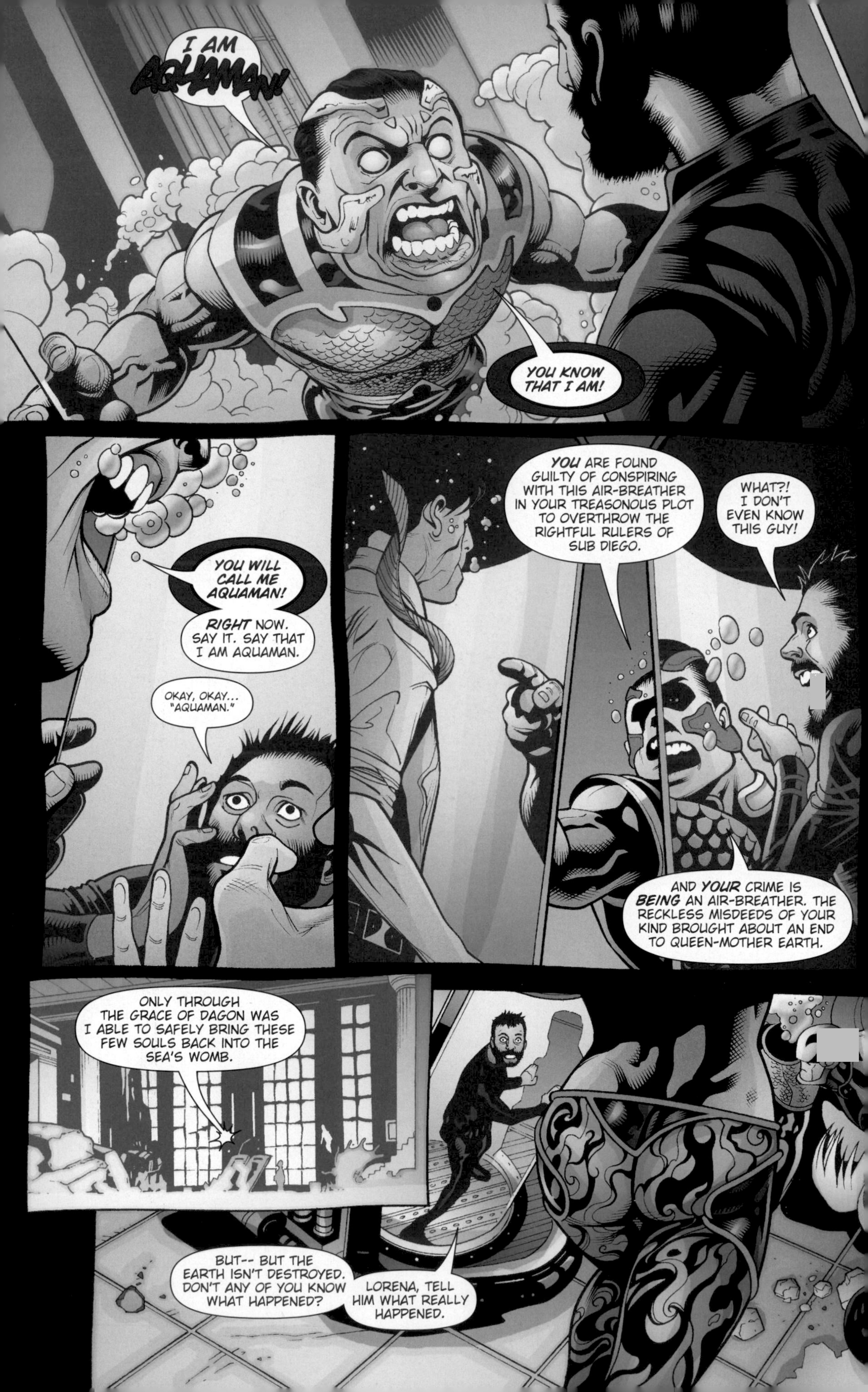

I AM AQUAMAN!
YOU KNOW THAT I AM!
YOU WILL CALL ME AQUAMAN!
RIGHT NOW. SAY IT. SAY THAT I AM AQUAMAN.
OKAY, OKAY... "AQUAMAN."
YOU ARE FOUND GUILTY OF CONSPIRING WITH THIS AIR-BREATHER IN YOUR TREASONOUS PLOT TO OVERTHROW THE RIGHTFUL RULERS OF SUB DIEGO.
WHAT?! I DON'T EVEN KNOW THIS GUY!
AND YOUR CRIME IS BEING AN AIR-BREATHER. THE RECKLESS MISDEEDS OF YOUR KIND BROUGHT ABOUT AN END TO QUEEN-MOTHER EARTH.
ONLY THROUGH THE GRACE OF DAGON WAS I ABLE TO SAFELY BRING THESE FEW SOULS BACK INTO THE SEA'S WOMB.
BUT-- BUT THE EARTH ISN'T DESTROYED. DON'T ANY OF YOU KNOW WHAT HAPPENED?
LORENA, TELL HIM WHAT REALLY HAPPENED.

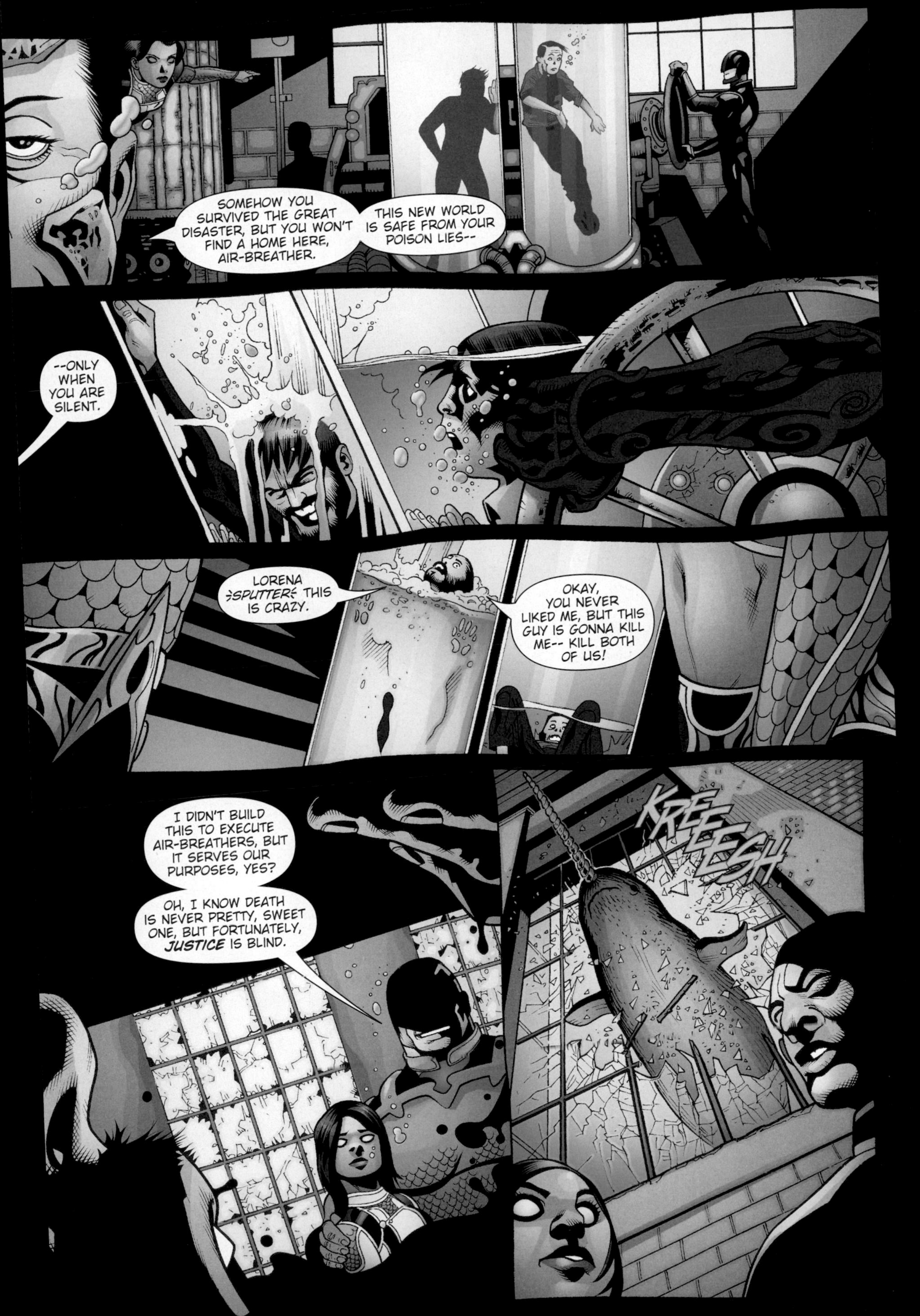
SOMEHOW YOU SURVIVED THE GREAT DISASTER, BUT YOU WON'T FIND A HOME HERE, AIR-BREATHER.
THIS NEW WORLD IS SAFE FROM YOUR POISON LIES--
--ONLY WHEN YOU ARE SILENT.
LORENA *SPUTTER* THIS IS CRAZY.
OKAY, YOU NEVER LIKED ME, BUT THIS GUY IS GONNA KILL ME-- KILL BOTH OF US!
I DIDN'T BUILD THIS TO EXECUTE AIR-BREATHERS, BUT IT SERVES OUR PURPOSES, YES?
OH, I KNOW DEATH IS NEVER PRETTY, SWEET ONE, BUT FORTUNATELY, JUSTICE IS BLIND.
KREEESH

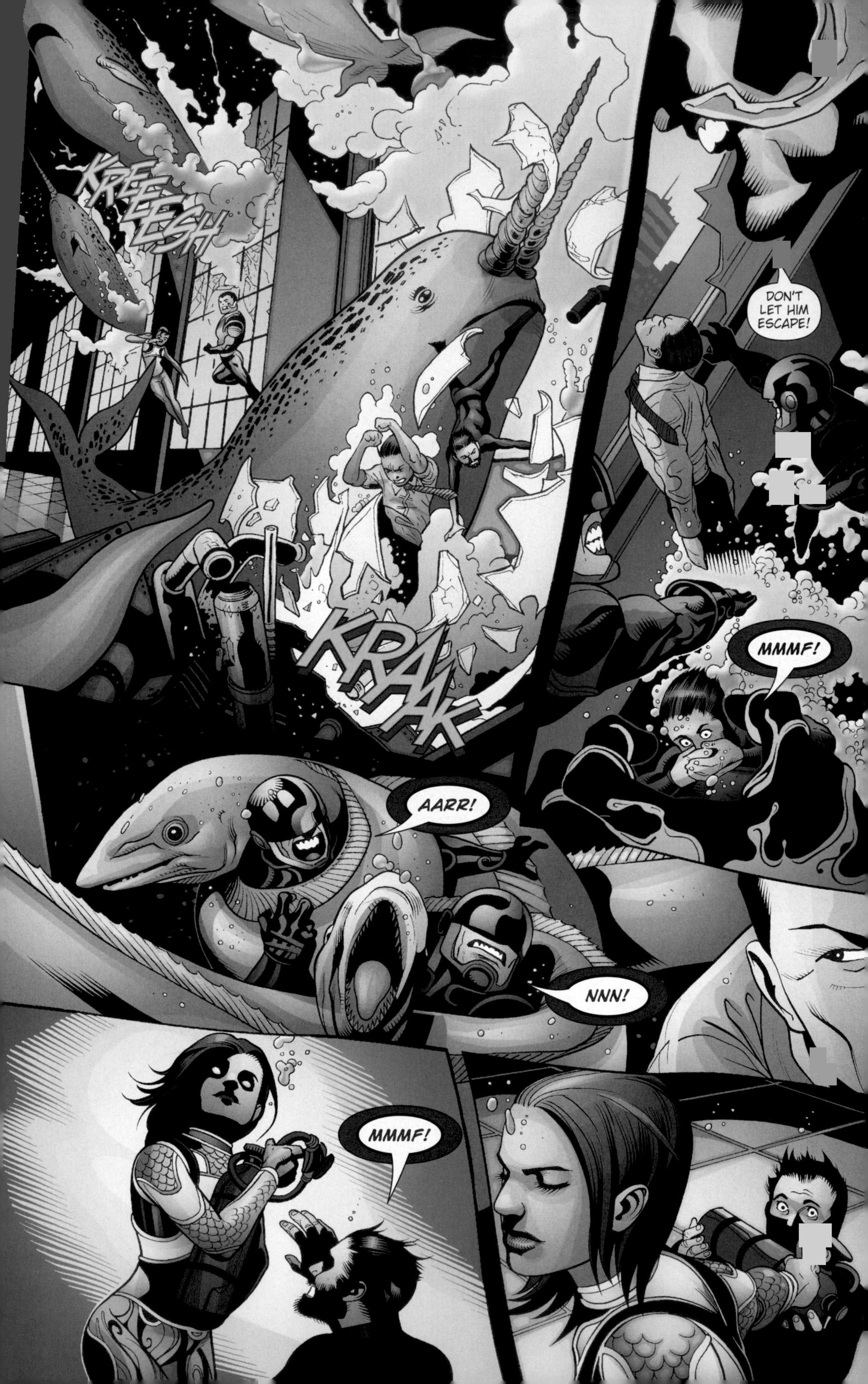
KREEESH
KRAAK
DON'T LET HIM ESCAPE!
MMMF!
AARR!
NNN!
MMMF!

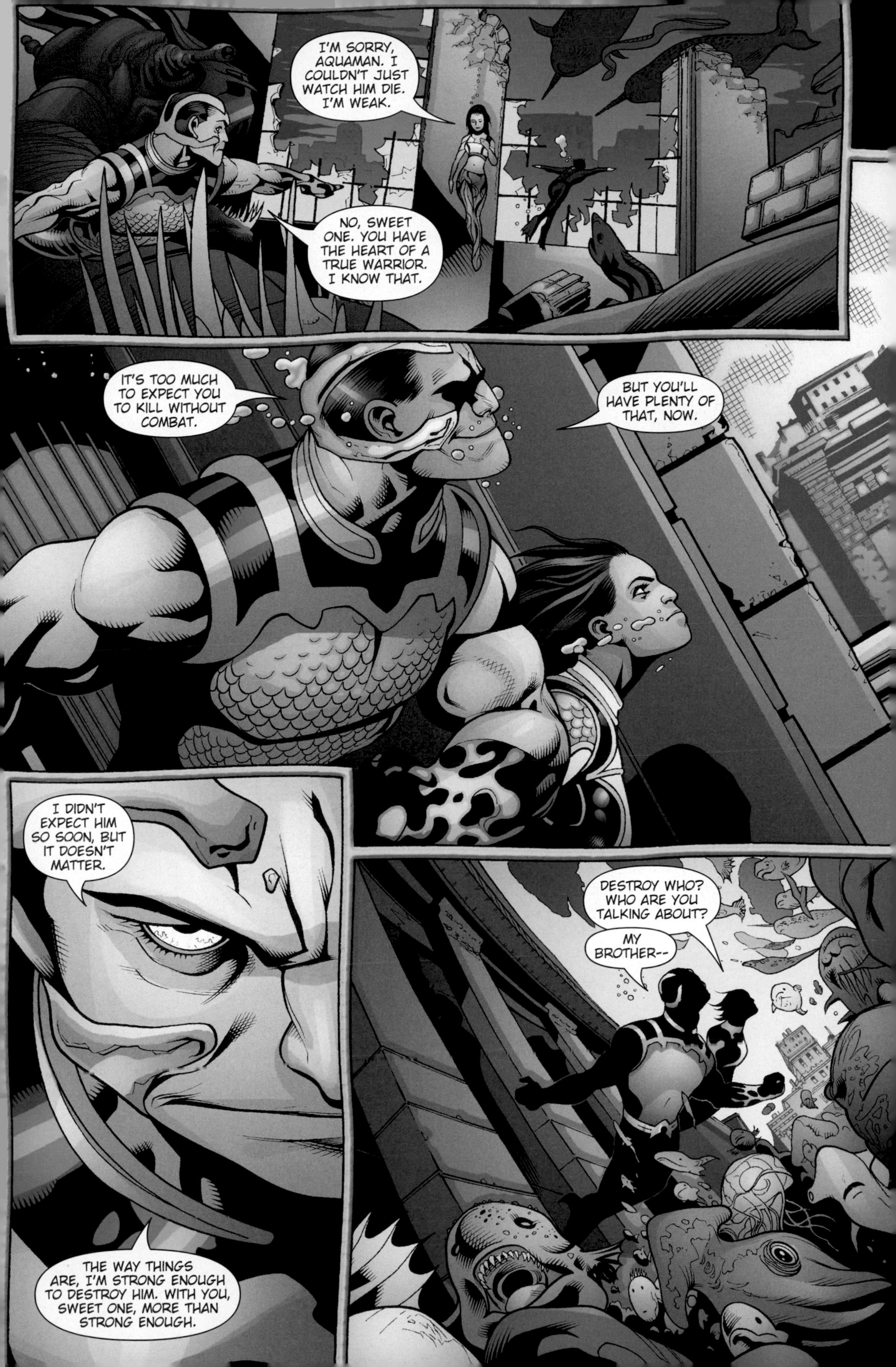
I'M SORRY, AQUAMAN. I COULDN'T JUST WATCH HIM DIE. I'M WEAK.
NO, SWEET ONE. YOU HAVE THE HEART OF A TRUE WARRIOR. I KNOW THAT.
IT'S TOO MUCH TO EXPECT YOU TO KILL WITHOUT COMBAT.
BUT YOU'LL HAVE PLENTY OF THAT, NOW.
I DIDN'T EXPECT HIM SO SOON, BUT IT DOESN'T MATTER.
THE WAY THINGS ARE, I'M STRONG ENOUGH TO DESTROY HIM. WITH YOU, SWEET ONE, MORE THAN STRONG ENOUGH.
DESTROY WHO? WHO ARE YOU TALKING ABOUT?
MY BROTHER--

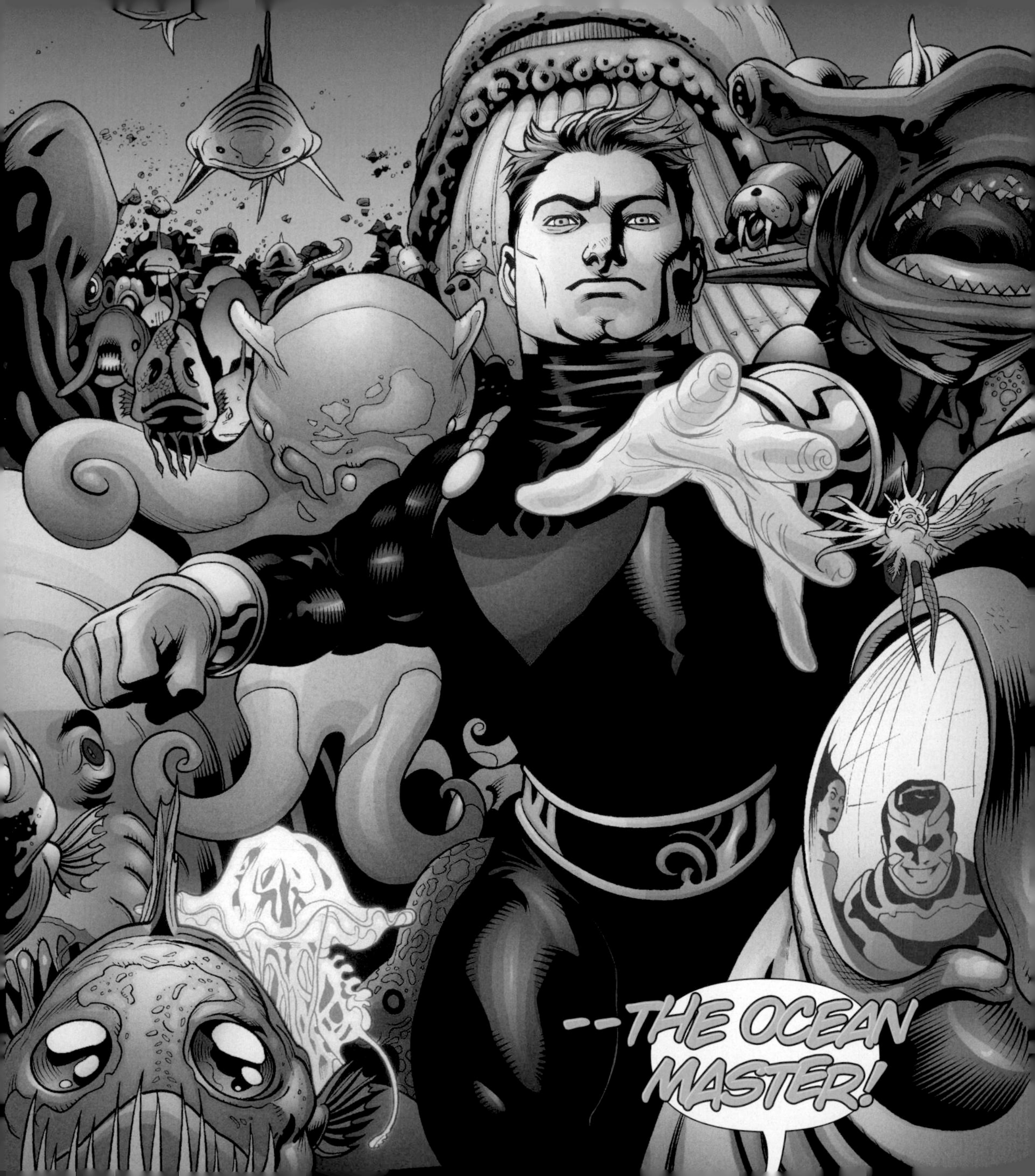
--THE OCEAN MASTER!

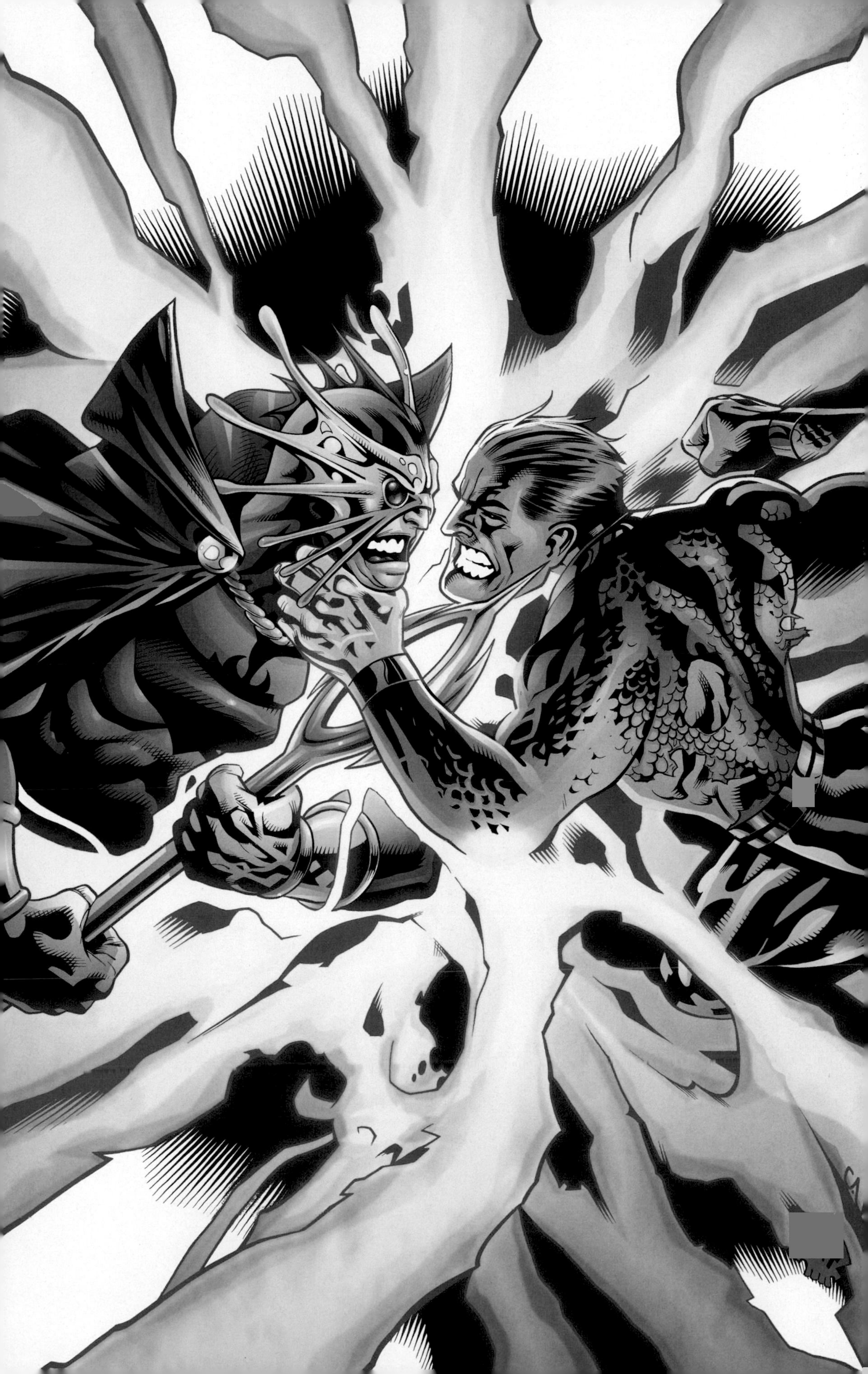

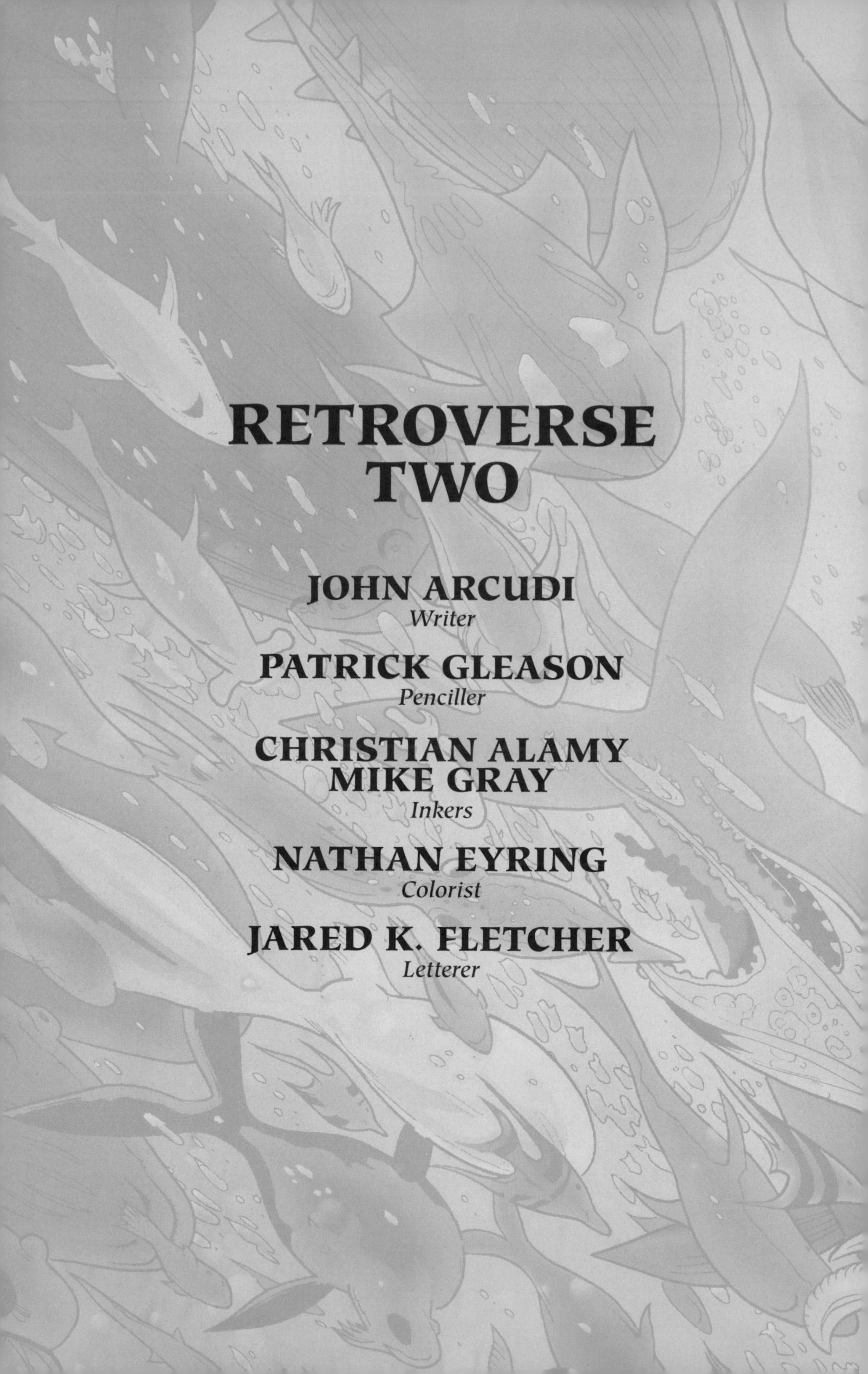

RETROVERSE TWO

JOHN ARCUDI
Writer

PATRICK GLEASON
Penciller

CHRISTIAN ALAMY
MIKE GRAY
Inkers

NATHAN EYRING
Colorist

JARED K. FLETCHER
Letterer

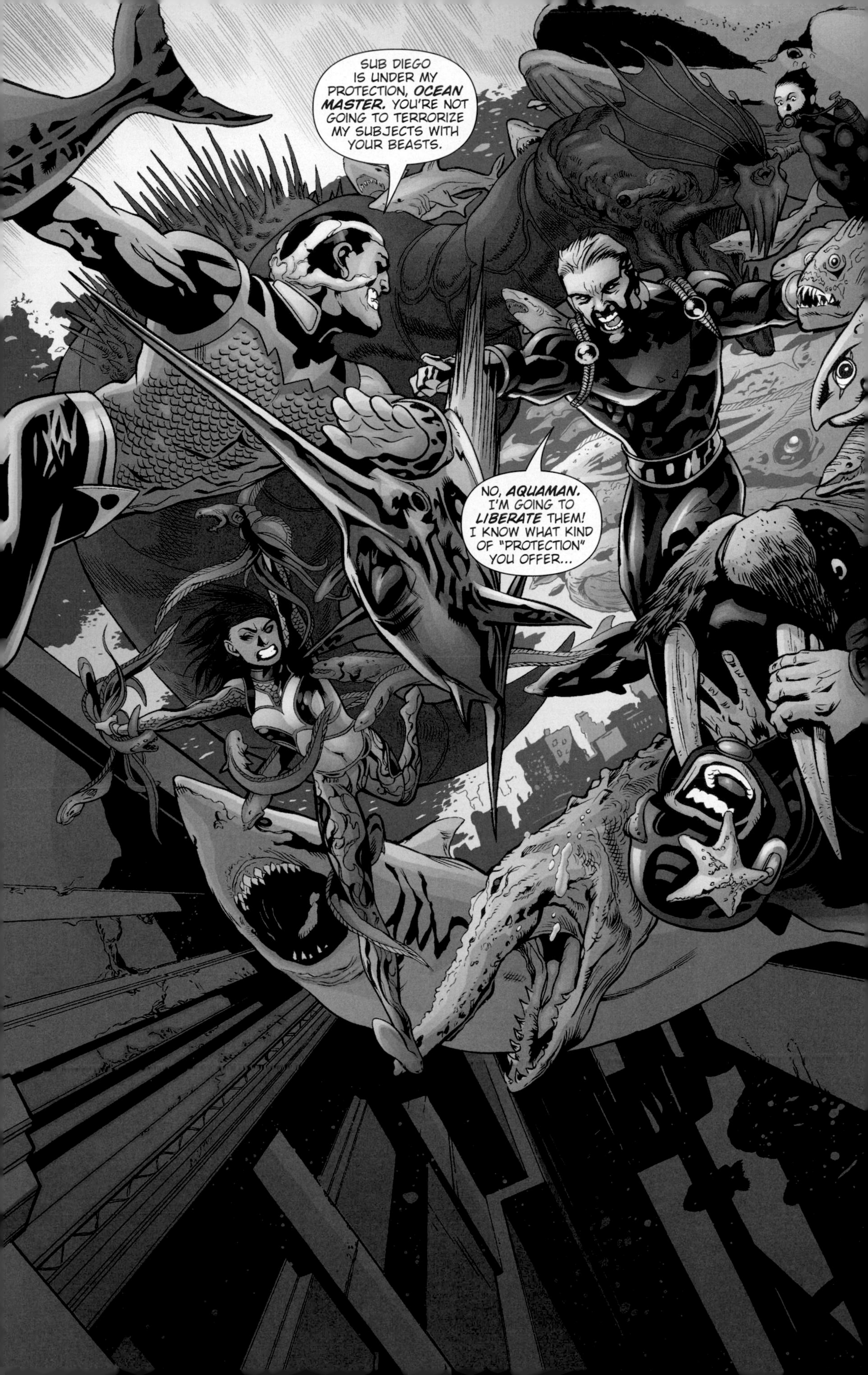
SUB DIEGO IS UNDER MY PROTECTION, OCEAN MASTER. YOU'RE NOT GOING TO TERRORIZE MY SUBJECTS WITH YOUR BEASTS.
NO, AQUAMAN. I'M GOING TO LIBERATE THEM! I KNOW WHAT KIND OF "PROTECTION" YOU OFFER...

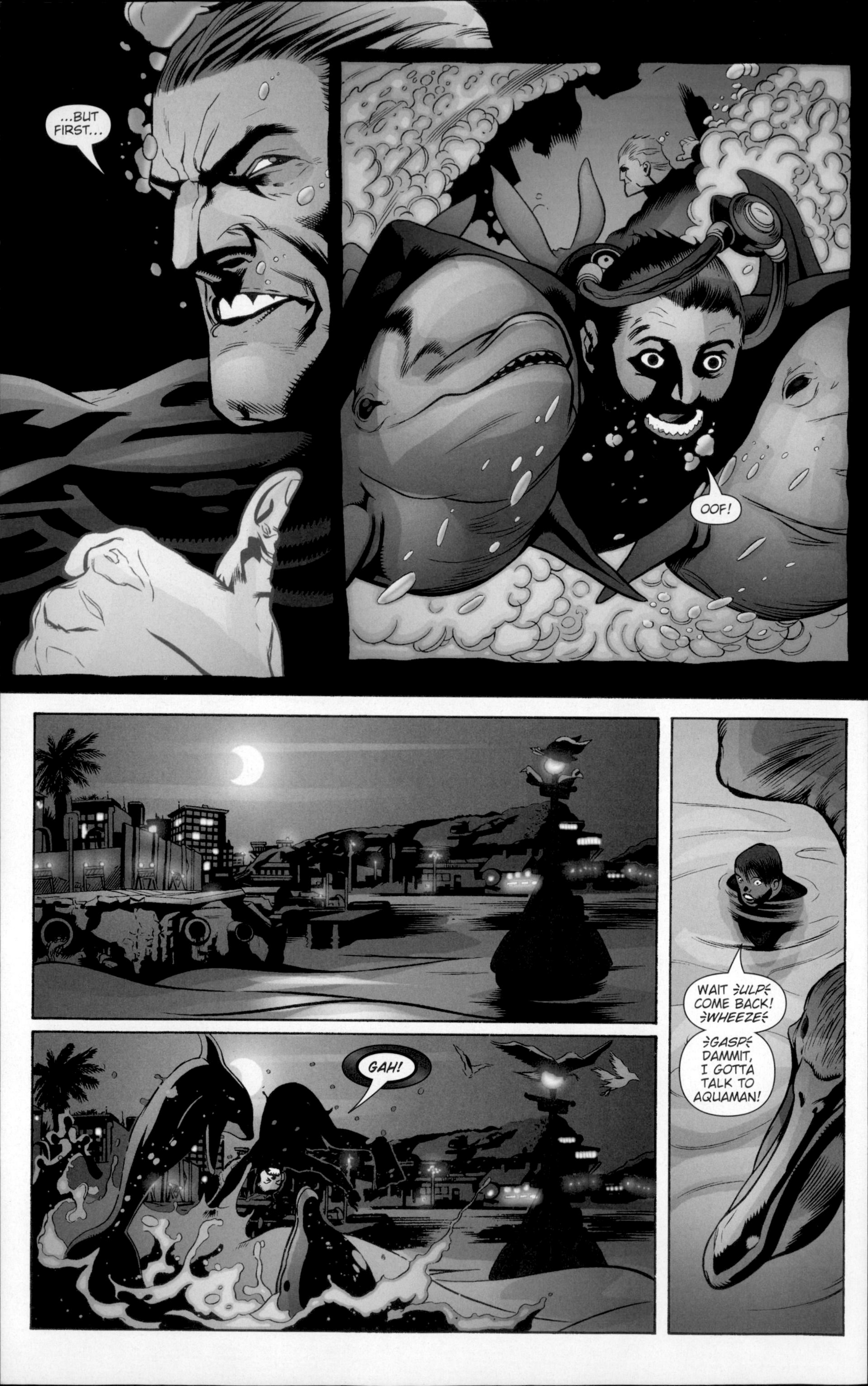
...BUT FIRST...
OOF!
GAH!
WAIT ~ULP~ COME BACK! ~WHEEZE~
~GASP~ DAMMIT, I GOTTA TALK TO AQUAMAN!

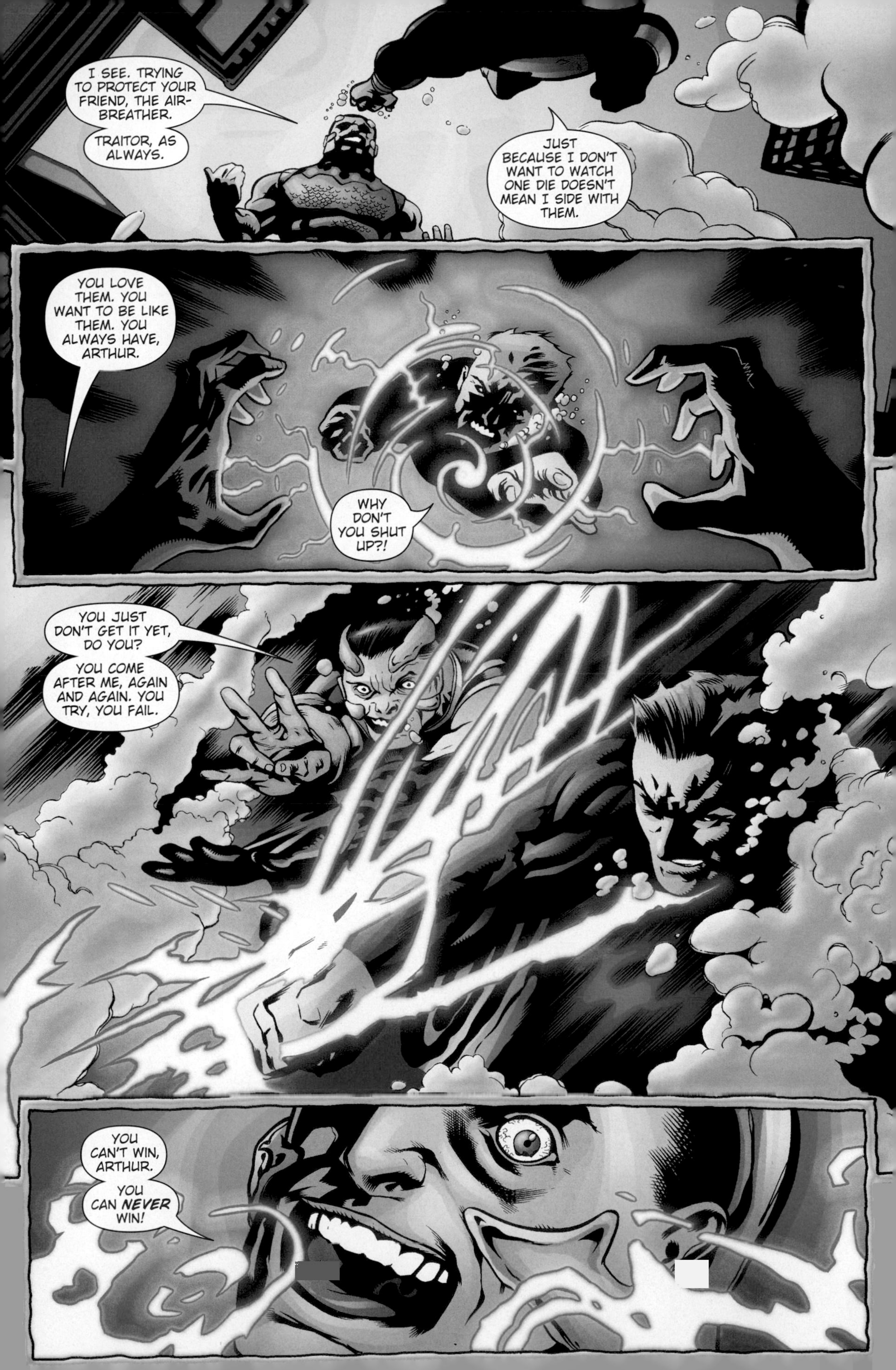

I SEE. TRYING TO PROTECT YOUR FRIEND, THE AIR-BREATHER.
TRAITOR, AS ALWAYS.
JUST BECAUSE I DON'T WANT TO WATCH ONE DIE DOESN'T MEAN I SIDE WITH THEM.
YOU LOVE THEM. YOU WANT TO BE LIKE THEM. YOU ALWAYS HAVE, ARTHUR.
WHY DON'T YOU SHUT UP?!
YOU JUST DON'T GET IT YET, DO YOU?
YOU COME AFTER ME, AGAIN AND AGAIN. YOU TRY, YOU FAIL.
YOU CAN'T WIN, ARTHUR.
YOU CAN *NEVER* WIN!

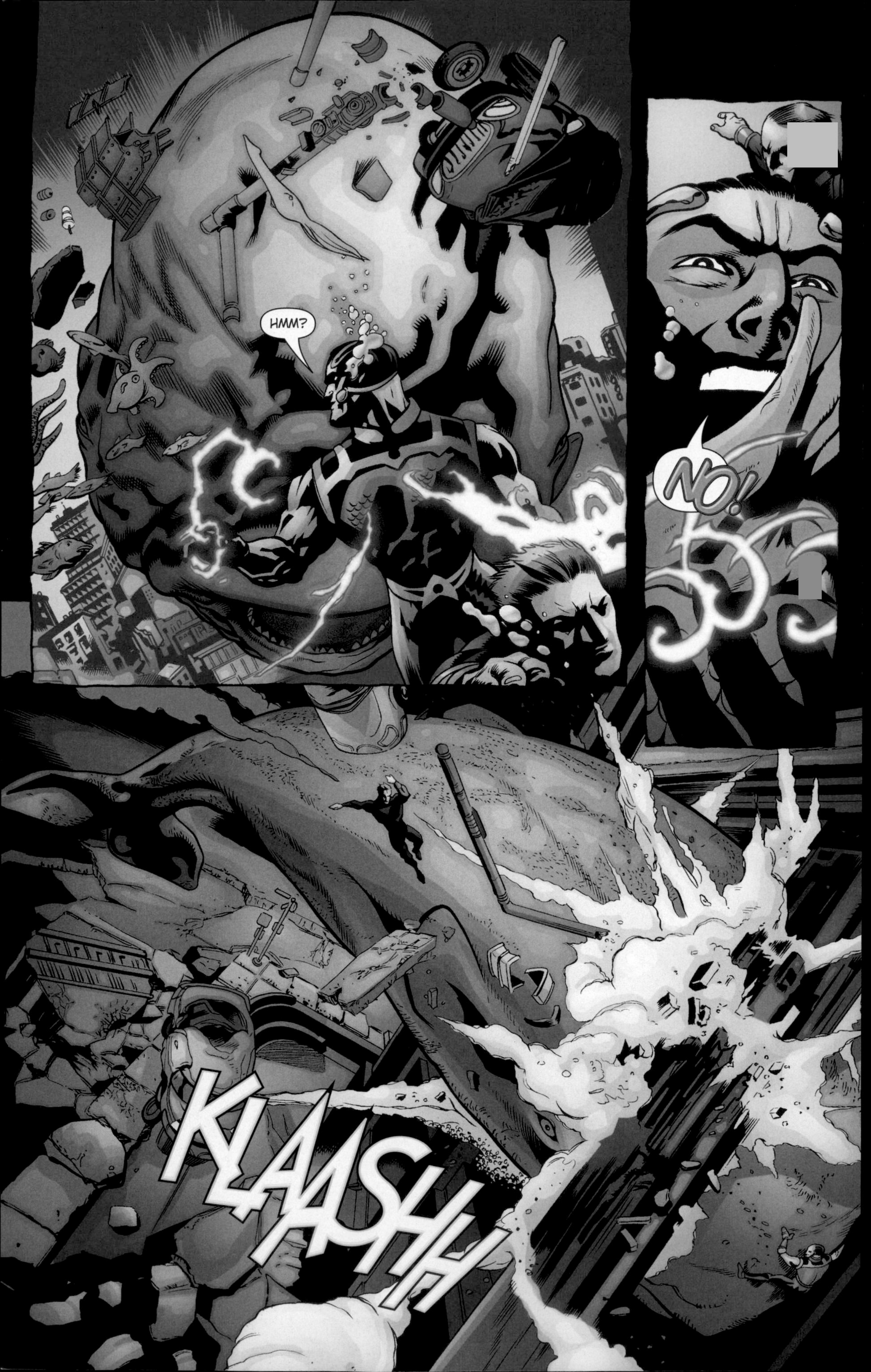
HMM?
NO!
KLAASHH

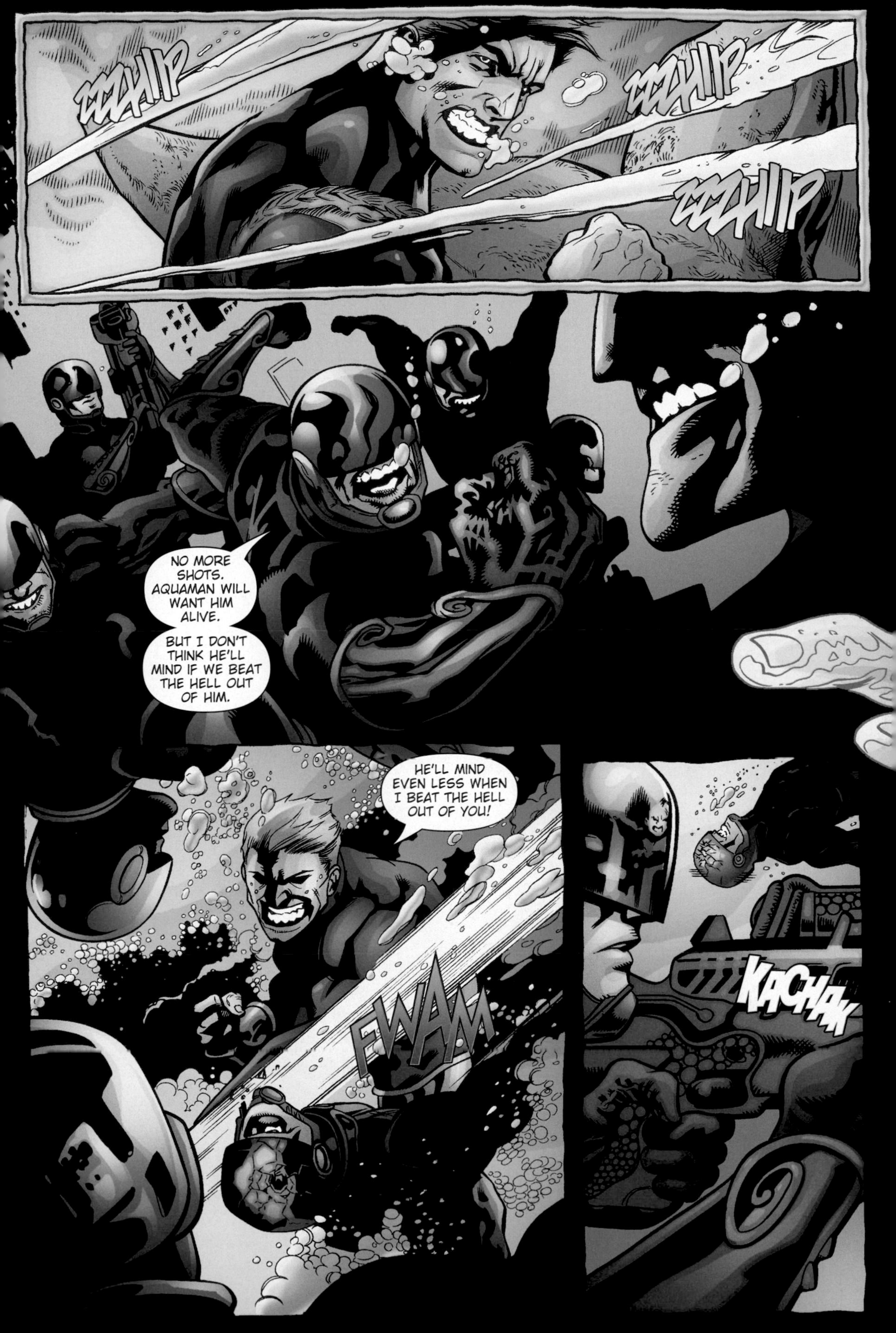
ZZZVIIIP
ZZZVIIIP
ZZZVIIIP
NO MORE SHOTS. AQUAMAN WILL WANT HIM ALIVE.
BUT I DON'T THINK HE'LL MIND IF WE BEAT THE HELL OUT OF HIM.
HE'LL MIND EVEN LESS WHEN I BEAT THE HELL OUT OF YOU!
FWAM
KACHAK

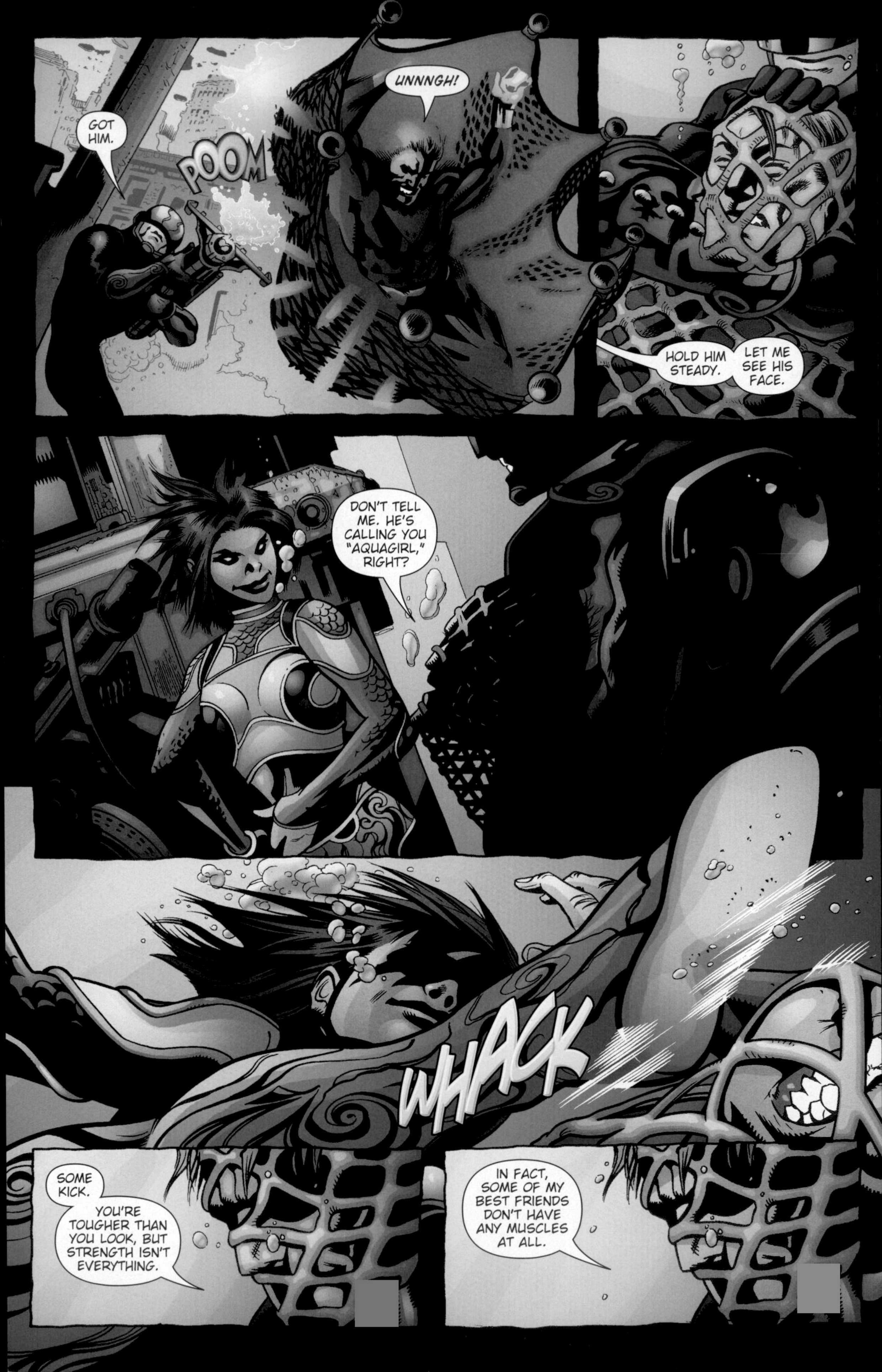
GOT HIM.
POOM
UNNNGH!
HOLD HIM STEADY.
LET ME SEE HIS FACE.
DON'T TELL ME. HE'S CALLING YOU "AQUAGIRL," RIGHT?
WHACK
SOME KICK.
YOU'RE TOUGHER THAN YOU LOOK, BUT STRENGTH ISN'T EVERYTHING.
IN FACT, SOME OF MY BEST FRIENDS DON'T HAVE ANY MUSCLES AT ALL.

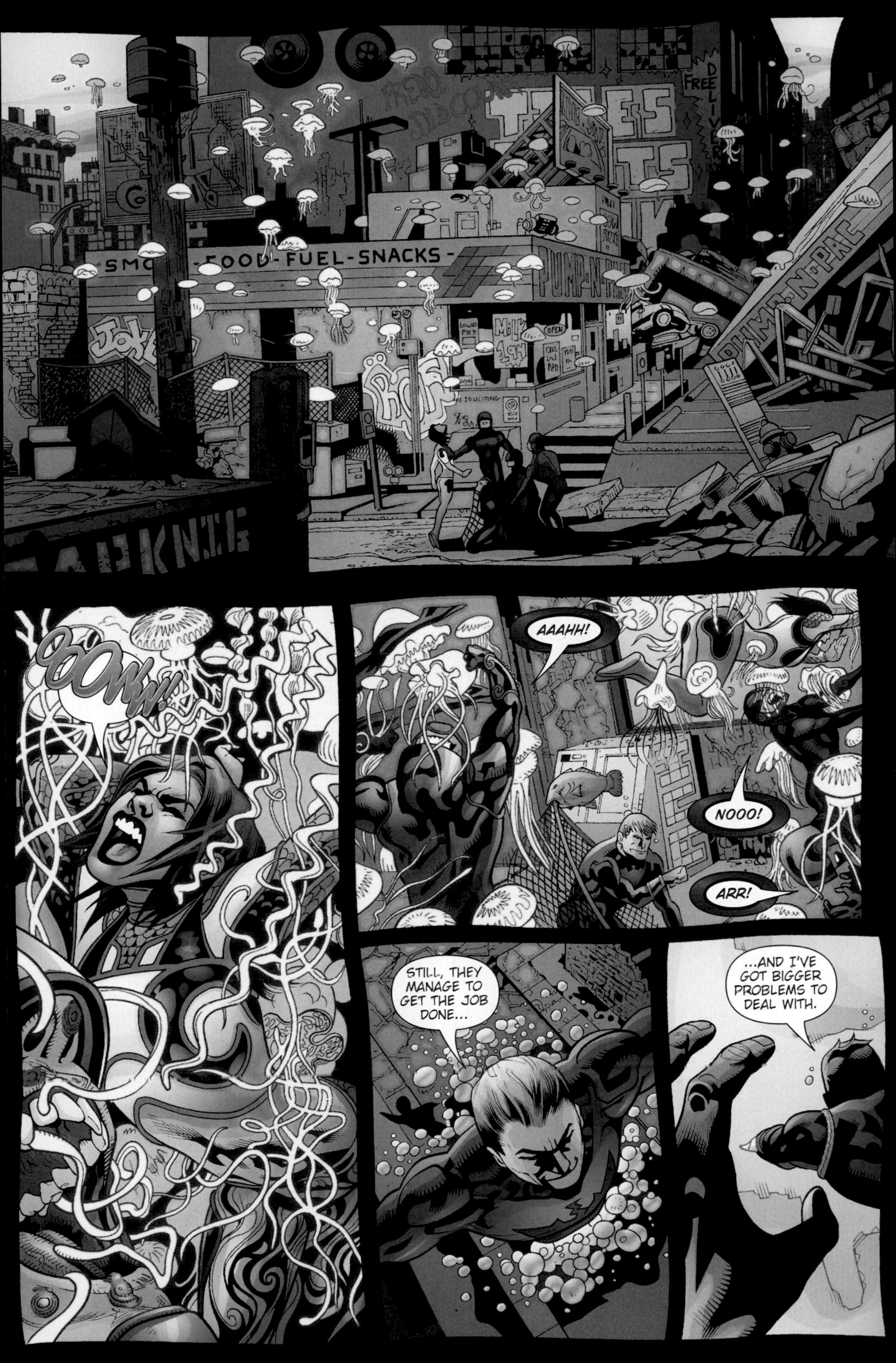
SMO -FOOD-FUEL-SNACKS-
PUMP-N-PAC
FREE DELIVERY
NO SOLICITING
OOOWW!
AAAHH!
NOOO!
ARR!
STILL, THEY MANAGE TO GET THE JOB DONE...
...AND I'VE GOT BIGGER PROBLEMS TO DEAL WITH.

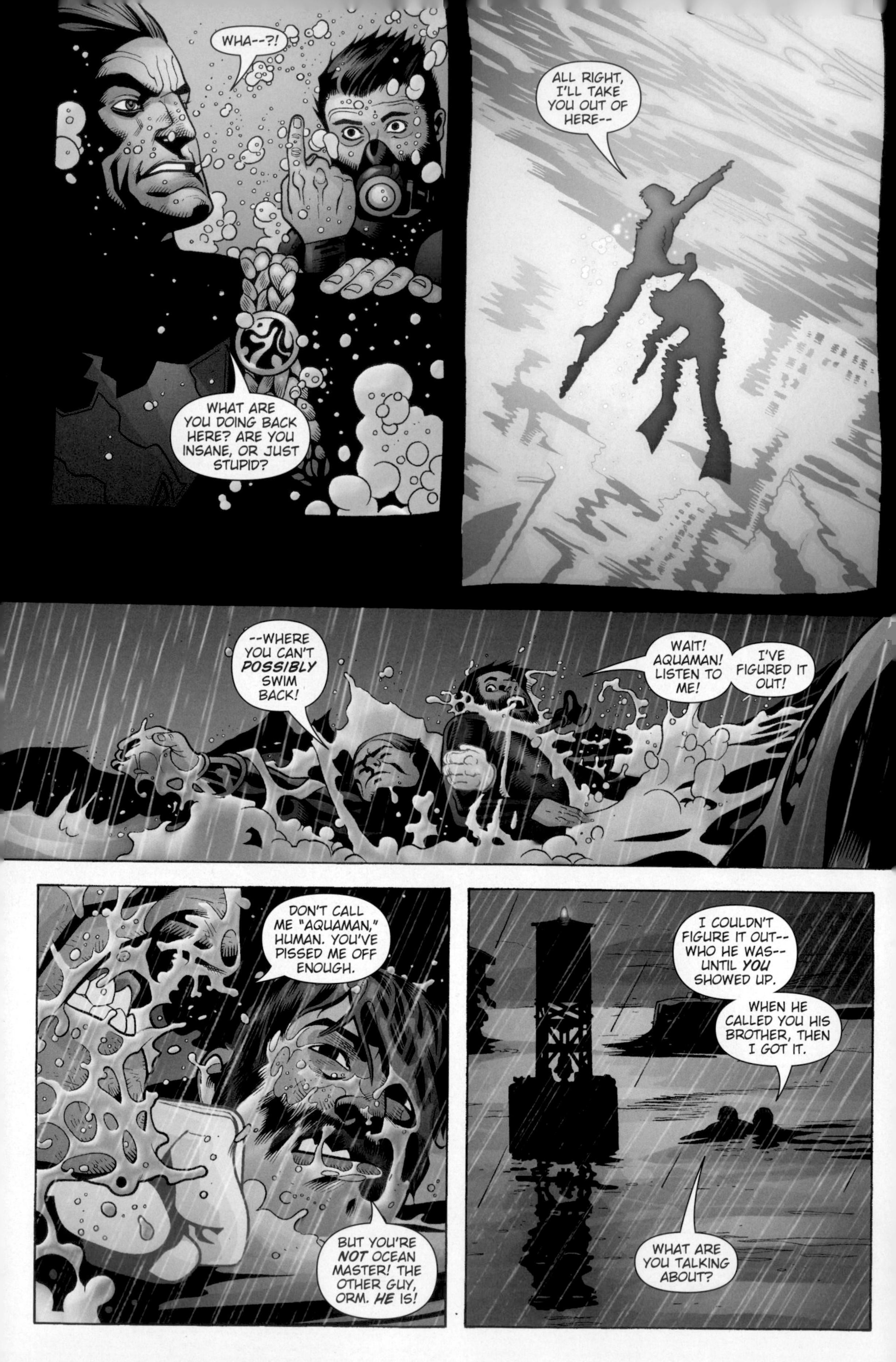
WHA--?!
WHAT ARE YOU DOING BACK HERE? ARE YOU INSANE, OR JUST STUPID?
ALL RIGHT, I'LL TAKE YOU OUT OF HERE--
--WHERE YOU CAN'T POSSIBLY SWIM BACK!
WAIT! AQUAMAN! LISTEN TO ME!
I'VE FIGURED IT OUT!
DON'T CALL ME "AQUAMAN," HUMAN. YOU'VE PISSED ME OFF ENOUGH.
BUT YOU'RE NOT OCEAN MASTER! THE OTHER GUY, ORM. HE IS!
I COULDN'T FIGURE IT OUT-- WHO HE WAS-- UNTIL YOU SHOWED UP.
WHEN HE CALLED YOU HIS BROTHER, THEN I GOT IT.
WHAT ARE YOU TALKING ABOUT?

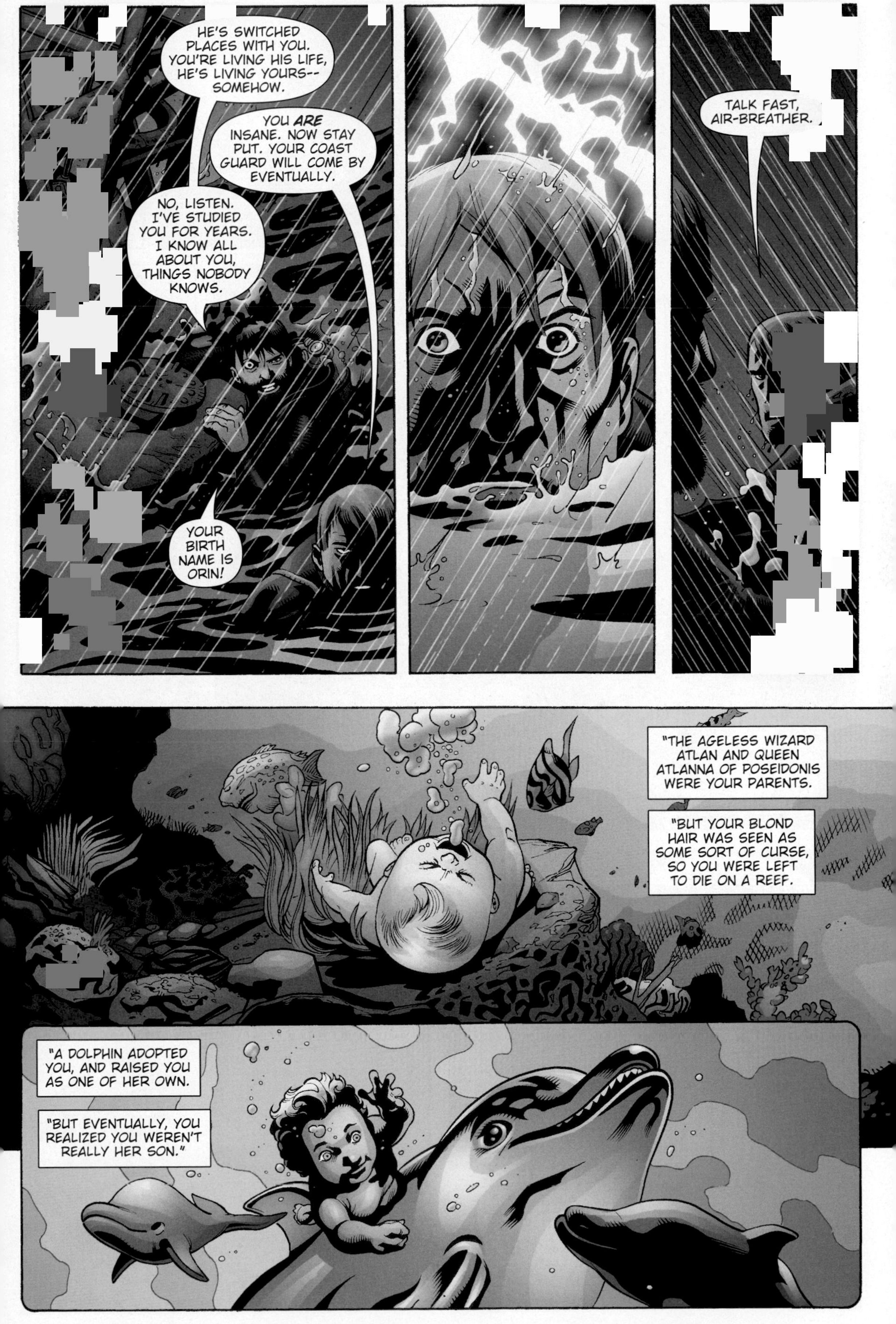
HE'S SWITCHED PLACES WITH YOU. YOU'RE LIVING HIS LIFE, HE'S LIVING YOURS-- SOMEHOW.
YOU ARE INSANE. NOW STAY PUT. YOUR COAST GUARD WILL COME BY EVENTUALLY.
NO, LISTEN. I'VE STUDIED YOU FOR YEARS. I KNOW ALL ABOUT YOU, THINGS NOBODY KNOWS.
YOUR BIRTH NAME IS ORIN!
TALK FAST, AIR-BREATHER.
"THE AGELESS WIZARD ATLAN AND QUEEN ATLANNA OF POSEIDONIS WERE YOUR PARENTS.
"BUT YOUR BLOND HAIR WAS SEEN AS SOME SORT OF CURSE, SO YOU WERE LEFT TO DIE ON A REEF.
"A DOLPHIN ADOPTED YOU, AND RAISED YOU AS ONE OF HER OWN.
"BUT EVENTUALLY, YOU REALIZED YOU WEREN'T REALLY HER SON."

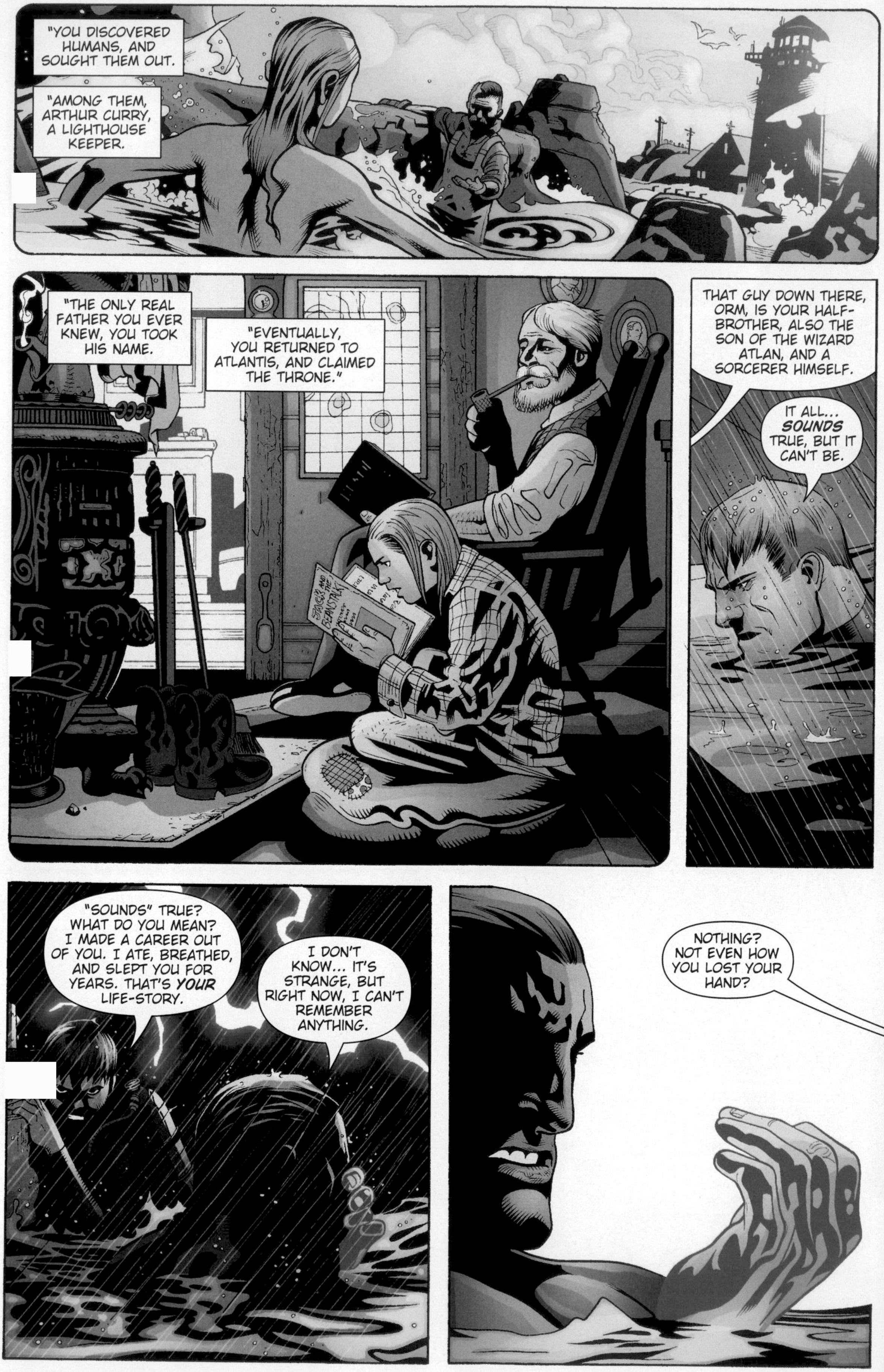
"YOU DISCOVERED HUMANS, AND SOUGHT THEM OUT.
"AMONG THEM, ARTHUR CURRY, A LIGHTHOUSE KEEPER.
"THE ONLY REAL FATHER YOU EVER KNEW, YOU TOOK HIS NAME.
"EVENTUALLY, YOU RETURNED TO ATLANTIS, AND CLAIMED THE THRONE."
THAT GUY DOWN THERE, ORM, IS YOUR HALF-BROTHER, ALSO THE SON OF THE WIZARD ATLAN, AND A SORCERER HIMSELF.
IT ALL... *SOUNDS* TRUE, BUT IT CAN'T BE.
"SOUNDS" TRUE? WHAT DO YOU MEAN? I MADE A CAREER OUT OF YOU. I ATE, BREATHED, AND SLEPT YOU FOR YEARS. THAT'S *YOUR* LIFE-STORY.
I DON'T KNOW... IT'S STRANGE, BUT RIGHT NOW, I CAN'T REMEMBER ANYTHING.
NOTHING? NOT EVEN HOW YOU LOST YOUR HAND?

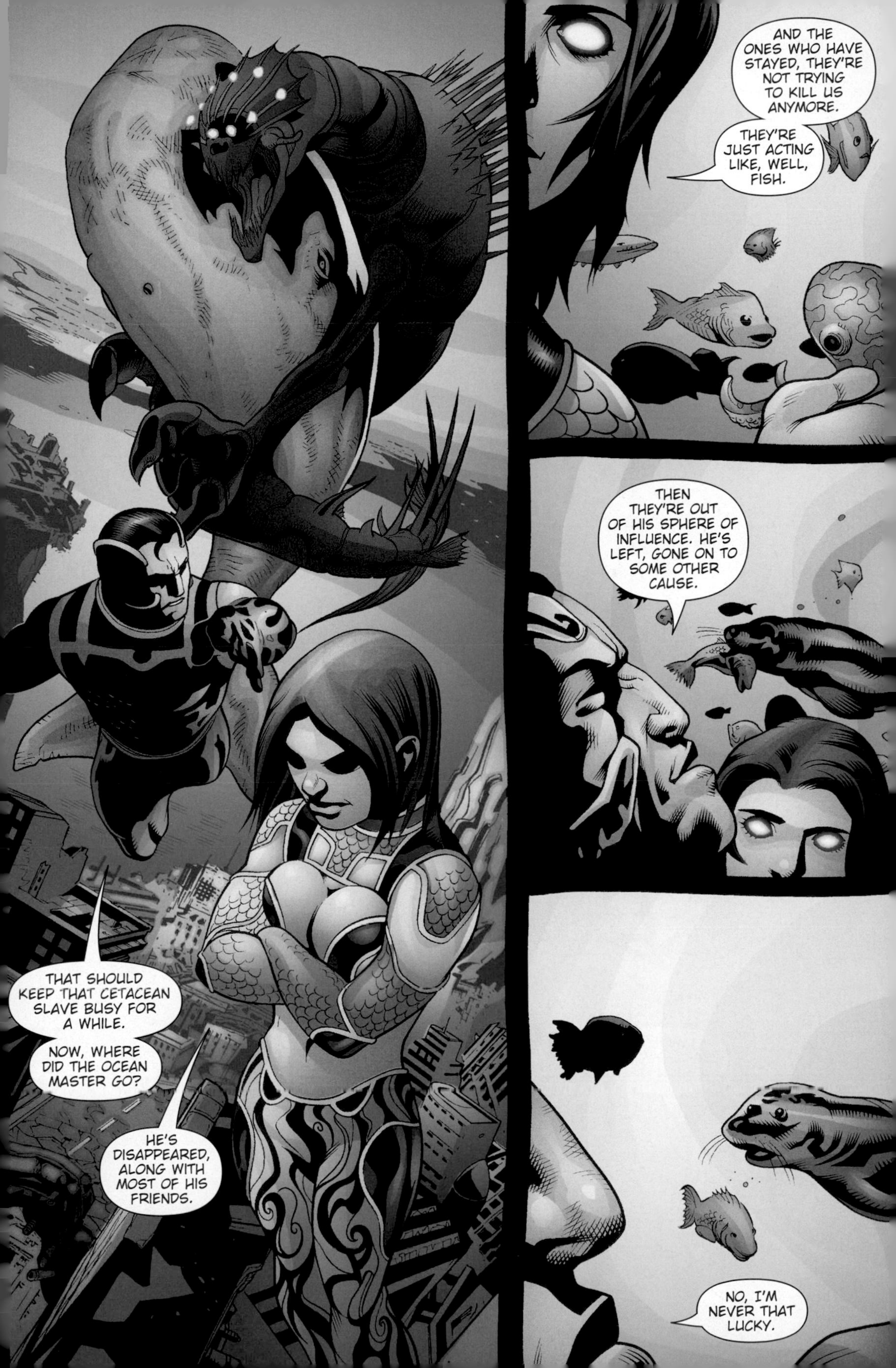
THAT SHOULD KEEP THAT CETACEAN SLAVE BUSY FOR A WHILE.
NOW, WHERE DID THE OCEAN MASTER GO?
HE'S DISAPPEARED, ALONG WITH MOST OF HIS FRIENDS.
AND THE ONES WHO HAVE STAYED, THEY'RE NOT TRYING TO KILL US ANYMORE.
THEY'RE JUST ACTING LIKE, WELL, FISH.
THEN THEY'RE OUT OF HIS SPHERE OF INFLUENCE. HE'S LEFT, GONE ON TO SOME OTHER CAUSE.
NO, I'M NEVER THAT LUCKY.

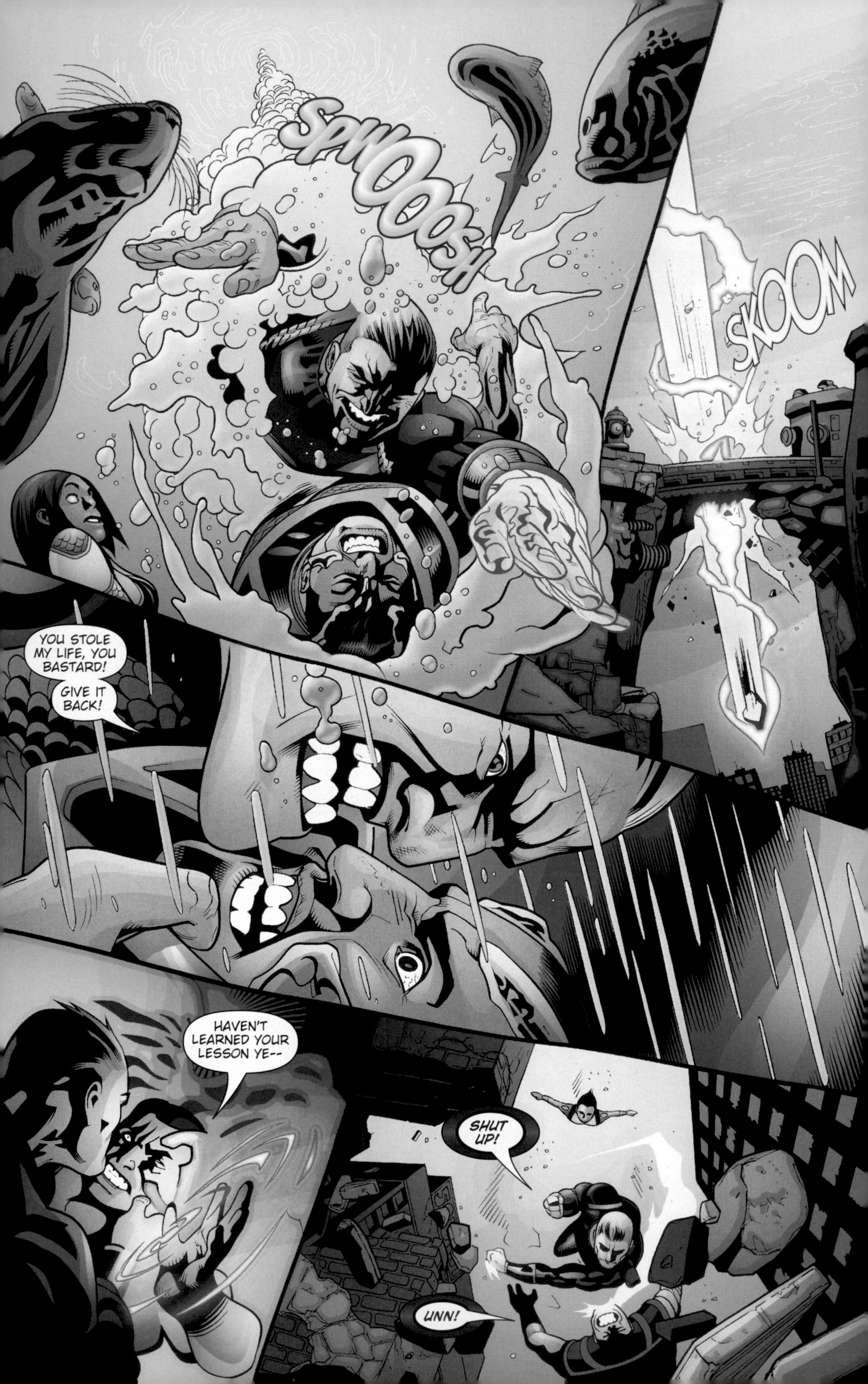
SPWOOOSH
SKOOM
YOU STOLE MY LIFE, YOU BASTARD!
GIVE IT BACK!
HAVEN'T LEARNED YOUR LESSON YE--
SHUT UP!
UNN!

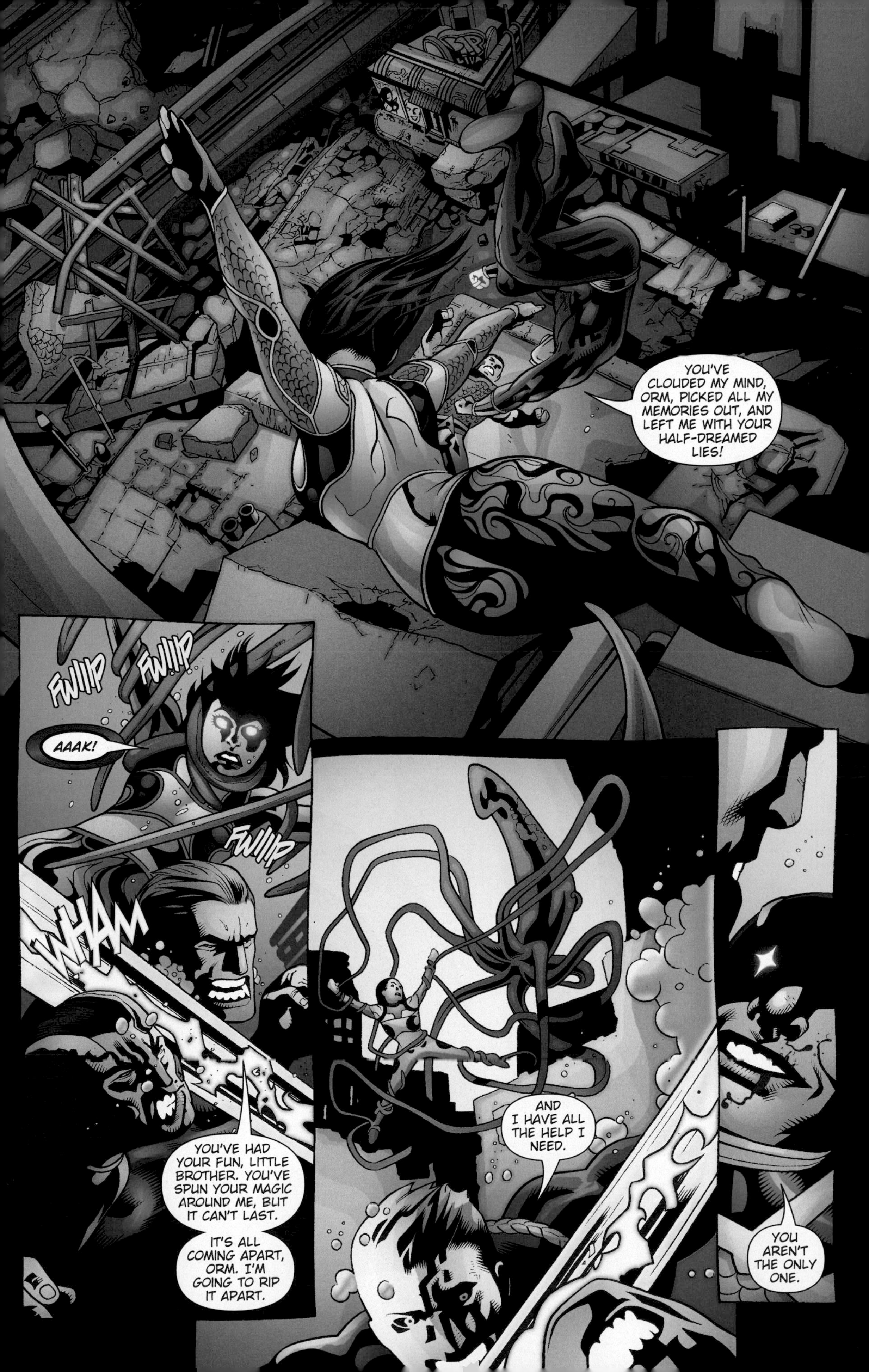
YOU'VE CLOUDED MY MIND, ORM, PICKED ALL MY MEMORIES OUT, AND LEFT ME WITH YOUR HALF-DREAMED LIES!
FWIIP
FWIIP
AAAK!
FWIIP
WHAM
YOU'VE HAD YOUR FUN, LITTLE BROTHER. YOU'VE SPUN YOUR MAGIC AROUND ME, BUT IT CAN'T LAST.
IT'S ALL COMING APART, ORM. I'M GOING TO RIP IT APART.
AND I HAVE ALL THE HELP I NEED.
YOU AREN'T THE ONLY ONE.

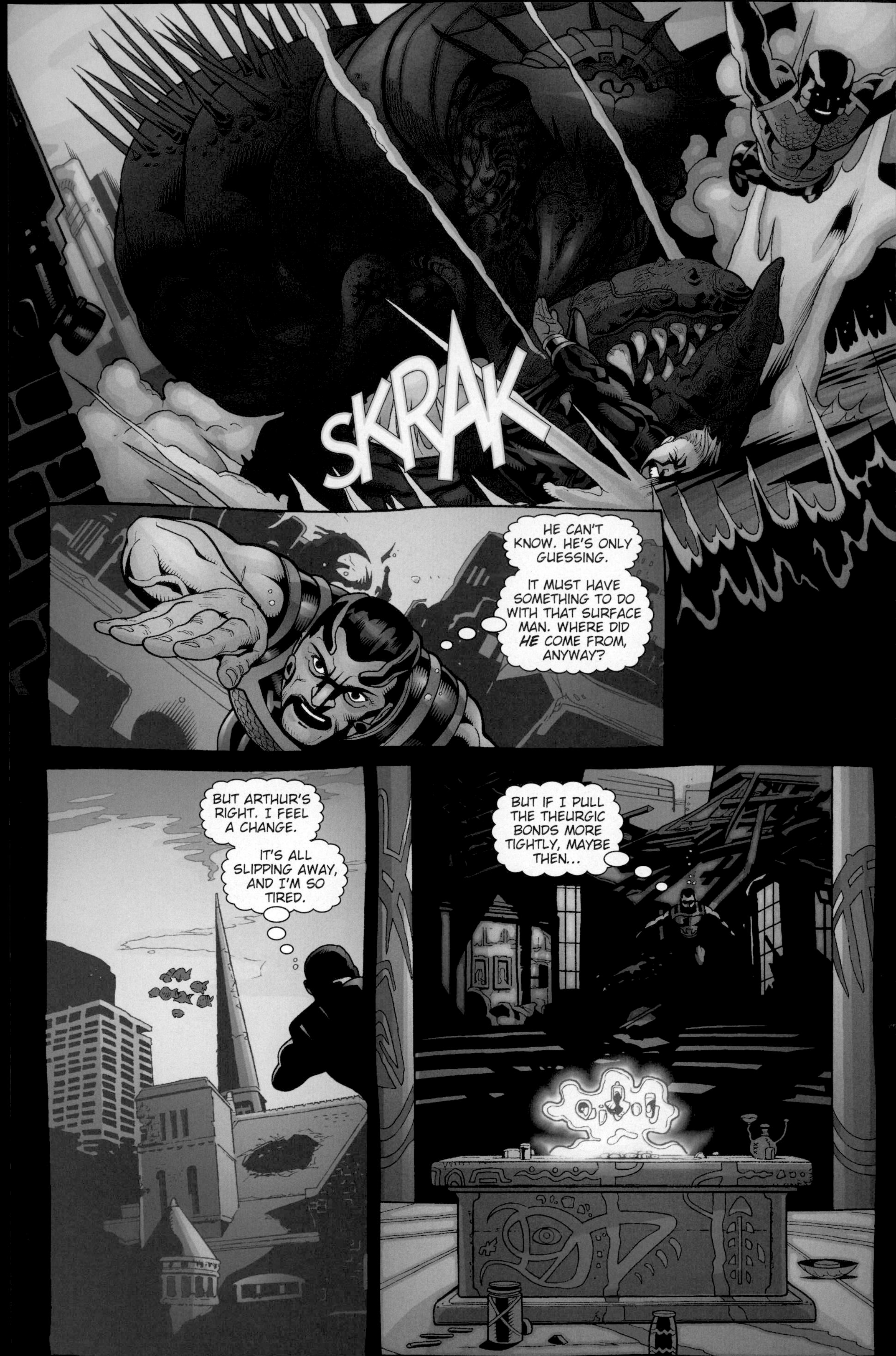
SKRAK
HE CAN'T KNOW. HE'S ONLY GUESSING.
IT MUST HAVE SOMETHING TO DO WITH THAT SURFACE MAN. WHERE DID HE COME FROM, ANYWAY?
BUT ARTHUR'S RIGHT. I FEEL A CHANGE.
IT'S ALL SLIPPING AWAY, AND I'M SO TIRED.
BUT IF I PULL THE THEURGIC BONDS MORE TIGHTLY, MAYBE THEN...

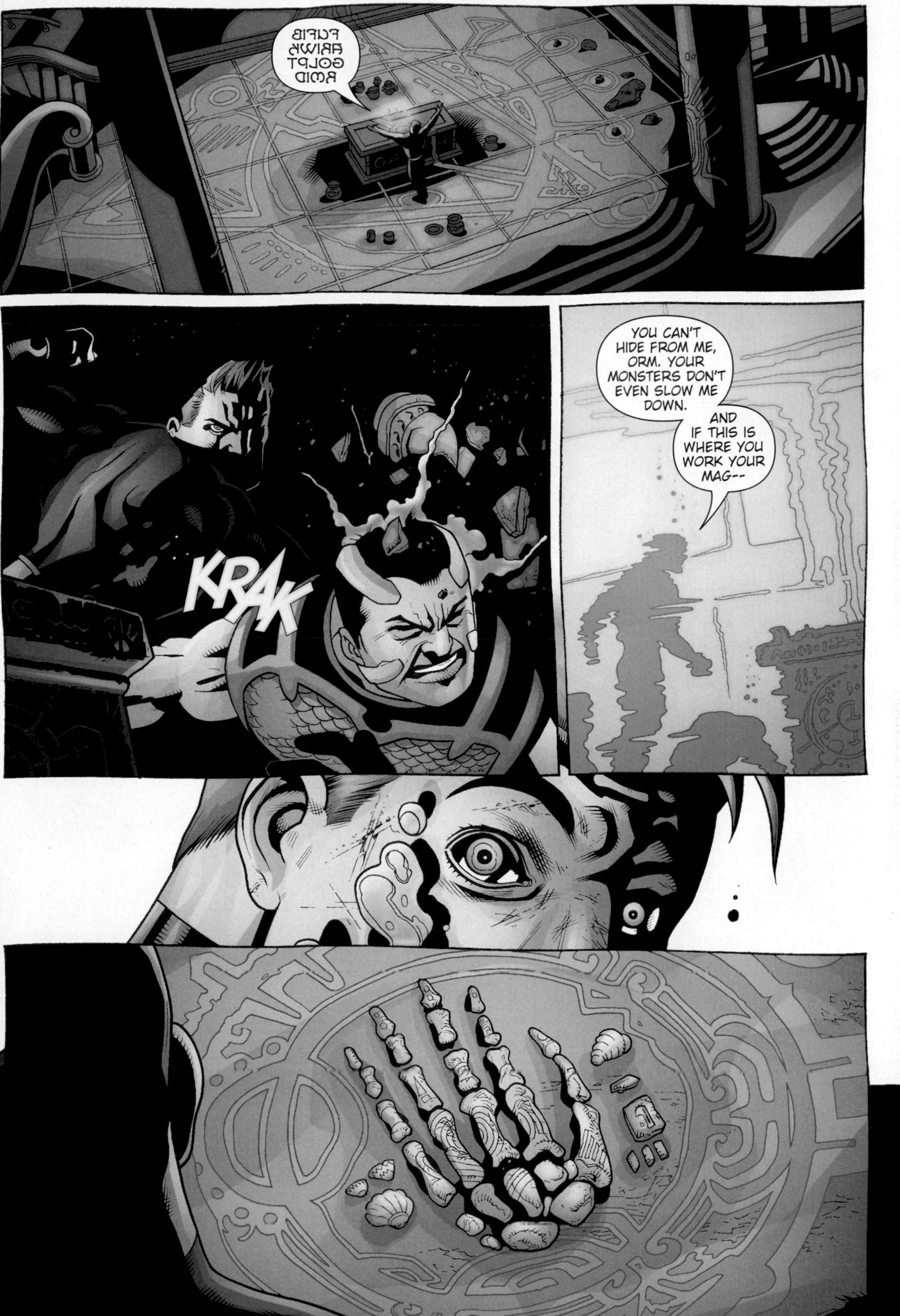
KRAK
YOU CAN'T HIDE FROM ME, ORM. YOUR MONSTERS DON'T EVEN SLOW ME DOWN.
AND IF THIS IS WHERE YOU WORK YOUR MAG--

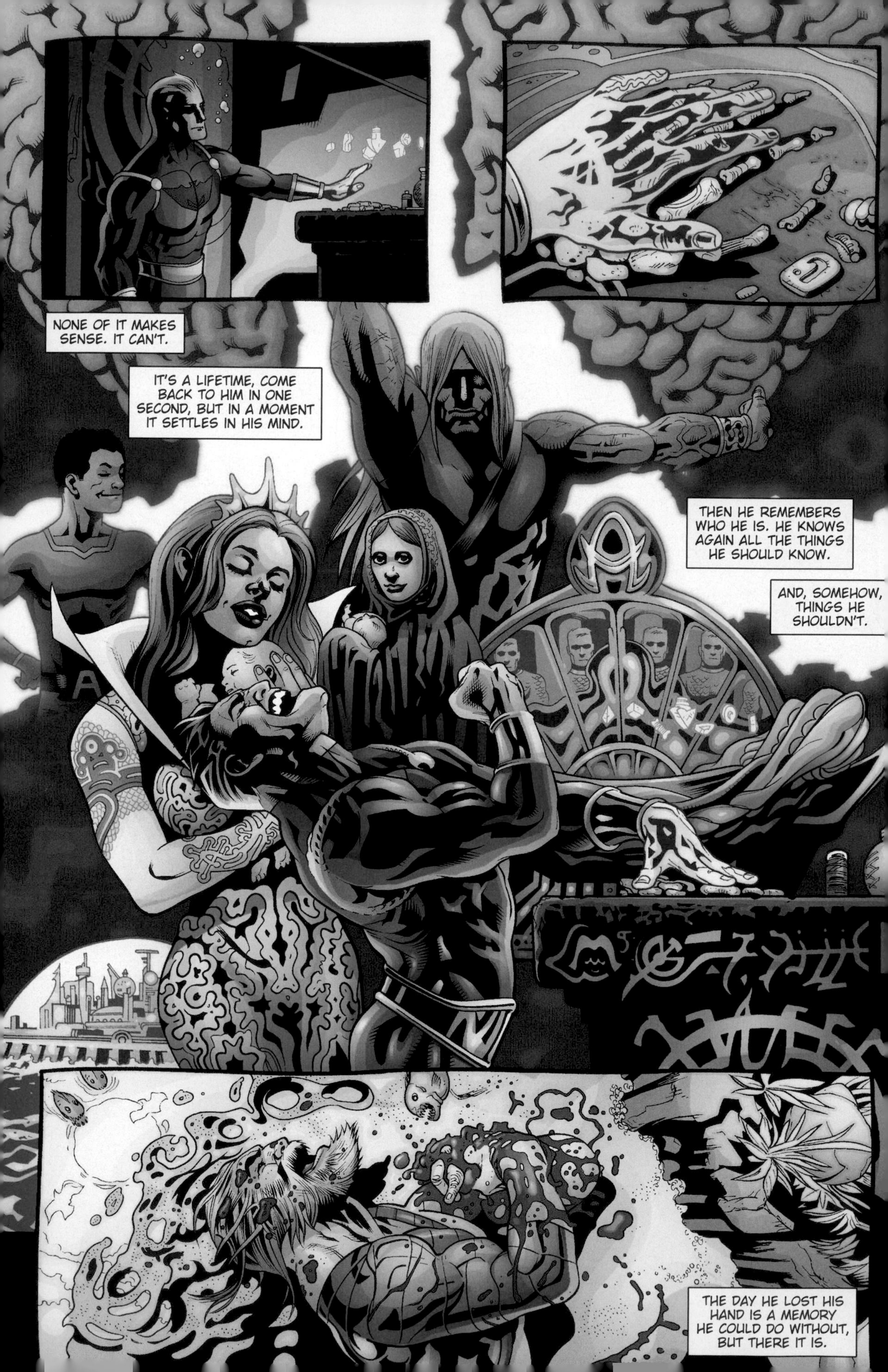
NONE OF IT MAKES SENSE. IT CAN'T.
IT'S A LIFETIME, COME BACK TO HIM IN ONE SECOND, BUT IN A MOMENT IT SETTLES IN HIS MIND.
THEN HE REMEMBERS WHO HE IS. HE KNOWS AGAIN ALL THE THINGS HE SHOULD KNOW.
AND, SOMEHOW, THINGS HE SHOULDN'T.
THE DAY HE LOST HIS HAND IS A MEMORY HE COULD DO WITHOUT, BUT THERE IT IS.

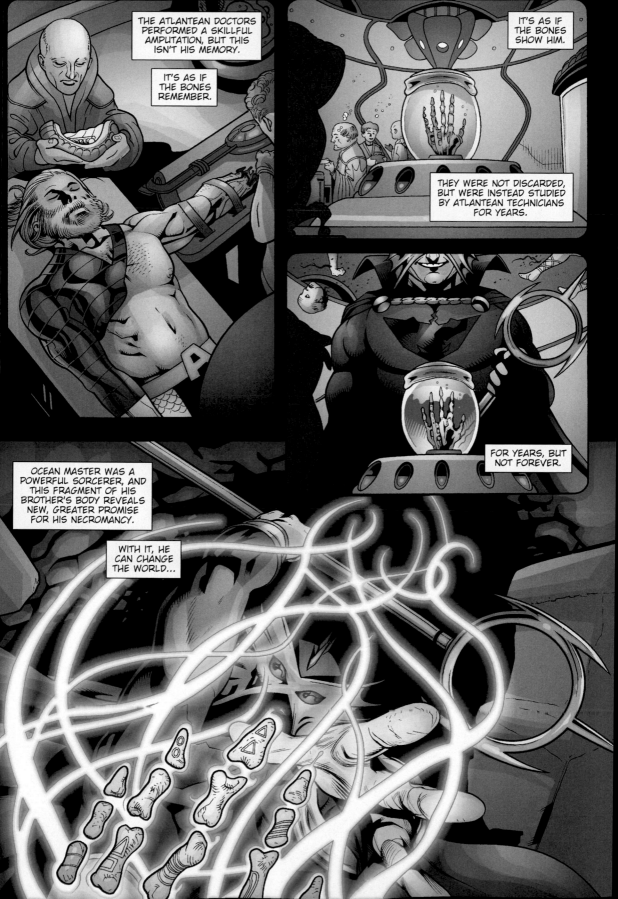

THE ATLANTEAN DOCTORS PERFORMED A SKILLFUL AMPUTATION, BUT THIS ISN'T HIS MEMORY.

IT'S AS IF THE BONES REMEMBER.

IT'S AS IF THE BONES SHOW HIM.

THEY WERE NOT DISCARDED, BUT WERE INSTEAD STUDIED BY ATLANTEAN TECHNICIANS FOR YEARS.

FOR YEARS, BUT NOT FOREVER.

OCEAN MASTER WAS A POWERFUL SORCERER, AND THIS FRAGMENT OF HIS BROTHER'S BODY REVEALS NEW, GREATER PROMISE FOR HIS NECROMANCY.

WITH IT, HE CAN CHANGE THE WORLD...

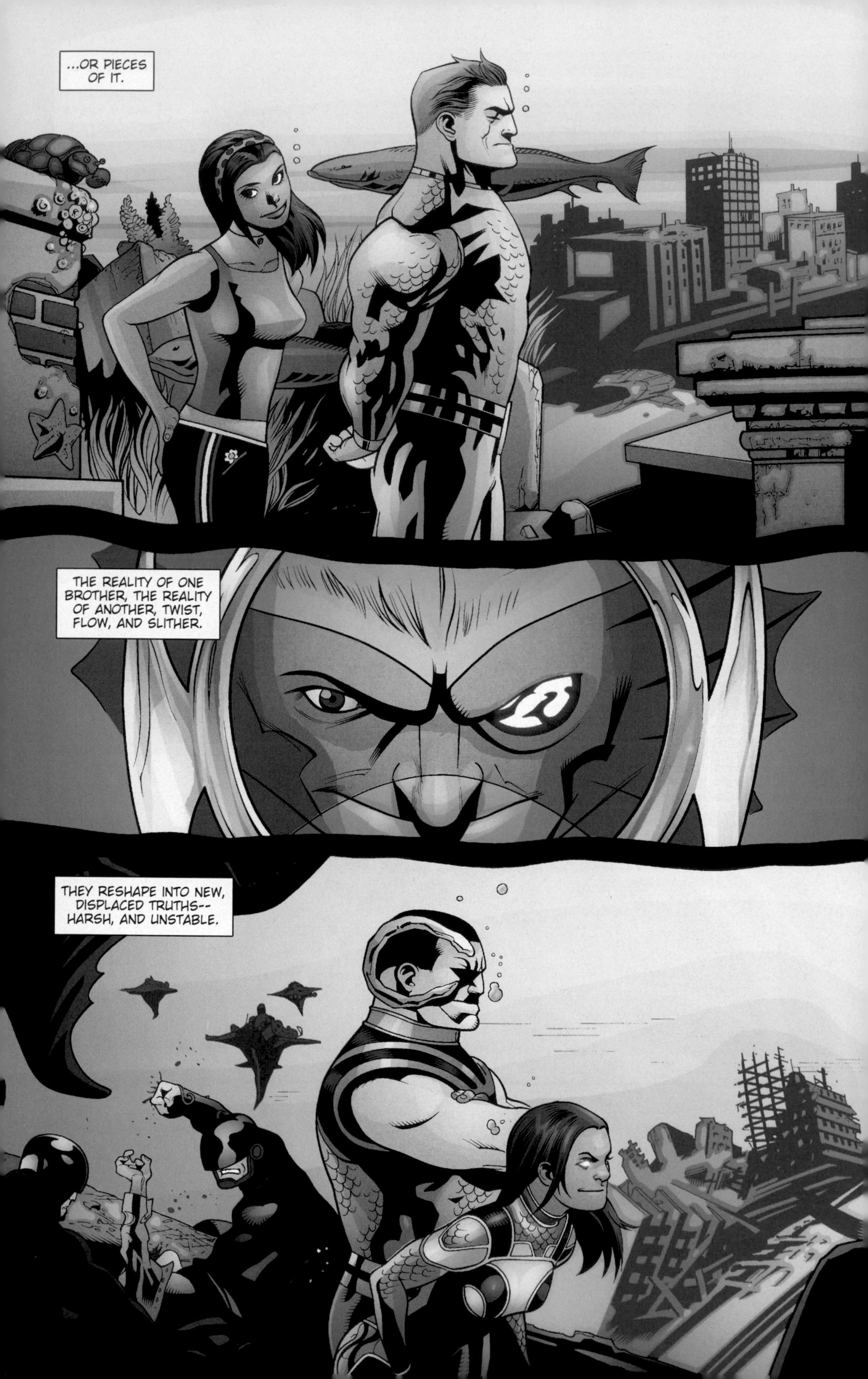
...OR PIECES OF IT.
THE REALITY OF ONE BROTHER, THE REALITY OF ANOTHER, TWIST, FLOW, AND SLITHER.
THEY RESHAPE INTO NEW, DISPLACED TRUTHS-- HARSH, AND UNSTABLE.

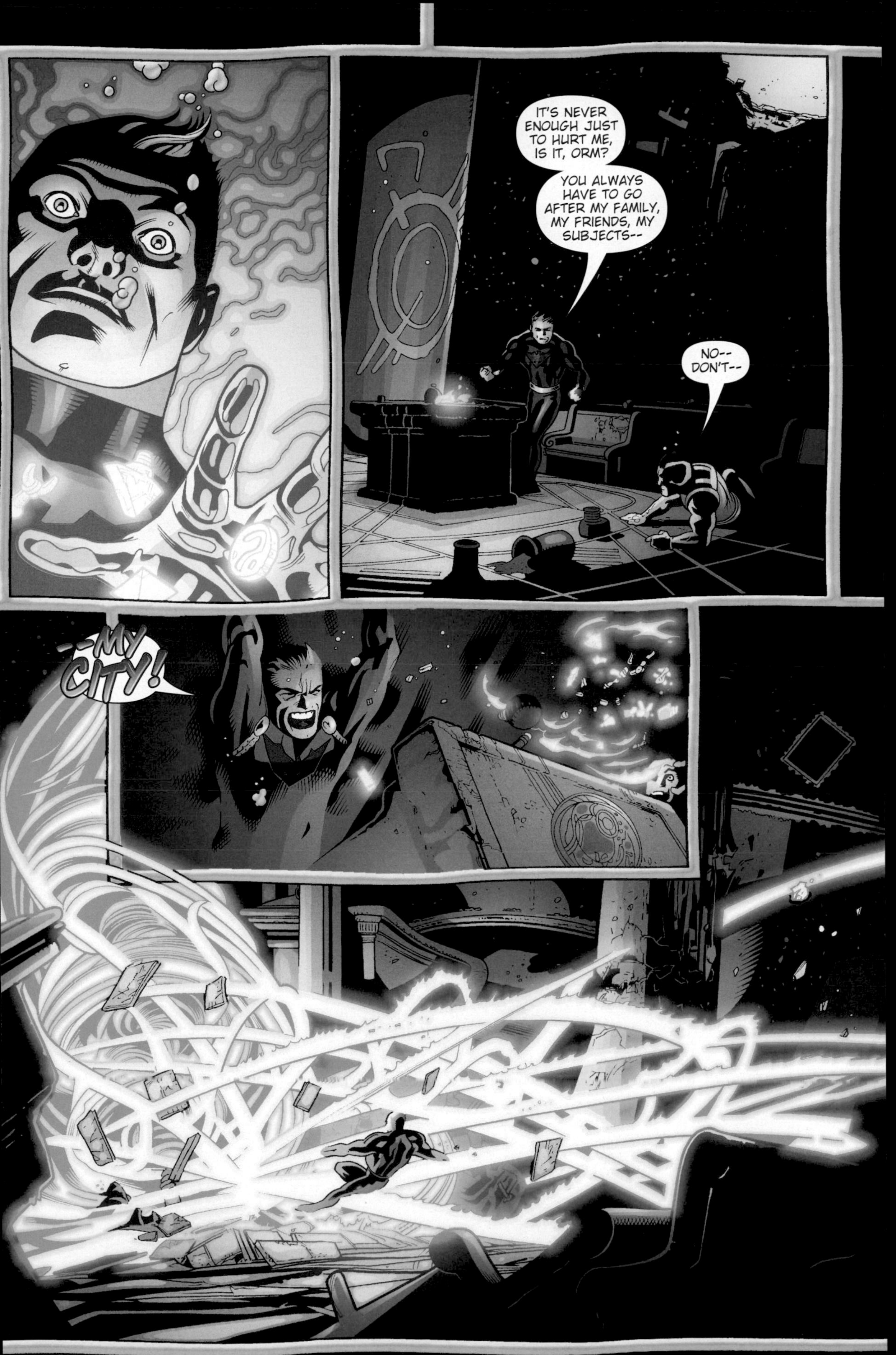

IT'S NEVER ENOUGH JUST TO HURT ME, IS IT, ORM?
YOU ALWAYS HAVE TO GO AFTER MY FAMILY, MY FRIENDS, MY SUBJECTS--
NO-- DON'T--
--MY CITY!

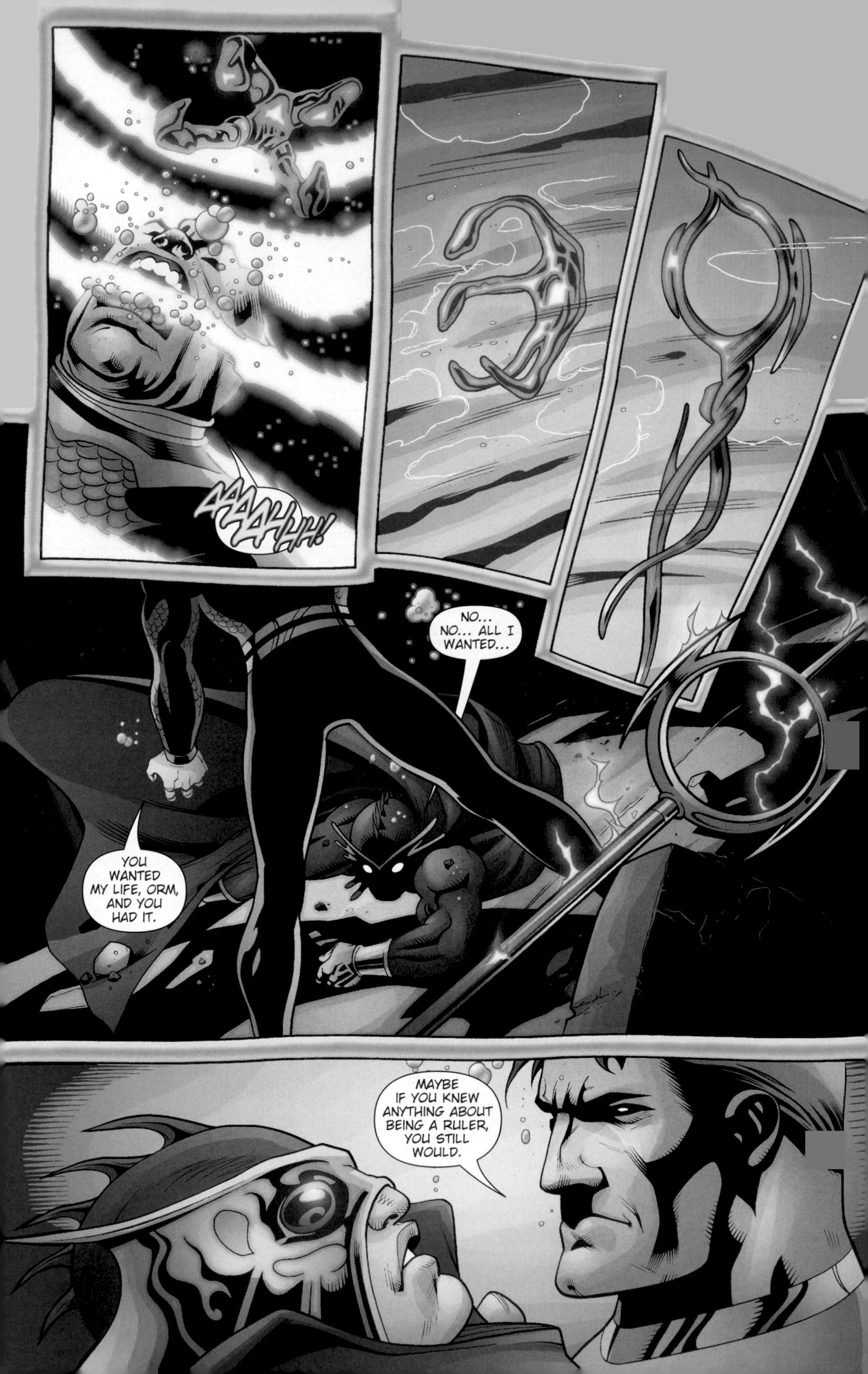
AAAAHHHH!
NO... NO... ALL I WANTED...
YOU WANTED MY LIFE, ORM, AND YOU HAD IT.
MAYBE IF YOU KNEW ANYTHING ABOUT BEING A RULER, YOU STILL WOULD.

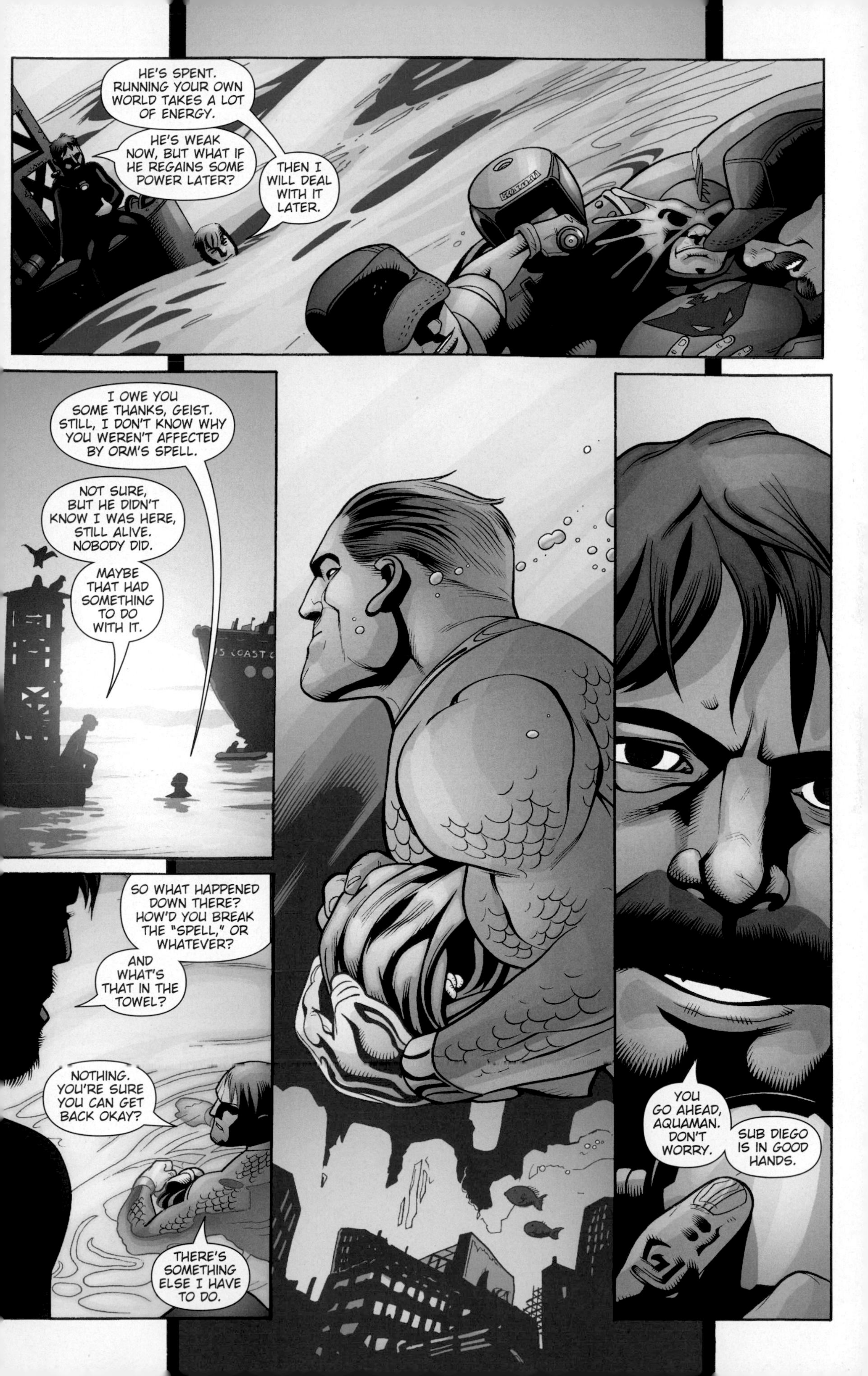
HE'S SPENT. RUNNING YOUR OWN WORLD TAKES A LOT OF ENERGY.
HE'S WEAK NOW, BUT WHAT IF HE REGAINS SOME POWER LATER?
THEN I WILL DEAL WITH IT LATER.
I OWE YOU SOME THANKS, GEIST. STILL, I DON'T KNOW WHY YOU WEREN'T AFFECTED BY ORM'S SPELL.
NOT SURE, BUT HE DIDN'T KNOW I WAS HERE, STILL ALIVE. NOBODY DID.
MAYBE THAT HAD SOMETHING TO DO WITH IT.
SO WHAT HAPPENED DOWN THERE? HOW'D YOU BREAK THE "SPELL," OR WHATEVER?
AND WHAT'S THAT IN THE TOWEL?
NOTHING. YOU'RE SURE YOU CAN GET BACK OKAY?
THERE'S SOMETHING ELSE I HAVE TO DO.
YOU GO AHEAD, AQUAMAN. DON'T WORRY.
SUB DIEGO IS IN GOOD HANDS.

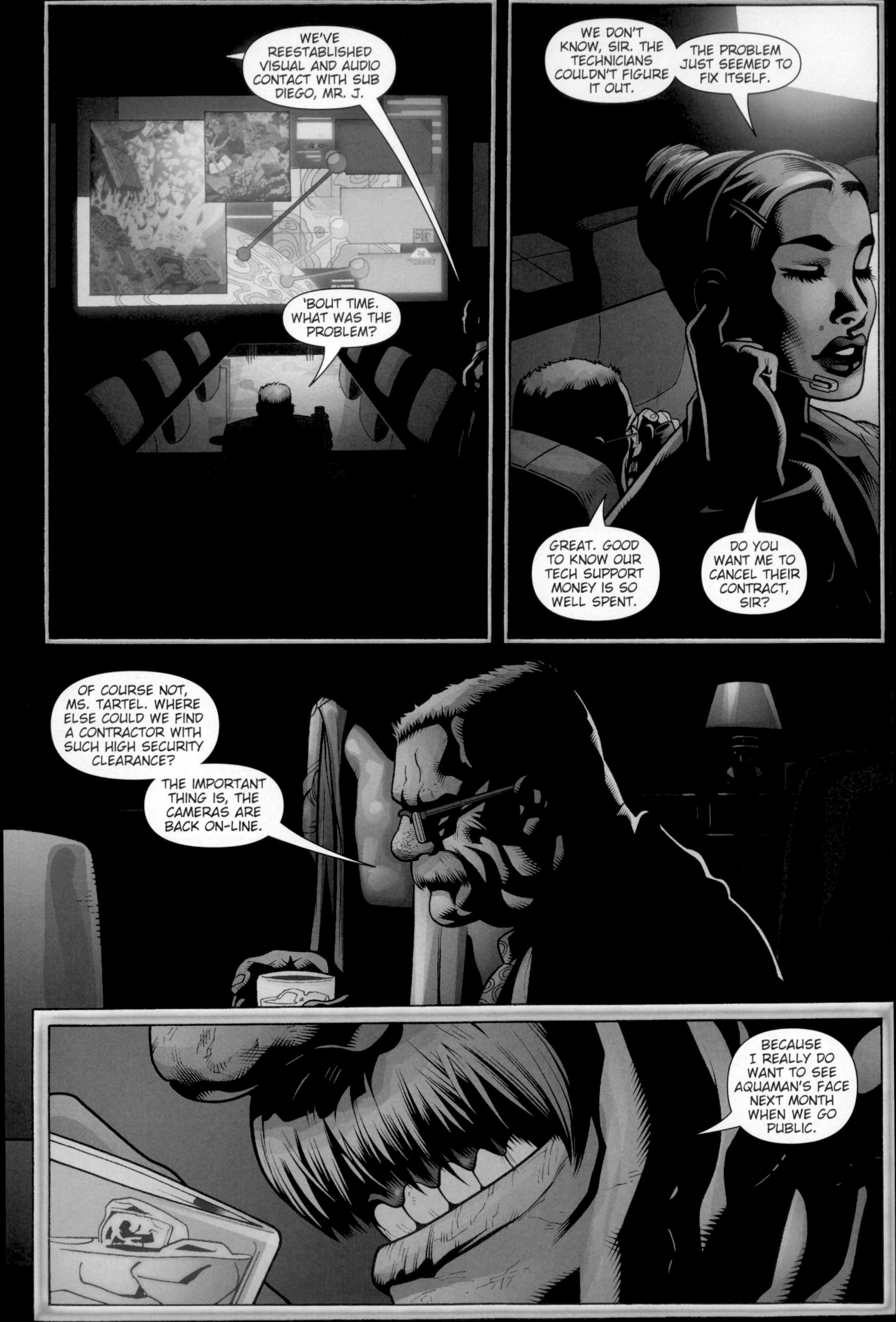
WE'VE REESTABLISHED VISUAL AND AUDIO CONTACT WITH SUB DIEGO, MR. J.
'BOUT TIME. WHAT WAS THE PROBLEM?
WE DON'T KNOW, SIR. THE TECHNICIANS COULDN'T FIGURE IT OUT.
THE PROBLEM JUST SEEMED TO FIX ITSELF.
GREAT. GOOD TO KNOW OUR TECH SUPPORT MONEY IS SO WELL SPENT.
DO YOU WANT ME TO CANCEL THEIR CONTRACT, SIR?
OF COURSE NOT, MS. TARTEL. WHERE ELSE COULD WE FIND A CONTRACTOR WITH SUCH HIGH SECURITY CLEARANCE?
THE IMPORTANT THING IS, THE CAMERAS ARE BACK ON-LINE.
BECAUSE I REALLY DO WANT TO SEE AQUAMAN'S FACE NEXT MONTH WHEN WE GO PUBLIC.

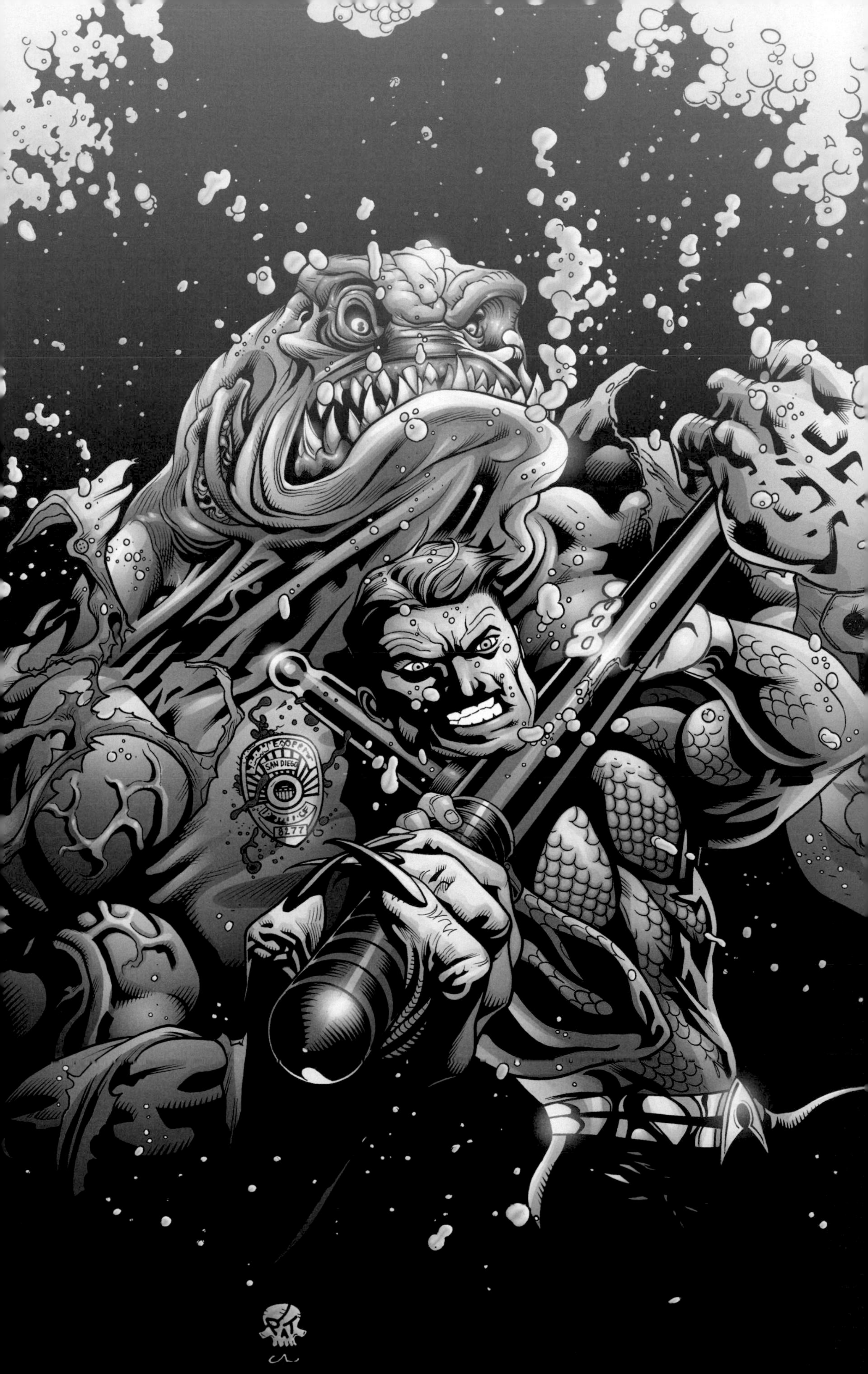
SAN DIEGO
8277

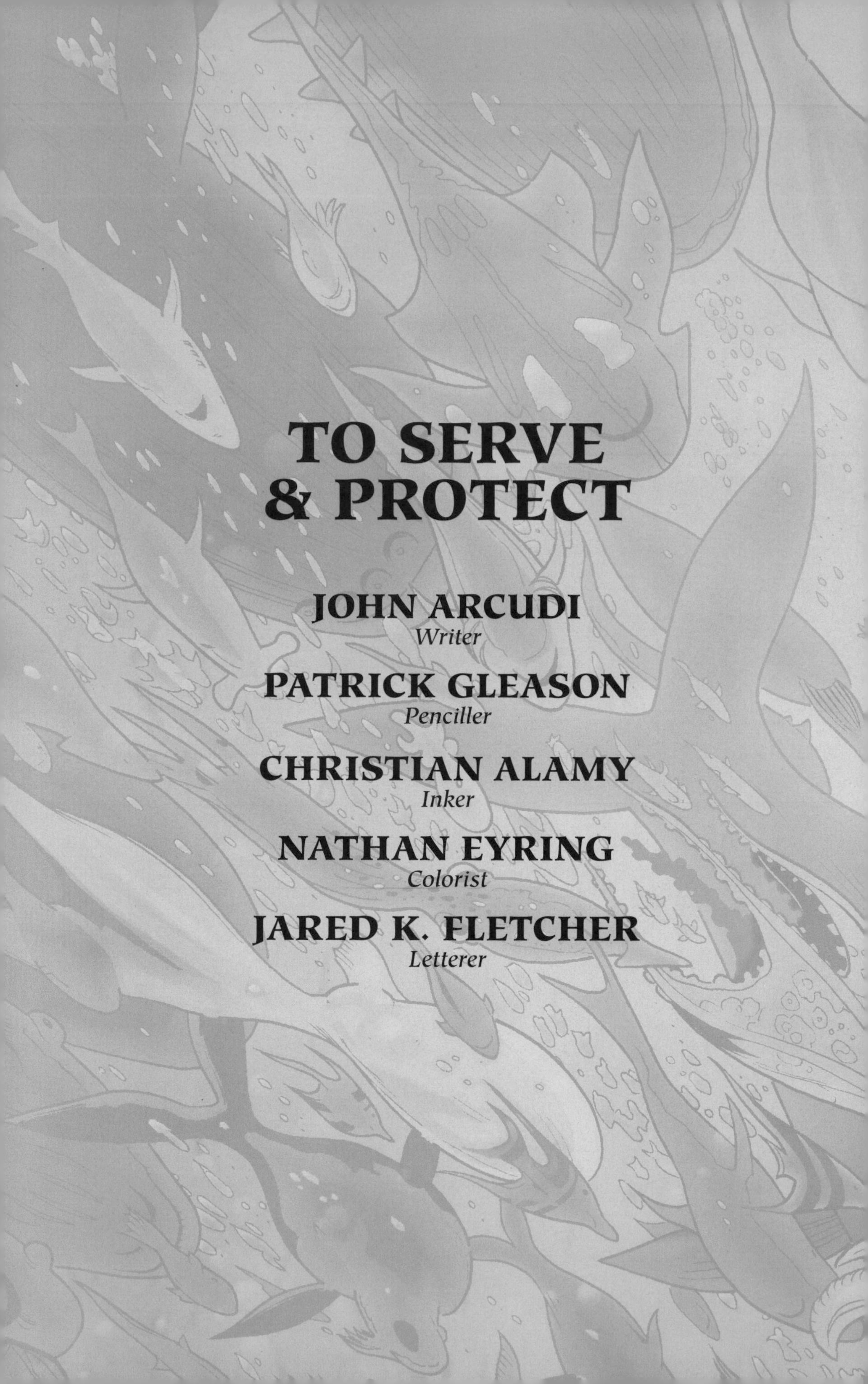

TO SERVE & PROTECT

JOHN ARCUDI
Writer

PATRICK GLEASON
Penciller

CHRISTIAN ALAMY
Inker

NATHAN EYRING
Colorist

JARED K. FLETCHER
Letterer

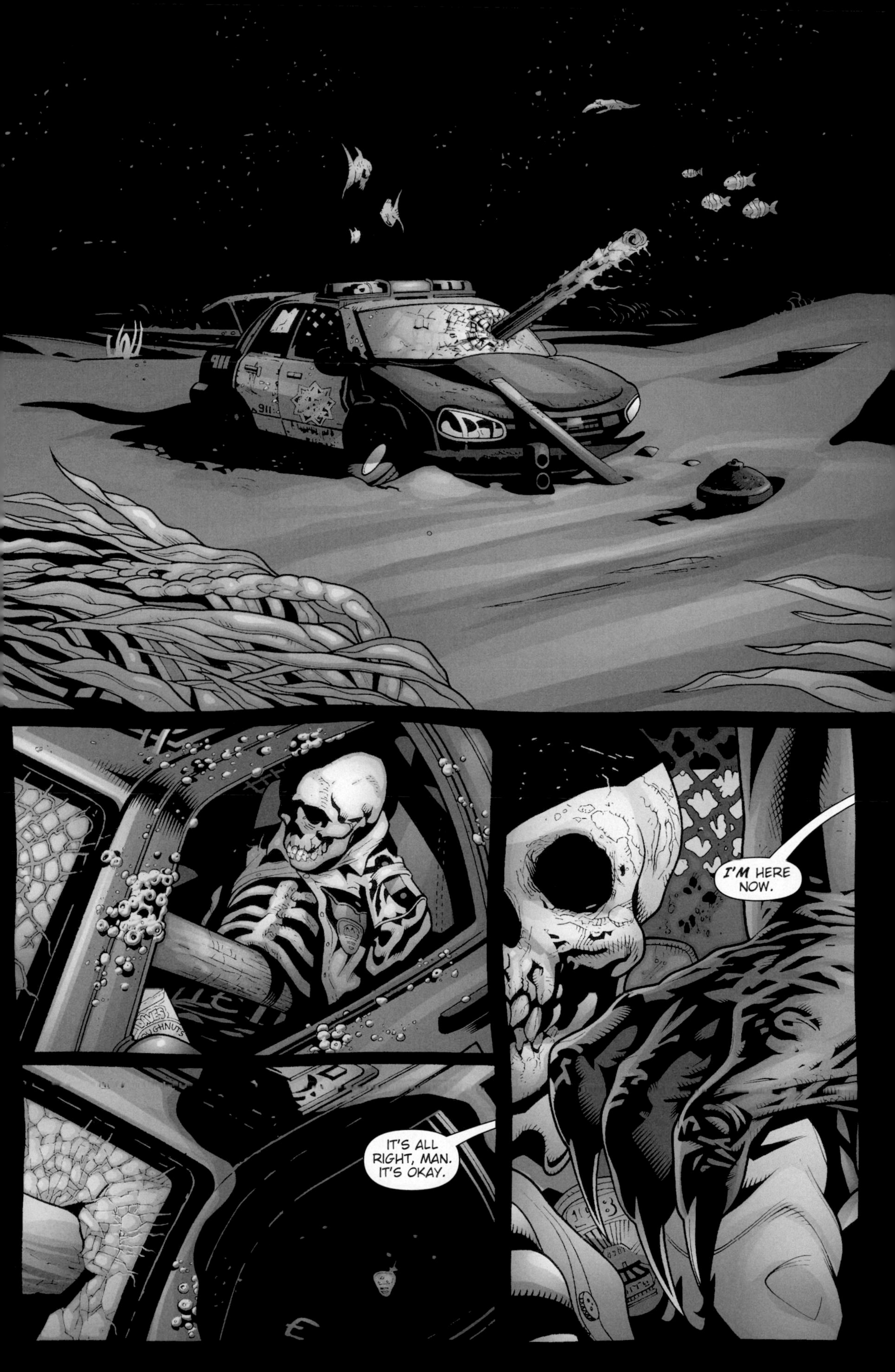

I'M HERE NOW.
IT'S ALL RIGHT, MAN. IT'S OKAY.

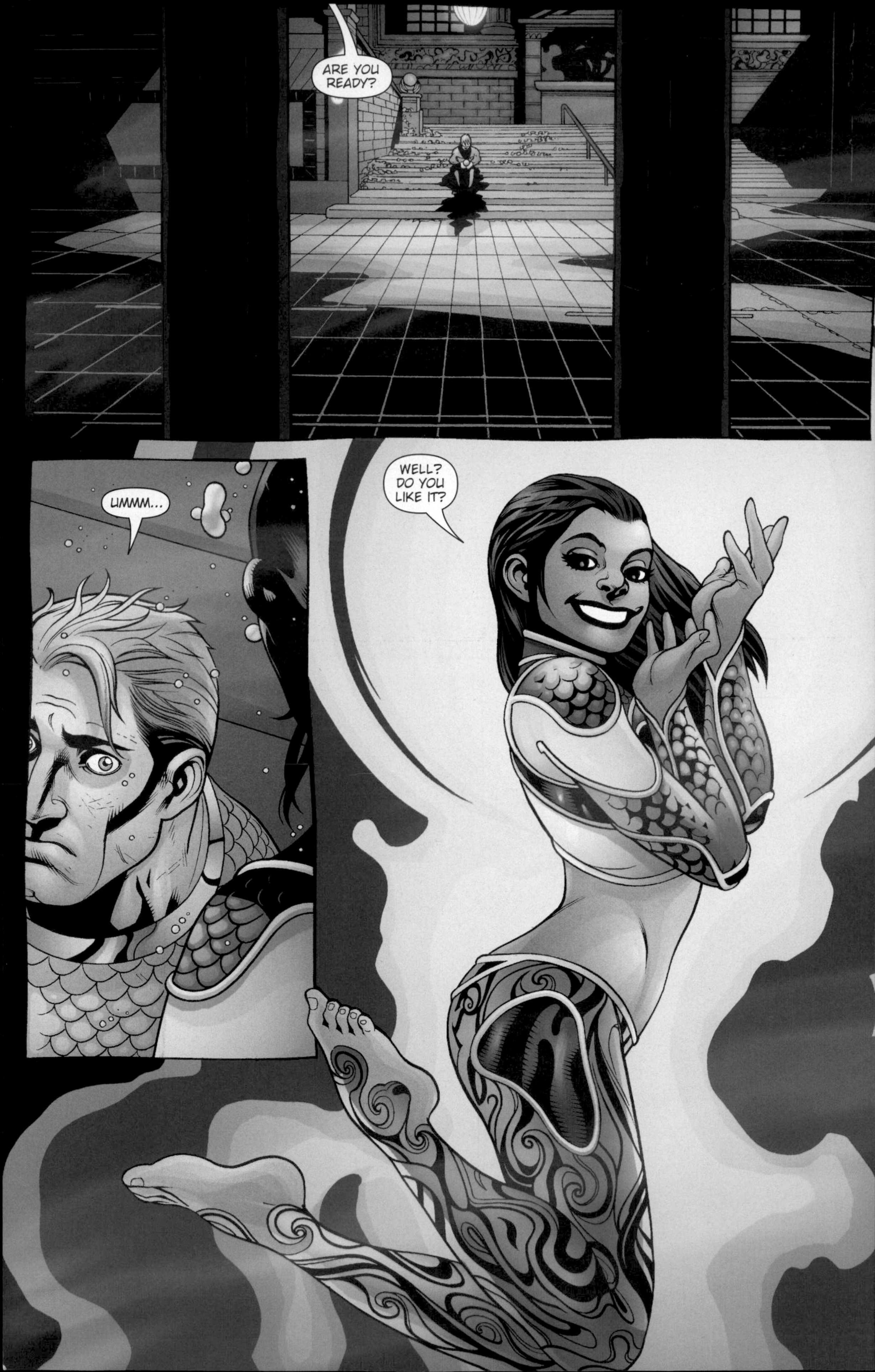
ARE YOU READY?
UMMM...
WELL? DO YOU LIKE IT?

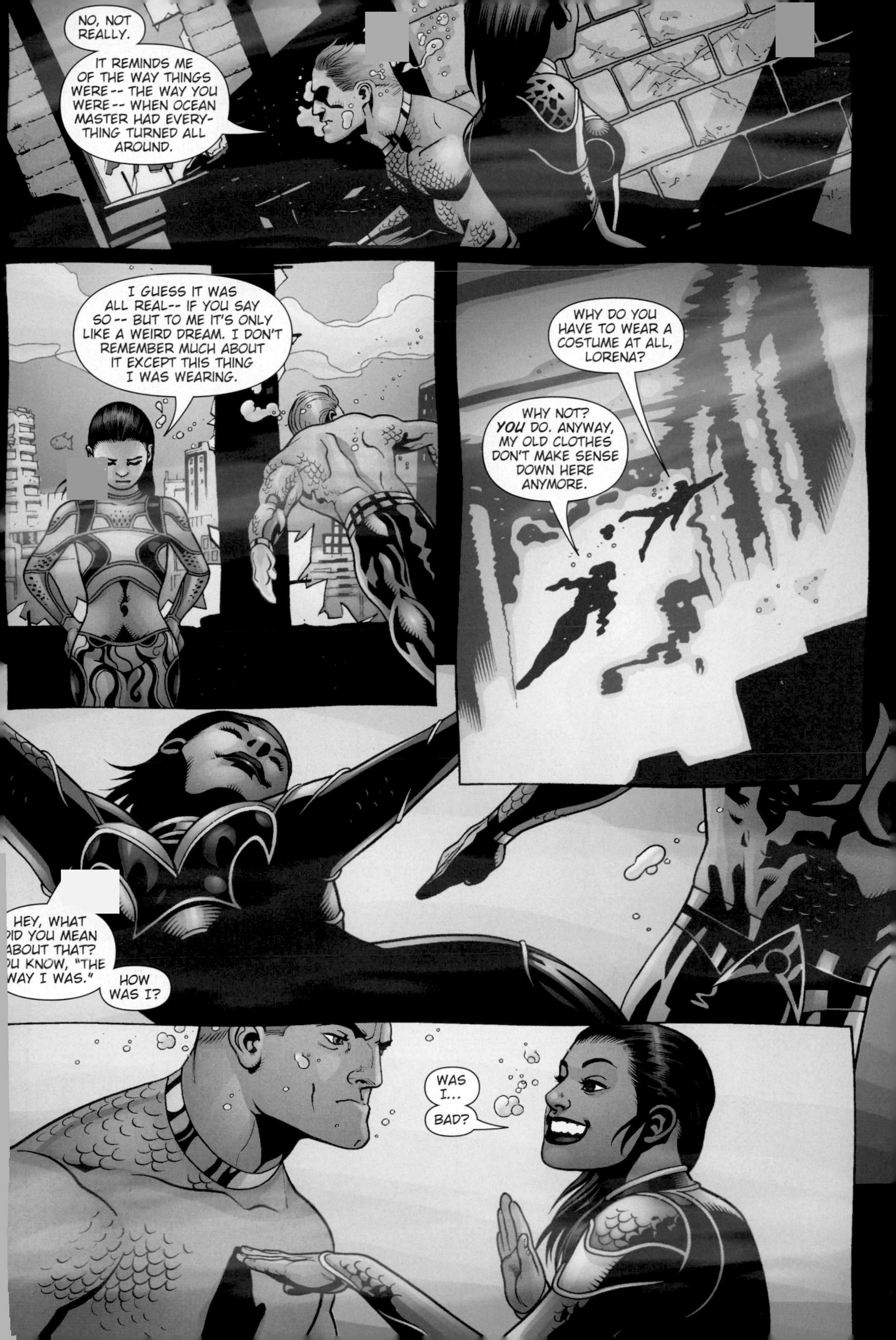

NO, NOT REALLY.
IT REMINDS ME OF THE WAY THINGS WERE-- THE WAY YOU WERE-- WHEN OCEAN MASTER HAD EVERY-THING TURNED ALL AROUND.
I GUESS IT WAS ALL REAL-- IF YOU SAY SO -- BUT TO ME IT'S ONLY LIKE A WEIRD DREAM. I DON'T REMEMBER MUCH ABOUT IT EXCEPT THIS THING I WAS WEARING.
WHY DO YOU HAVE TO WEAR A COSTUME AT ALL, LORENA?
WHY NOT? YOU DO. ANYWAY, MY OLD CLOTHES DON'T MAKE SENSE DOWN HERE ANYMORE.
HEY, WHAT DID YOU MEAN ABOUT THAT? YOU KNOW, "THE WAY I WAS."
HOW WAS I?
WAS I... BAD?

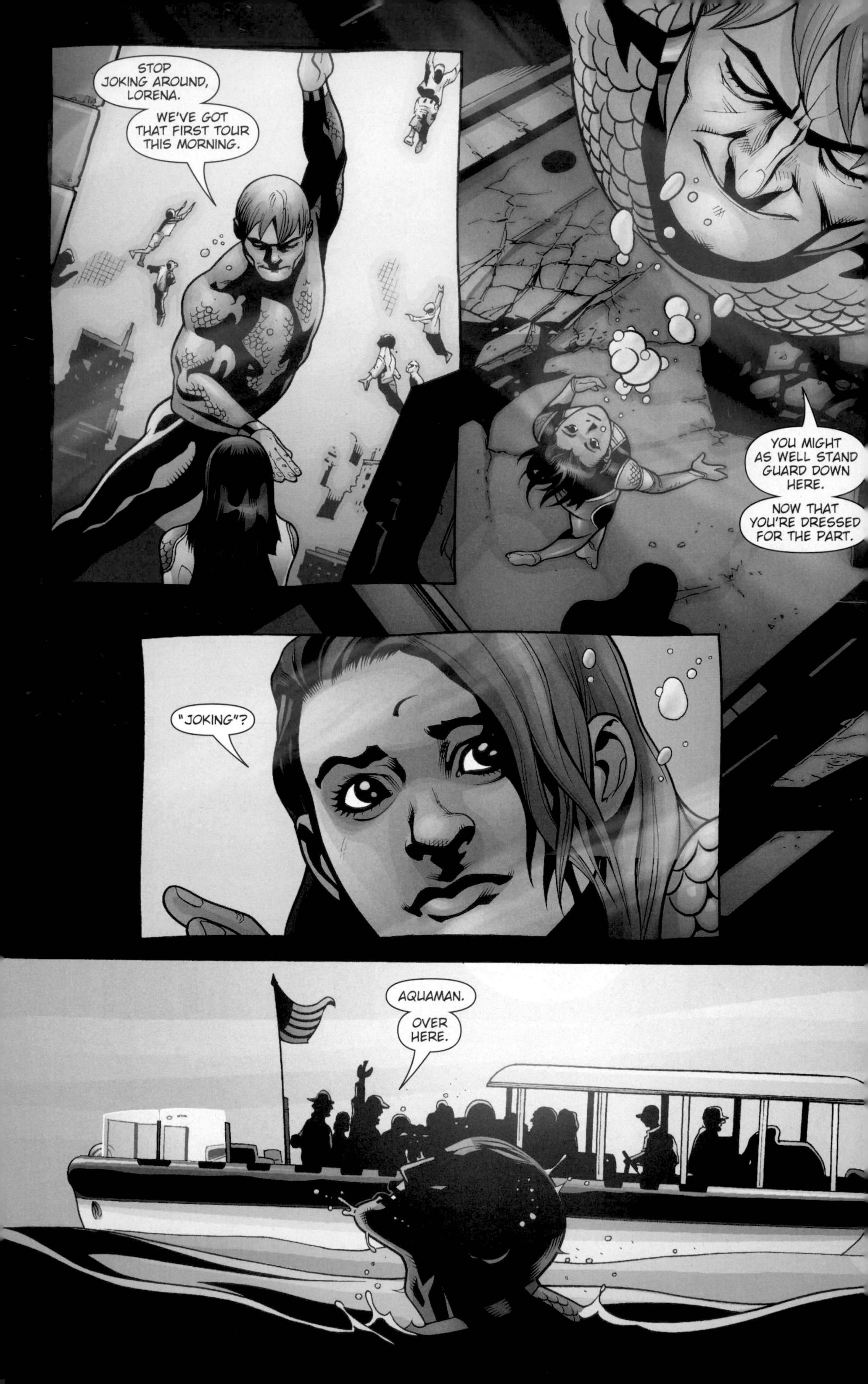
STOP JOKING AROUND, LORENA.
WE'VE GOT THAT FIRST TOUR THIS MORNING.
YOU MIGHT AS WELL STAND GUARD DOWN HERE.
NOW THAT YOU'RE DRESSED FOR THE PART.
"JOKING"?
AQUAMAN.
OVER HERE.

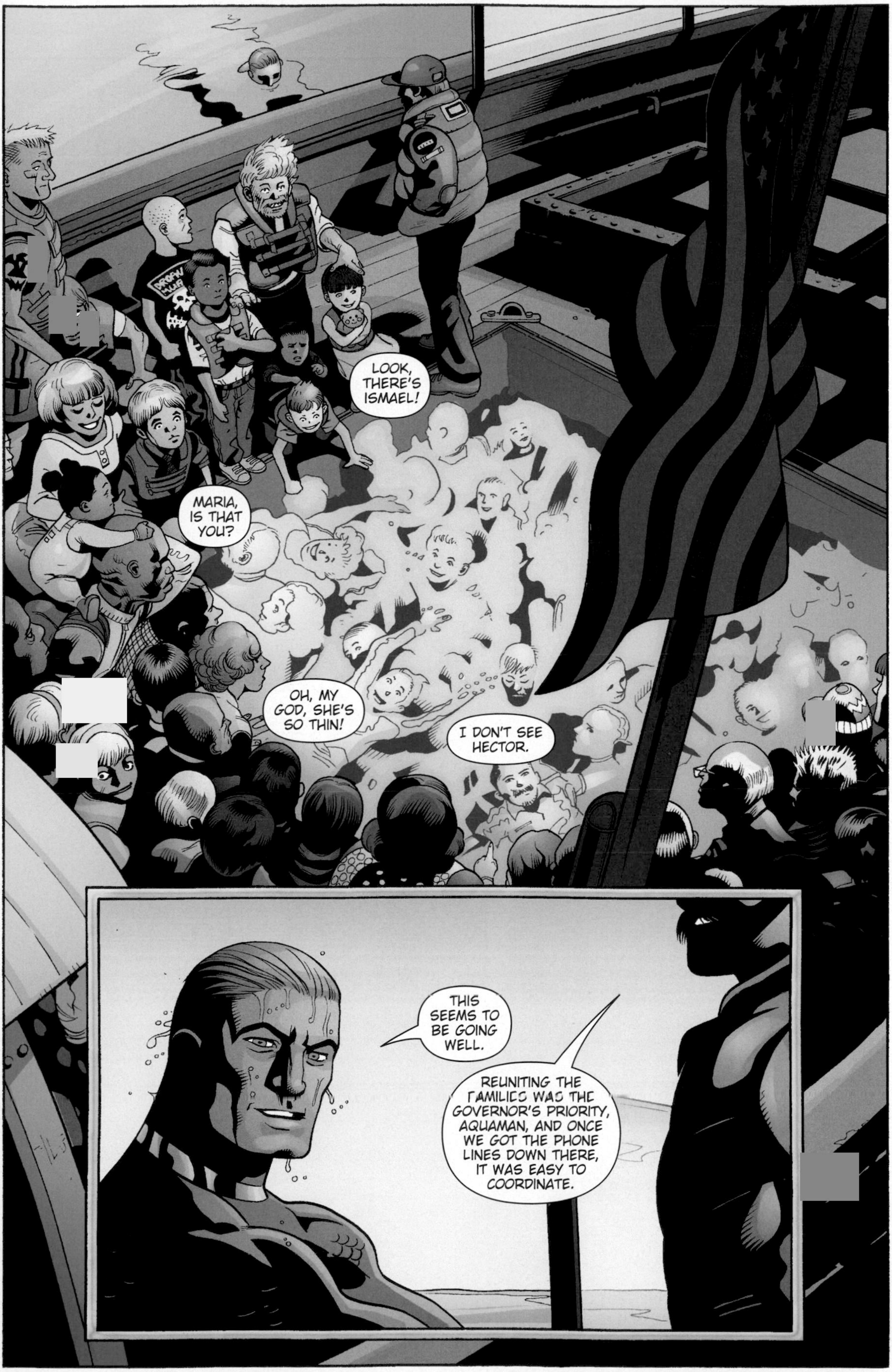
LOOK, THERE'S ISMAEL!
MARIA, IS THAT YOU?
OH, MY GOD, SHE'S SO THIN!
I DON'T SEE HECTOR.
THIS SEEMS TO BE GOING WELL.
REUNITING THE FAMILIES WAS THE GOVERNOR'S PRIORITY, AQUAMAN, AND ONCE WE GOT THE PHONE LINES DOWN THERE, IT WAS EASY TO COORDINATE.

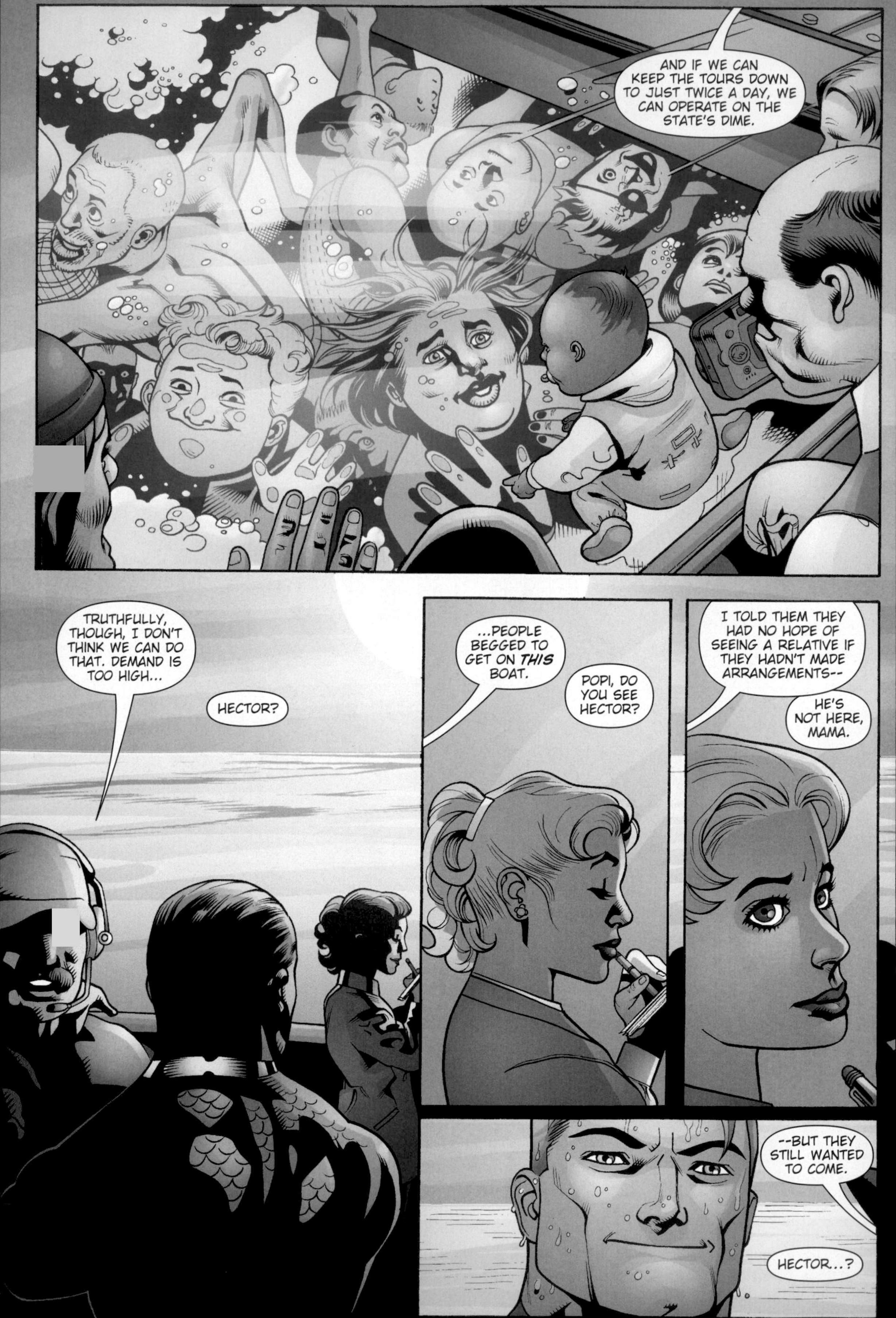
AND IF WE CAN KEEP THE TOURS DOWN TO JUST TWICE A DAY, WE CAN OPERATE ON THE STATE'S DIME.
TRUTHFULLY, THOUGH, I DON'T THINK WE CAN DO THAT. DEMAND IS TOO HIGH...
HECTOR?
...PEOPLE BEGGED TO GET ON *THIS* BOAT.
POPI, DO YOU SEE HECTOR?
I TOLD THEM THEY HAD NO HOPE OF SEEING A RELATIVE IF THEY HADN'T MADE ARRANGEMENTS--
HE'S NOT HERE, MAMA.
--BUT THEY STILL WANTED TO COME.
HECTOR...?

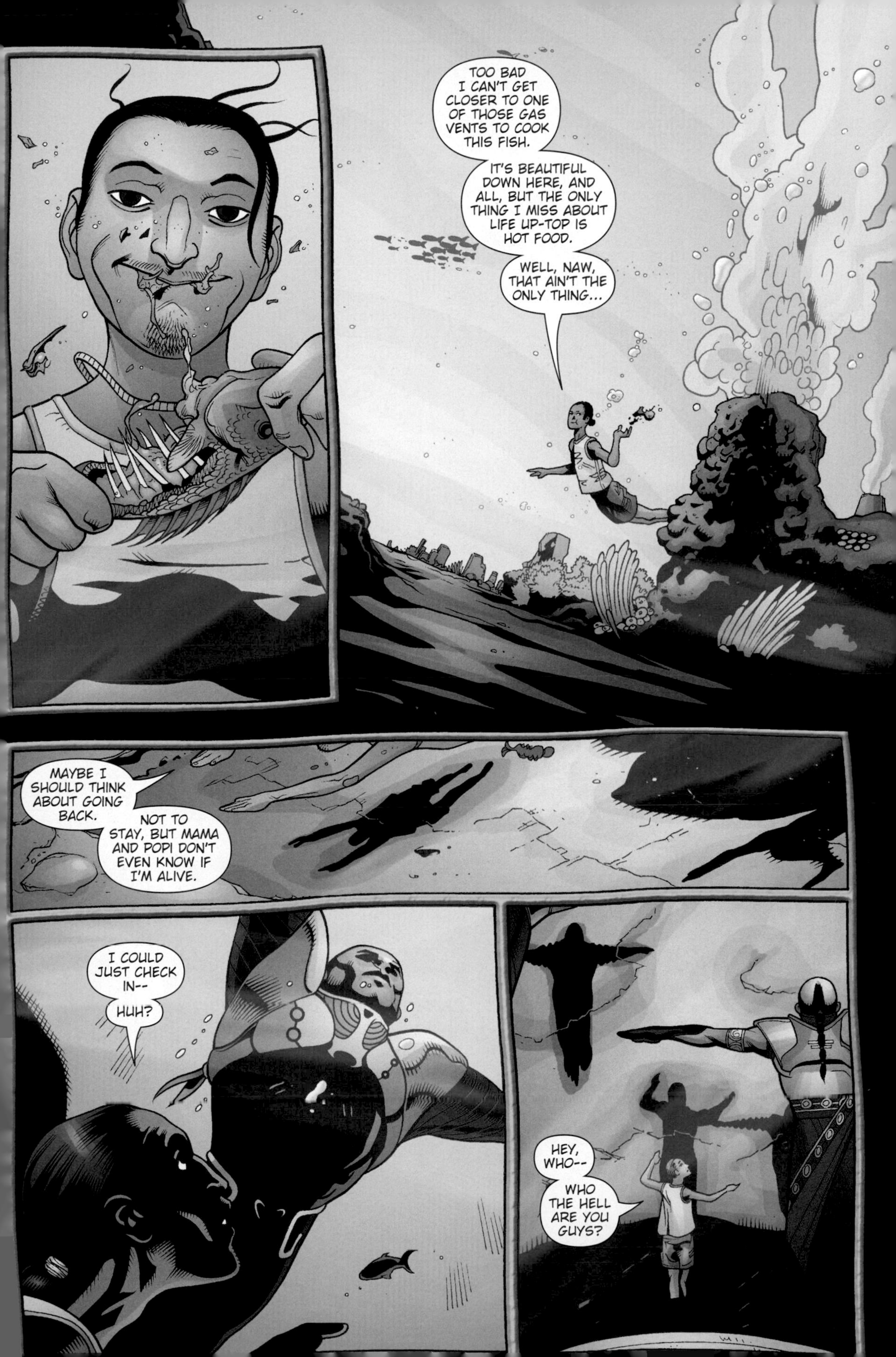

TOO BAD I CAN'T GET CLOSER TO ONE OF THOSE GAS VENTS TO COOK THIS FISH.
IT'S BEAUTIFUL DOWN HERE, AND ALL, BUT THE ONLY THING I MISS ABOUT LIFE UP-TOP IS HOT FOOD.
WELL, NAW, THAT AIN'T THE ONLY THING...
MAYBE I SHOULD THINK ABOUT GOING BACK.
NOT TO STAY, BUT MAMA AND POPI DON'T EVEN KNOW IF I'M ALIVE.
I COULD JUST CHECK IN--
HUH?
HEY, WHO--
WHO THE HELL ARE YOU GUYS?

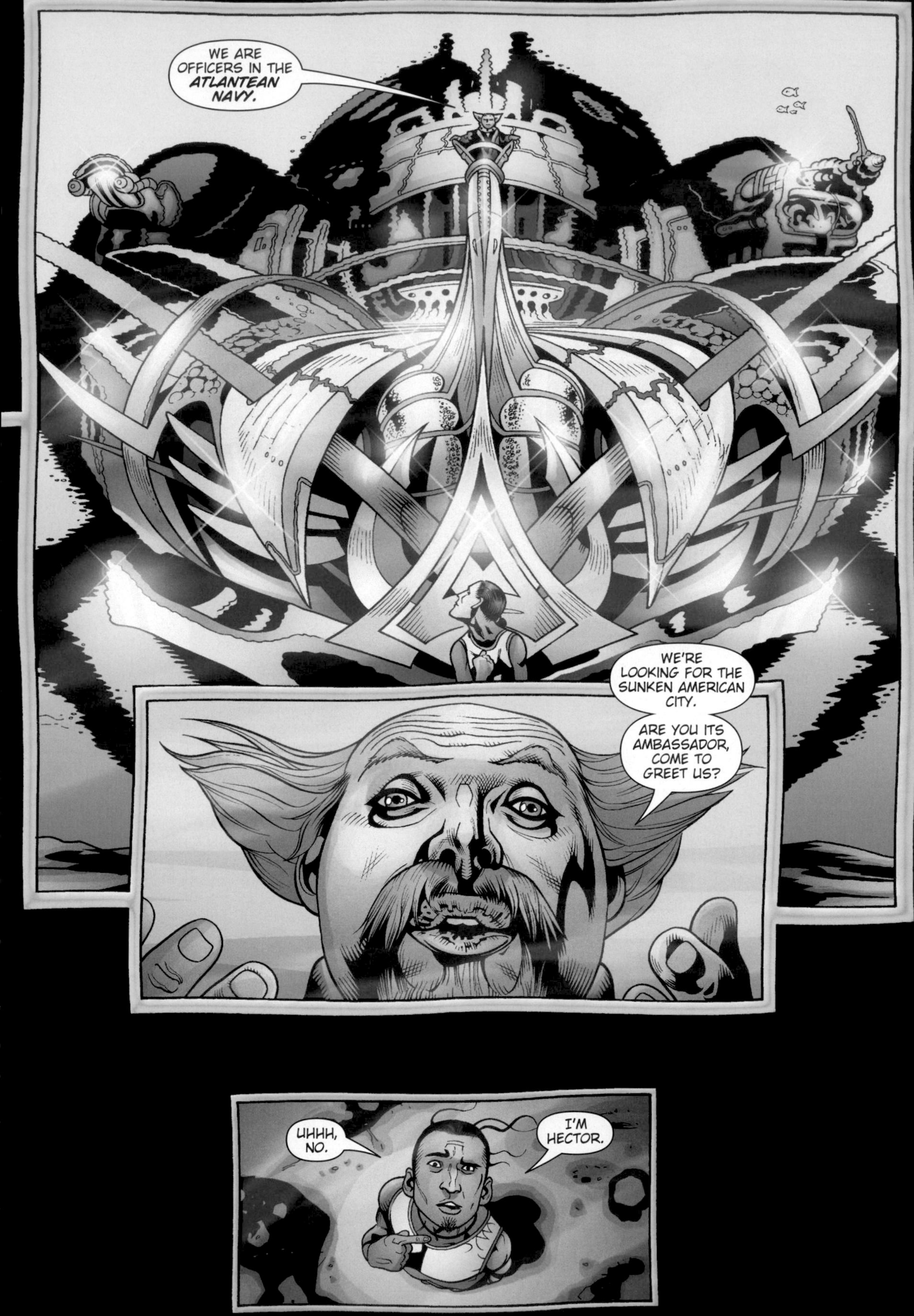
WE ARE OFFICERS IN THE ATLANTEAN NAVY.
WE'RE LOOKING FOR THE SUNKEN AMERICAN CITY.
ARE YOU ITS AMBASSADOR, COME TO GREET US?
UHHH, NO.
I'M HECTOR.

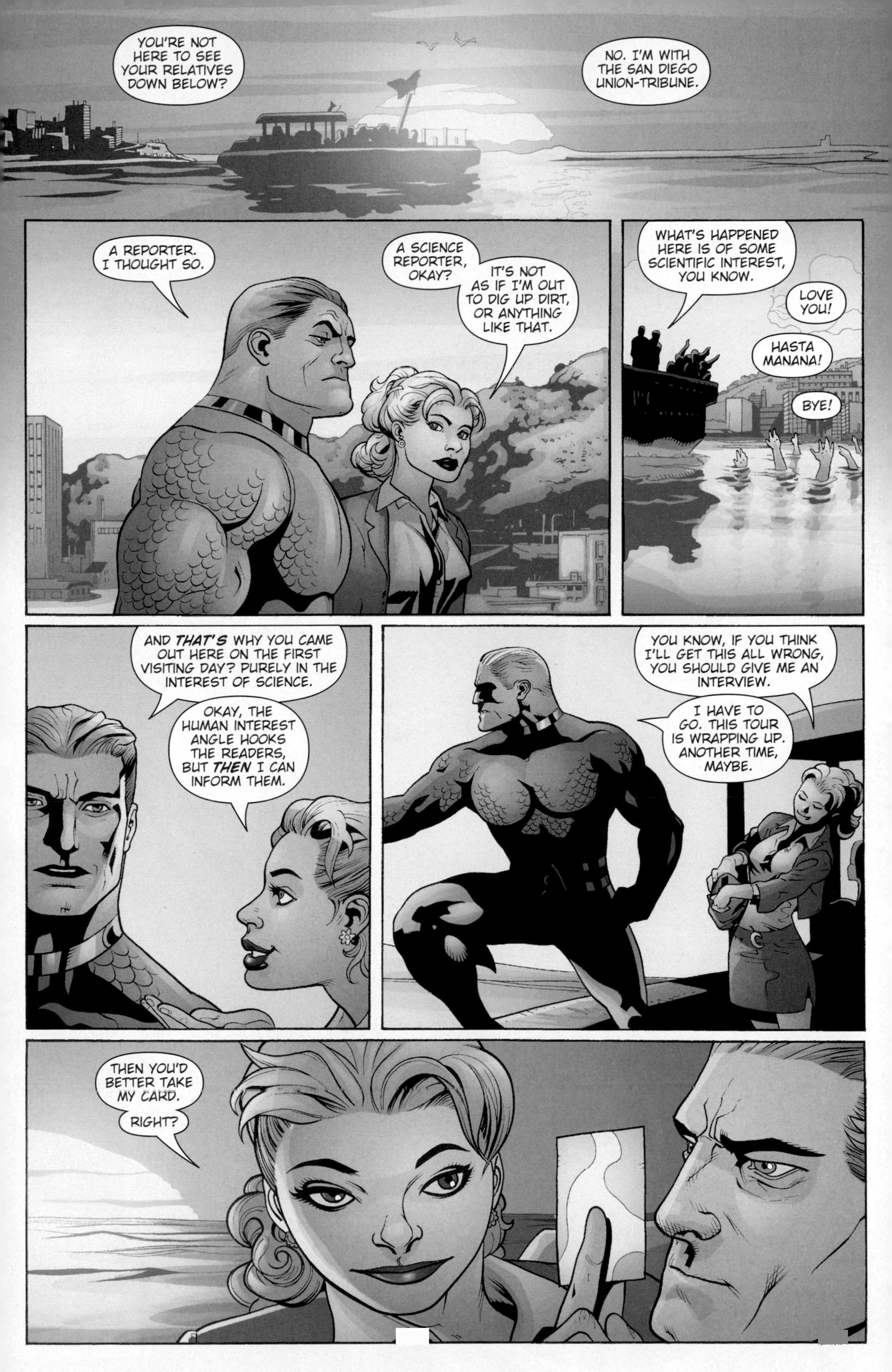
YOU'RE NOT HERE TO SEE YOUR RELATIVES DOWN BELOW?
NO. I'M WITH THE SAN DIEGO UNION-TRIBUNE.
A REPORTER. I THOUGHT SO.
A SCIENCE REPORTER, OKAY?
IT'S NOT AS IF I'M OUT TO DIG UP DIRT, OR ANYTHING LIKE THAT.
WHAT'S HAPPENED HERE IS OF SOME SCIENTIFIC INTEREST, YOU KNOW.
LOVE YOU!
HASTA MANANA!
BYE!
AND THAT'S WHY YOU CAME OUT HERE ON THE FIRST VISITING DAY? PURELY IN THE INTEREST OF SCIENCE.
OKAY, THE HUMAN INTEREST ANGLE HOOKS THE READERS, BUT THEN I CAN INFORM THEM.
YOU KNOW, IF YOU THINK I'LL GET THIS ALL WRONG, YOU SHOULD GIVE ME AN INTERVIEW.
I HAVE TO GO. THIS TOUR IS WRAPPING UP. ANOTHER TIME, MAYBE.
THEN YOU'D BETTER TAKE MY CARD.
RIGHT?

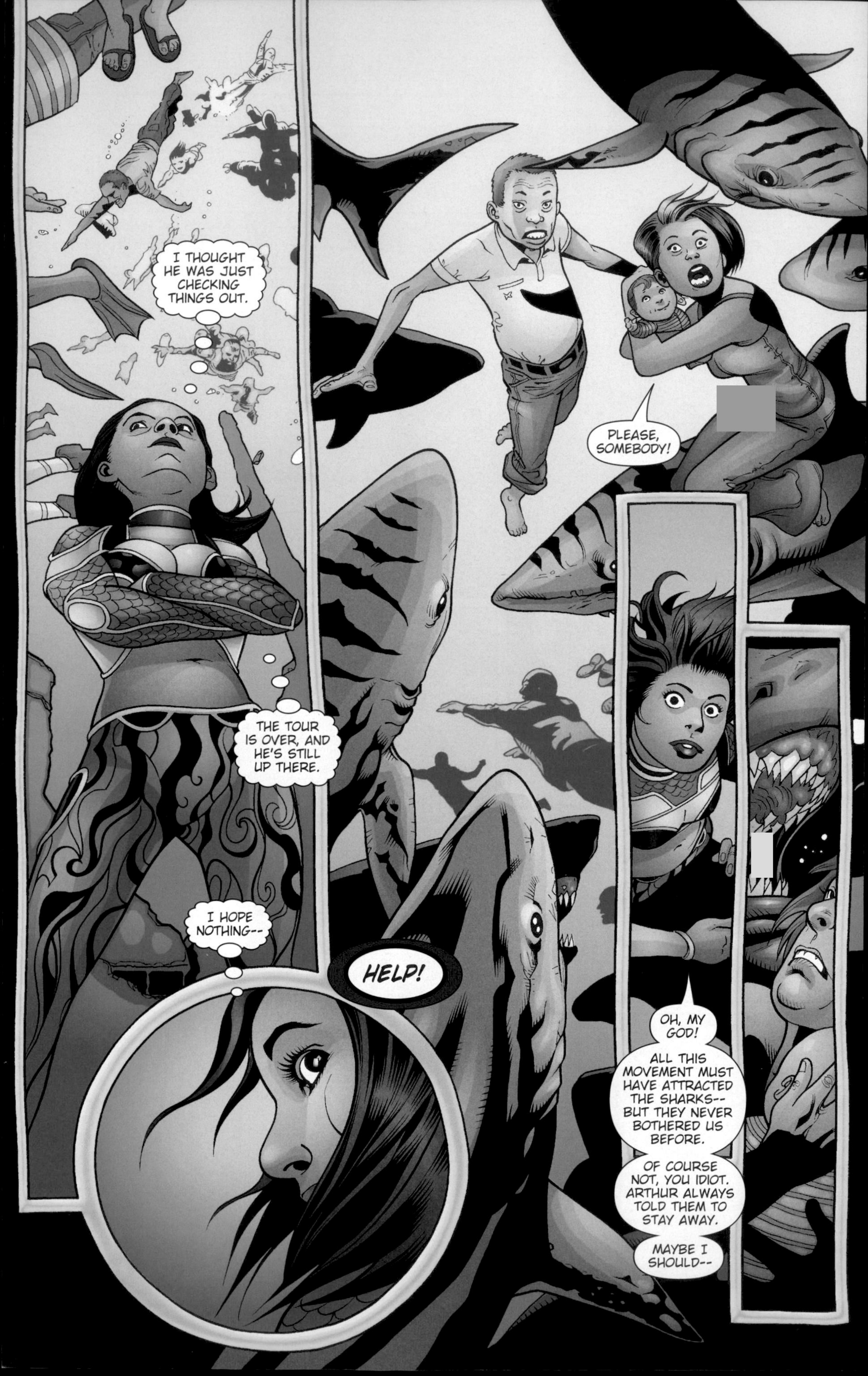
I THOUGHT HE WAS JUST CHECKING THINGS OUT.
THE TOUR IS OVER, AND HE'S STILL UP THERE.
I HOPE NOTHING--
PLEASE, SOMEBODY!
HELP!
OH, MY GOD!
ALL THIS MOVEMENT MUST HAVE ATTRACTED THE SHARKS-- BUT THEY NEVER BOTHERED US BEFORE.
OF COURSE NOT, YOU IDIOT. ARTHUR ALWAYS TOLD THEM TO STAY AWAY.
MAYBE I SHOULD--

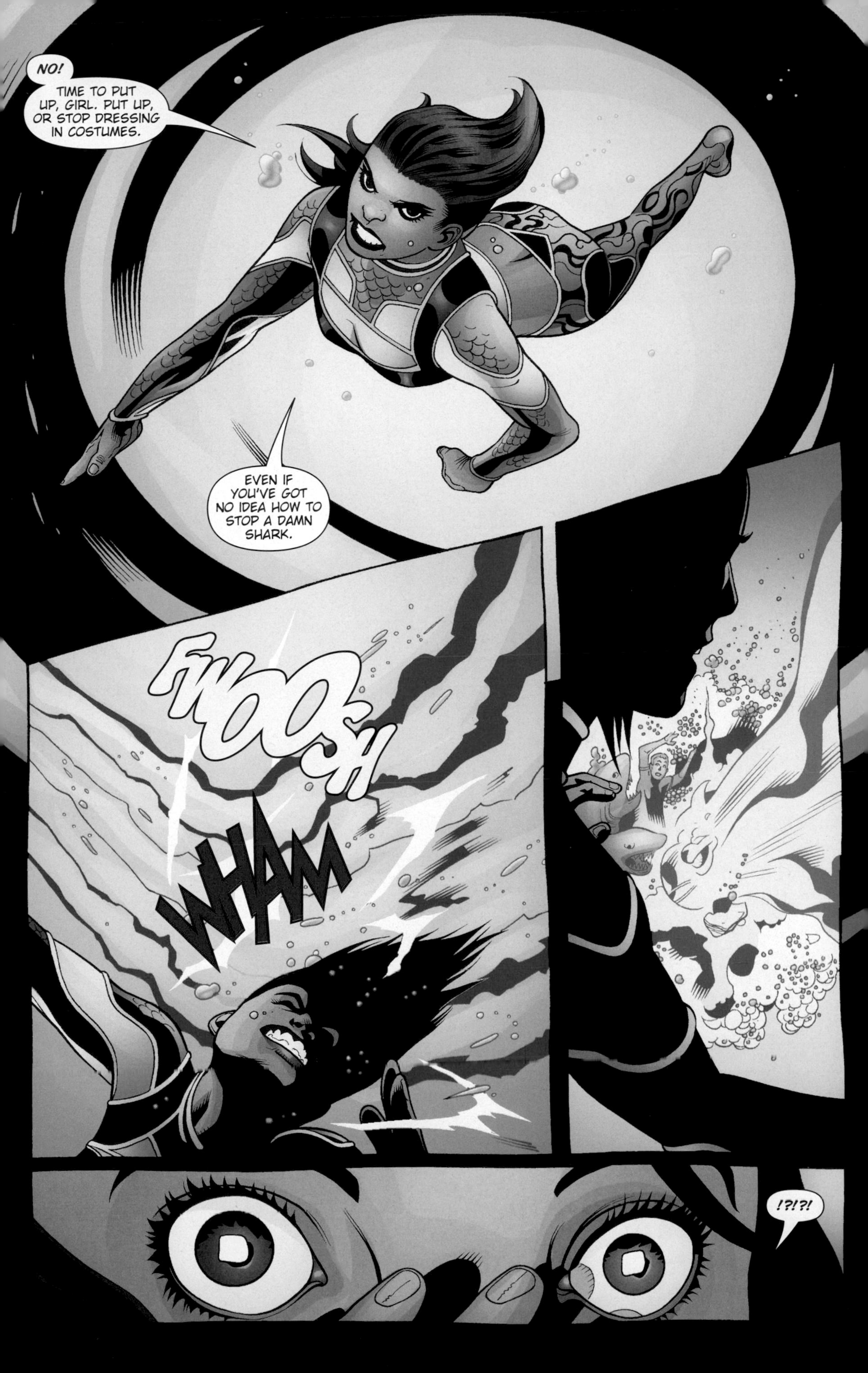
NO!
TIME TO PUT UP, GIRL. PUT UP, OR STOP DRESSING IN COSTUMES.
EVEN IF YOU'VE GOT NO IDEA HOW TO STOP A DAMN SHARK.
FWOOSH
WHAM
!?!?!

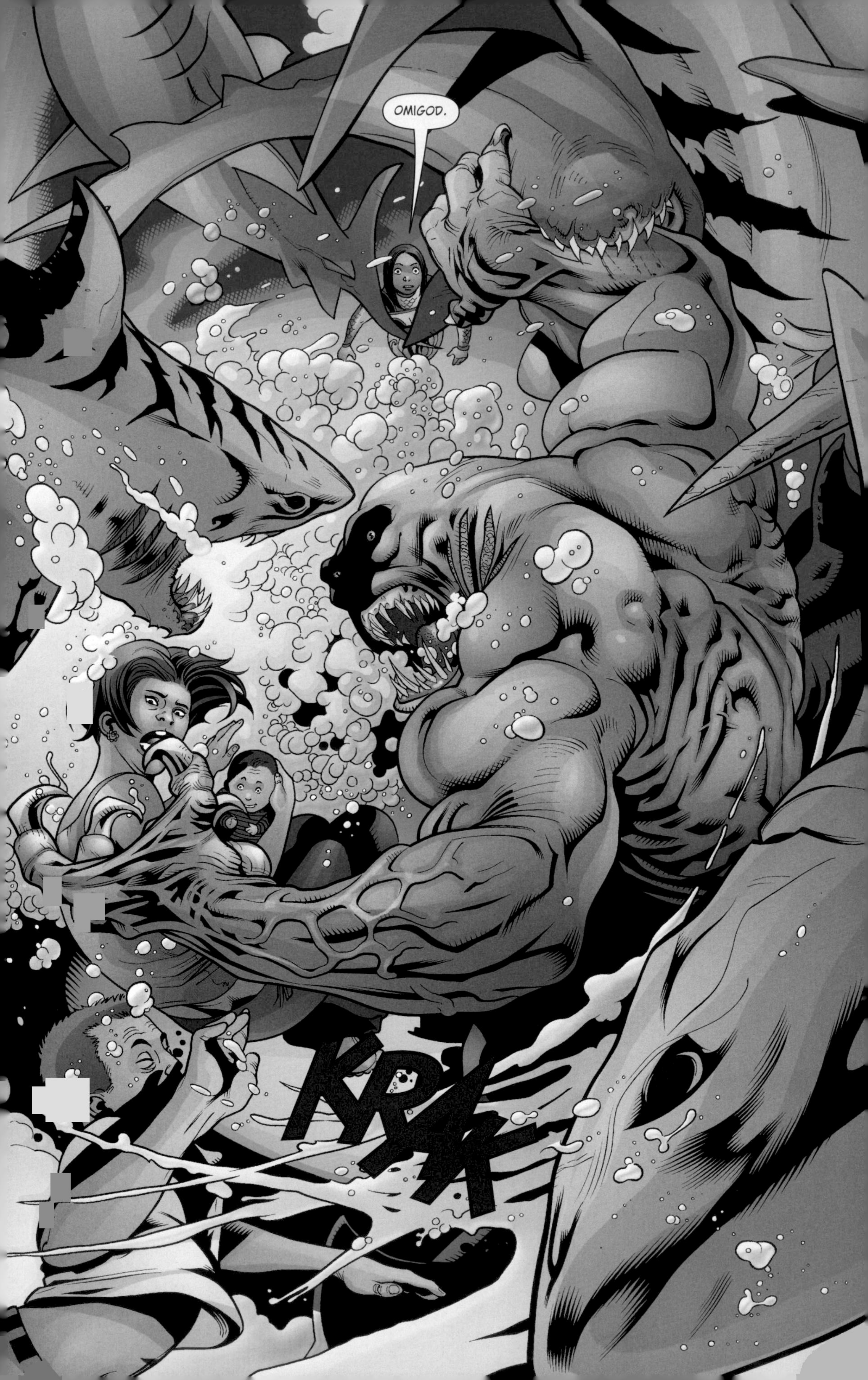
OMIGOD.
KRAK

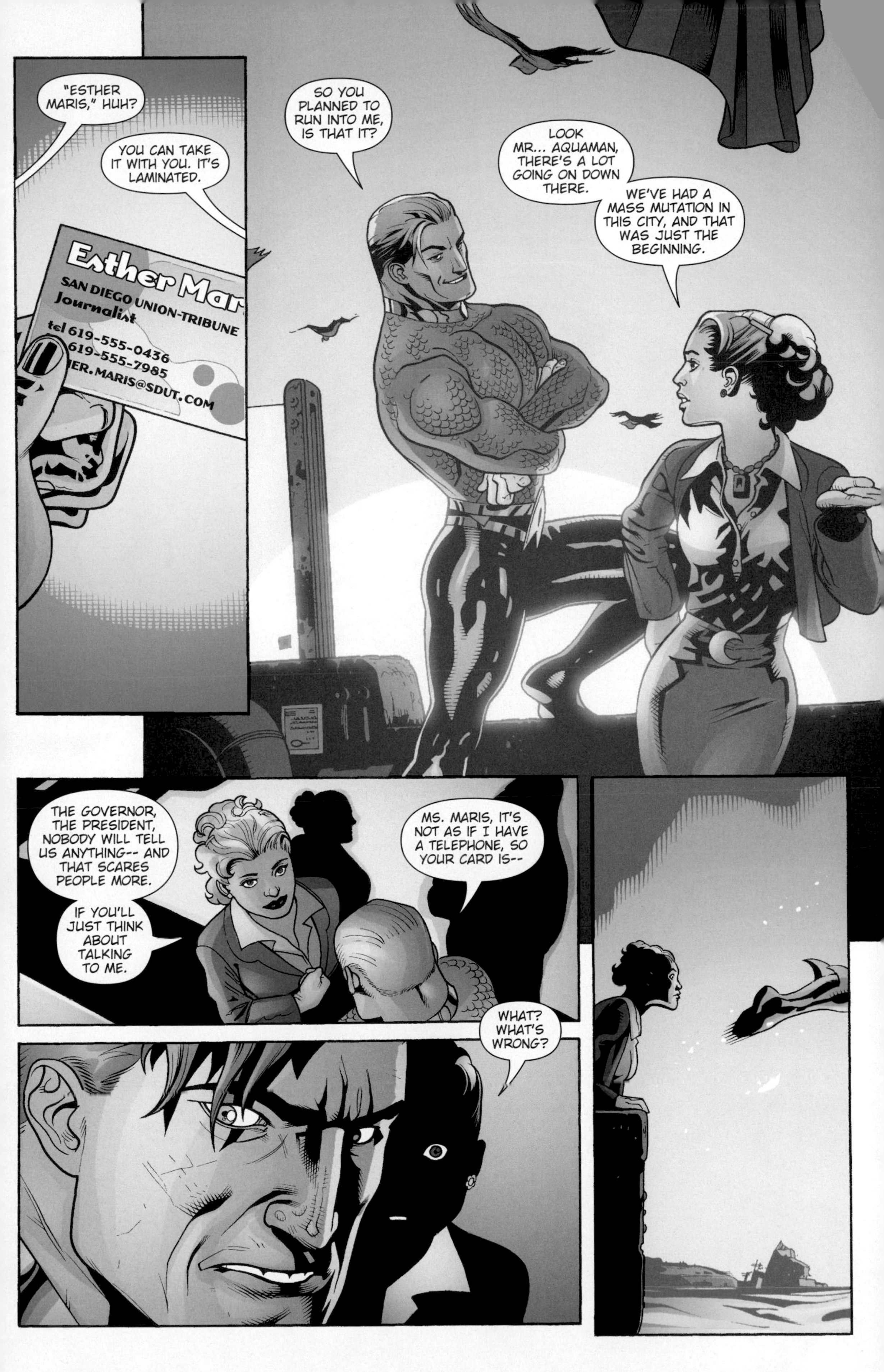
"ESTHER MARIS," HUH?
YOU CAN TAKE IT WITH YOU. IT'S LAMINATED.
Esther Mar
SAN DIEGO UNION-TRIBUNE
Journalist
tel 619-555-0436
619-555-7985
ER.MARIS@SDUT.COM
SO YOU PLANNED TO RUN INTO ME, IS THAT IT?
LOOK MR... AQUAMAN, THERE'S A LOT GOING ON DOWN THERE.
WE'VE HAD A MASS MUTATION IN THIS CITY, AND THAT WAS JUST THE BEGINNING.
THE GOVERNOR, THE PRESIDENT, NOBODY WILL TELL US ANYTHING-- AND THAT SCARES PEOPLE MORE.
IF YOU'LL JUST THINK ABOUT TALKING TO ME.
MS. MARIS, IT'S NOT AS IF I HAVE A TELEPHONE, SO YOUR CARD IS--
WHAT? WHAT'S WRONG?

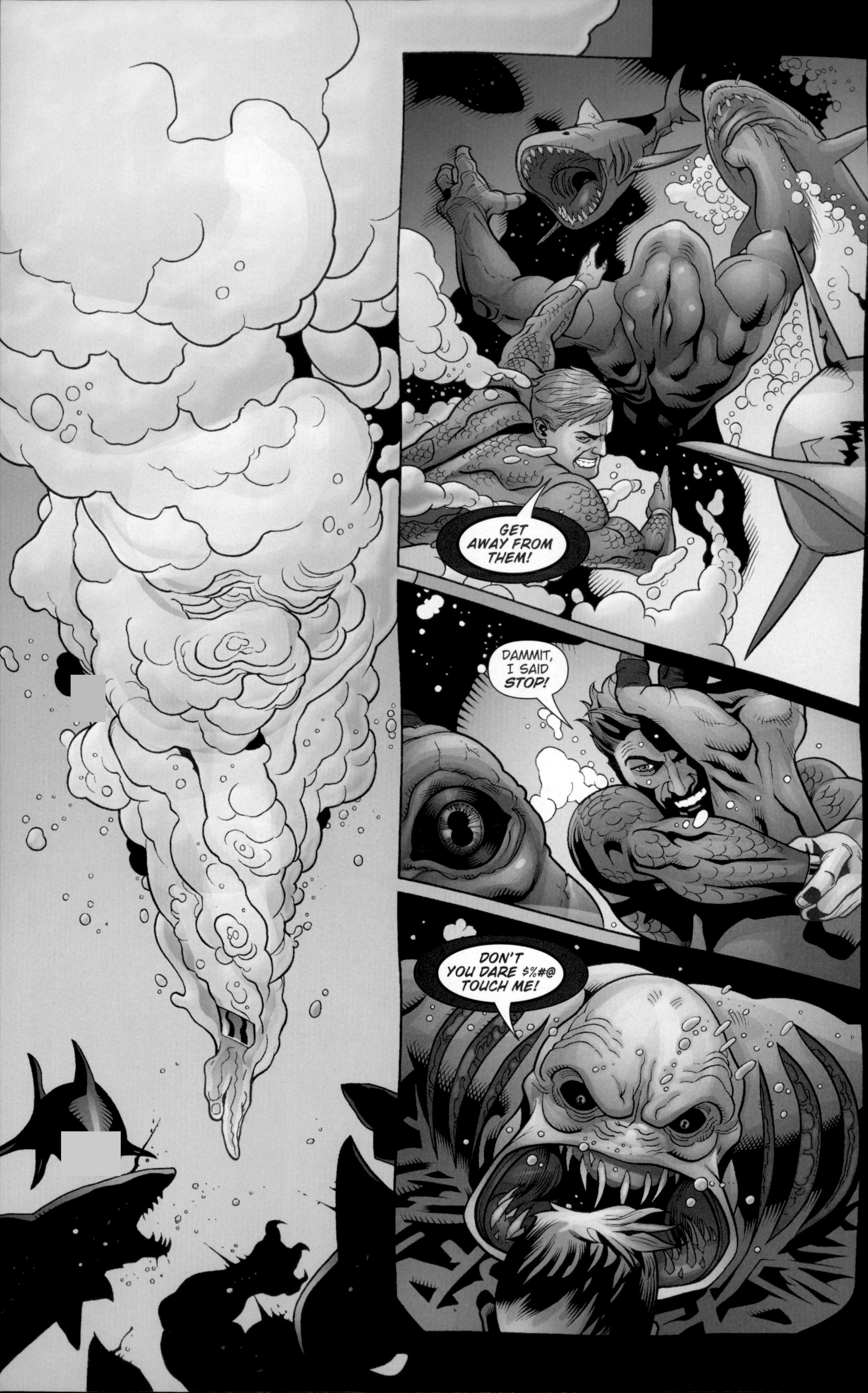
GET AWAY FROM THEM!
DAMMIT, I SAID STOP!
DON'T YOU DARE $%#@ TOUCH ME!

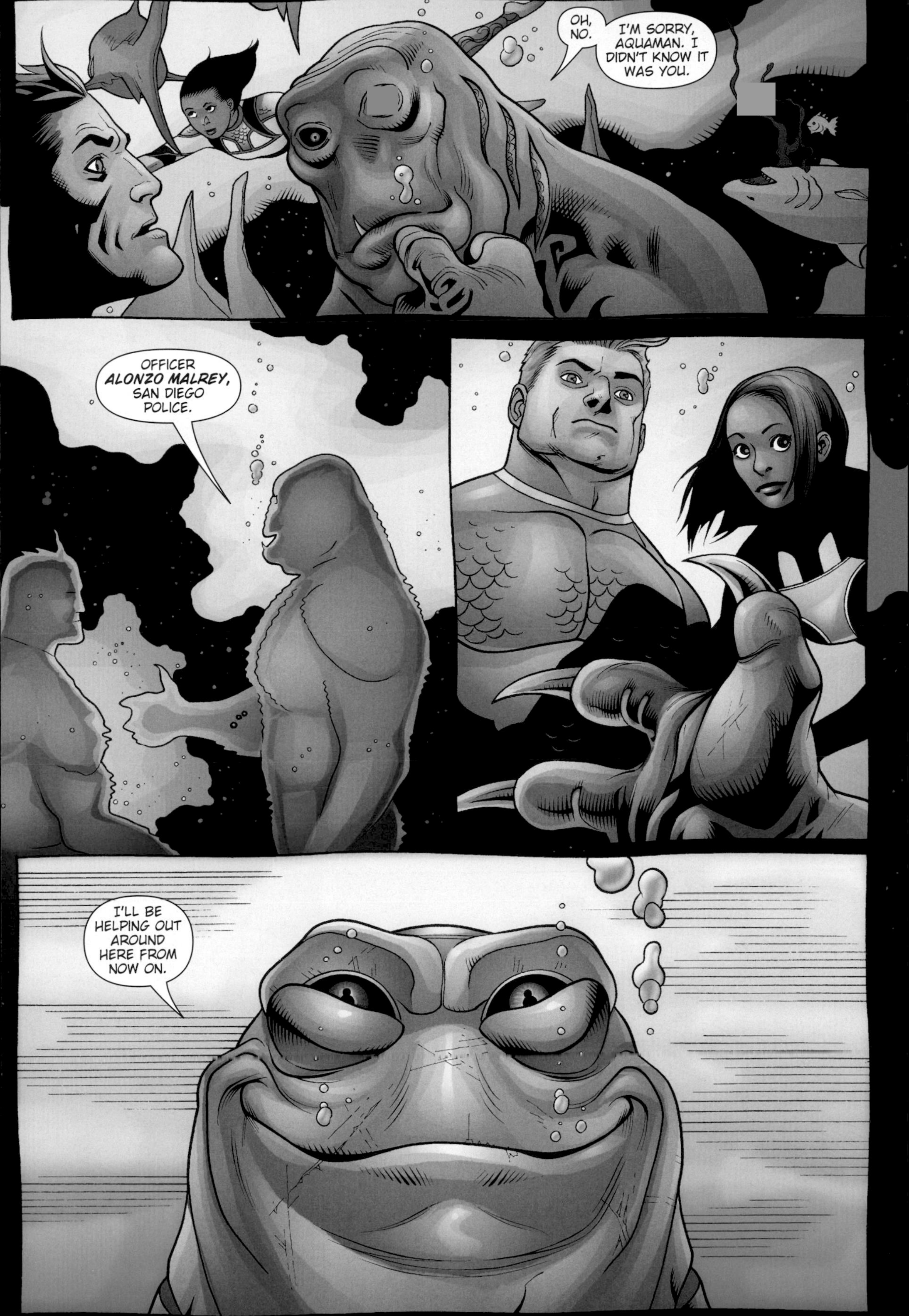
OH, NO.
I'M SORRY, AQUAMAN. I DIDN'T KNOW IT WAS YOU.
OFFICER ALONZO MALREY, SAN DIEGO POLICE.
I'LL BE HELPING OUT AROUND HERE FROM NOW ON.

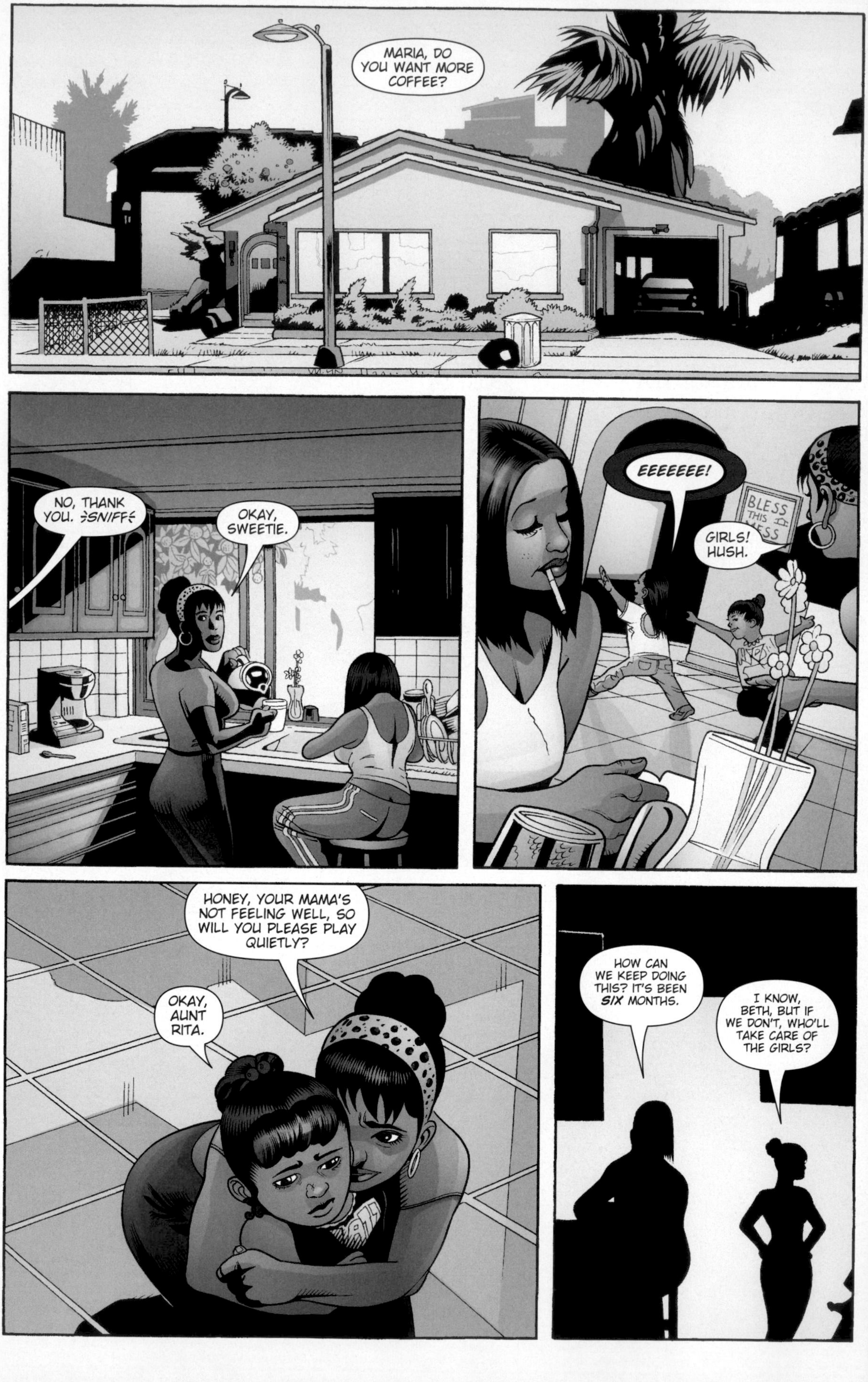
MARIA, DO YOU WANT MORE COFFEE?
NO, THANK YOU. *SNIFF*
OKAY, SWEETIE.
EEEEEEE!
BLESS THIS MESS
GIRLS! HUSH.
HONEY, YOUR MAMA'S NOT FEELING WELL, SO WILL YOU PLEASE PLAY QUIETLY?
OKAY, AUNT RITA.
HOW CAN WE KEEP DOING THIS? IT'S BEEN SIX MONTHS.
I KNOW, BETH, BUT IF WE DON'T, WHO'LL TAKE CARE OF THE GIRLS?

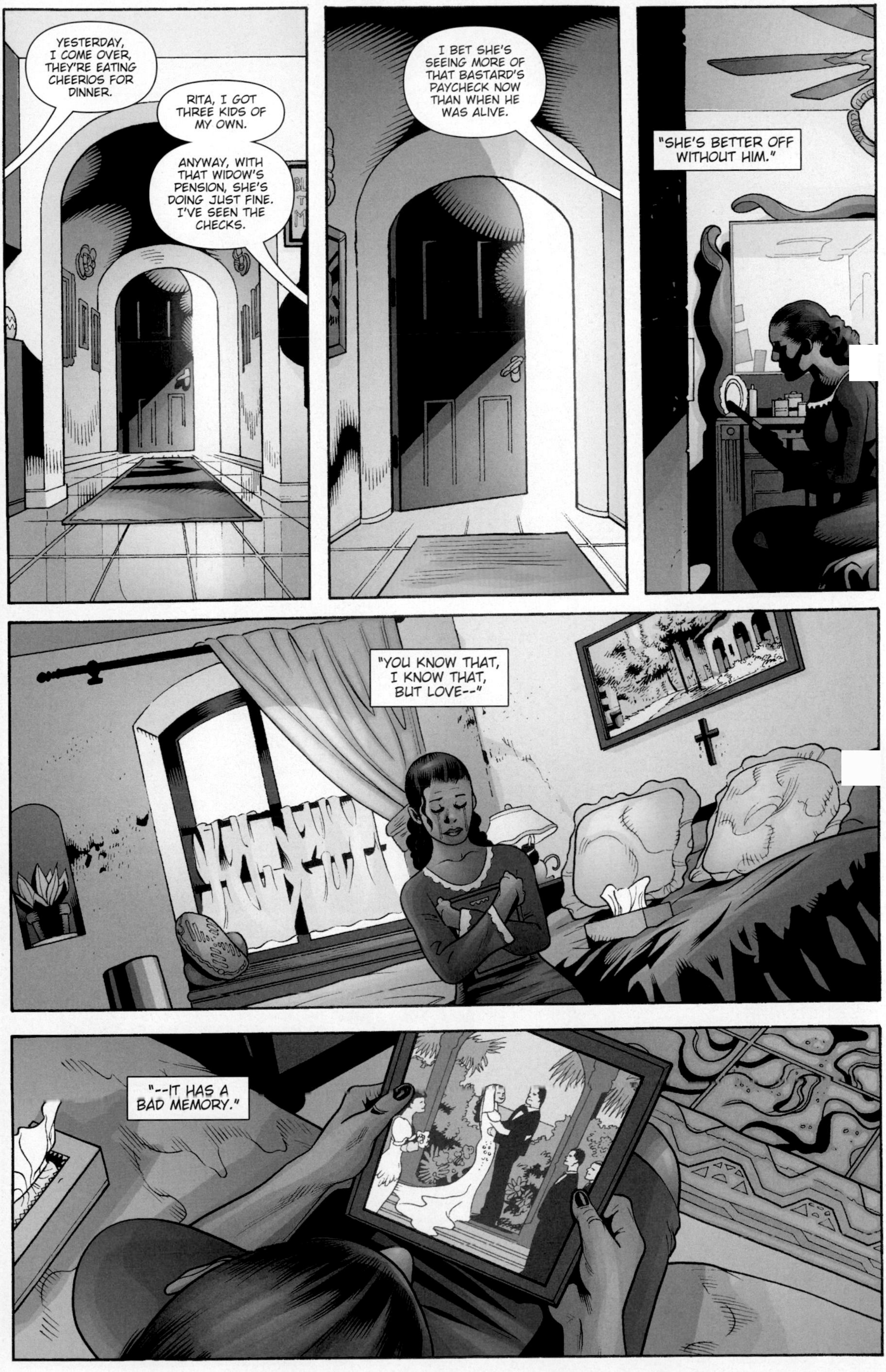
YESTERDAY, I COME OVER, THEY'RE EATING CHEERIOS FOR DINNER.
RITA, I GOT THREE KIDS OF MY OWN.
ANYWAY, WITH THAT WIDOW'S PENSION, SHE'S DOING JUST FINE. I'VE SEEN THE CHECKS.
I BET SHE'S SEEING MORE OF THAT BASTARD'S PAYCHECK NOW THAN WHEN HE WAS ALIVE.
"SHE'S BETTER OFF WITHOUT HIM."
"YOU KNOW THAT, I KNOW THAT, BUT LOVE--"
"--IT HAS A BAD MEMORY."

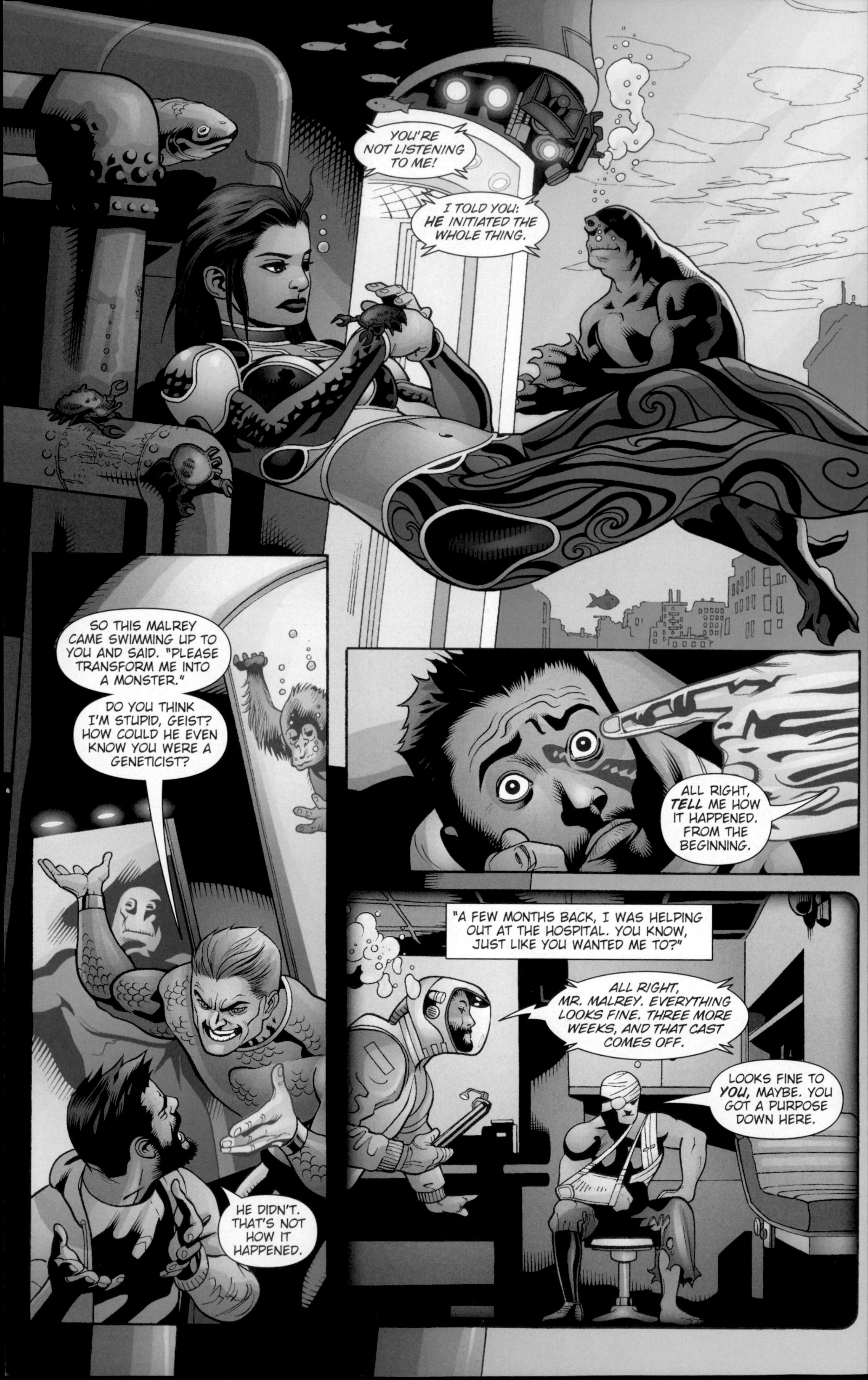

YOU'RE NOT LISTENING TO ME!
I TOLD YOU: HE INITIATED THE WHOLE THING.
SO THIS MALREY CAME SWIMMING UP TO YOU AND SAID. "PLEASE TRANSFORM ME INTO A MONSTER."
DO YOU THINK I'M STUPID, GEIST? HOW COULD HE EVEN KNOW YOU WERE A GENETICIST?
HE DIDN'T. THAT'S NOT HOW IT HAPPENED.
ALL RIGHT, TELL ME HOW IT HAPPENED. FROM THE BEGINNING.
"A FEW MONTHS BACK, I WAS HELPING OUT AT THE HOSPITAL. YOU KNOW, JUST LIKE YOU WANTED ME TO?"
ALL RIGHT, MR. MALREY. EVERYTHING LOOKS FINE. THREE MORE WEEKS, AND THAT CAST COMES OFF.
LOOKS FINE TO YOU, MAYBE. YOU GOT A PURPOSE DOWN HERE.

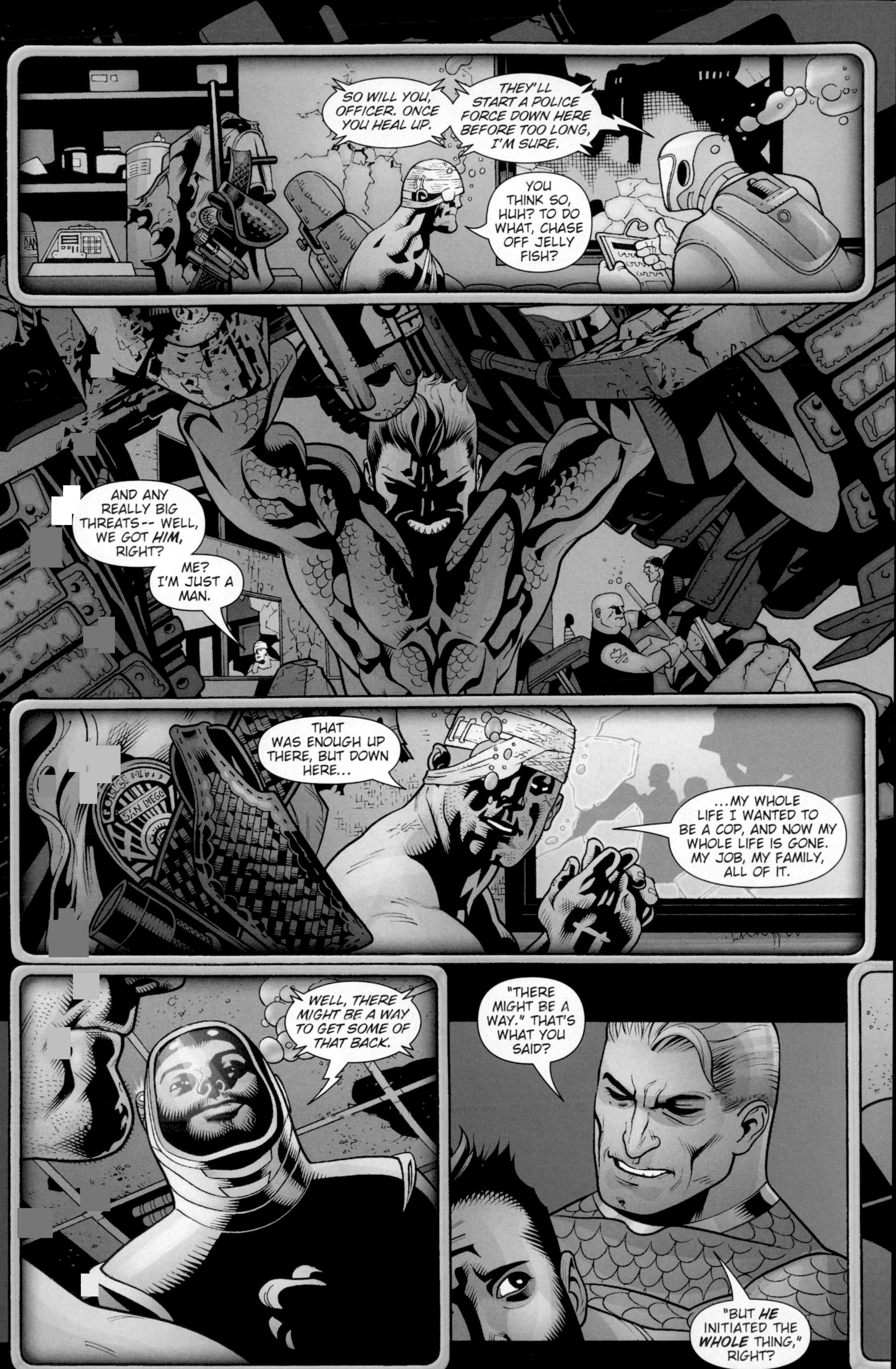
SO WILL YOU, OFFICER. ONCE YOU HEAL UP.
THEY'LL START A POLICE FORCE DOWN HERE BEFORE TOO LONG, I'M SURE.
YOU THINK SO, HUH? TO DO WHAT, CHASE OFF JELLY FISH?
AND ANY REALLY BIG THREATS-- WELL, WE GOT HIM, RIGHT?
ME? I'M JUST A MAN.
THAT WAS ENOUGH UP THERE, BUT DOWN HERE...
...MY WHOLE LIFE I WANTED TO BE A COP, AND NOW MY WHOLE LIFE IS GONE. MY JOB, MY FAMILY, ALL OF IT.
WELL, THERE MIGHT BE A WAY TO GET SOME OF THAT BACK.
"THERE MIGHT BE A WAY." THAT'S WHAT YOU SAID?
"BUT HE INITIATED THE WHOLE THING," RIGHT?

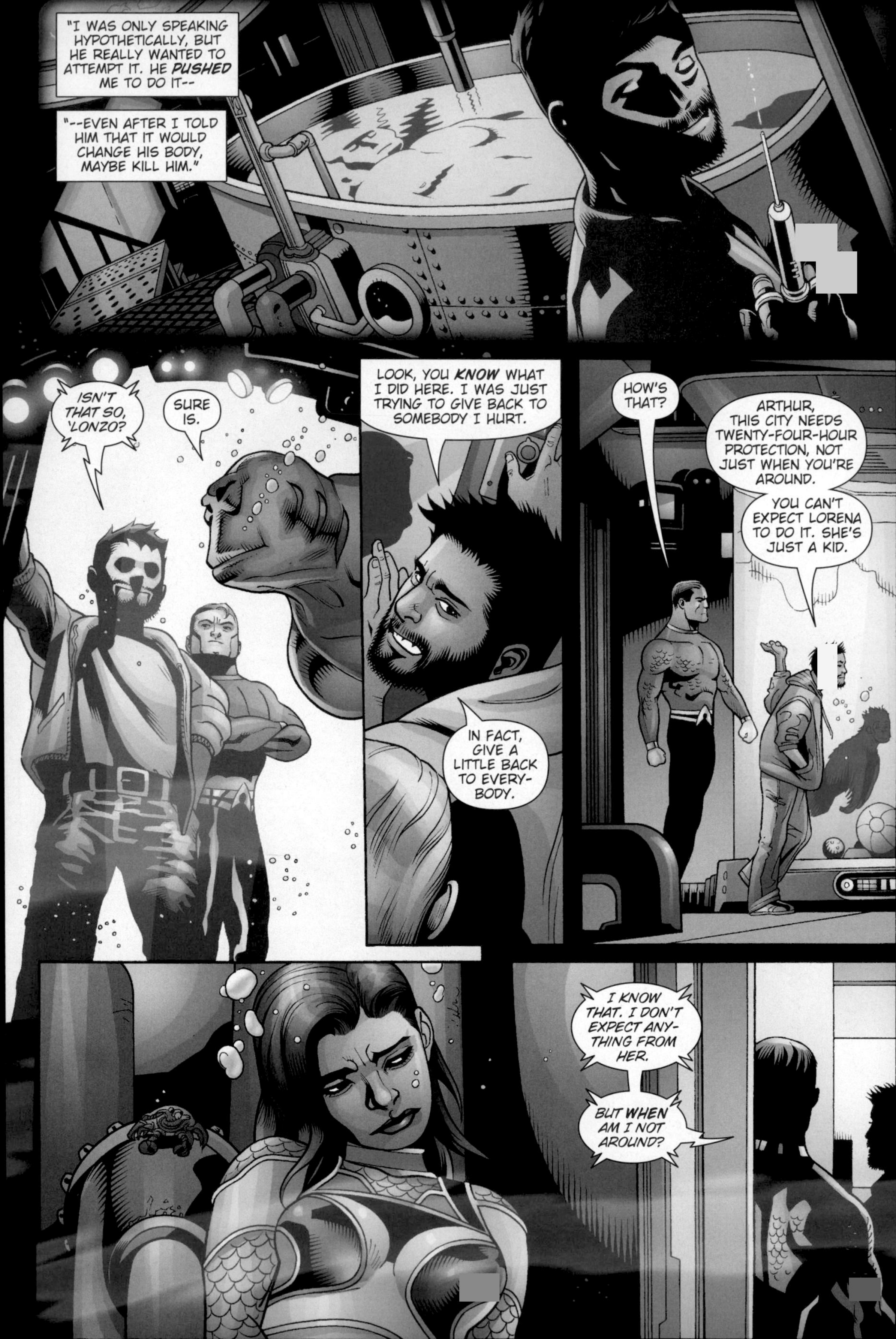
"I WAS ONLY SPEAKING HYPOTHETICALLY, BUT HE REALLY WANTED TO ATTEMPT IT. HE PUSHED ME TO DO IT--
"--EVEN AFTER I TOLD HIM THAT IT WOULD CHANGE HIS BODY, MAYBE KILL HIM."
ISN'T THAT SO, 'LONZO?
SURE IS.
LOOK, YOU KNOW WHAT I DID HERE. I WAS JUST TRYING TO GIVE BACK TO SOMEBODY I HURT.
IN FACT, GIVE A LITTLE BACK TO EVERY-BODY.
HOW'S THAT?
ARTHUR, THIS CITY NEEDS TWENTY-FOUR-HOUR PROTECTION, NOT JUST WHEN YOU'RE AROUND.
YOU CAN'T EXPECT LORENA TO DO IT. SHE'S JUST A KID.
I KNOW THAT. I DON'T EXPECT ANY-THING FROM HER.
BUT WHEN AM I NOT AROUND?

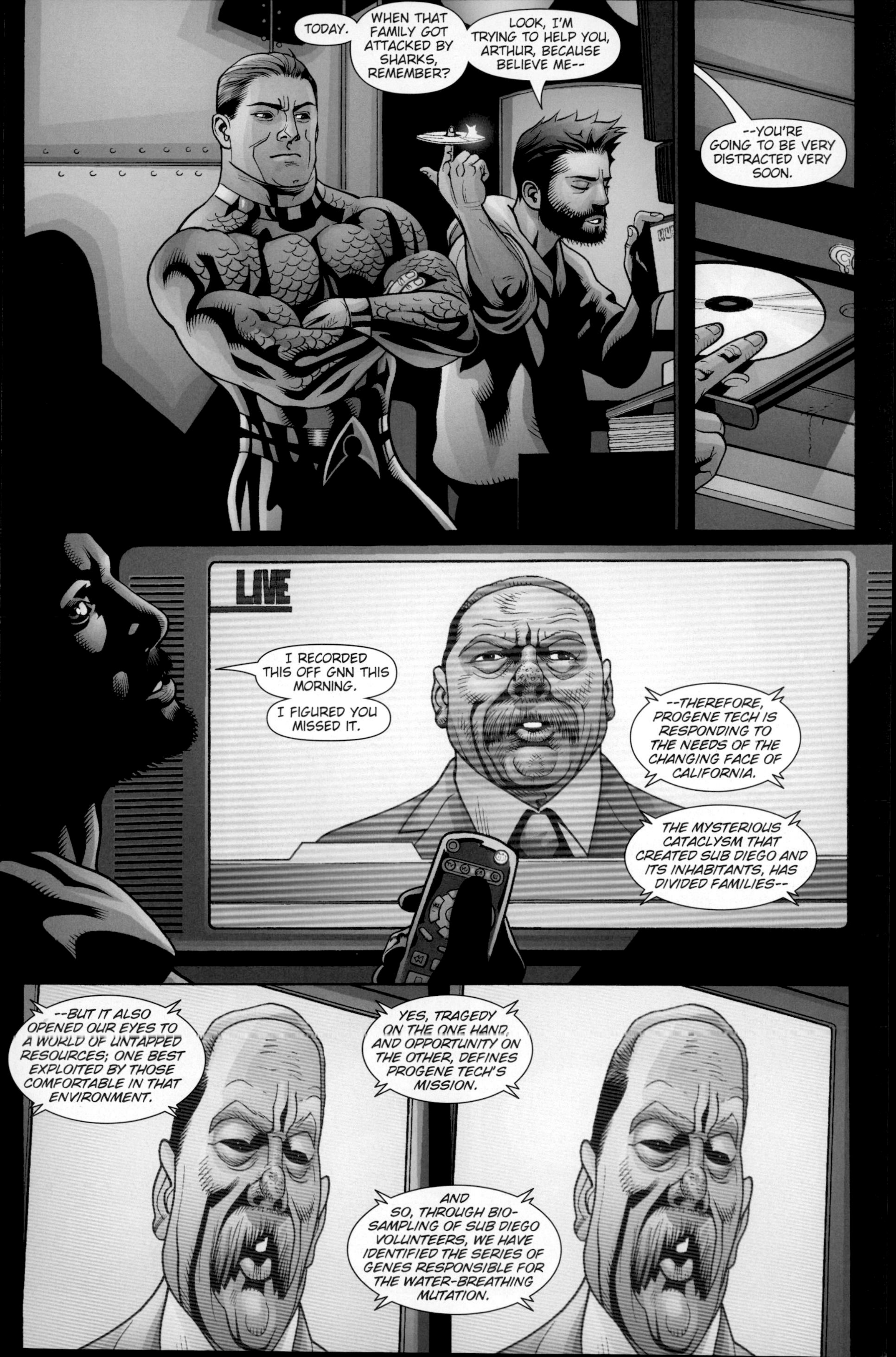
TODAY.
WHEN THAT FAMILY GOT ATTACKED BY SHARKS, REMEMBER?
LOOK, I'M TRYING TO HELP YOU, ARTHUR, BECAUSE BELIEVE ME--
--YOU'RE GOING TO BE VERY DISTRACTED VERY SOON.
LIVE
I RECORDED THIS OFF GNN THIS MORNING.
I FIGURED YOU MISSED IT.
--THEREFORE, PROGENE TECH IS RESPONDING TO THE NEEDS OF THE CHANGING FACE OF CALIFORNIA.
THE MYSTERIOUS CATACLYSM THAT CREATED SUB DIEGO AND ITS INHABITANTS, HAS DIVIDED FAMILIES--
--BUT IT ALSO OPENED OUR EYES TO A WORLD OF UNTAPPED RESOURCES; ONE BEST EXPLOITED BY THOSE COMFORTABLE IN THAT ENVIRONMENT.
YES, TRAGEDY ON THE ONE HAND, AND OPPORTUNITY ON THE OTHER, DEFINES PROGENE TECH'S MISSION.
AND SO, THROUGH BIO-SAMPLING OF SUB DIEGO VOLUNTEERS, WE HAVE IDENTIFIED THE SERIES OF GENES RESPONSIBLE FOR THE WATER-BREATHING MUTATION.

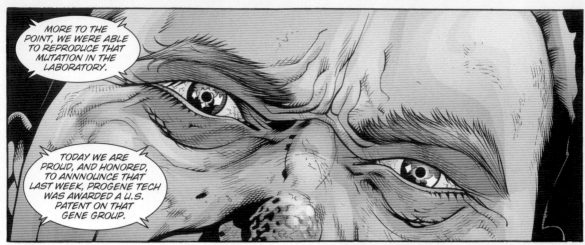

MORE TO THE POINT, WE WERE ABLE TO REPRODUCE THAT MUTATION IN THE LABORATORY.

TODAY WE ARE PROUD, AND HONORED, TO ANNNOUNCE THAT LAST WEEK, PROGENE TECH WAS AWARDED A U.S. PATENT ON THAT GENE GROUP.

SOON, WE WILL DEVELOP A GENE THERAPY THAT, WE HOPE, WILL REUNITIE FAMILIES, AND BRING THE OCEAN FLOOR'S RICHES TO OUR DOORSTEP.

AND NOW, I'LL TAKE ANY QUESTIONS.

I'LL BET *YOU* HAVE A FEW.

FROM SUB DIEGO VOLUNTEERS? BUT THAT MEANS...

KLIK

RIGHT. THAT MEANS THEY OBSERVED THE GENETIC ANOMALY I INTRODUCED INTO THE SAN DIEGO POPULATION YEARS AGO.

THE ANOMALY I EXTRACTED FROM *YOU*.

AND IF THEY'VE PATENTED IT, DO YOU SEE WHAT *THAT* MEANS?

THEY *OWN* YOUR DNA!

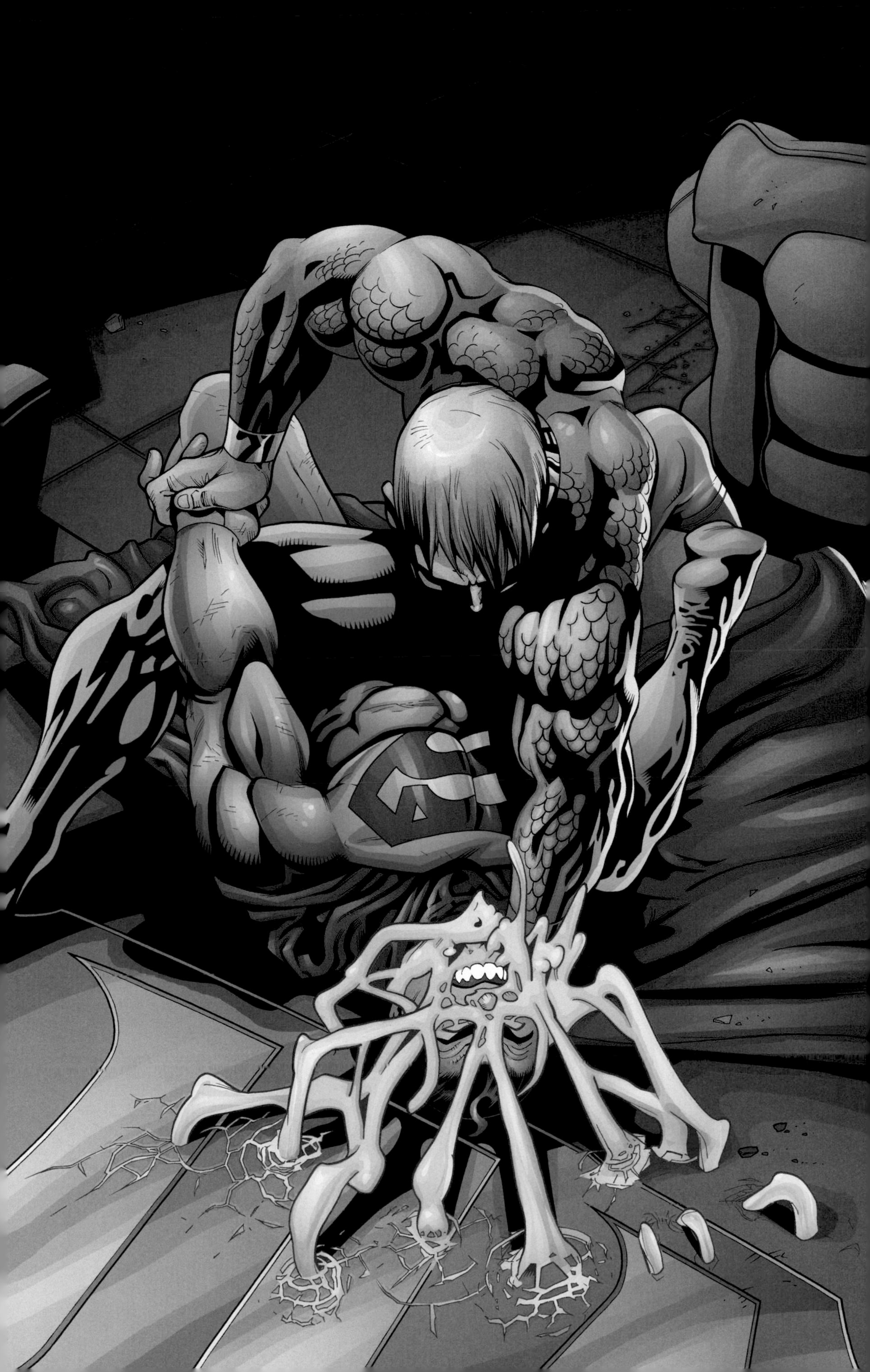

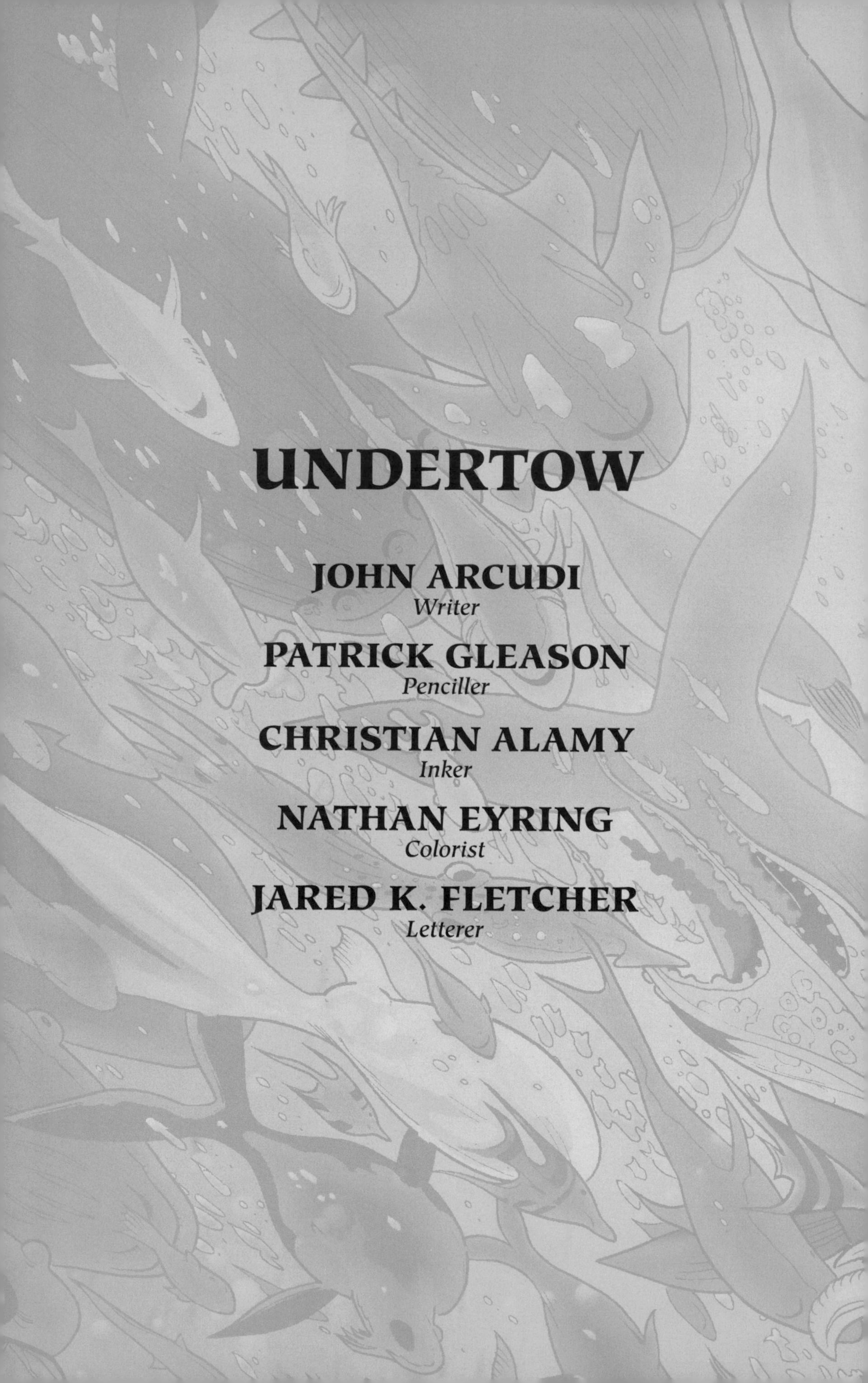

UNDERTOW

JOHN ARCUDI
Writer

PATRICK GLEASON
Penciller

CHRISTIAN ALAMY
Inker

NATHAN EYRING
Colorist

JARED K. FLETCHER
Letterer

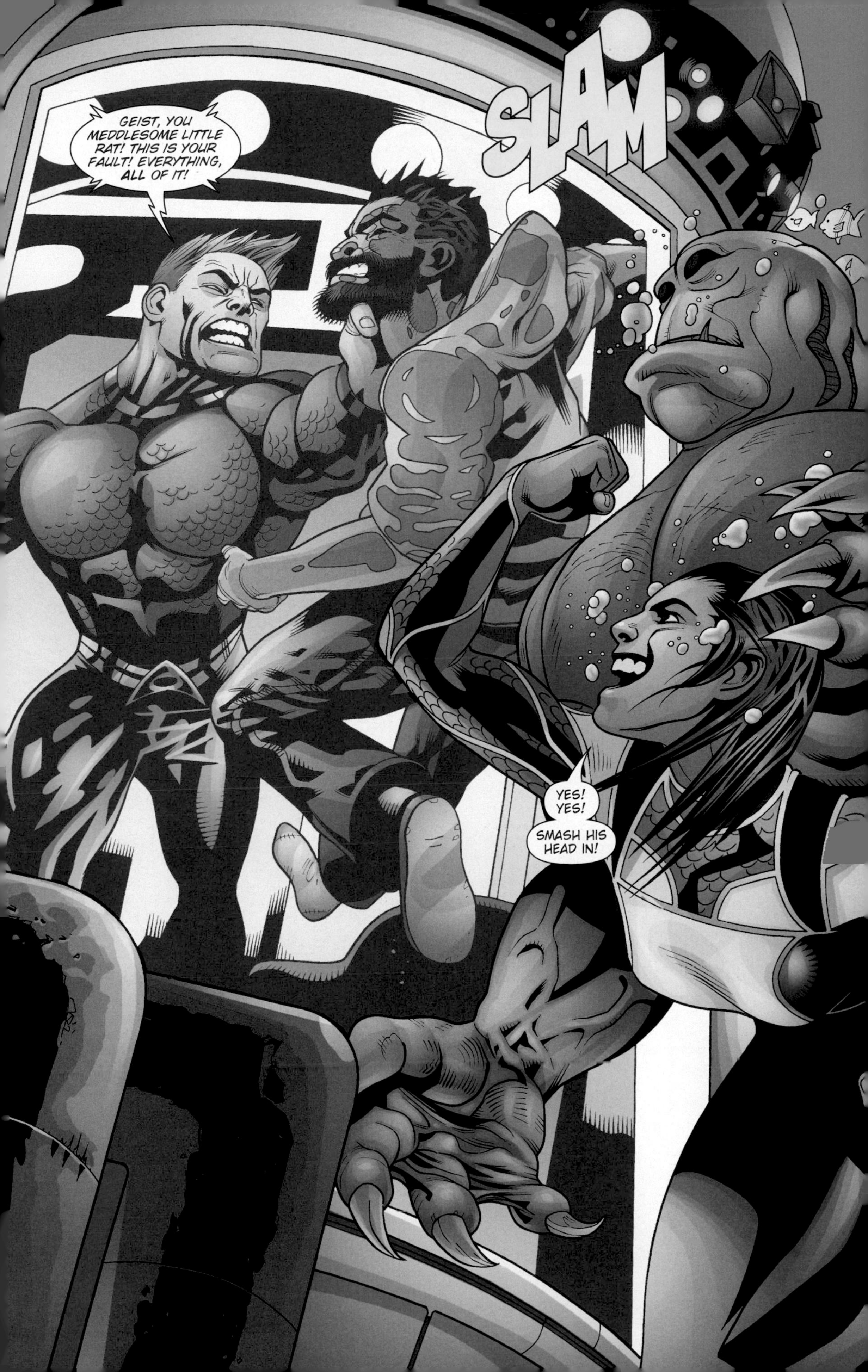
GEIST, YOU MEDDLESOME LITTLE RAT! THIS IS YOUR FAULT! EVERYTHING, ALL OF IT!
SLAM
YES! YES!
SMASH HIS HEAD IN!

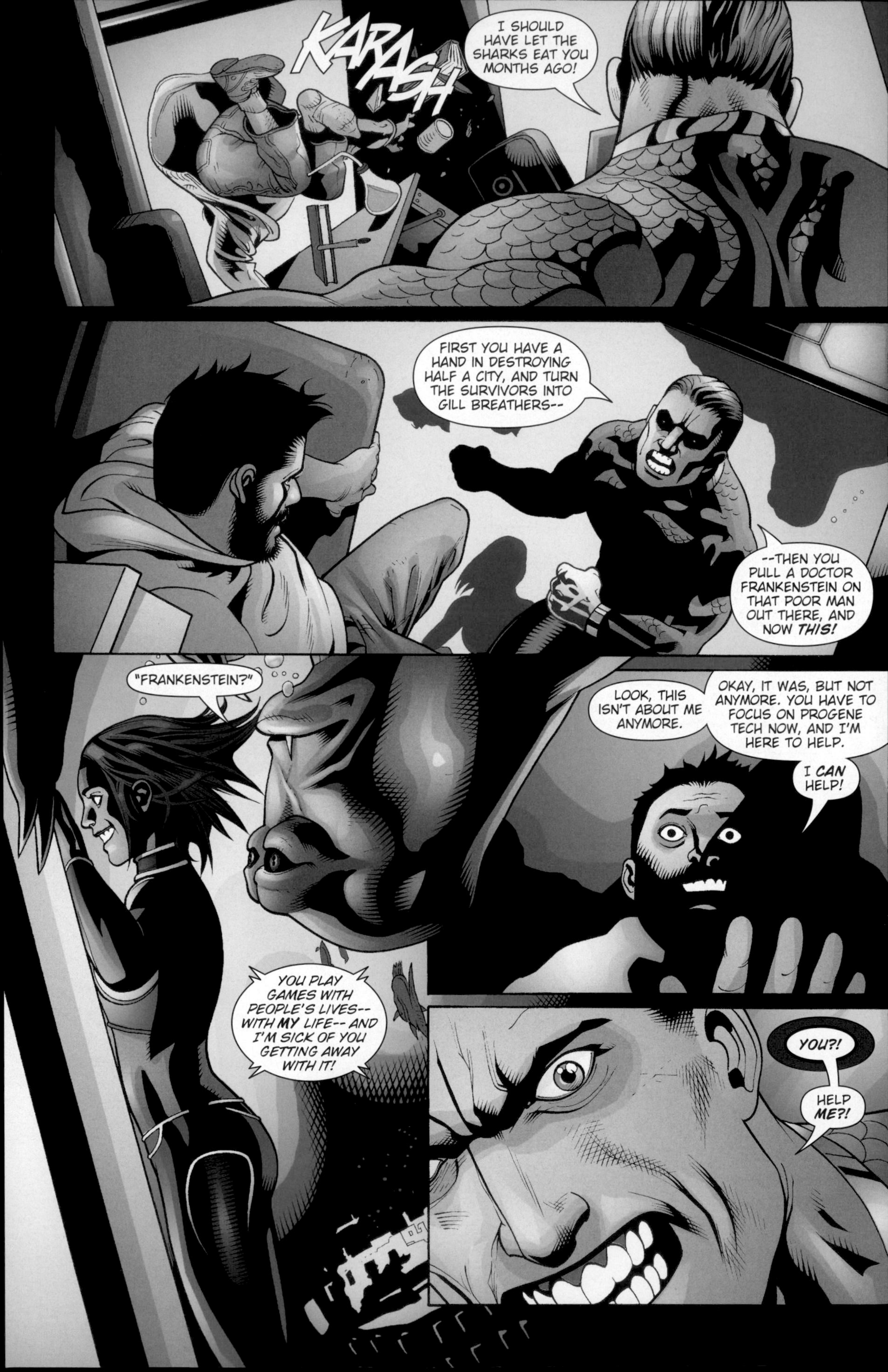
KARASH
I SHOULD HAVE LET THE SHARKS EAT YOU MONTHS AGO!
FIRST YOU HAVE A HAND IN DESTROYING HALF A CITY, AND TURN THE SURVIVORS INTO GILL BREATHERS--
--THEN YOU PULL A DOCTOR FRANKENSTEIN ON THAT POOR MAN OUT THERE, AND NOW THIS!
"FRANKENSTEIN?"
LOOK, THIS ISN'T ABOUT ME ANYMORE.
OKAY, IT WAS, BUT NOT ANYMORE. YOU HAVE TO FOCUS ON PROGENE TECH NOW, AND I'M HERE TO HELP.
I CAN HELP!
YOU PLAY GAMES WITH PEOPLE'S LIVES-- WITH MY LIFE-- AND I'M SICK OF YOU GETTING AWAY WITH IT!
YOU?!
HELP ME?!

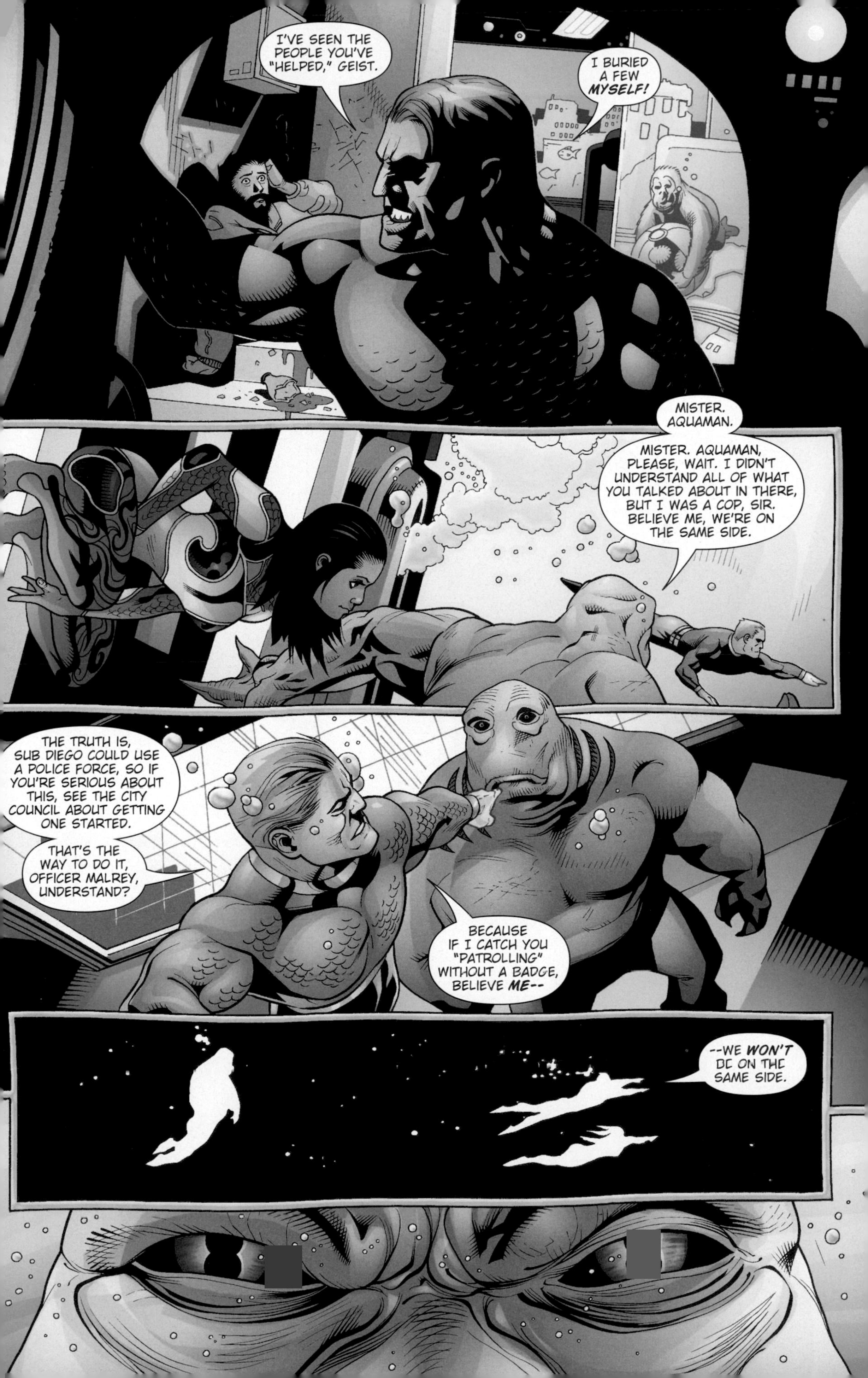
I'VE SEEN THE PEOPLE YOU'VE "HELPED," GEIST.
I BURIED A FEW *MYSELF!*
MISTER. AQUAMAN.
MISTER. AQUAMAN, PLEASE, WAIT. I DIDN'T UNDERSTAND ALL OF WHAT YOU TALKED ABOUT IN THERE, BUT I WAS A COP, SIR. BELIEVE ME, WE'RE ON THE SAME SIDE.
THE TRUTH IS, SUB DIEGO COULD USE A POLICE FORCE, SO IF YOU'RE SERIOUS ABOUT THIS, SEE THE CITY COUNCIL ABOUT GETTING ONE STARTED.
THAT'S THE WAY TO DO IT, OFFICER MALREY, UNDERSTAND?
BECAUSE IF I CATCH YOU "PATROLLING" WITHOUT A BADGE, BELIEVE *ME*--
--WE *WON'T* BE ON THE SAME SIDE.

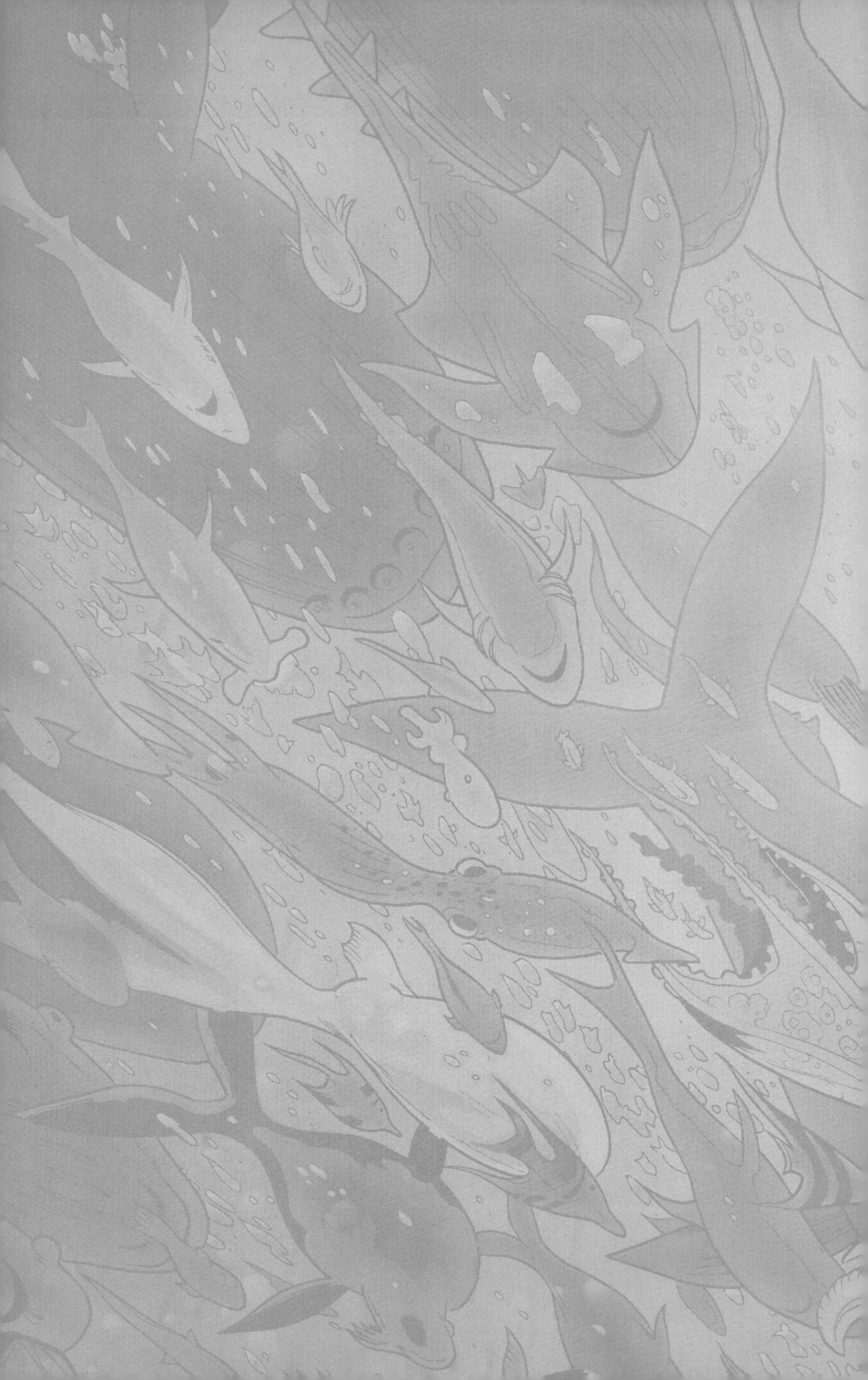

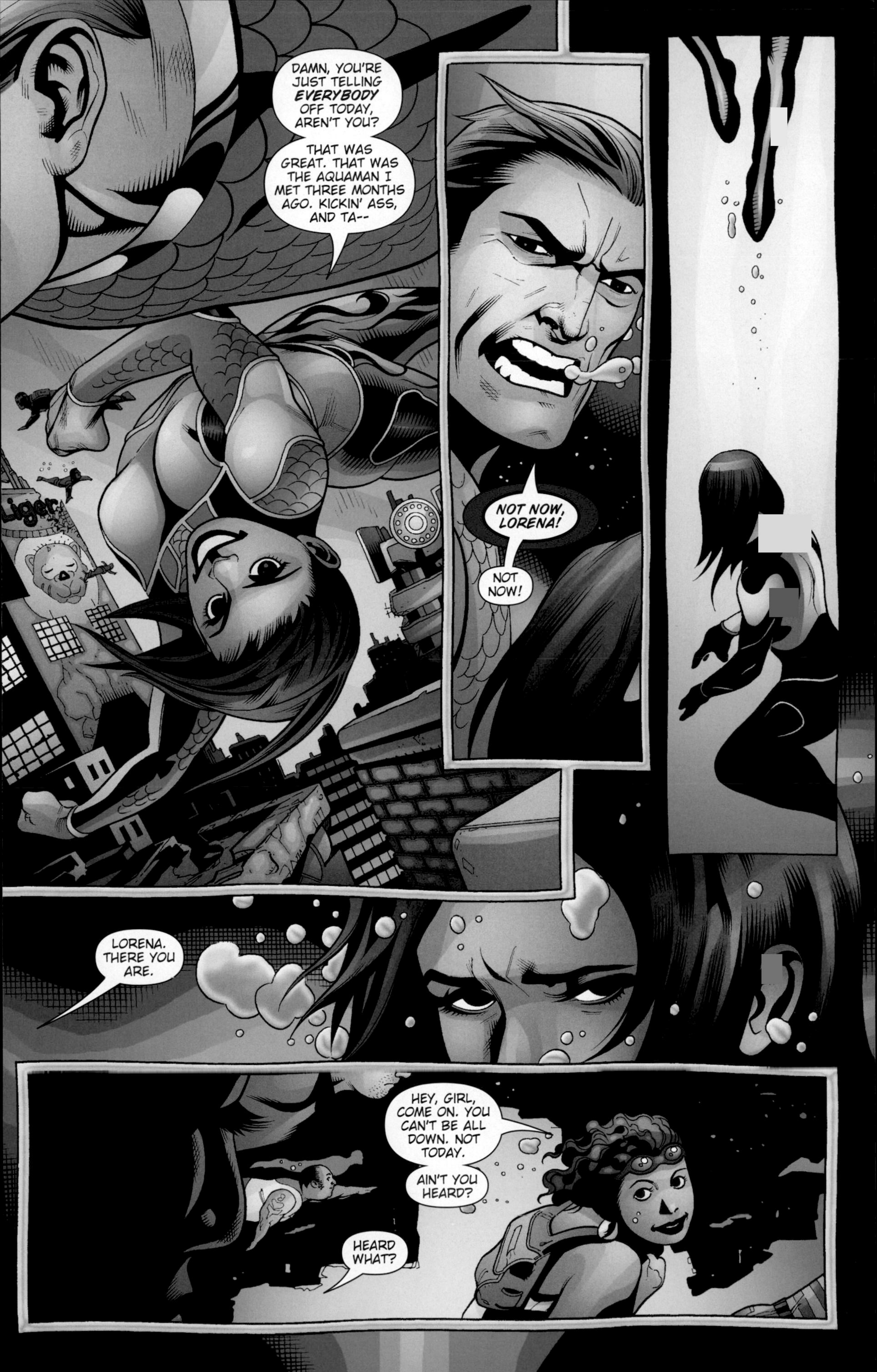
DAMN, YOU'RE JUST TELLING ***EVERYBODY*** OFF TODAY, AREN'T YOU?
THAT WAS GREAT. THAT WAS THE AQUAMAN I MET THREE MONTHS AGO. KICKIN' ASS, AND TA--
NOT NOW, LORENA!
NOT NOW!
Liger
LORENA. THERE YOU ARE.
HEY, GIRL, COME ON. YOU CAN'T BE ALL DOWN. NOT TODAY.
AIN'T YOU HEARD?
HEARD WHAT?

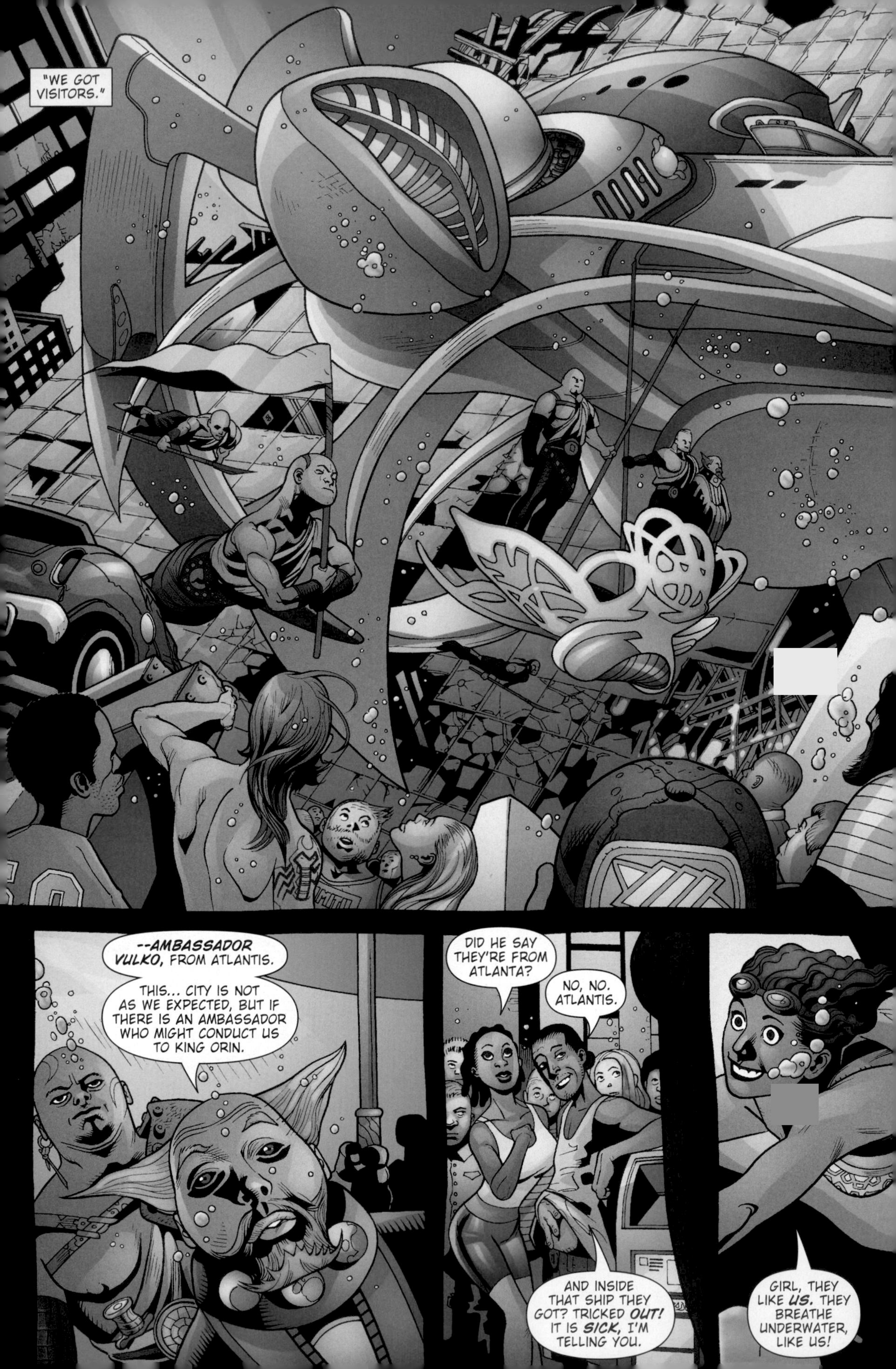
"WE GOT VISITORS."
--AMBASSADOR VULKO, FROM ATLANTIS.
THIS... CITY IS NOT AS WE EXPECTED, BUT IF THERE IS AN AMBASSADOR WHO MIGHT CONDUCT US TO KING ORIN.
DID HE SAY THEY'RE FROM ATLANTA?
NO, NO. ATLANTIS.
AND INSIDE THAT SHIP THEY GOT? TRICKED OUT! IT IS SICK, I'M TELLING YOU.
GIRL, THEY LIKE US. THEY BREATHE UNDERWATER, LIKE US!

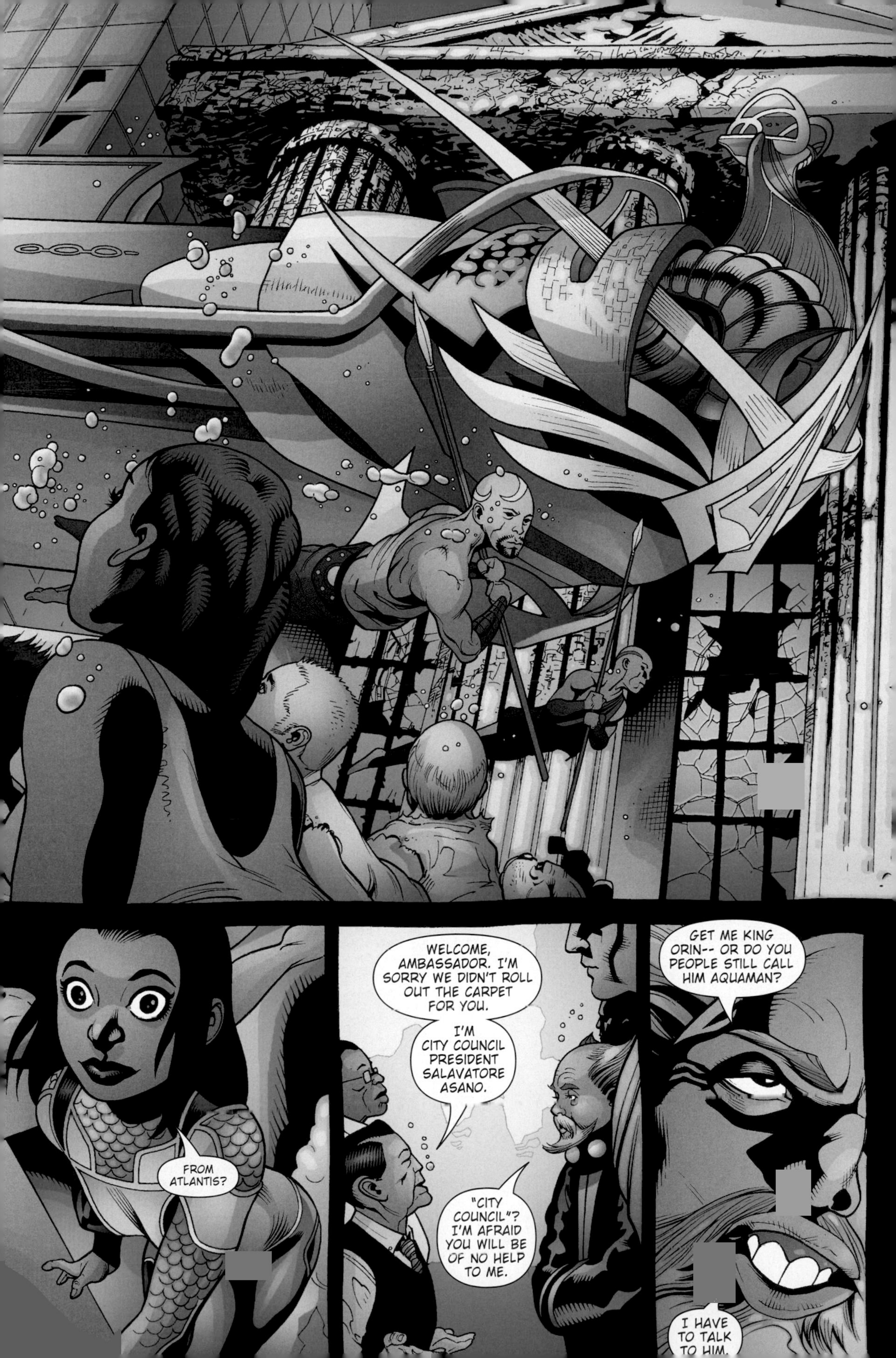
FROM ATLANTIS?
WELCOME, AMBASSADOR. I'M SORRY WE DIDN'T ROLL OUT THE CARPET FOR YOU.
I'M CITY COUNCIL PRESIDENT SALVATORE ASANO.
"CITY COUNCIL"? I'M AFRAID YOU WILL BE OF NO HELP TO ME.
GET ME KING ORIN-- OR DO YOU PEOPLE STILL CALL HIM AQUAMAN?
I HAVE TO TALK TO HIM.

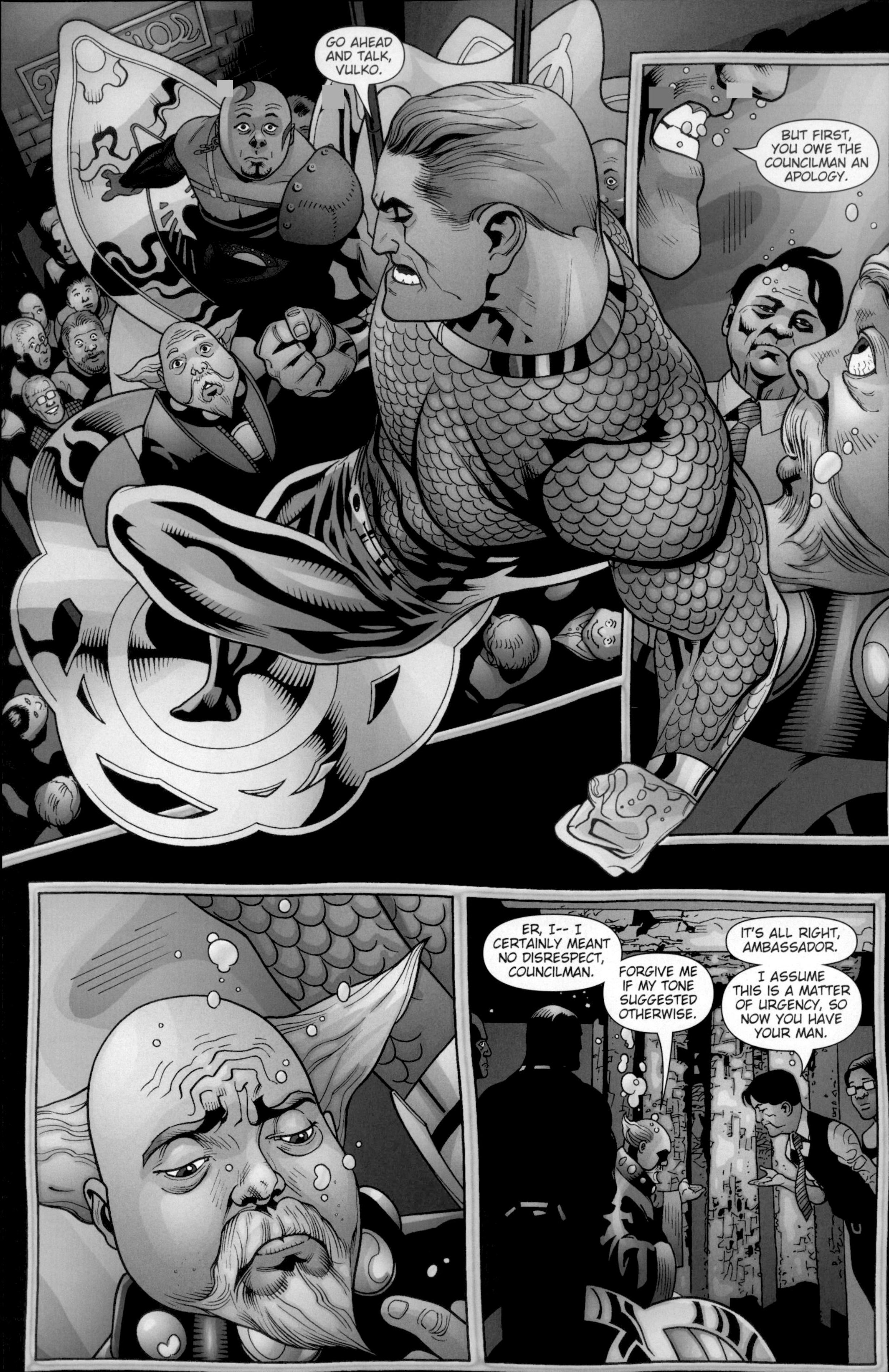
GO AHEAD AND TALK, VULKO.
BUT FIRST, YOU OWE THE COUNCILMAN AN APOLOGY.
ER, I-- I CERTAINLY MEANT NO DISRESPECT, COUNCILMAN.
FORGIVE ME IF MY TONE SUGGESTED OTHERWISE.
IT'S ALL RIGHT, AMBASSADOR.
I ASSUME THIS IS A MATTER OF URGENCY, SO NOW YOU HAVE YOUR MAN.

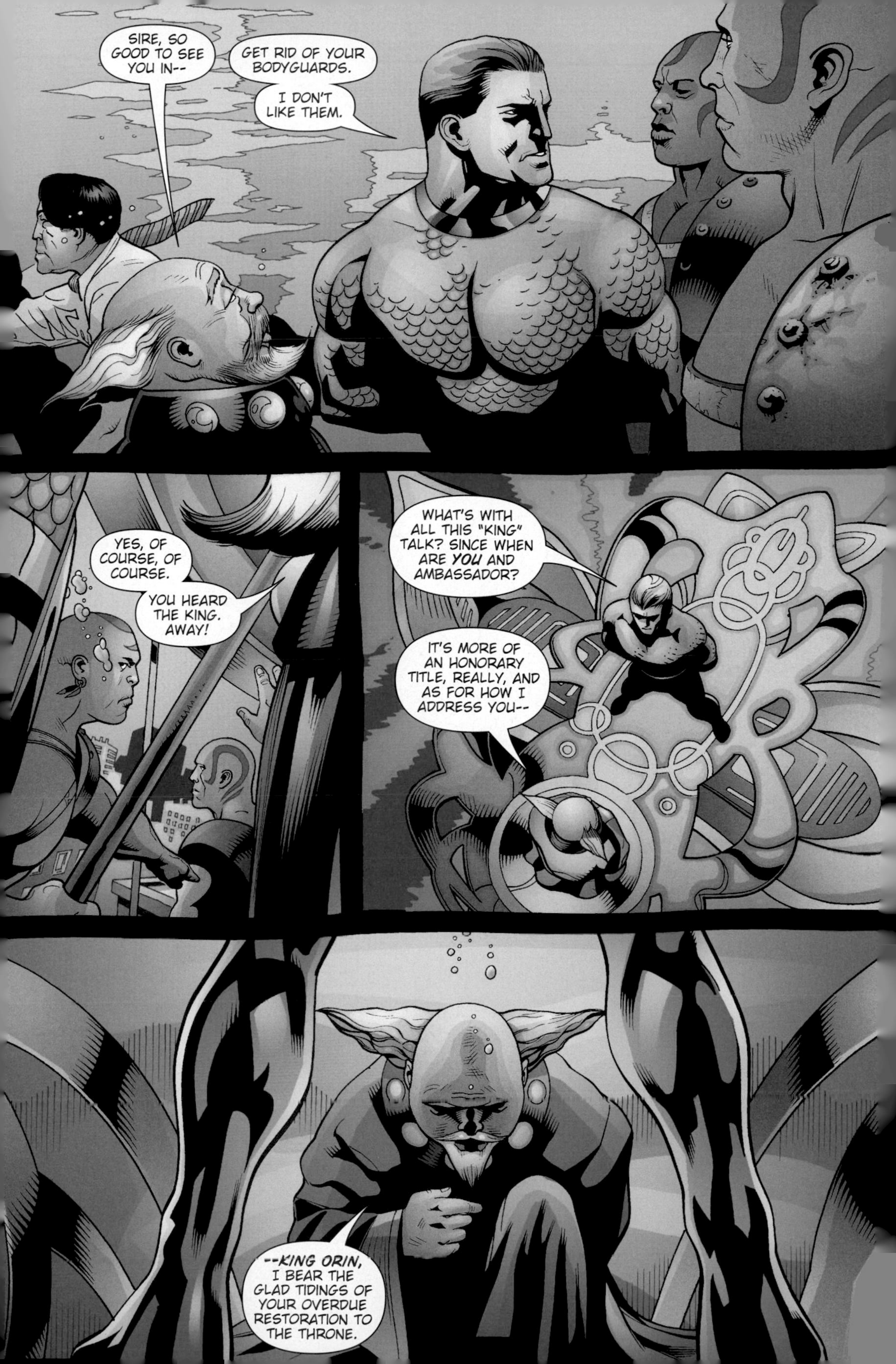

SIRE, SO GOOD TO SEE YOU IN--
GET RID OF YOUR BODYGUARDS.
I DON'T LIKE THEM.
YES, OF COURSE, OF COURSE.
YOU HEARD THE KING. AWAY!
WHAT'S WITH ALL THIS "KING" TALK? SINCE WHEN ARE *YOU* AND AMBASSADOR?
IT'S MORE OF AN HONORARY TITLE, REALLY, AND AS FOR HOW I ADDRESS YOU--
--*KING ORIN*, I BEAR THE GLAD TIDINGS OF YOUR OVERDUE RESTORATION TO THE THRONE.

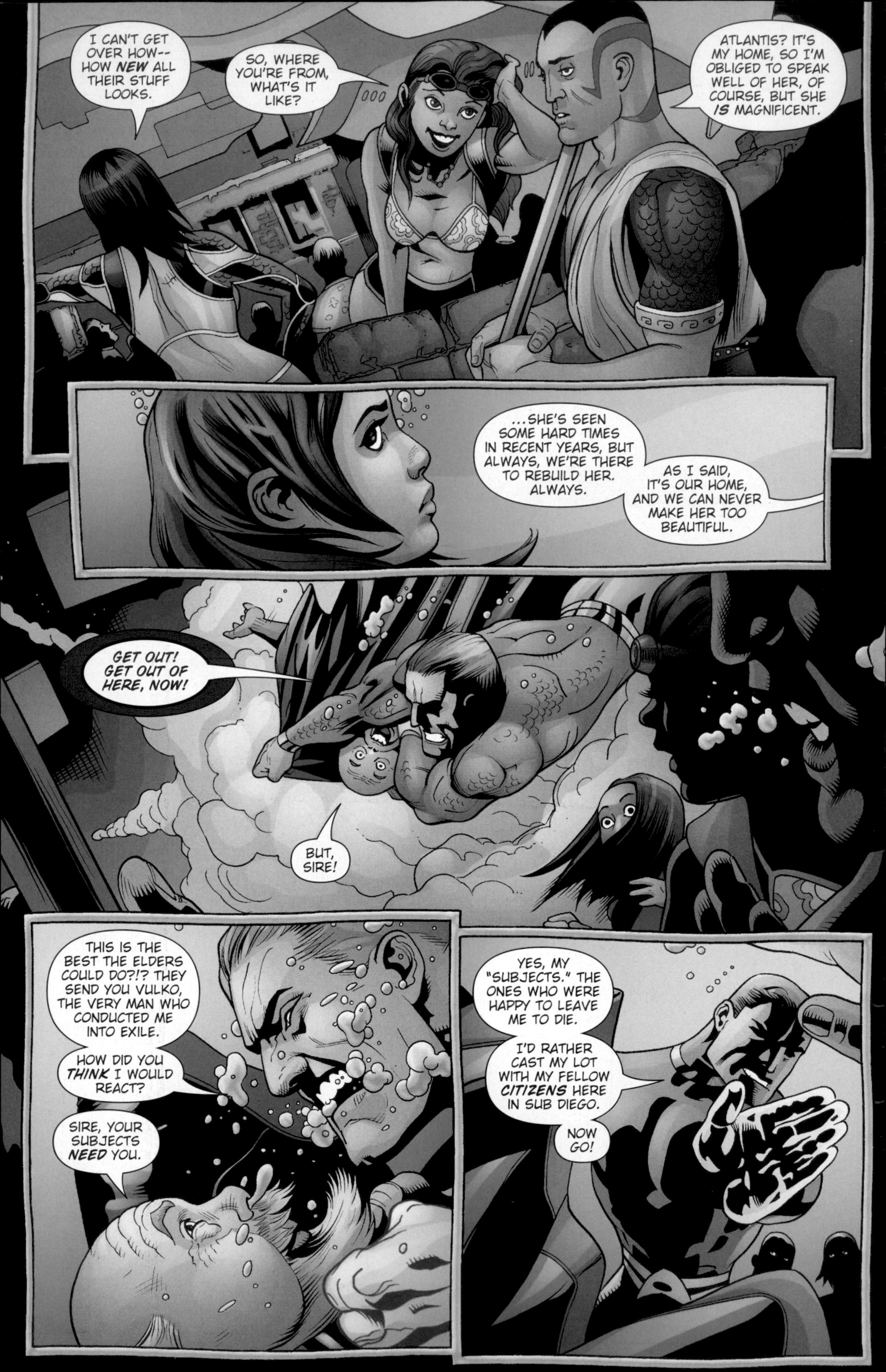
I CAN'T GET OVER HOW-- HOW NEW ALL THEIR STUFF LOOKS.
SO, WHERE YOU'RE FROM, WHAT'S IT LIKE?
ATLANTIS? IT'S MY HOME, SO I'M OBLIGED TO SPEAK WELL OF HER, OF COURSE, BUT SHE IS MAGNIFICENT.
...SHE'S SEEN SOME HARD TIMES IN RECENT YEARS, BUT ALWAYS, WE'RE THERE TO REBUILD HER. ALWAYS.
AS I SAID, IT'S OUR HOME, AND WE CAN NEVER MAKE HER TOO BEAUTIFUL.
GET OUT! GET OUT OF HERE, NOW!
BUT, SIRE!
THIS IS THE BEST THE ELDERS COULD DO?!? THEY SEND YOU VULKO, THE VERY MAN WHO CONDUCTED ME INTO EXILE.
HOW DID YOU THINK I WOULD REACT?
SIRE, YOUR SUBJECTS NEED YOU.
YES, MY "SUBJECTS." THE ONES WHO WERE HAPPY TO LEAVE ME TO DIE.
I'D RATHER CAST MY LOT WITH MY FELLOW CITIZENS HERE IN SUB DIEGO.
NOW GO!

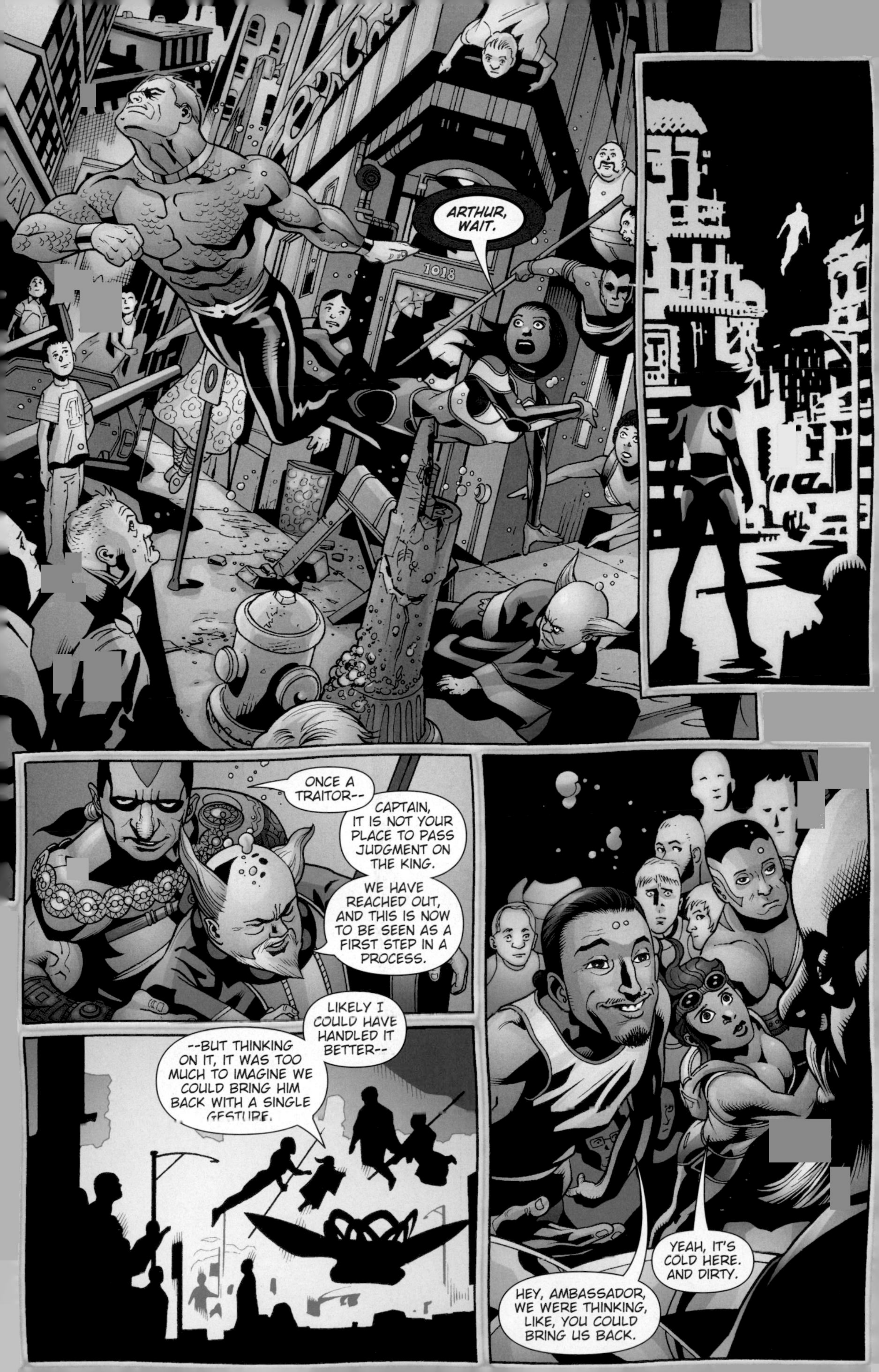
ARTHUR, WAIT.
1018
ONCE A TRAITOR--
CAPTAIN, IT IS NOT YOUR PLACE TO PASS JUDGMENT ON THE KING.
WE HAVE REACHED OUT, AND THIS IS NOW TO BE SEEN AS A FIRST STEP IN A PROCESS.
LIKELY I COULD HAVE HANDLED IT BETTER--
--BUT THINKING ON IT, IT WAS TOO MUCH TO IMAGINE WE COULD BRING HIM BACK WITH A SINGLE GESTURE.
HEY, AMBASSADOR, WE WERE THINKING, LIKE, YOU COULD BRING US BACK.
YEAH, IT'S COLD HERE. AND DIRTY.

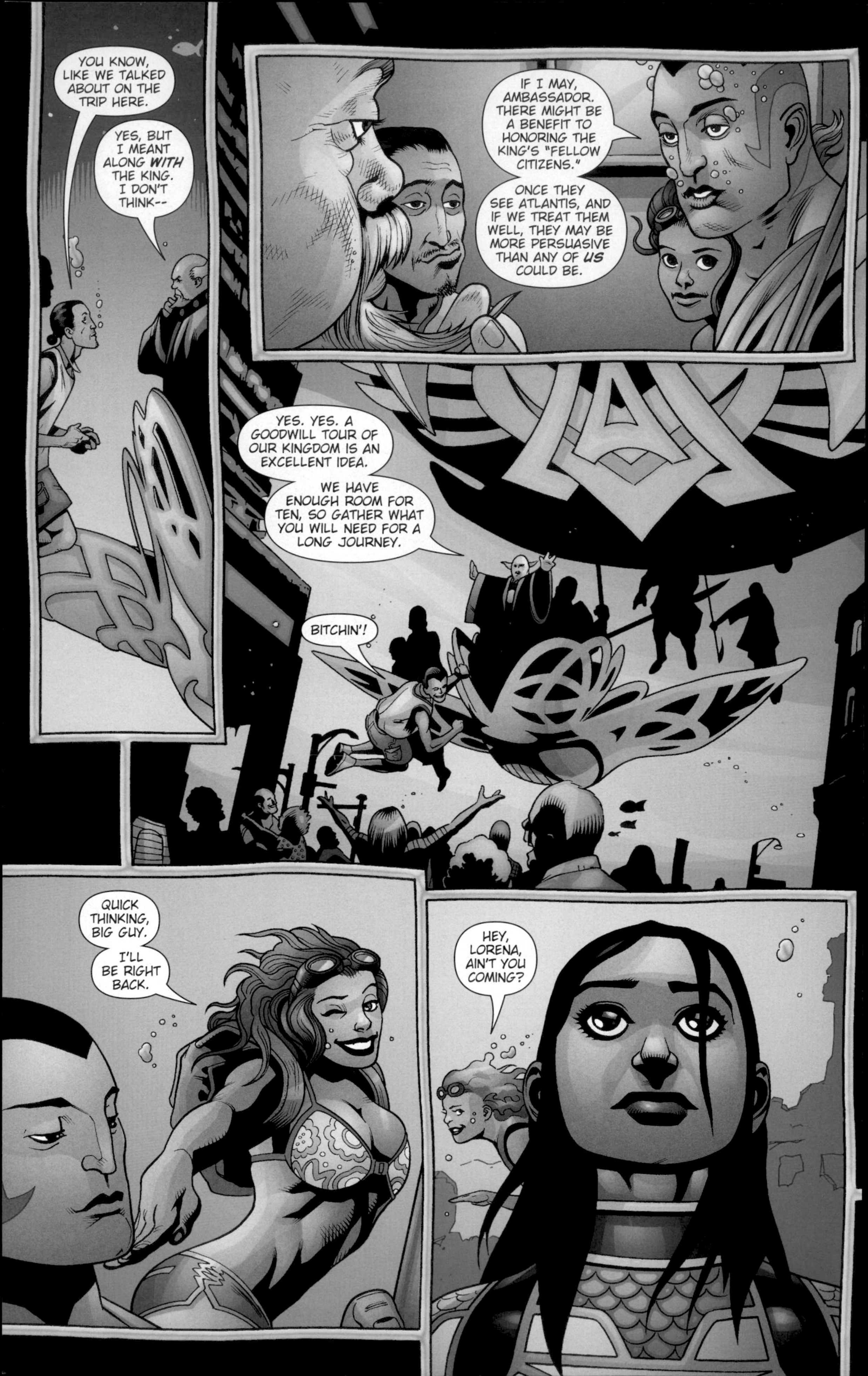
YOU KNOW, LIKE WE TALKED ABOUT ON THE TRIP HERE.
YES, BUT I MEANT ALONG *WITH* THE KING. I DON'T THINK--
IF I MAY, AMBASSADOR. THERE MIGHT BE A BENEFIT TO HONORING THE KING'S "FELLOW CITIZENS."
ONCE THEY SEE ATLANTIS, AND IF WE TREAT THEM WELL, THEY MAY BE MORE PERSUASIVE THAN ANY OF *US* COULD BE.
YES. YES. A GOODWILL TOUR OF OUR KINGDOM IS AN EXCELLENT IDEA.
WE HAVE ENOUGH ROOM FOR TEN, SO GATHER WHAT YOU WILL NEED FOR A LONG JOURNEY.
BITCHIN'!
QUICK THINKING, BIG GUY.
I'LL BE RIGHT BACK.
HEY, LORENA, AIN'T YOU COMING?

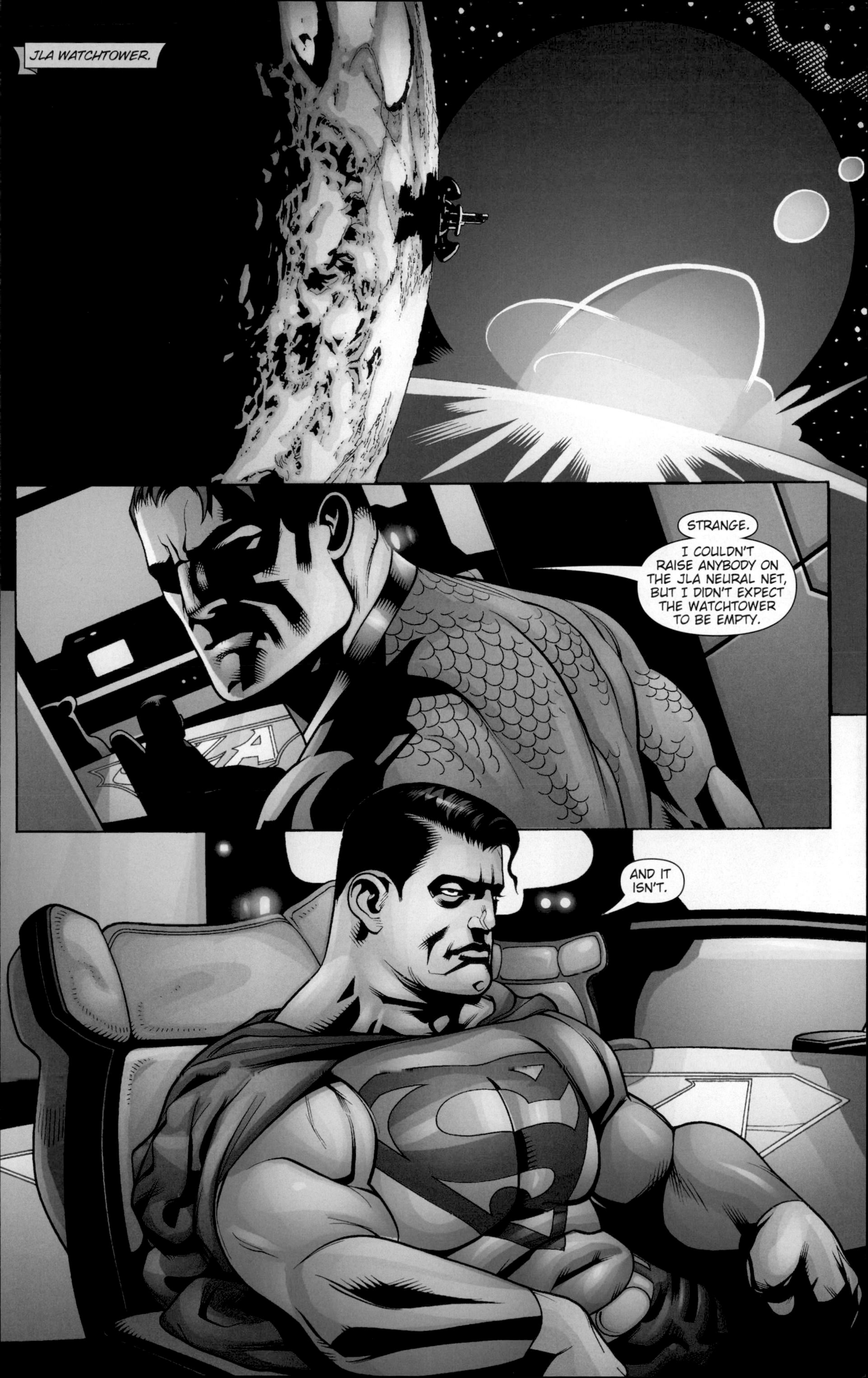

JLA WATCHTOWER.
STRANGE.
I COULDN'T RAISE ANYBODY ON THE JLA NEURAL NET, BUT I DIDN'T EXPECT THE WATCHTOWER TO BE EMPTY.
AND IT ISN'T.

OH. HELLO, KAL.

WELL, MAYBE YOU CAN TELL ME WHY I CAN'T SEEM TO ACCESS THE NEURAL NET.

WE'VE ALL BEEN VERY BUSY. THE AMERICAN WEST-COAST IS NOT THE WHOLE WORLD, YOU KNOW.

EXCUSE ME.

WHAT'S TROUBLING, YOU ARTHUR? YOU DON'T SEEM YOURSELF.

I TOLD YOU ABOUT THE MAN NAMED GEIST, WHO MANAGED TO GET SOME OF MY GENETIC MATERIAL--

"--WHICH HE USED TO DEVELOP A SELF-REPLICATING DNA STRAND."

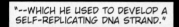

"HE INTRODUCED THIS STRAND INTO THE GENERAL POPULATION OF THE CITY BEFORE IT SANK--"

"--CAUSING THE WIDESPREAD MUTATION THAT ALLOWED THE SURVIVORS OF THE CATASTROPHE TO BREATHE UNDERWATER."

"THEN THIS MORNING, A COMPANY NAMED PROGENE TECH ANNOUNCED THAT THEY HAD ISOLATED THIS SAME GENETIC ANOMALY."

"THAT THEY WERE AWARDED A PATENT ON IT."

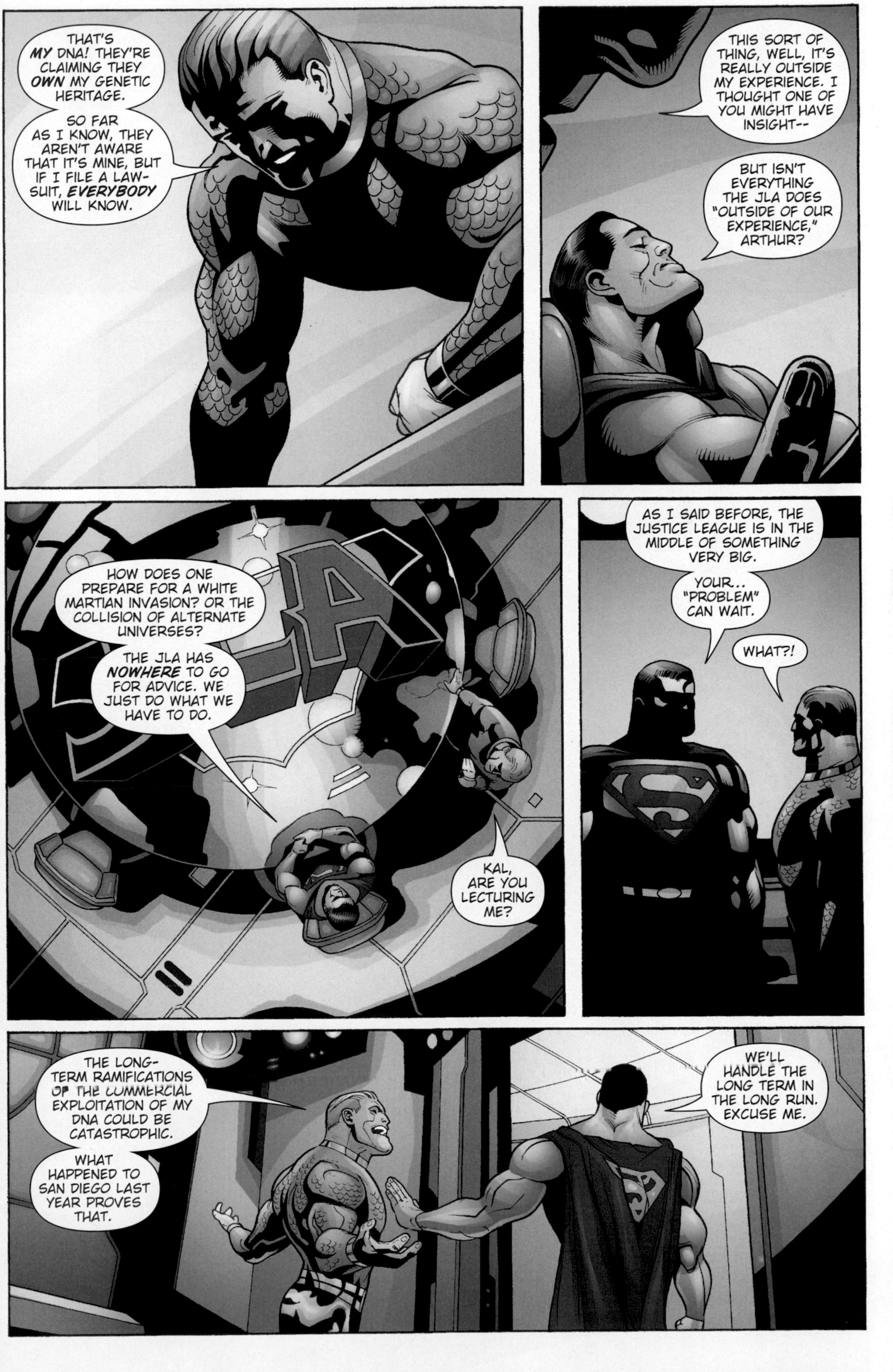
THAT'S MY DNA! THEY'RE CLAIMING THEY OWN MY GENETIC HERITAGE.
SO FAR AS I KNOW, THEY AREN'T AWARE THAT IT'S MINE, BUT IF I FILE A LAW-SUIT, EVERYBODY WILL KNOW.
THIS SORT OF THING, WELL, IT'S REALLY OUTSIDE MY EXPERIENCE. I THOUGHT ONE OF YOU MIGHT HAVE INSIGHT--
BUT ISN'T EVERYTHING THE JLA DOES "OUTSIDE OF OUR EXPERIENCE," ARTHUR?
HOW DOES ONE PREPARE FOR A WHITE MARTIAN INVASION? OR THE COLLISION OF ALTERNATE UNIVERSES?
THE JLA HAS NOWHERE TO GO FOR ADVICE. WE JUST DO WHAT WE HAVE TO DO.
KAL, ARE YOU LECTURING ME?
AS I SAID BEFORE, THE JUSTICE LEAGUE IS IN THE MIDDLE OF SOMETHING VERY BIG.
YOUR... "PROBLEM" CAN WAIT.
WHAT?!
THE LONG-TERM RAMIFICATIONS OF THE COMMERCIAL EXPLOITATION OF MY DNA COULD BE CATASTROPHIC.
WHAT HAPPENED TO SAN DIEGO LAST YEAR PROVES THAT.
WE'LL HANDLE THE LONG TERM IN THE LONG RUN. EXCUSE ME.

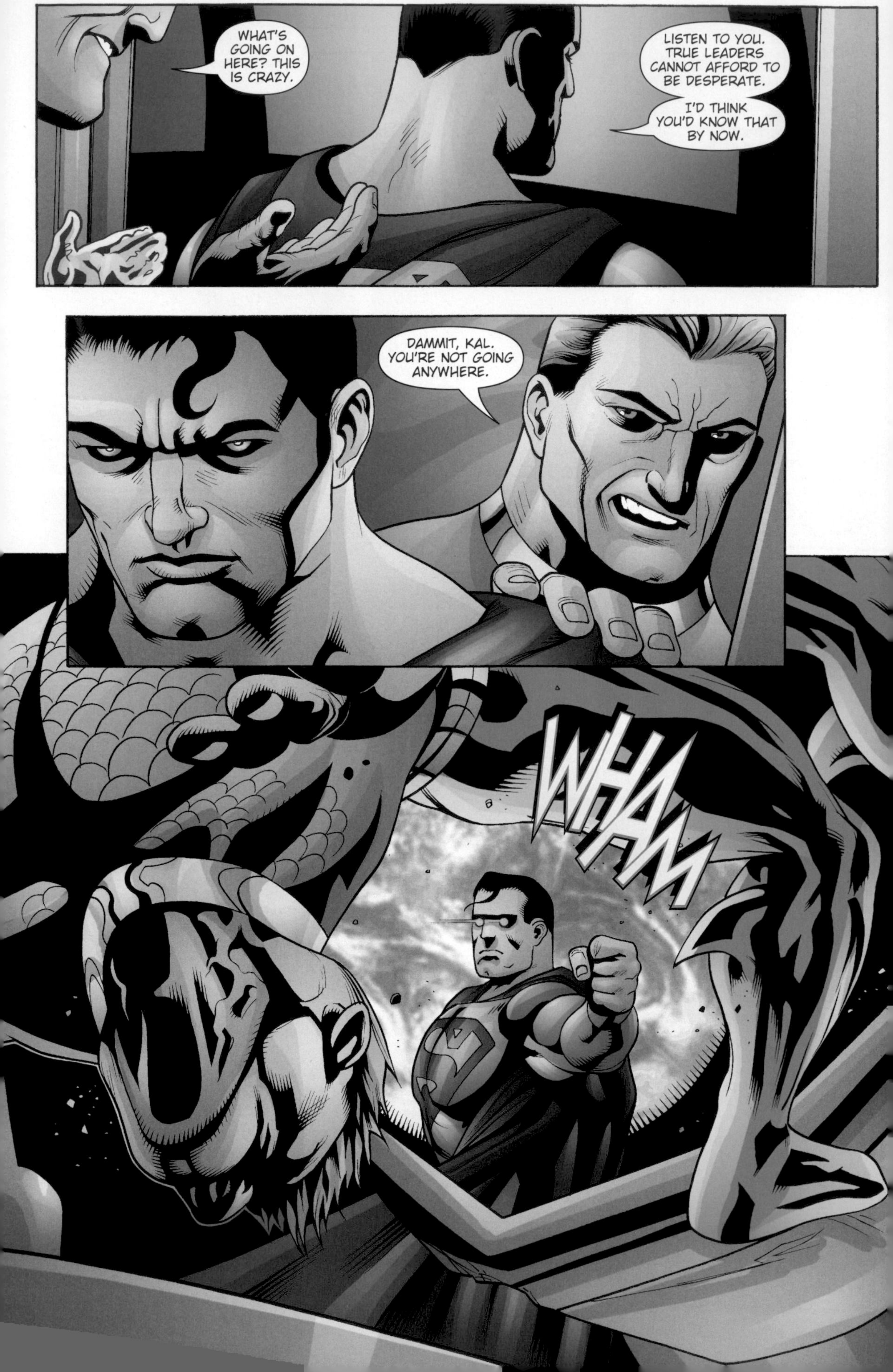
WHAT'S GOING ON HERE? THIS IS CRAZY.
LISTEN TO YOU. TRUE LEADERS CANNOT AFFORD TO BE DESPERATE.
I'D THINK YOU'D KNOW THAT BY NOW.
DAMMIT, KAL. YOU'RE NOT GOING ANYWHERE.
WHAM

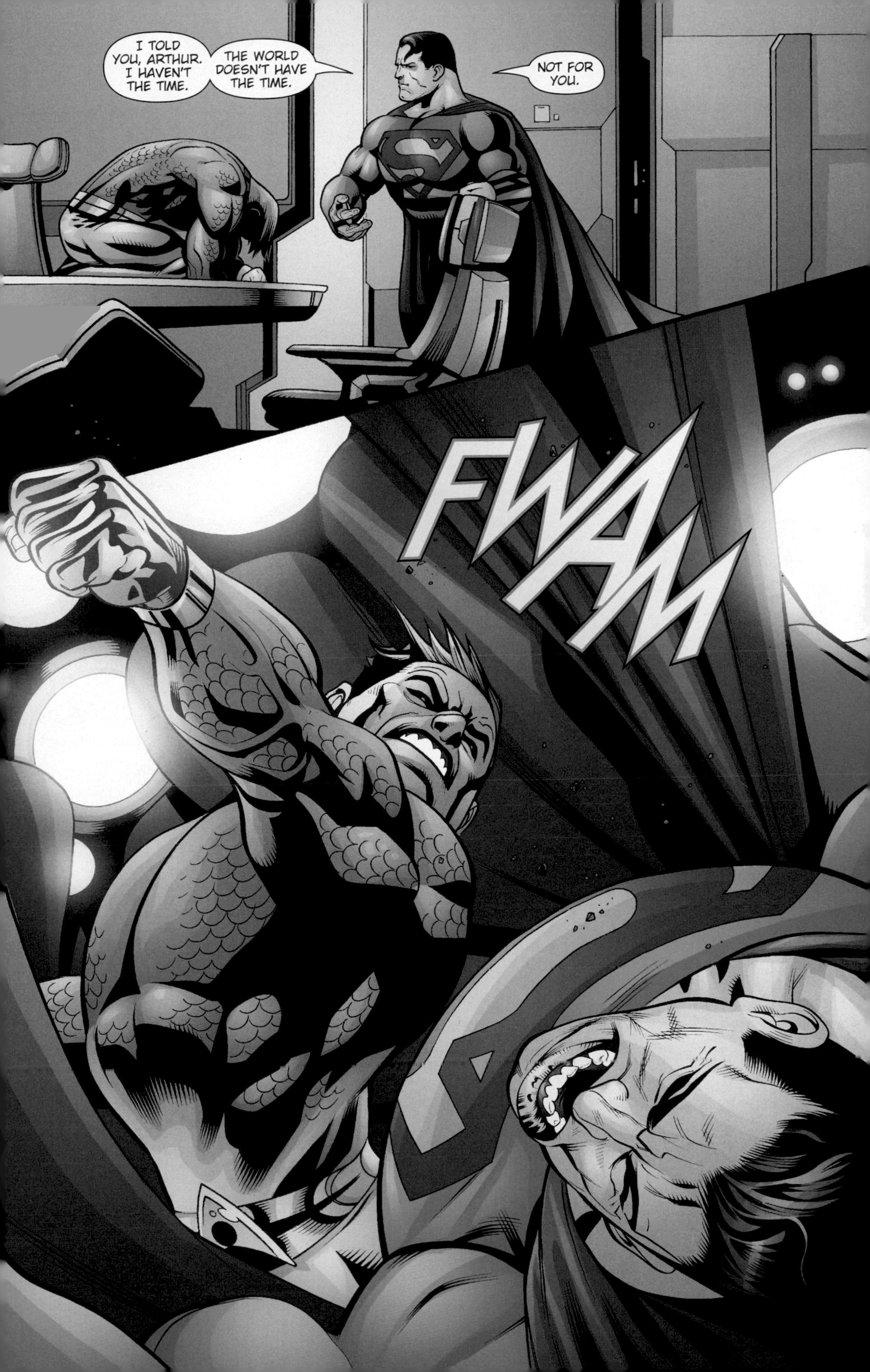
I TOLD YOU, ARTHUR. I HAVEN'T THE TIME.
THE WORLD DOESN'T HAVE THE TIME.
NOT FOR YOU.
FWAM

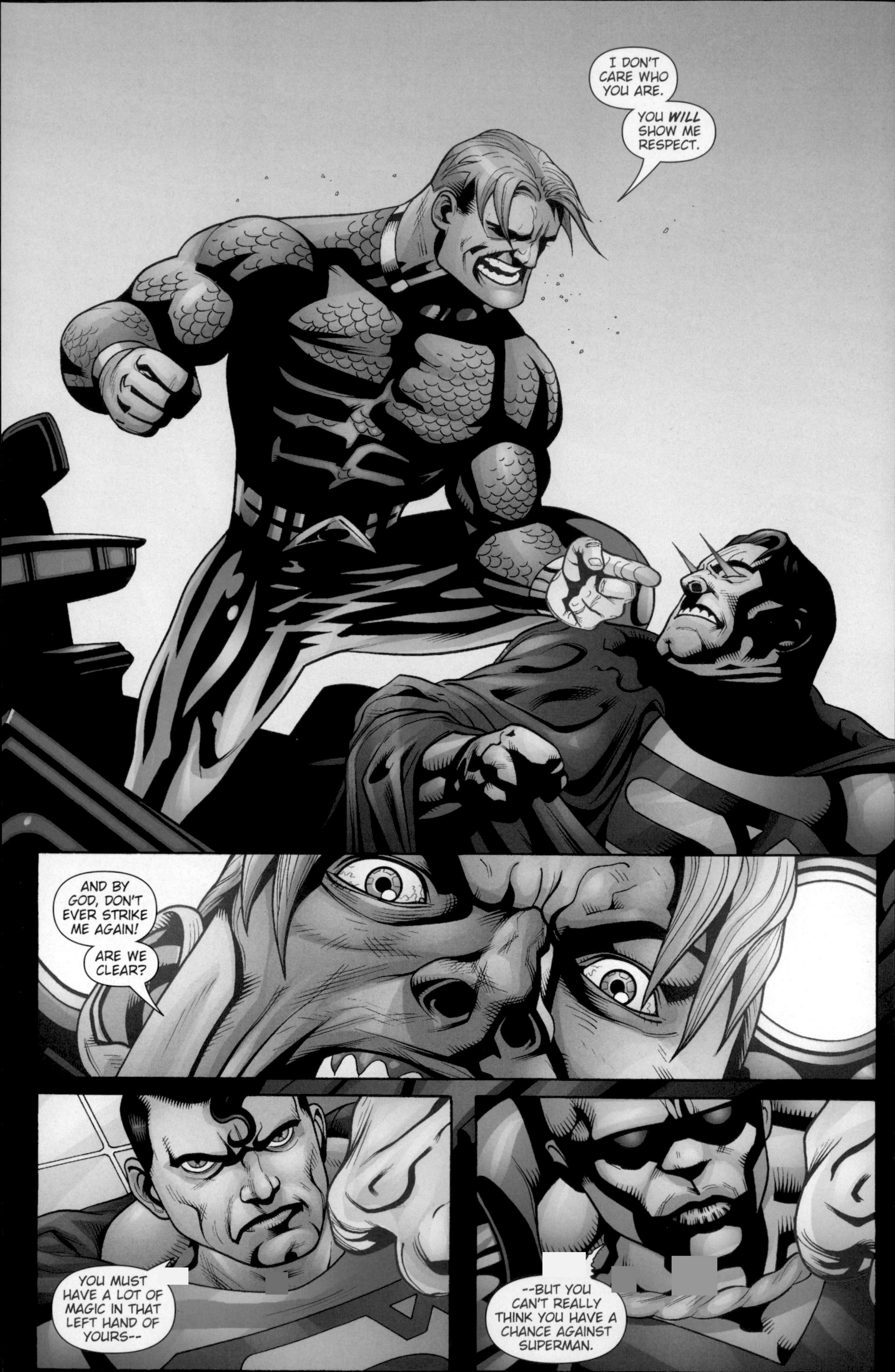
I DON'T CARE WHO YOU ARE.
YOU *WILL* SHOW ME RESPECT.
AND BY GOD, DON'T EVER STRIKE ME AGAIN!
ARE WE CLEAR?
YOU MUST HAVE A LOT OF MAGIC IN THAT LEFT HAND OF YOURS--
--BUT YOU CAN'T REALLY THINK YOU HAVE A CHANCE AGAINST SUPERMAN.

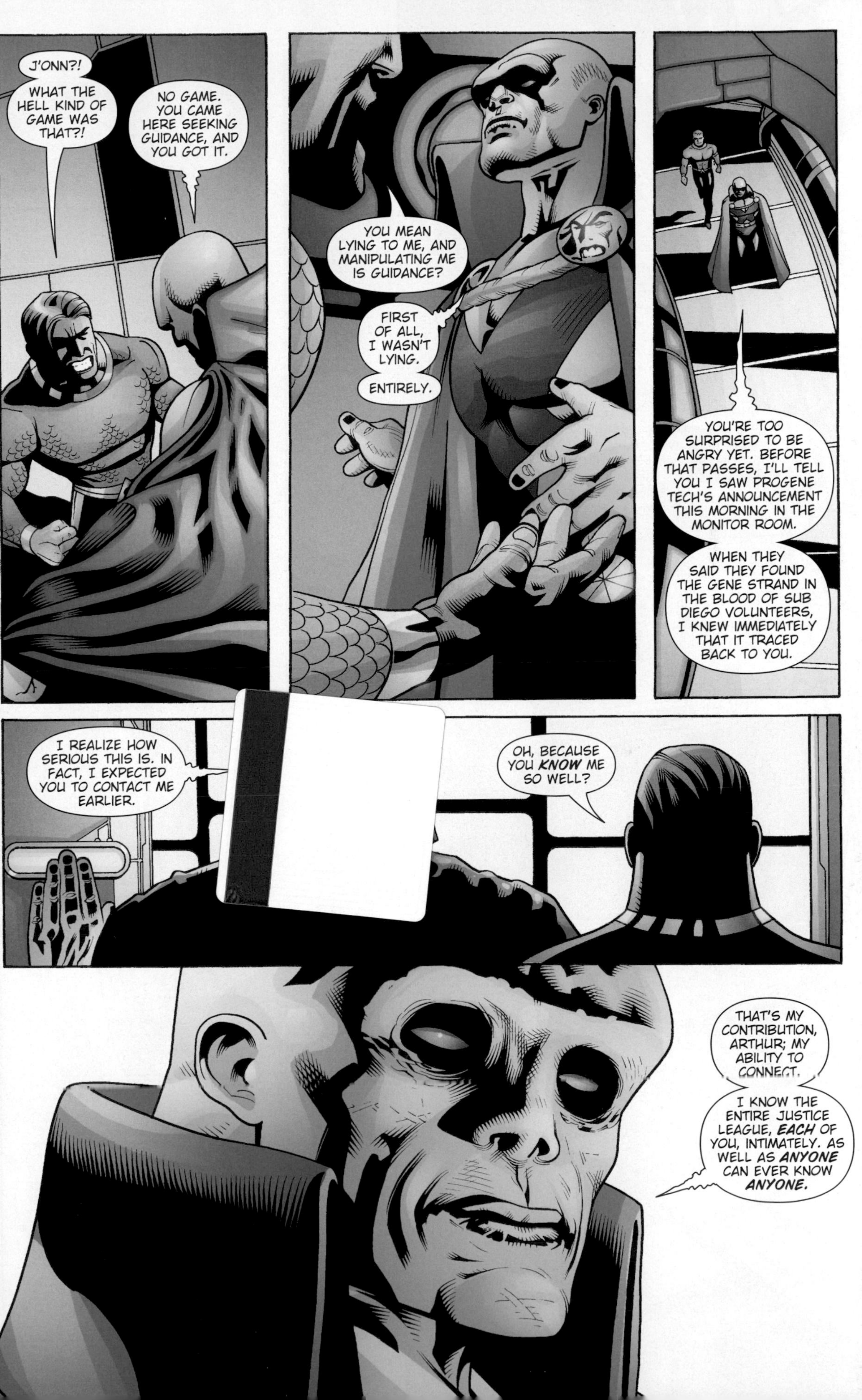
J'ONN?!
WHAT THE HELL KIND OF GAME WAS THAT?!
NO GAME. YOU CAME HERE SEEKING GUIDANCE, AND YOU GOT IT.
YOU MEAN LYING TO ME, AND MANIPULATING ME IS GUIDANCE?
FIRST OF ALL, I WASN'T LYING.
ENTIRELY.
YOU'RE TOO SURPRISED TO BE ANGRY YET. BEFORE THAT PASSES, I'LL TELL YOU I SAW PROGENE TECH'S ANNOUNCEMENT THIS MORNING IN THE MONITOR ROOM.
WHEN THEY SAID THEY FOUND THE GENE STRAND IN THE BLOOD OF SUB DIEGO VOLUNTEERS, I KNEW IMMEDIATELY THAT IT TRACED BACK TO YOU.
I REALIZE HOW SERIOUS THIS IS. IN FACT, I EXPECTED YOU TO CONTACT ME EARLIER.
OH, BECAUSE YOU KNOW ME SO WELL?
THAT'S MY CONTRIBUTION, ARTHUR; MY ABILITY TO CONNECT.
I KNOW THE ENTIRE JUSTICE LEAGUE, EACH OF YOU, INTIMATELY. AS WELL AS ANYONE CAN EVER KNOW ANYONE.

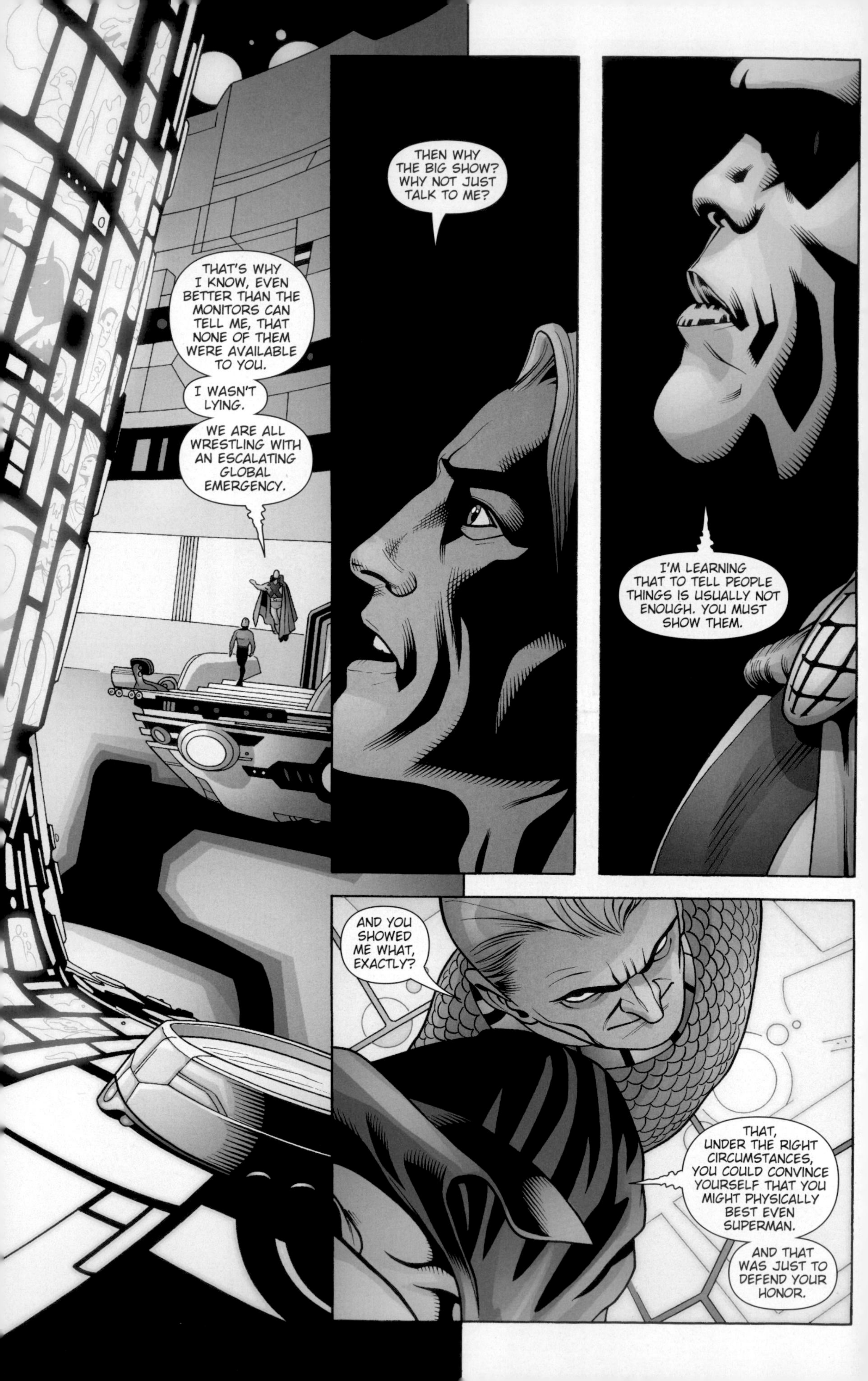
THAT'S WHY I KNOW, EVEN BETTER THAN THE MONITORS CAN TELL ME, THAT NONE OF THEM WERE AVAILABLE TO YOU.
I WASN'T LYING.
WE ARE ALL WRESTLING WITH AN ESCALATING GLOBAL EMERGENCY.
THEN WHY THE BIG SHOW? WHY NOT JUST TALK TO ME?
I'M LEARNING THAT TO TELL PEOPLE THINGS IS USUALLY NOT ENOUGH. YOU MUST SHOW THEM.
AND YOU SHOWED ME WHAT, EXACTLY?
THAT, UNDER THE RIGHT CIRCUMSTANCES, YOU COULD CONVINCE YOURSELF THAT YOU MIGHT PHYSICALLY BEST EVEN SUPERMAN.
AND THAT WAS JUST TO DEFEND YOUR HONOR.

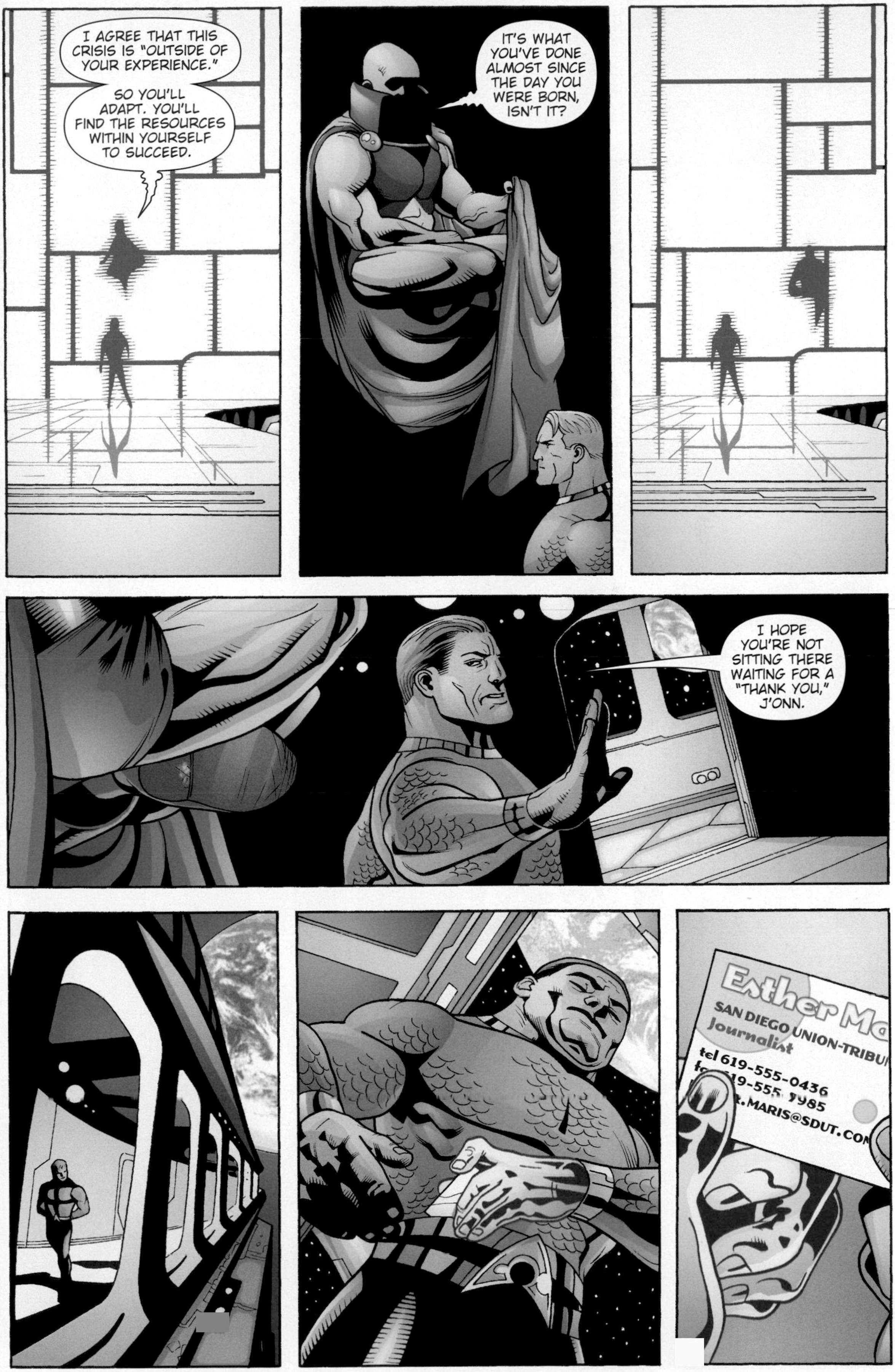
I AGREE THAT THIS CRISIS IS "OUTSIDE OF YOUR EXPERIENCE."
SO YOU'LL ADAPT. YOU'LL FIND THE RESOURCES WITHIN YOURSELF TO SUCCEED.
IT'S WHAT YOU'VE DONE ALMOST SINCE THE DAY YOU WERE BORN, ISN'T IT?
I HOPE YOU'RE NOT SITTING THERE WAITING FOR A "THANK YOU," J'ONN.
Esther Ma
SAN DIEGO UNION-TRIBU
Journalist
tel 619-555-0436

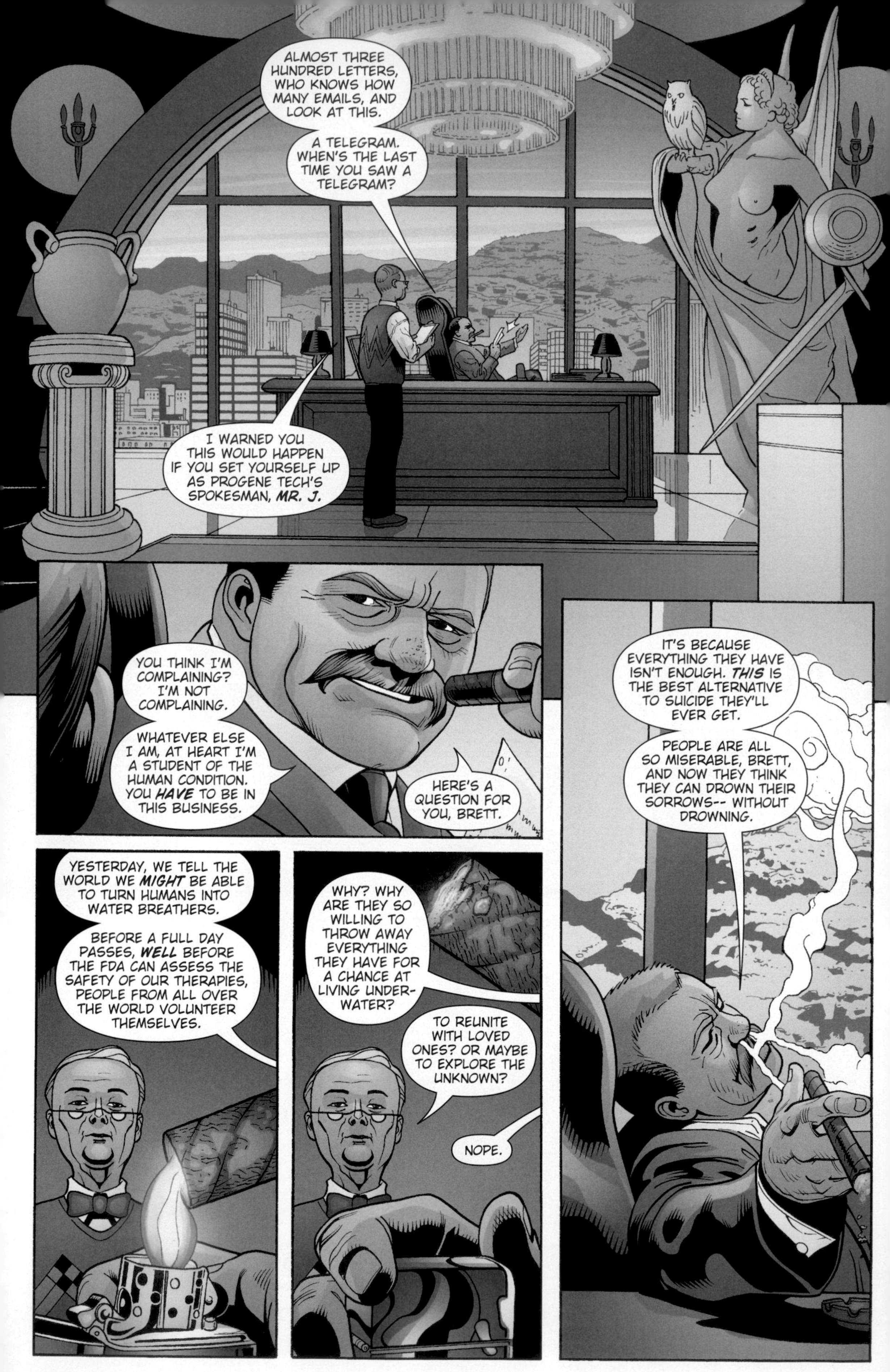
ALMOST THREE HUNDRED LETTERS, WHO KNOWS HOW MANY EMAILS, AND LOOK AT THIS.
A TELEGRAM. WHEN'S THE LAST TIME YOU SAW A TELEGRAM?
I WARNED YOU THIS WOULD HAPPEN IF YOU SET YOURSELF UP AS PROGENE TECH'S SPOKESMAN, MR. J.
YOU THINK I'M COMPLAINING? I'M NOT COMPLAINING.
WHATEVER ELSE I AM, AT HEART I'M A STUDENT OF THE HUMAN CONDITION. YOU HAVE TO BE IN THIS BUSINESS.
HERE'S A QUESTION FOR YOU, BRETT.
YESTERDAY, WE TELL THE WORLD WE MIGHT BE ABLE TO TURN HUMANS INTO WATER BREATHERS.
BEFORE A FULL DAY PASSES, WELL BEFORE THE FDA CAN ASSESS THE SAFETY OF OUR THERAPIES, PEOPLE FROM ALL OVER THE WORLD VOLUNTEER THEMSELVES.
WHY? WHY ARE THEY SO WILLING TO THROW AWAY EVERYTHING THEY HAVE FOR A CHANCE AT LIVING UNDER-WATER?
TO REUNITE WITH LOVED ONES? OR MAYBE TO EXPLORE THE UNKNOWN?
NOPE.
IT'S BECAUSE EVERYTHING THEY HAVE ISN'T ENOUGH. THIS IS THE BEST ALTERNATIVE TO SUICIDE THEY'LL EVER GET.
PEOPLE ARE ALL SO MISERABLE, BRETT, AND NOW THEY THINK THEY CAN DROWN THEIR SORROWS-- WITHOUT DROWNING.

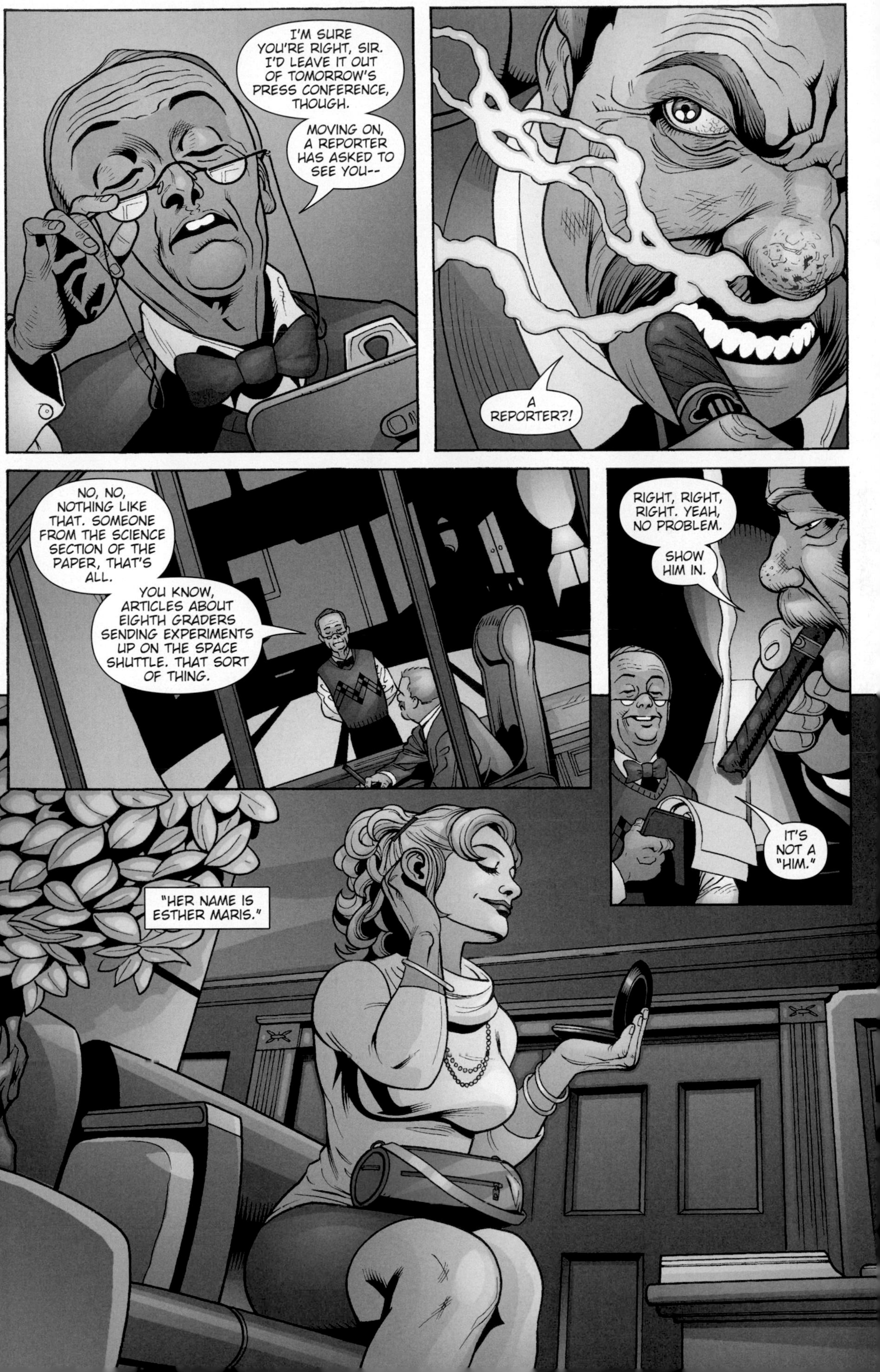
I'M SURE YOU'RE RIGHT, SIR. I'D LEAVE IT OUT OF TOMORROW'S PRESS CONFERENCE, THOUGH.
MOVING ON, A REPORTER HAS ASKED TO SEE YOU--
A REPORTER?!
NO, NO, NOTHING LIKE THAT. SOMEONE FROM THE SCIENCE SECTION OF THE PAPER, THAT'S ALL.
YOU KNOW, ARTICLES ABOUT EIGHTH GRADERS SENDING EXPERIMENTS UP ON THE SPACE SHUTTLE. THAT SORT OF THING.
RIGHT, RIGHT, RIGHT. YEAH, NO PROBLEM.
SHOW HIM IN.
IT'S NOT A "HIM."
"HER NAME IS ESTHER MARIS."

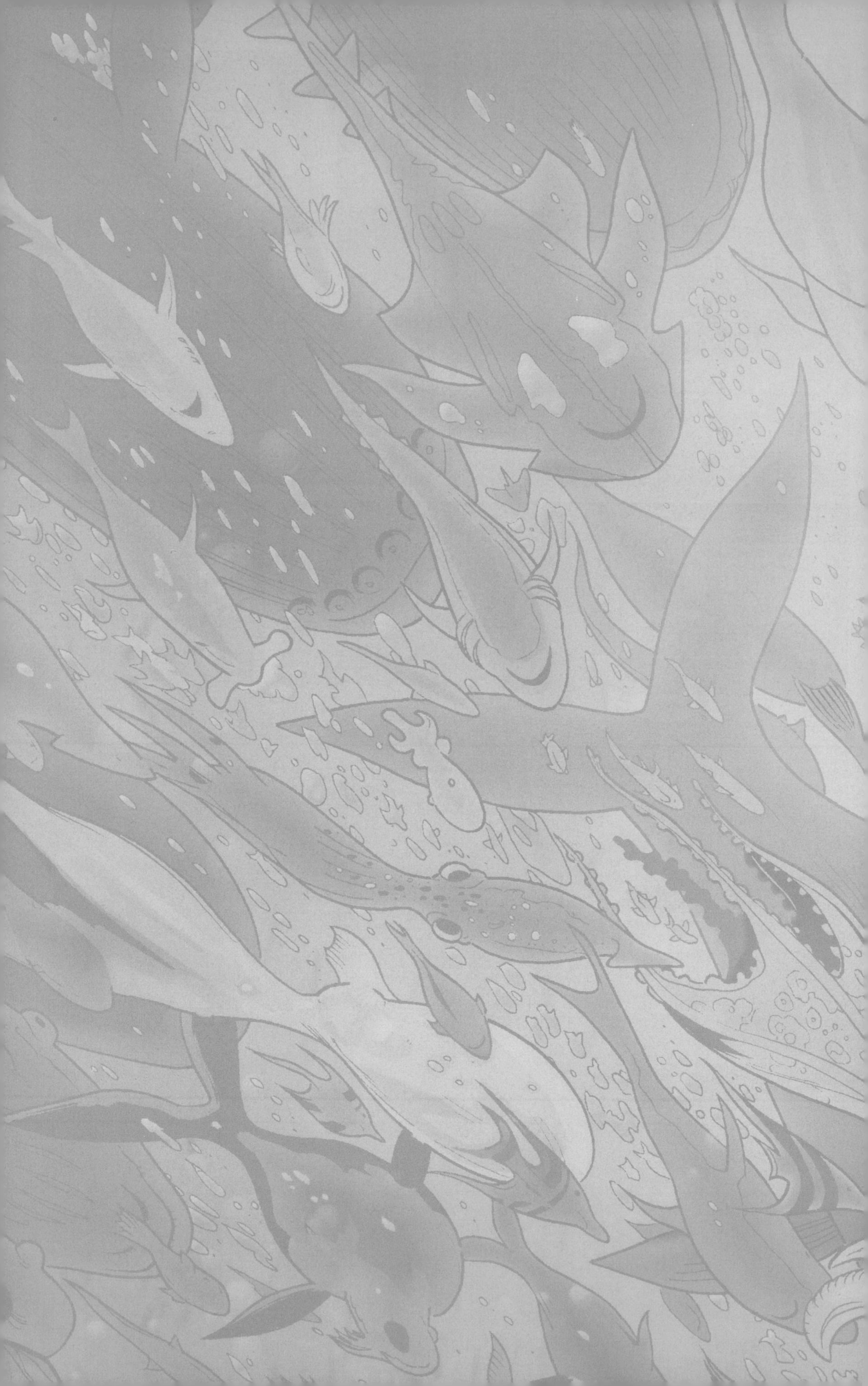

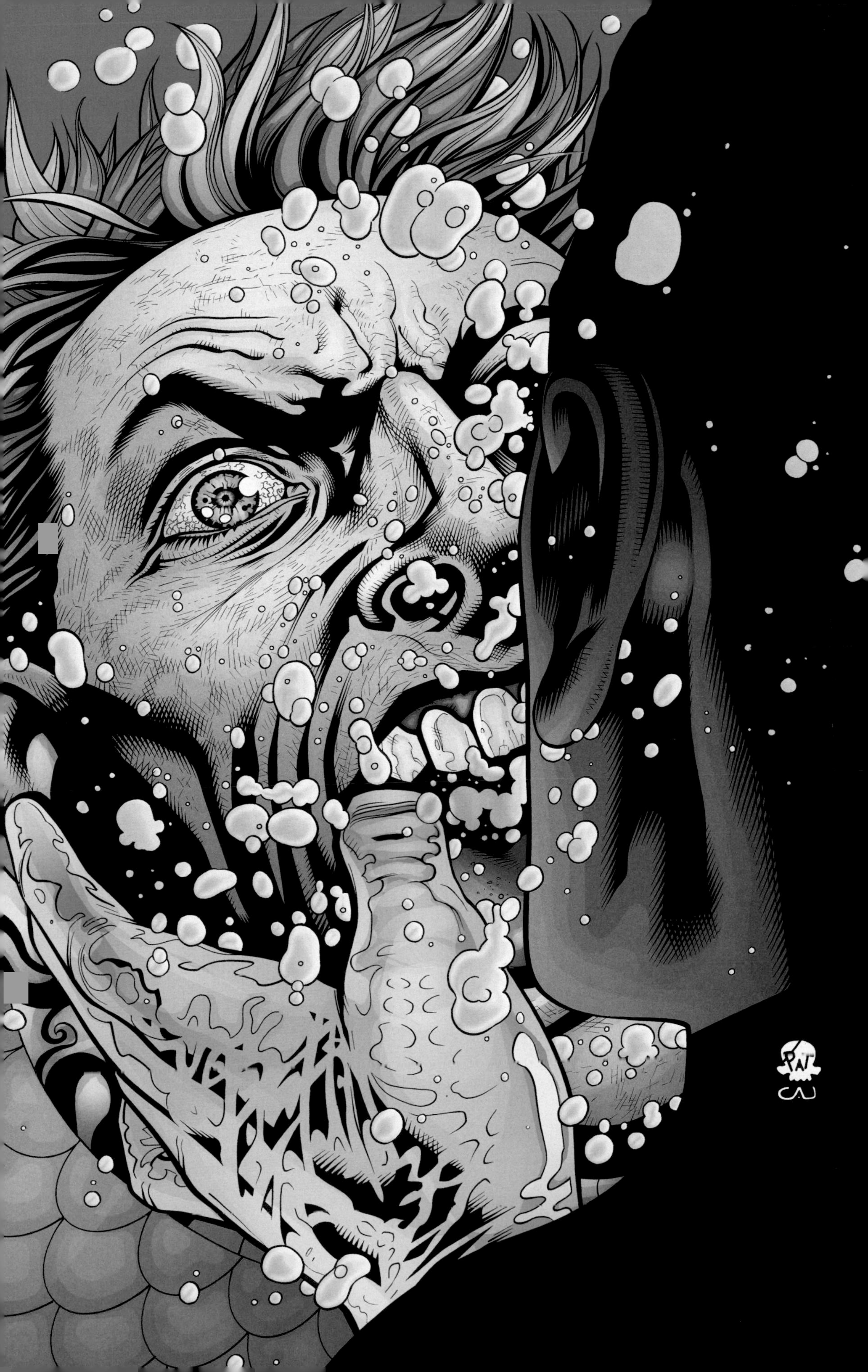

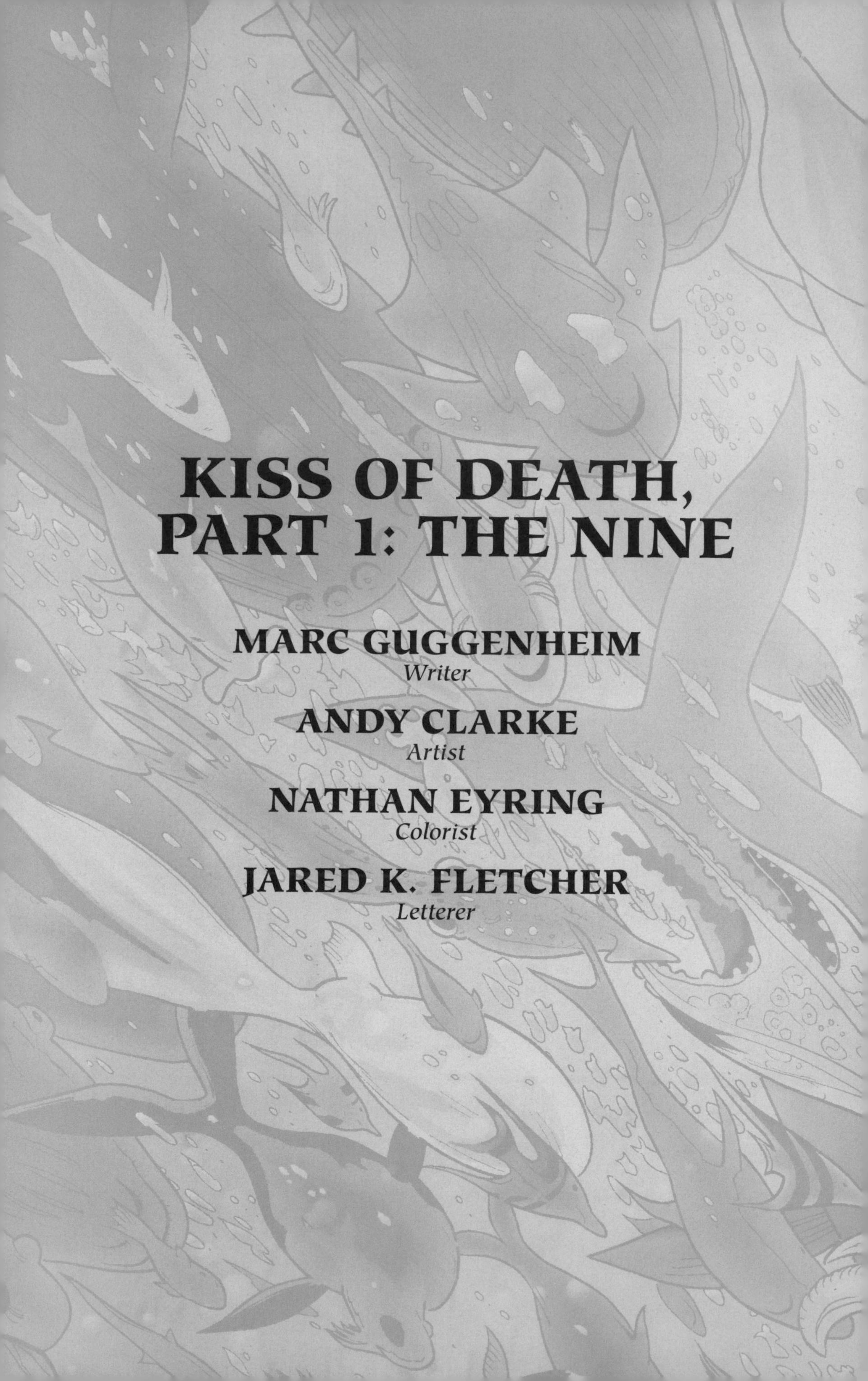

KISS OF DEATH, PART 1: THE NINE

MARC GUGGENHEIM
Writer

ANDY CLARKE
Artist

NATHAN EYRING
Colorist

JARED K. FLETCHER
Letterer

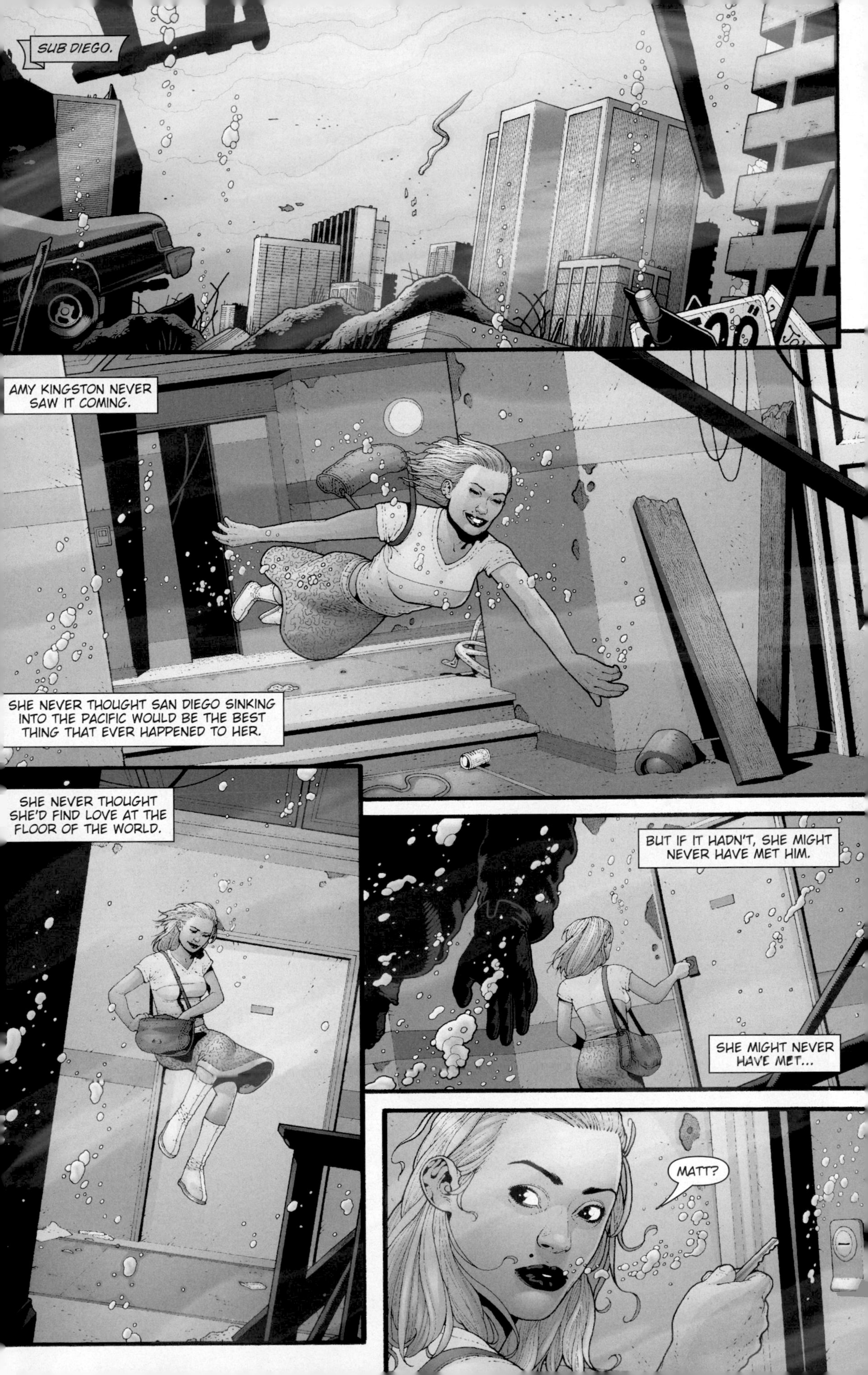
SUB DIEGO.
AMY KINGSTON NEVER SAW IT COMING.
SHE NEVER THOUGHT SAN DIEGO SINKING INTO THE PACIFIC WOULD BE THE BEST THING THAT EVER HAPPENED TO HER.
SHE NEVER THOUGHT SHE'D FIND LOVE AT THE FLOOR OF THE WORLD.
BUT IF IT HADN'T, SHE MIGHT NEVER HAVE MET HIM.
SHE MIGHT NEVER HAVE MET...
MATT?

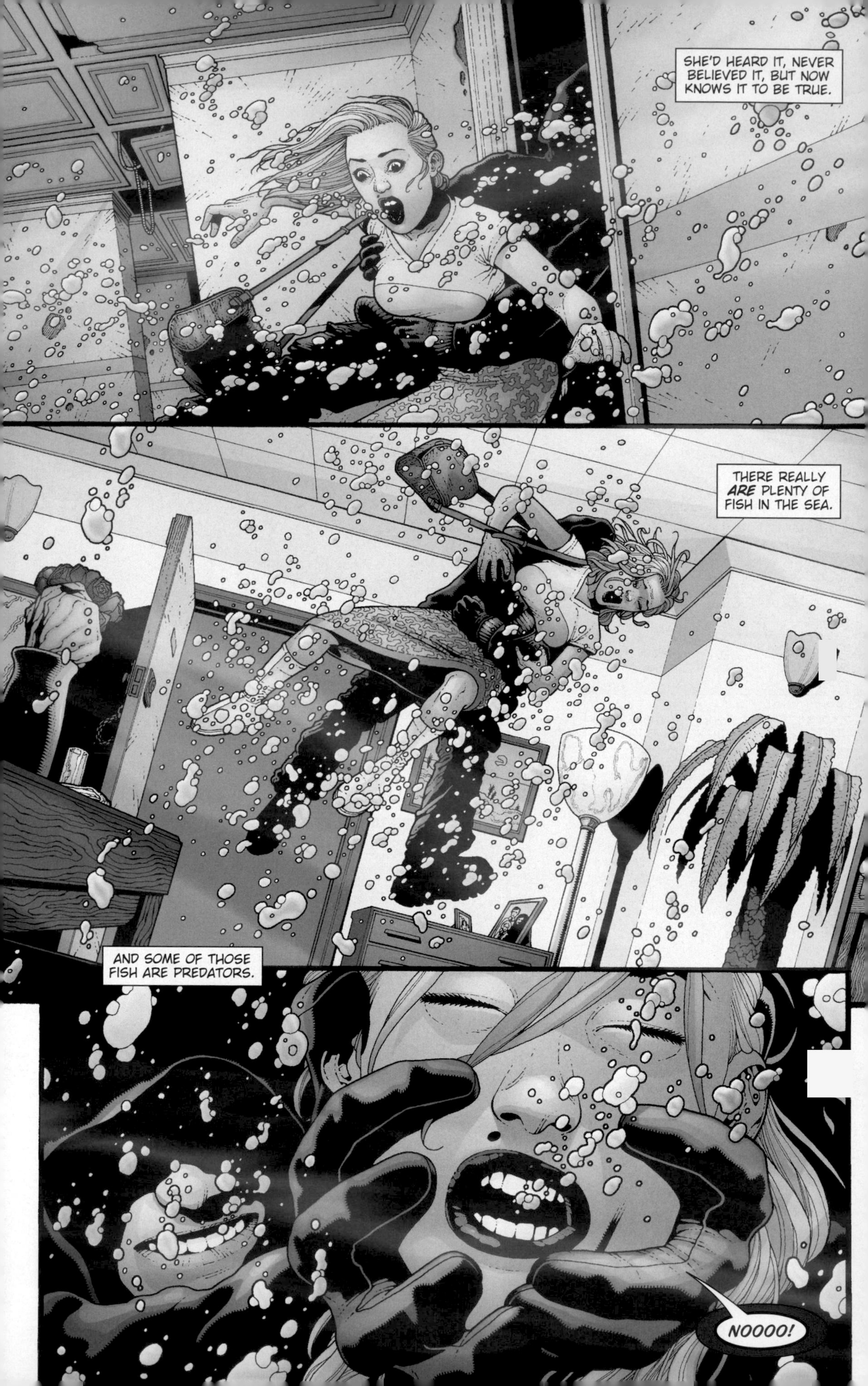
SHE'D HEARD IT, NEVER BELIEVED IT, BUT NOW KNOWS IT TO BE TRUE.
THERE REALLY ARE PLENTY OF FISH IN THE SEA.
AND SOME OF THOSE FISH ARE PREDATORS.
NOOOO!

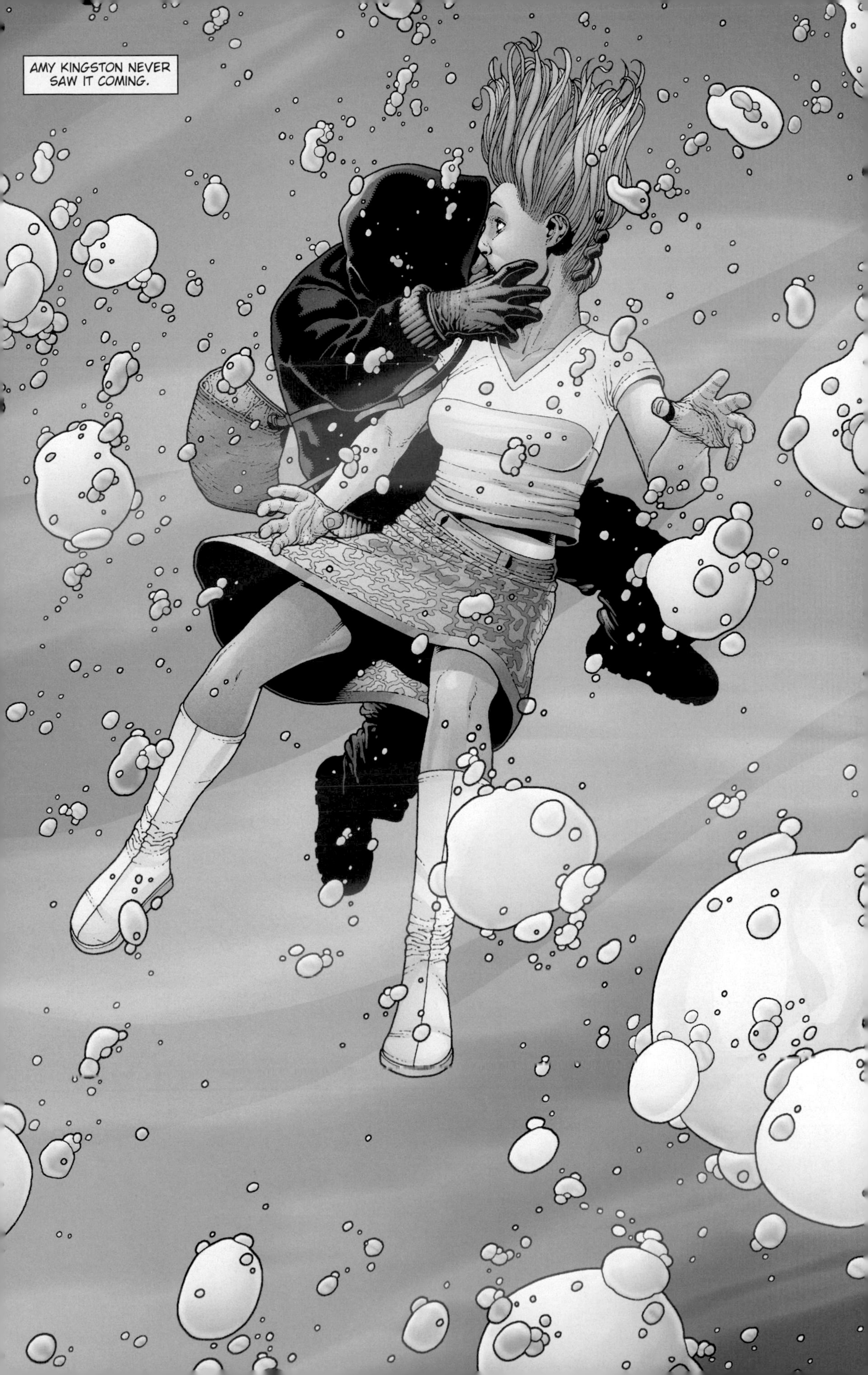
AMY KINGSTON NEVER SAW IT COMING.

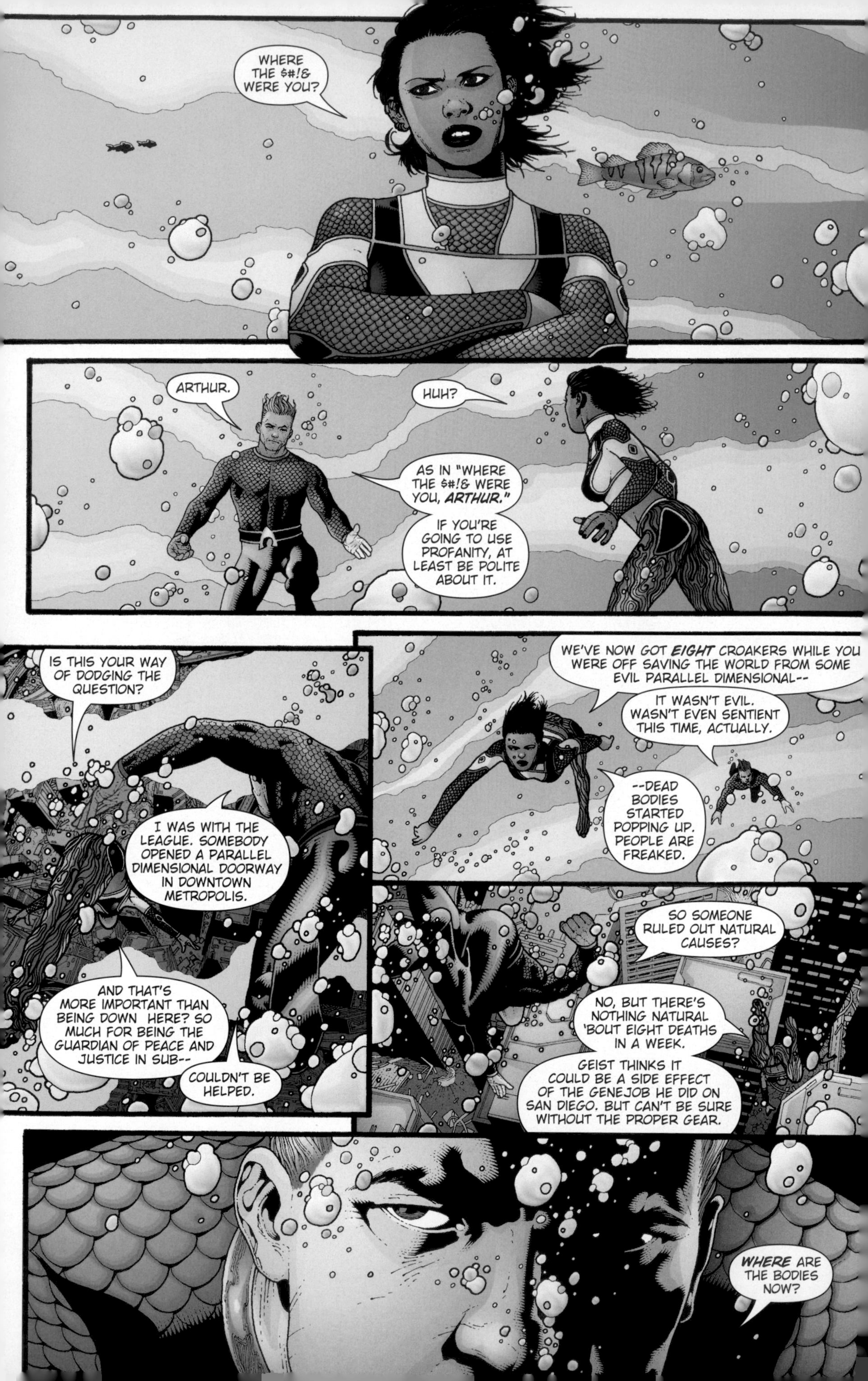

WHERE THE $#!& WERE YOU?
ARTHUR.
HUH?
AS IN "WHERE THE $#!& WERE YOU, ARTHUR."
IF YOU'RE GOING TO USE PROFANITY, AT LEAST BE POLITE ABOUT IT.
IS THIS YOUR WAY OF DODGING THE QUESTION?
I WAS WITH THE LEAGUE. SOMEBODY OPENED A PARALLEL DIMENSIONAL DOORWAY IN DOWNTOWN METROPOLIS.
AND THAT'S MORE IMPORTANT THAN BEING DOWN HERE? SO MUCH FOR BEING THE GUARDIAN OF PEACE AND JUSTICE IN SUB--
COULDN'T BE HELPED.
WE'VE NOW GOT EIGHT CROAKERS WHILE YOU WERE OFF SAVING THE WORLD FROM SOME EVIL PARALLEL DIMENSIONAL--
IT WASN'T EVIL. WASN'T EVEN SENTIENT THIS TIME, ACTUALLY.
--DEAD BODIES STARTED POPPING UP. PEOPLE ARE FREAKED.
SO SOMEONE RULED OUT NATURAL CAUSES?
NO, BUT THERE'S NOTHING NATURAL 'BOUT EIGHT DEATHS IN A WEEK.
GEIST THINKS IT COULD BE A SIDE EFFECT OF THE GENEJOB HE DID ON SAN DIEGO. BUT CAN'T BE SURE WITHOUT THE PROPER GEAR.
WHERE ARE THE BODIES NOW?

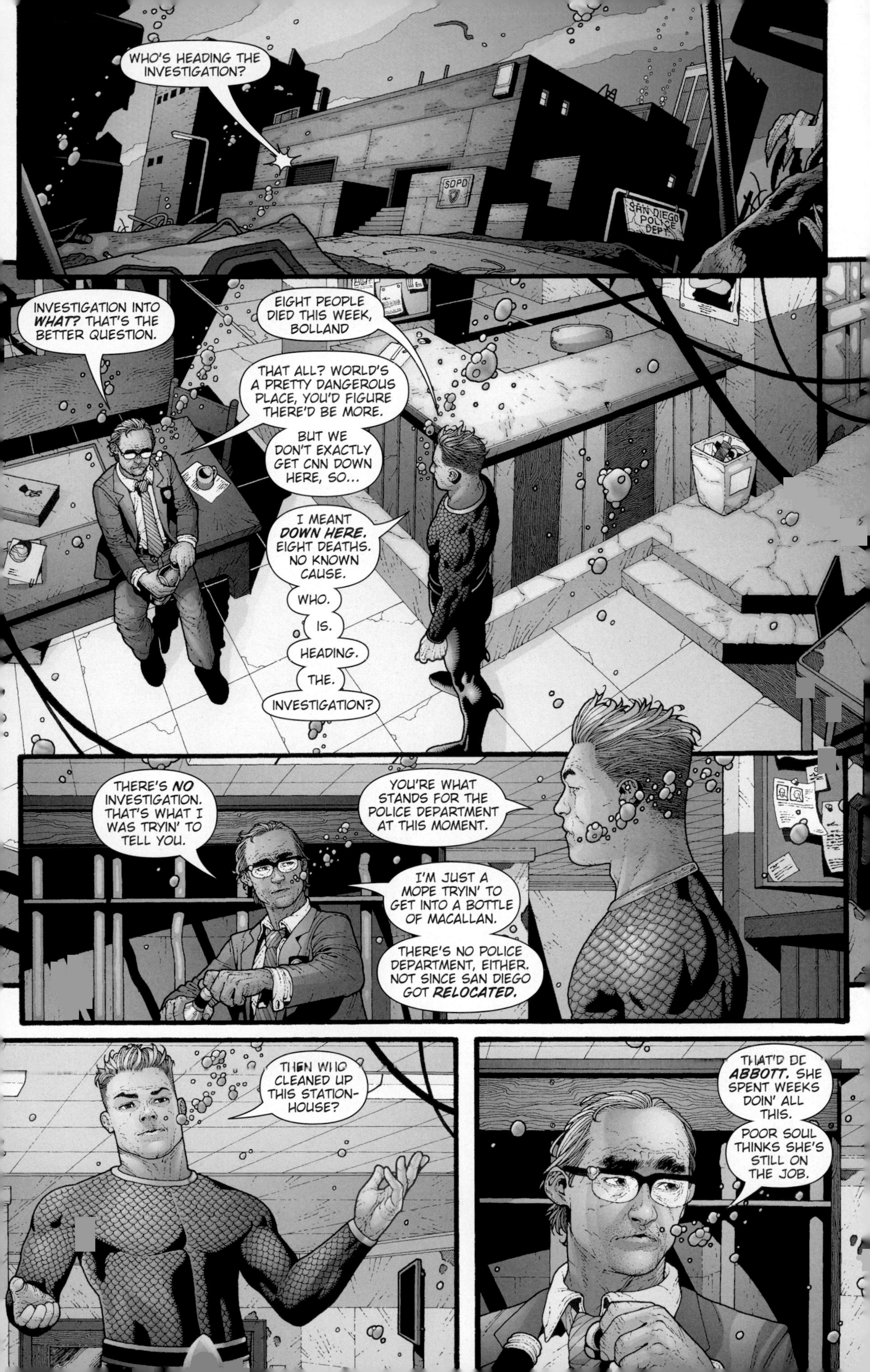
WHO'S HEADING THE INVESTIGATION?
INVESTIGATION INTO WHAT? THAT'S THE BETTER QUESTION.
EIGHT PEOPLE DIED THIS WEEK, BOLLAND
THAT ALL? WORLD'S A PRETTY DANGEROUS PLACE, YOU'D FIGURE THERE'D BE MORE.
BUT WE DON'T EXACTLY GET CNN DOWN HERE, SO...
I MEANT DOWN HERE. EIGHT DEATHS. NO KNOWN CAUSE.
WHO.
IS.
HEADING.
THE.
INVESTIGATION?
THERE'S NO INVESTIGATION. THAT'S WHAT I WAS TRYIN' TO TELL YOU.
YOU'RE WHAT STANDS FOR THE POLICE DEPARTMENT AT THIS MOMENT.
I'M JUST A MOPE TRYIN' TO GET INTO A BOTTLE OF MACALLAN.
THERE'S NO POLICE DEPARTMENT, EITHER. NOT SINCE SAN DIEGO GOT RELOCATED.
THEN WHO CLEANED UP THIS STATION-HOUSE?
THAT'D BE ABBOTT. SHE SPENT WEEKS DOIN' ALL THIS.
POOR SOUL THINKS SHE'S STILL ON THE JOB.

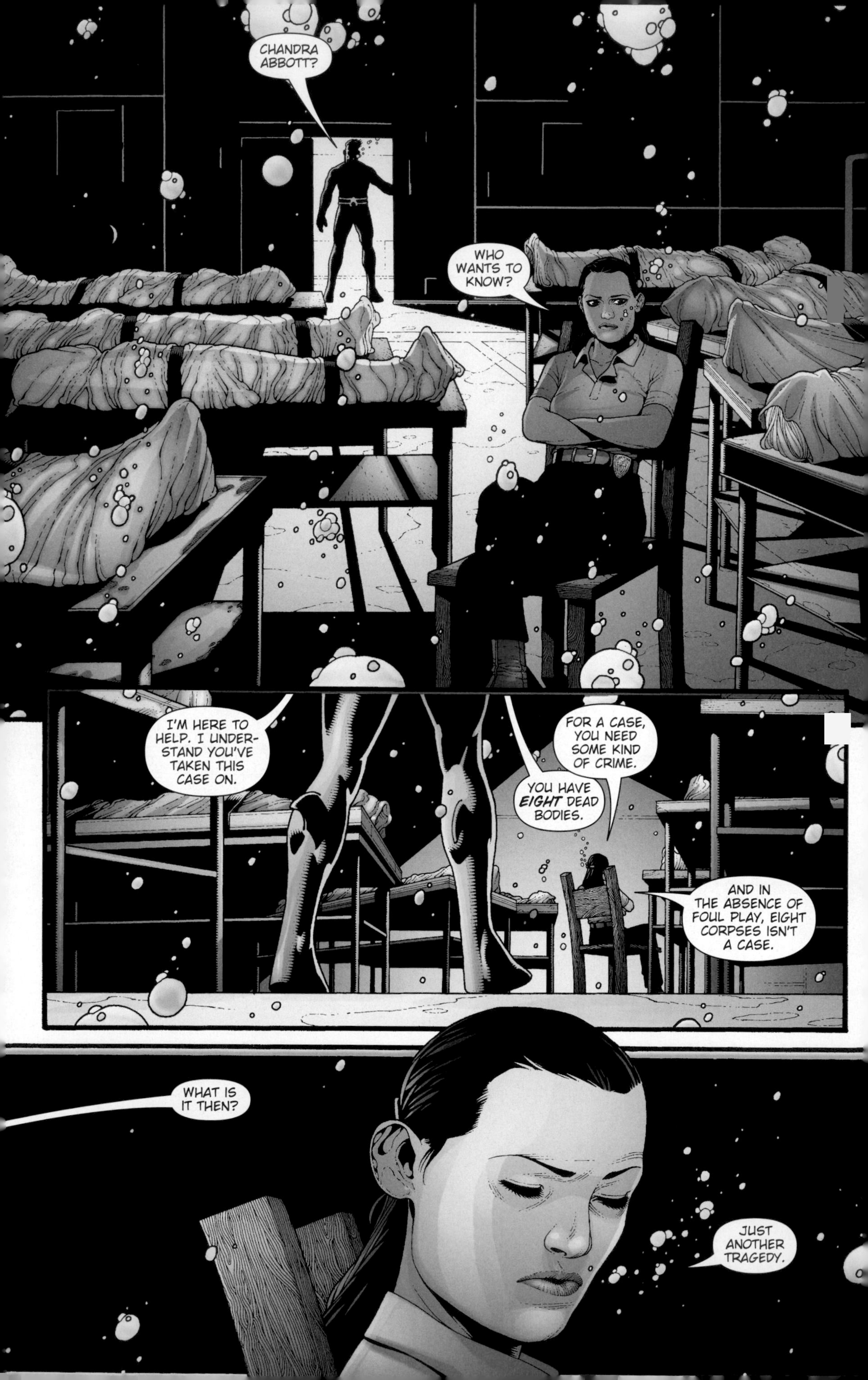
CHANDRA ABBOTT?
WHO WANTS TO KNOW?
I'M HERE TO HELP. I UNDERSTAND YOU'VE TAKEN THIS CASE ON.
FOR A CASE, YOU NEED SOME KIND OF CRIME.
YOU HAVE EIGHT DEAD BODIES.
AND IN THE ABSENCE OF FOUL PLAY, EIGHT CORPSES ISN'T A CASE.
WHAT IS IT THEN?
JUST ANOTHER TRAGEDY.

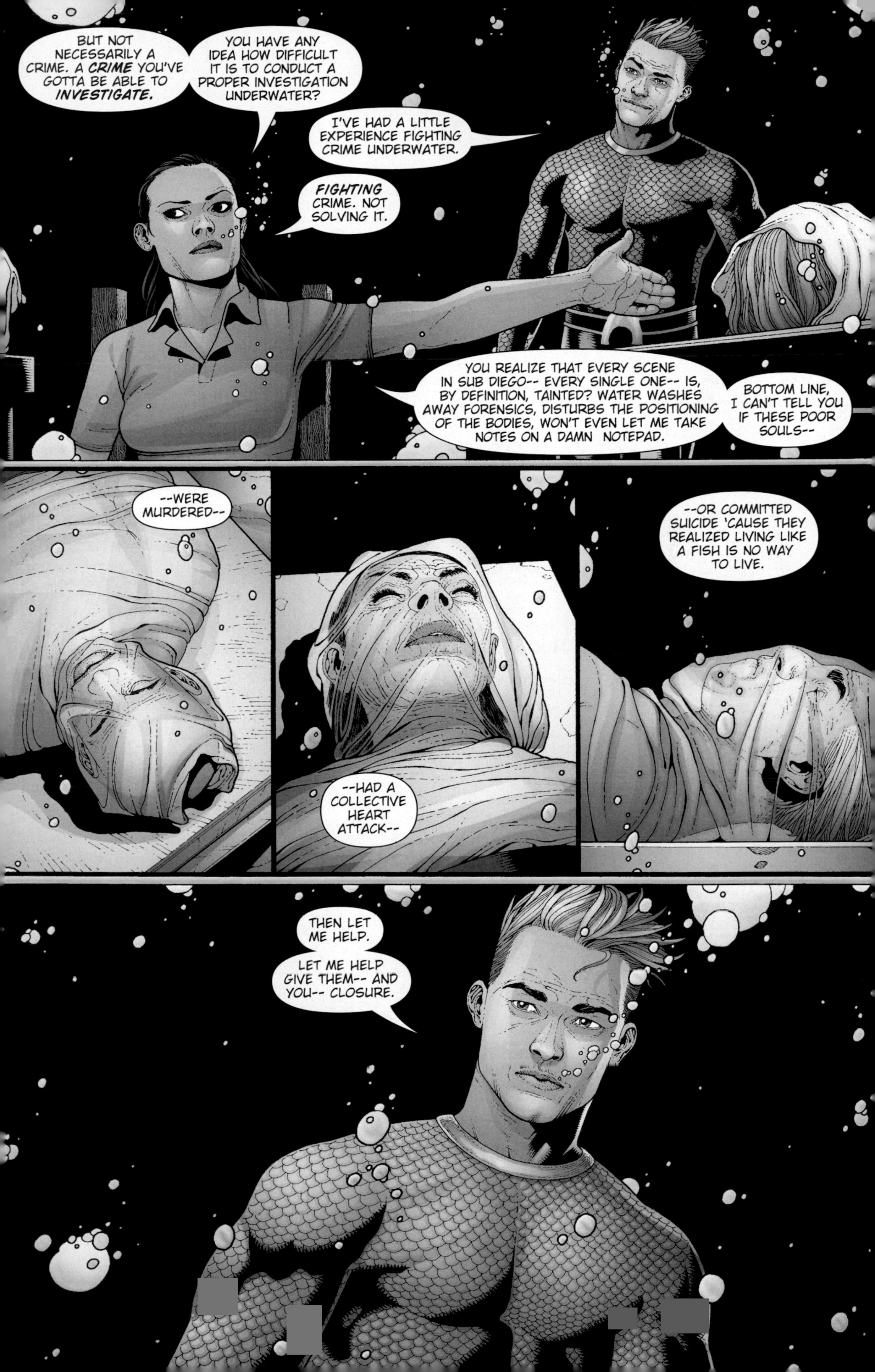
BUT NOT NECESSARILY A CRIME. A CRIME YOU'VE GOTTA BE ABLE TO INVESTIGATE.
YOU HAVE ANY IDEA HOW DIFFICULT IT IS TO CONDUCT A PROPER INVESTIGATION UNDERWATER?
I'VE HAD A LITTLE EXPERIENCE FIGHTING CRIME UNDERWATER.
FIGHTING CRIME. NOT SOLVING IT.
YOU REALIZE THAT EVERY SCENE IN SUB DIEGO-- EVERY SINGLE ONE-- IS, BY DEFINITION, TAINTED? WATER WASHES AWAY FORENSICS, DISTURBS THE POSITIONING OF THE BODIES, WON'T EVEN LET ME TAKE NOTES ON A DAMN NOTEPAD.
BOTTOM LINE, I CAN'T TELL YOU IF THESE POOR SOULS--
--WERE MURDERED--
--HAD A COLLECTIVE HEART ATTACK--
--OR COMMITTED SUICIDE 'CAUSE THEY REALIZED LIVING LIKE A FISH IS NO WAY TO LIVE.
THEN LET ME HELP.
LET ME HELP GIVE THEM-- AND YOU-- CLOSURE.

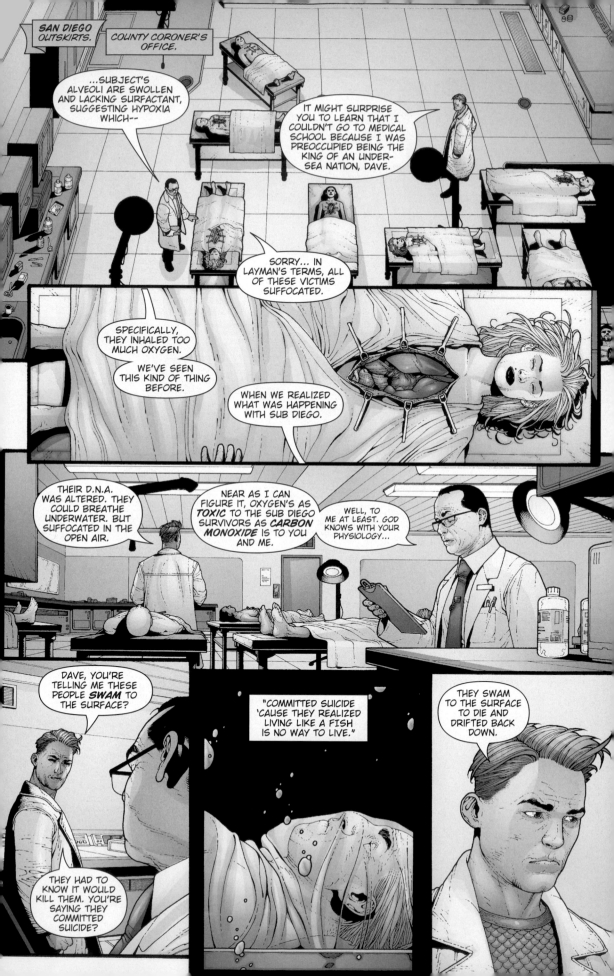

SAN DIEGO OUTSKIRTS. COUNTY CORONER'S OFFICE.

...SUBJECT'S ALVEOLI ARE SWOLLEN AND LACKING SURFACTANT, SUGGESTING HYPOXIA WHICH--

IT MIGHT SURPRISE YOU TO LEARN THAT I COULDN'T GO TO MEDICAL SCHOOL BECAUSE I WAS PREOCCUPIED BEING THE KING OF AN UNDER-SEA NATION, DAVE.

SORRY... IN LAYMAN'S TERMS, ALL OF THESE VICTIMS SUFFOCATED.

SPECIFICALLY, THEY INHALED TOO MUCH OXYGEN.

WE'VE SEEN THIS KIND OF THING BEFORE.

WHEN WE REALIZED WHAT WAS HAPPENING WITH SUB DIEGO.

THEIR D.N.A. WAS ALTERED. THEY COULD BREATHE UNDERWATER. BUT SUFFOCATED IN THE OPEN AIR.

NEAR AS I CAN FIGURE IT, OXYGEN'S AS *TOXIC* TO THE SUB DIEGO SURVIVORS AS *CARBON MONOXIDE* IS TO YOU AND ME.

WELL, TO ME AT LEAST. GOD KNOWS WITH YOUR PHYSIOLOGY...

DAVE, YOU'RE TELLING ME THESE PEOPLE *SWAM* TO THE SURFACE?

THEY HAD TO KNOW IT WOULD KILL THEM. YOU'RE SAYING THEY COMMITTED SUICIDE?

"COMMITTED SUICIDE 'CAUSE THEY REALIZED LIVING LIKE A FISH IS NO WAY TO LIVE."

THEY SWAM TO THE SURFACE TO DIE AND DRIFTED BACK DOWN.

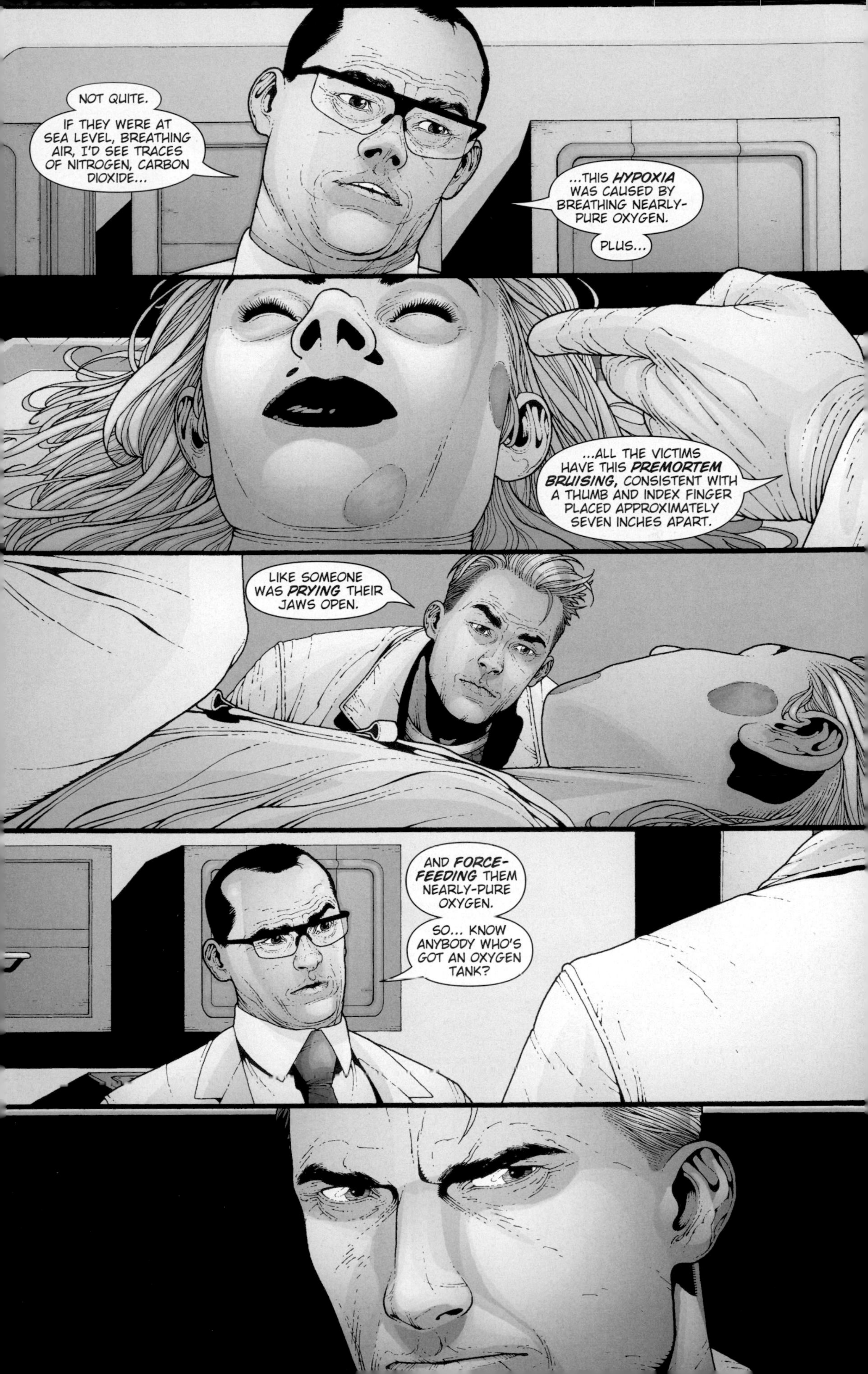
NOT QUITE.
IF THEY WERE AT SEA LEVEL, BREATHING AIR, I'D SEE TRACES OF NITROGEN, CARBON DIOXIDE...
...THIS *HYPOXIA* WAS CAUSED BY BREATHING NEARLY-PURE OXYGEN.
PLUS...
...ALL THE VICTIMS HAVE THIS *PREMORTEM BRUISING*, CONSISTENT WITH A THUMB AND INDEX FINGER PLACED APPROXIMATELY SEVEN INCHES APART.
LIKE SOMEONE WAS *PRYING* THEIR JAWS OPEN.
AND *FORCE-FEEDING* THEM NEARLY-PURE OXYGEN.
SO... KNOW ANYBODY WHO'S GOT AN OXYGEN TANK?

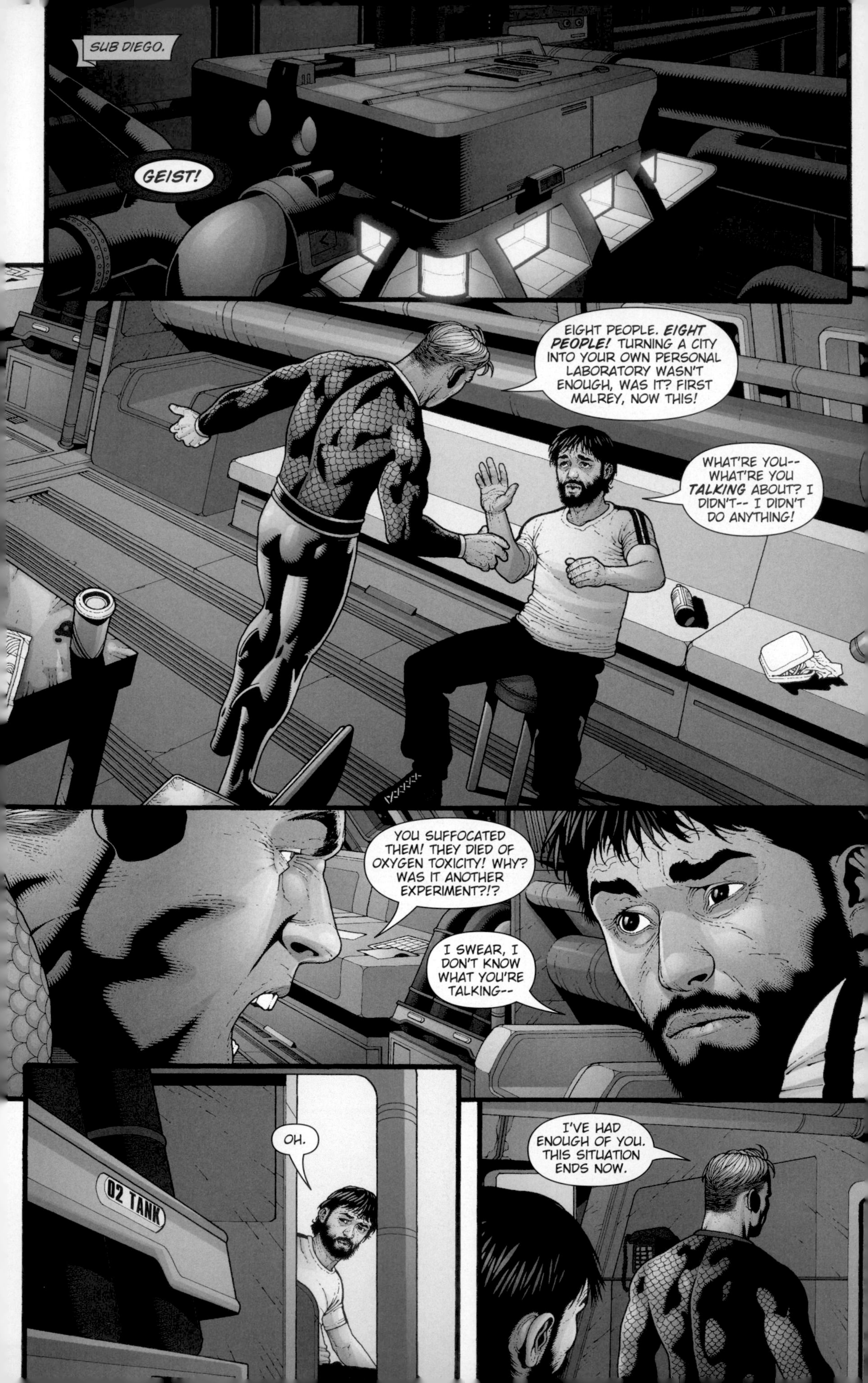
SUB DIEGO.
GEIST!
EIGHT PEOPLE. EIGHT PEOPLE! TURNING A CITY INTO YOUR OWN PERSONAL LABORATORY WASN'T ENOUGH, WAS IT? FIRST MALREY, NOW THIS!
WHAT'RE YOU-- WHAT'RE YOU TALKING ABOUT? I DIDN'T-- I DIDN'T DO ANYTHING!
YOU SUFFOCATED THEM! THEY DIED OF OXYGEN TOXICITY! WHY? WAS IT ANOTHER EXPERIMENT?!?
I SWEAR, I DON'T KNOW WHAT YOU'RE TALKING--
O2 TANK
OH.
I'VE HAD ENOUGH OF YOU. THIS SITUATION ENDS NOW.

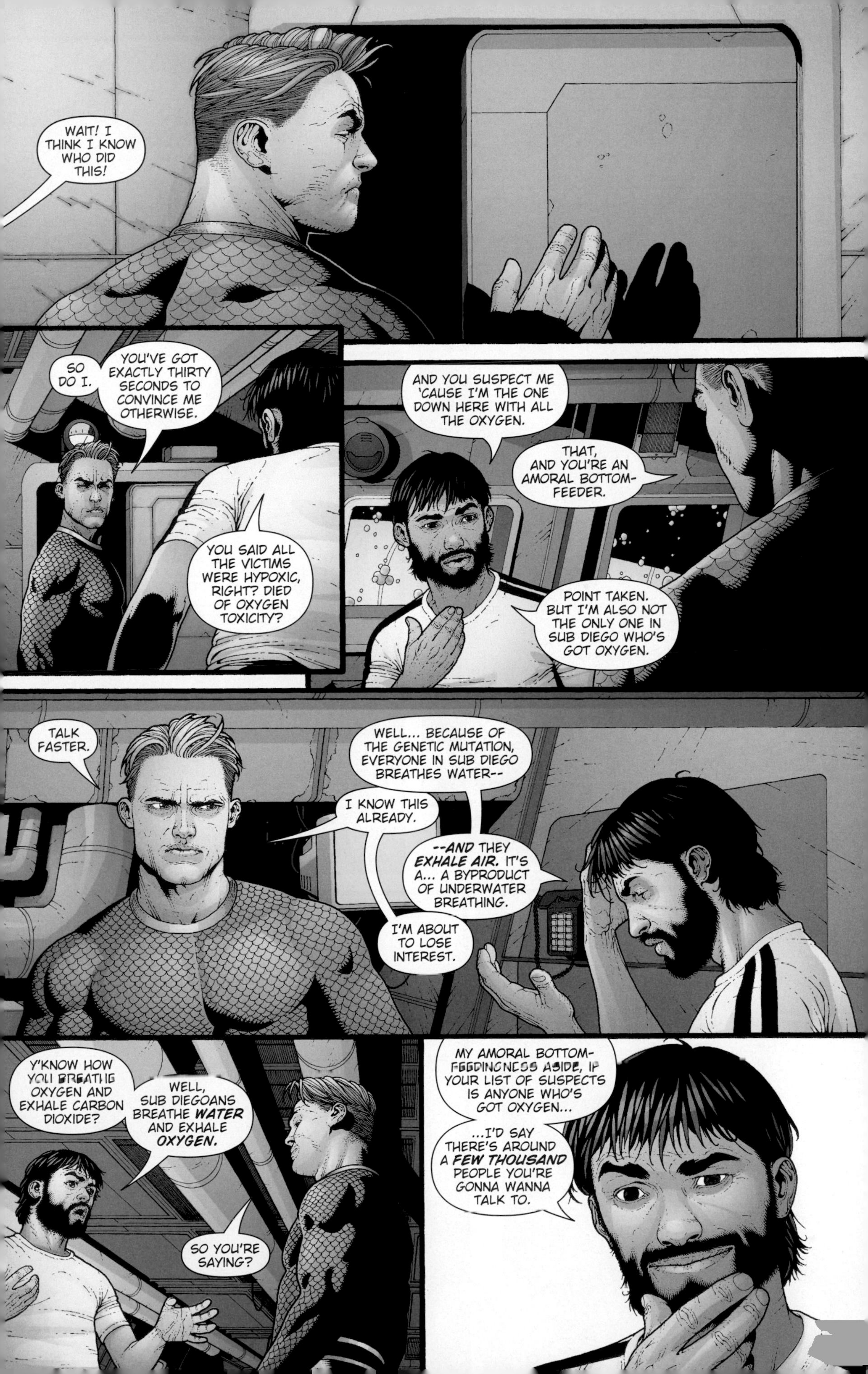
WAIT! I THINK I KNOW WHO DID THIS!
SO DO I.
YOU'VE GOT EXACTLY THIRTY SECONDS TO CONVINCE ME OTHERWISE.
YOU SAID ALL THE VICTIMS WERE HYPOXIC, RIGHT? DIED OF OXYGEN TOXICITY?
AND YOU SUSPECT ME 'CAUSE I'M THE ONE DOWN HERE WITH ALL THE OXYGEN.
THAT, AND YOU'RE AN AMORAL BOTTOM-FEEDER.
POINT TAKEN. BUT I'M ALSO NOT THE ONLY ONE IN SUB DIEGO WHO'S GOT OXYGEN.
TALK FASTER.
WELL... BECAUSE OF THE GENETIC MUTATION, EVERYONE IN SUB DIEGO BREATHES WATER--
I KNOW THIS ALREADY.
--AND THEY EXHALE AIR. IT'S A... A BYPRODUCT OF UNDERWATER BREATHING.
I'M ABOUT TO LOSE INTEREST.
Y'KNOW HOW YOU BREATHE OXYGEN AND EXHALE CARBON DIOXIDE?
WELL, SUB DIEGOANS BREATHE WATER AND EXHALE OXYGEN.
SO YOU'RE SAYING?
MY AMORAL BOTTOM-FEEDINGNESS ASIDE, IF YOUR LIST OF SUSPECTS IS ANYONE WHO'S GOT OXYGEN...
...I'D SAY THERE'S AROUND A FEW THOUSAND PEOPLE YOU'RE GONNA WANNA TALK TO.

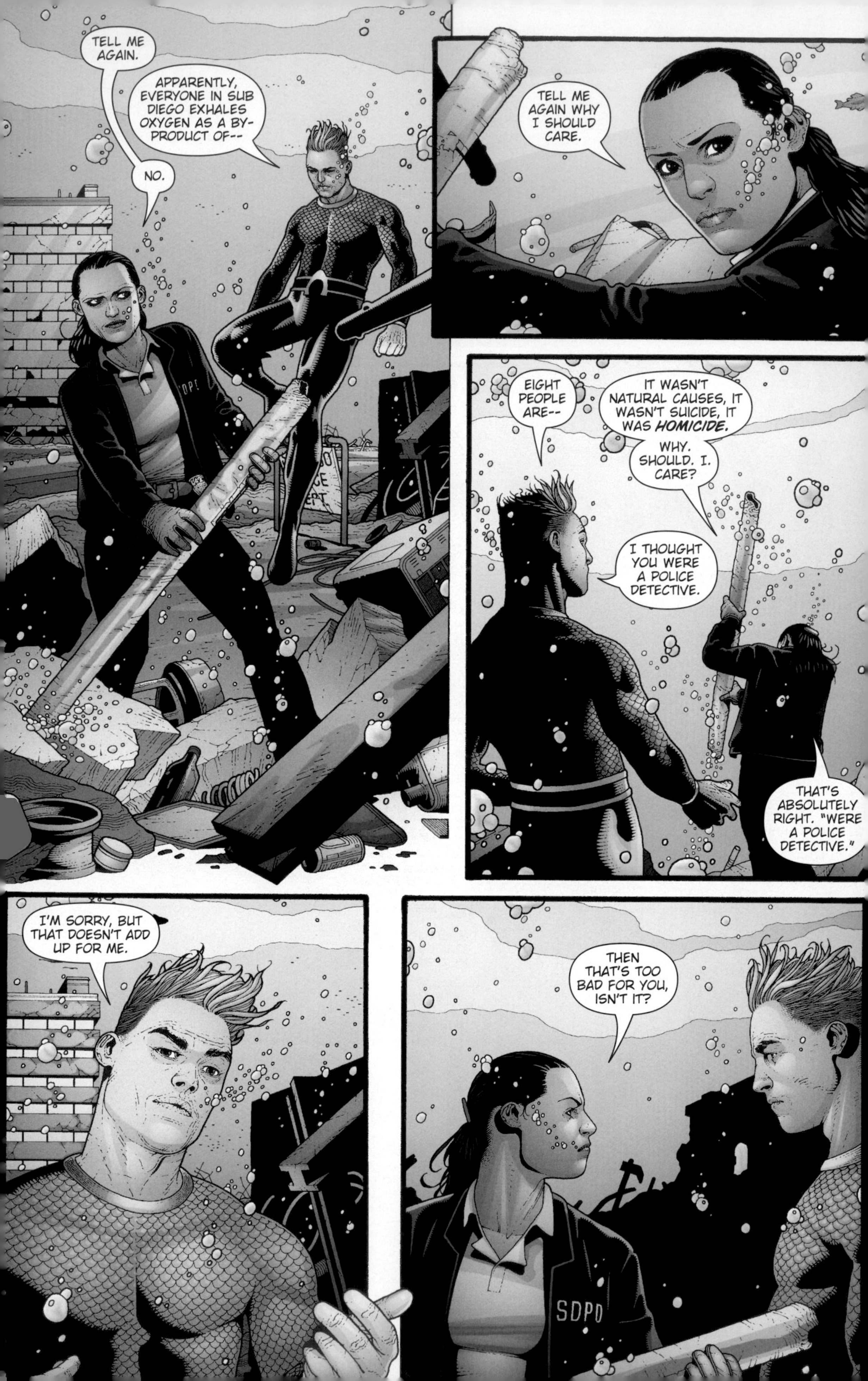
TELL ME AGAIN.
APPARENTLY, EVERYONE IN SUB DIEGO EXHALES OXYGEN AS A BY-PRODUCT OF--
NO.
TELL ME AGAIN WHY I SHOULD CARE.
EIGHT PEOPLE ARE--
IT WASN'T NATURAL CAUSES, IT WASN'T SUICIDE, IT WAS *HOMICIDE.*
WHY. SHOULD. I. CARE?
I THOUGHT YOU WERE A POLICE DETECTIVE.
THAT'S ABSOLUTELY RIGHT. "WERE A POLICE DETECTIVE."
I'M SORRY, BUT THAT DOESN'T ADD UP FOR ME.
THEN THAT'S TOO BAD FOR YOU, ISN'T IT?
SDPD

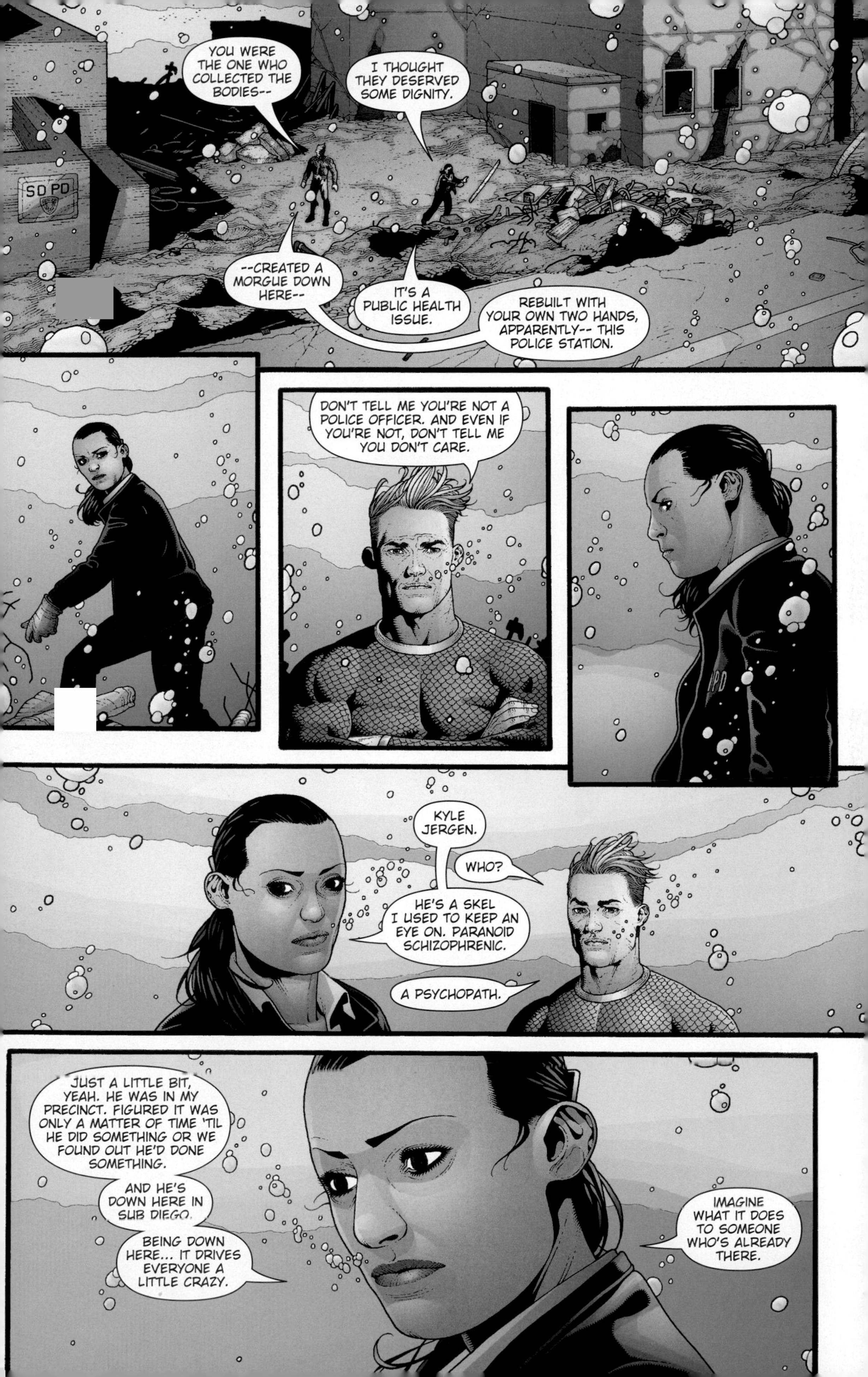
YOU WERE THE ONE WHO COLLECTED THE BODIES--
I THOUGHT THEY DESERVED SOME DIGNITY.
SD PD
--CREATED A MORGUE DOWN HERE--
IT'S A PUBLIC HEALTH ISSUE.
REBUILT WITH YOUR OWN TWO HANDS, APPARENTLY-- THIS POLICE STATION.
DON'T TELL ME YOU'RE NOT A POLICE OFFICER. AND EVEN IF YOU'RE NOT, DON'T TELL ME YOU DON'T CARE.
KYLE JERGEN.
WHO?
HE'S A SKEL I USED TO KEEP AN EYE ON. PARANOID SCHIZOPHRENIC.
A PSYCHOPATH.
JUST A LITTLE BIT, YEAH. HE WAS IN MY PRECINCT. FIGURED IT WAS ONLY A MATTER OF TIME 'TIL HE DID SOMETHING OR WE FOUND OUT HE'D DONE SOMETHING.
AND HE'S DOWN HERE IN SUB DIEGO.
BEING DOWN HERE... IT DRIVES EVERYONE A LITTLE CRAZY.
IMAGINE WHAT IT DOES TO SOMEONE WHO'S ALREADY THERE.

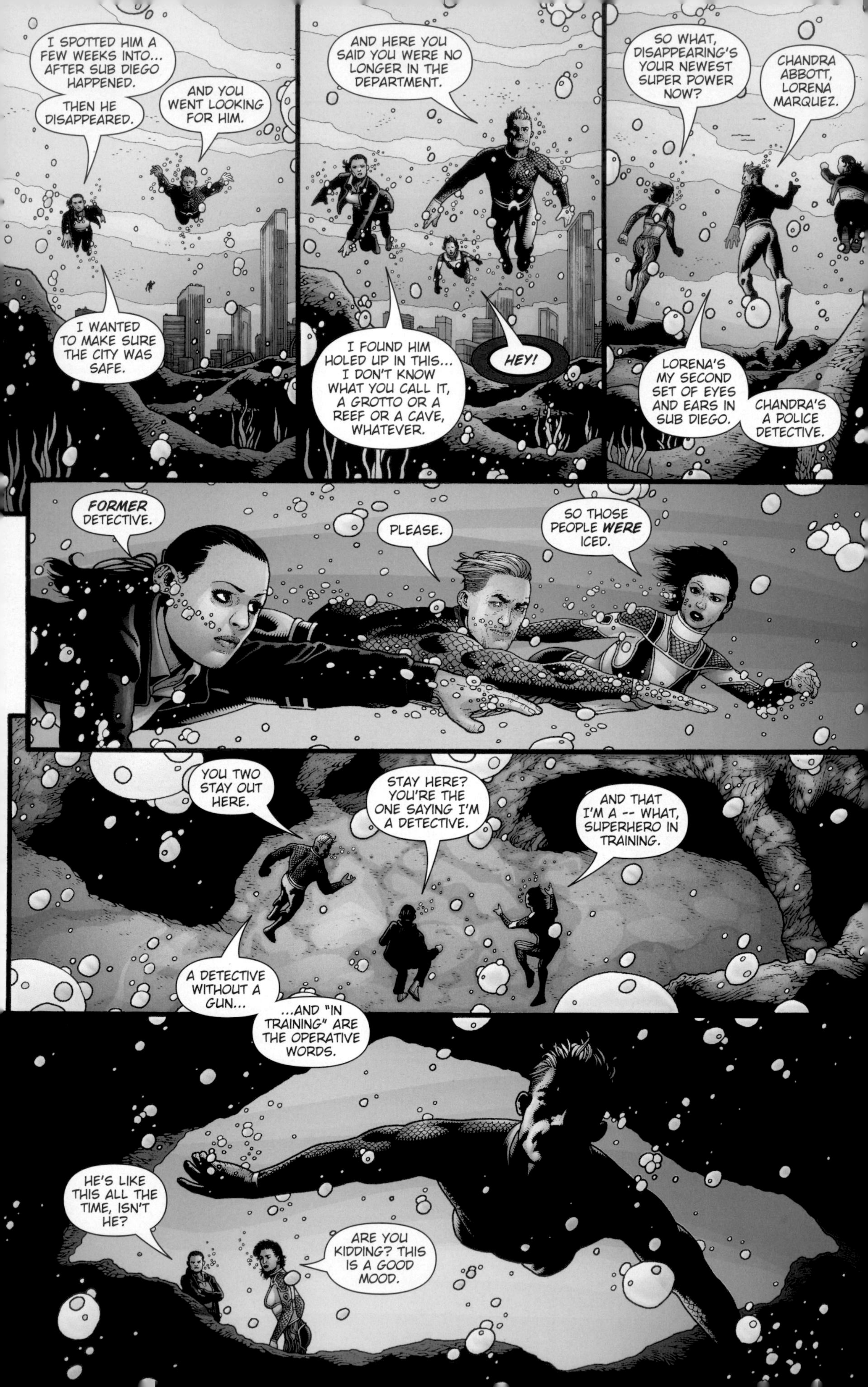
I SPOTTED HIM A FEW WEEKS INTO... AFTER SUB DIEGO HAPPENED.
THEN HE DISAPPEARED.
AND YOU WENT LOOKING FOR HIM.
I WANTED TO MAKE SURE THE CITY WAS SAFE.
AND HERE YOU SAID YOU WERE NO LONGER IN THE DEPARTMENT.
I FOUND HIM HOLED UP IN THIS... I DON'T KNOW WHAT YOU CALL IT, A GROTTO OR A REEF OR A CAVE, WHATEVER.
HEY!
SO WHAT, DISAPPEARING'S YOUR NEWEST SUPER POWER NOW?
CHANDRA ABBOTT, LORENA MARQUEZ.
LORENA'S MY SECOND SET OF EYES AND EARS IN SUB DIEGO.
CHANDRA'S A POLICE DETECTIVE.
FORMER DETECTIVE.
PLEASE.
SO THOSE PEOPLE *WERE* ICED.
YOU TWO STAY OUT HERE.
STAY HERE? YOU'RE THE ONE SAYING I'M A DETECTIVE.
AND THAT I'M A -- WHAT, SUPERHERO IN TRAINING.
A DETECTIVE WITHOUT A GUN...
...AND "IN TRAINING" ARE THE OPERATIVE WORDS.
HE'S LIKE THIS ALL THE TIME, ISN'T HE?
ARE YOU KIDDING? THIS IS A GOOD MOOD.

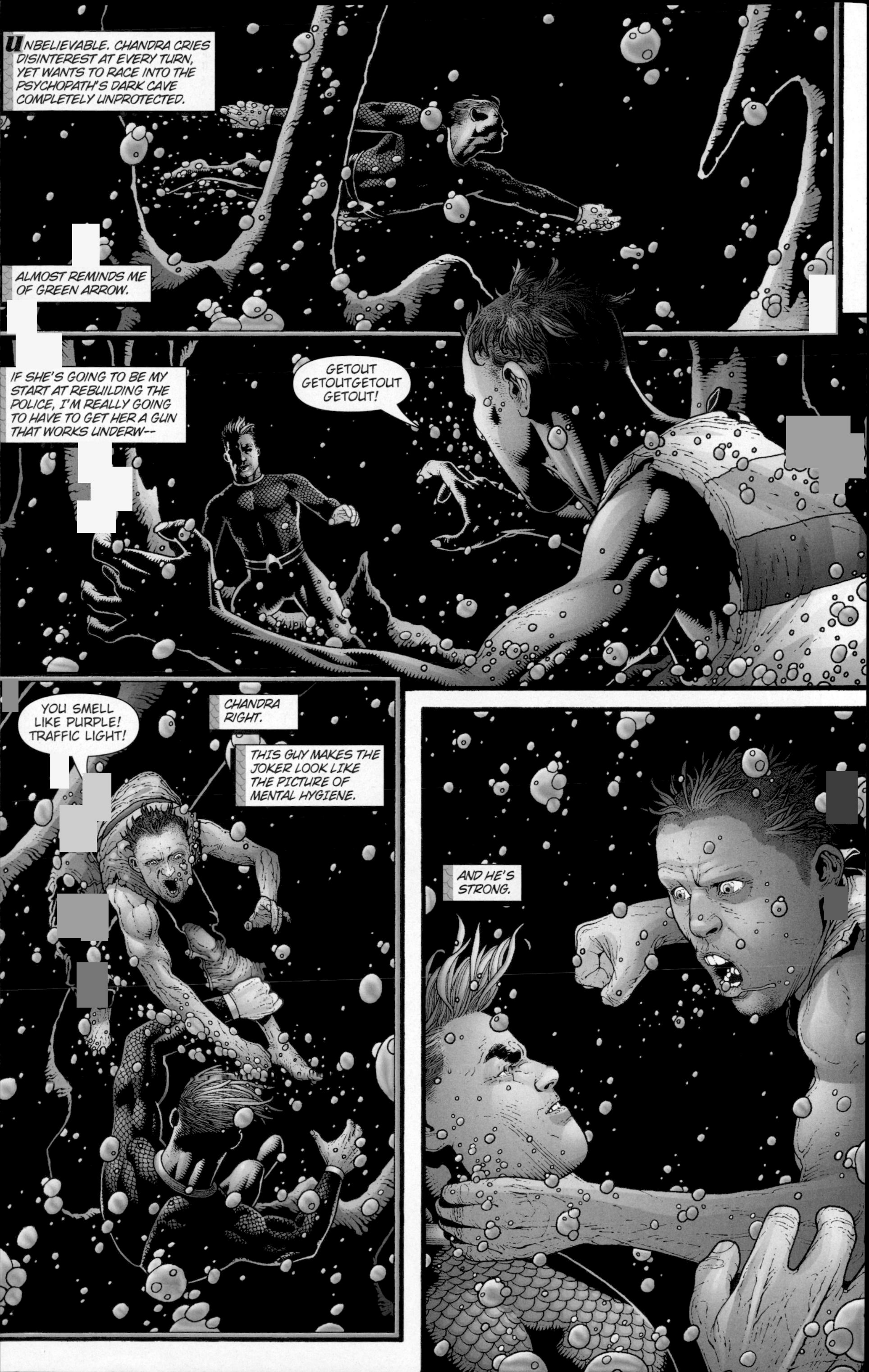
UNBELIEVABLE. CHANDRA CRIES DISINTEREST AT EVERY TURN, YET WANTS TO RACE INTO THE PSYCHOPATH'S DARK CAVE COMPLETELY UNPROTECTED.
ALMOST REMINDS ME OF GREEN ARROW.
IF SHE'S GOING TO BE MY START AT REBUILDING THE POLICE, I'M REALLY GOING TO HAVE TO GET HER A GUN THAT WORKS UNDERW--
GETOUT GETOUTGETOUT GETOUT!
YOU SMELL LIKE PURPLE! TRAFFIC LIGHT!
CHANDRA RIGHT.
THIS GUY MAKES THE JOKER LOOK LIKE THE PICTURE OF MENTAL HYGIENE.
AND HE'S STRONG.

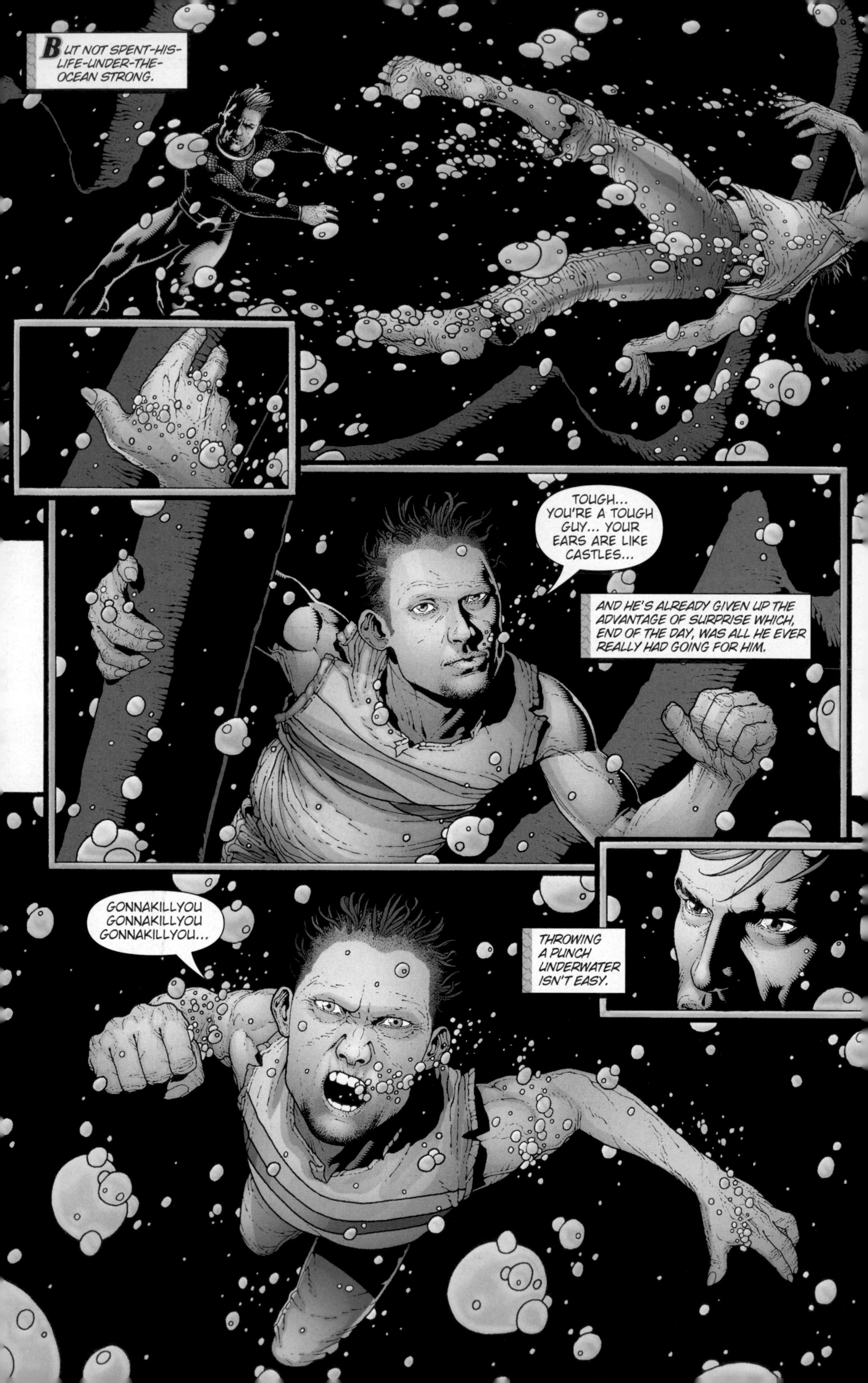
BUT NOT SPENT-HIS-LIFE-UNDER-THE-OCEAN STRONG.
TOUGH... YOU'RE A TOUGH GUY... YOUR EARS ARE LIKE CASTLES...
AND HE'S ALREADY GIVEN UP THE ADVANTAGE OF SURPRISE WHICH, END OF THE DAY, WAS ALL HE EVER REALLY HAD GOING FOR HIM.
GONNAKILLYOU GONNAKILLYOU GONNAKILLYOU...
THROWING A PUNCH UNDERWATER ISN'T EASY.

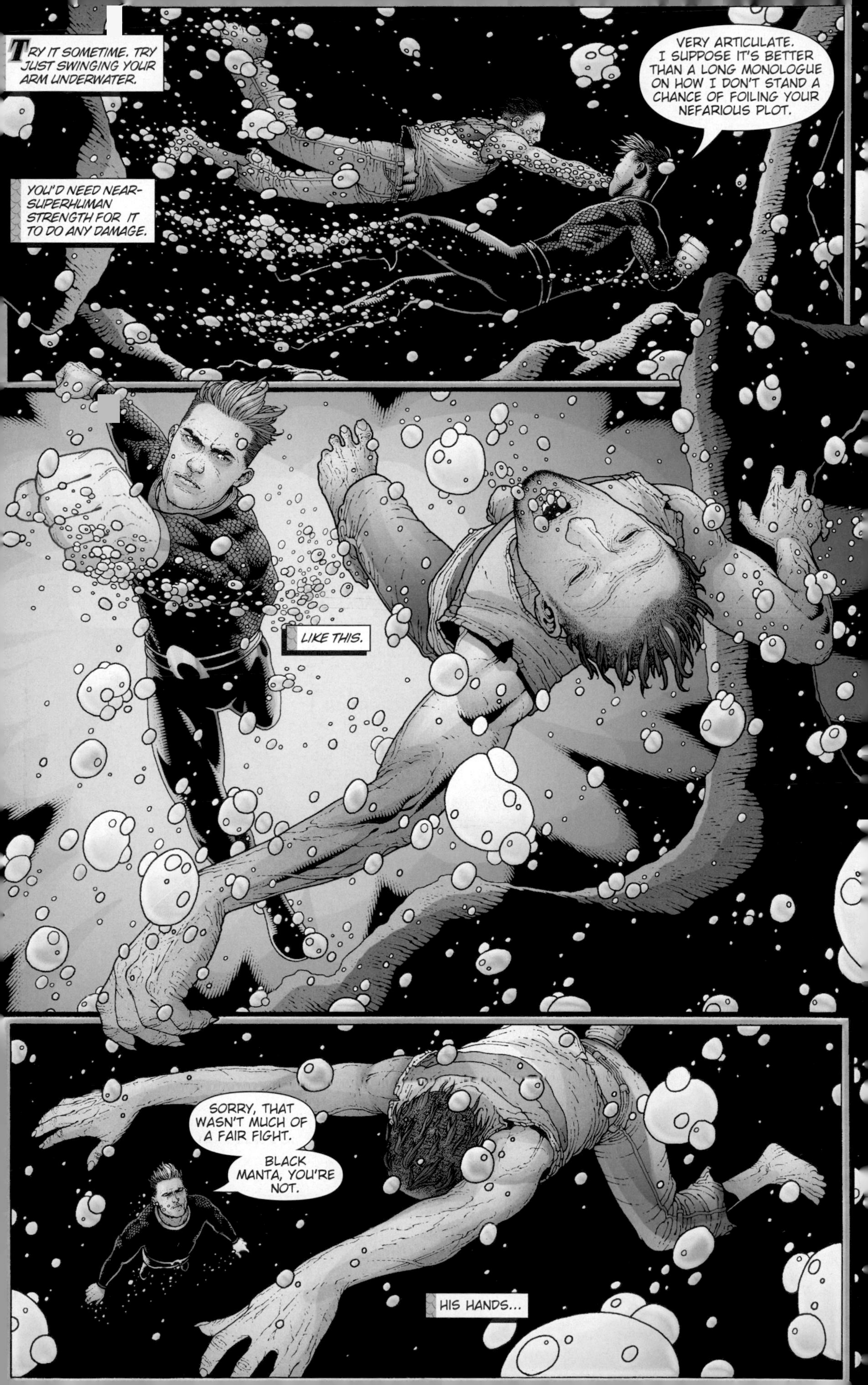
TRY IT SOMETIME. TRY JUST SWINGING YOUR ARM UNDERWATER.
YOU'D NEED NEAR-SUPERHUMAN STRENGTH FOR IT TO DO ANY DAMAGE.
VERY ARTICULATE. I SUPPOSE IT'S BETTER THAN A LONG MONOLOGUE ON HOW I DON'T STAND A CHANCE OF FOILING YOUR NEFARIOUS PLOT.
LIKE THIS.
SORRY, THAT WASN'T MUCH OF A FAIR FIGHT.
BLACK MANTA, YOU'RE NOT.
HIS HANDS...

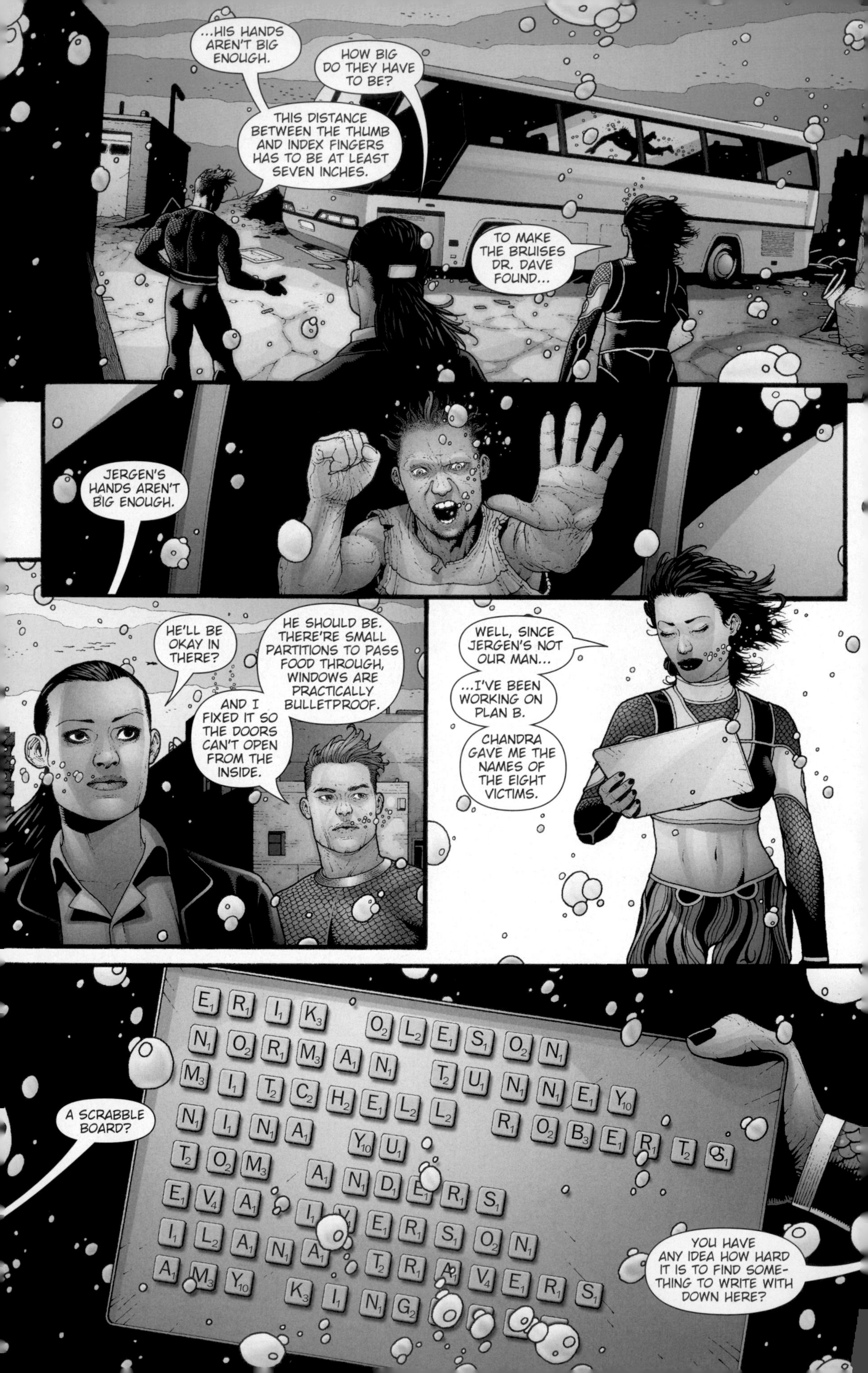
...HIS HANDS AREN'T BIG ENOUGH.
HOW BIG DO THEY HAVE TO BE?
THIS DISTANCE BETWEEN THE THUMB AND INDEX FINGERS HAS TO BE AT LEAST SEVEN INCHES.
TO MAKE THE BRUISES DR. DAVE FOUND...
JERGEN'S HANDS AREN'T BIG ENOUGH.
HE'LL BE OKAY IN THERE?
HE SHOULD BE. THERE'RE SMALL PARTITIONS TO PASS FOOD THROUGH, WINDOWS ARE PRACTICALLY BULLETPROOF.
AND I FIXED IT SO THE DOORS CAN'T OPEN FROM THE INSIDE.
WELL, SINCE JERGEN'S NOT OUR MAN...
...I'VE BEEN WORKING ON PLAN B.
CHANDRA GAVE ME THE NAMES OF THE EIGHT VICTIMS.
A SCRABBLE BOARD?
ERIK OLESON
NORMAN TUNNEY
MITCHELL ROBERTS
NINA YU
TOM ANDERS
EVA IVERSON
ILANA TRAVERS
AMY KING
YOU HAVE ANY IDEA HOW HARD IT IS TO FIND SOME-THING TO WRITE WITH DOWN HERE?

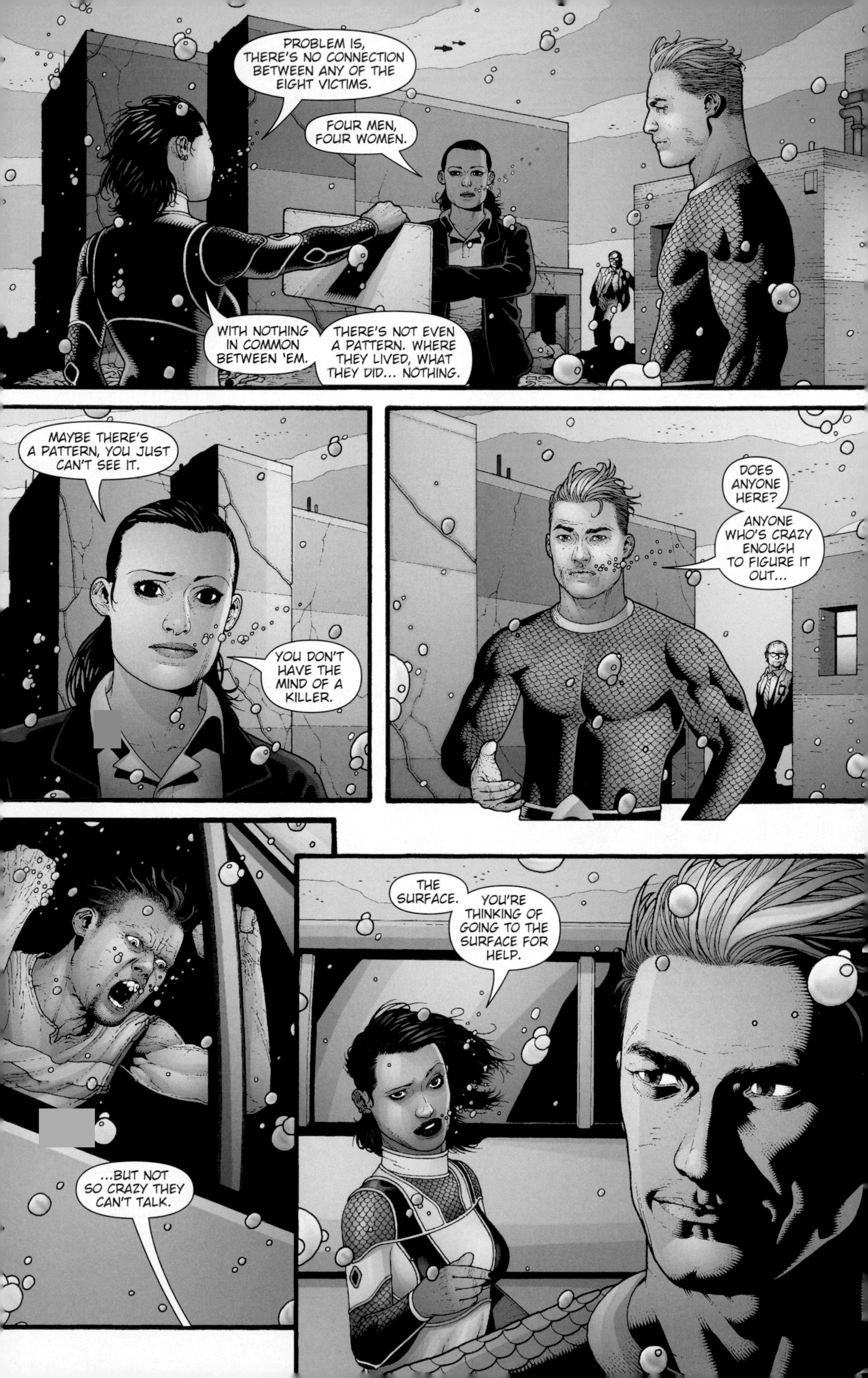
PROBLEM IS, THERE'S NO CONNECTION BETWEEN ANY OF THE EIGHT VICTIMS.
FOUR MEN, FOUR WOMEN.
WITH NOTHING IN COMMON BETWEEN 'EM.
THERE'S NOT EVEN A PATTERN. WHERE THEY LIVED, WHAT THEY DID... NOTHING.
MAYBE THERE'S A PATTERN, YOU JUST CAN'T SEE IT.
YOU DON'T HAVE THE MIND OF A KILLER.
DOES ANYONE HERE?
ANYONE WHO'S CRAZY ENOUGH TO FIGURE IT OUT...
...BUT NOT SO CRAZY THEY CAN'T TALK.
THE SURFACE.
YOU'RE THINKING OF GOING TO THE SURFACE FOR HELP.

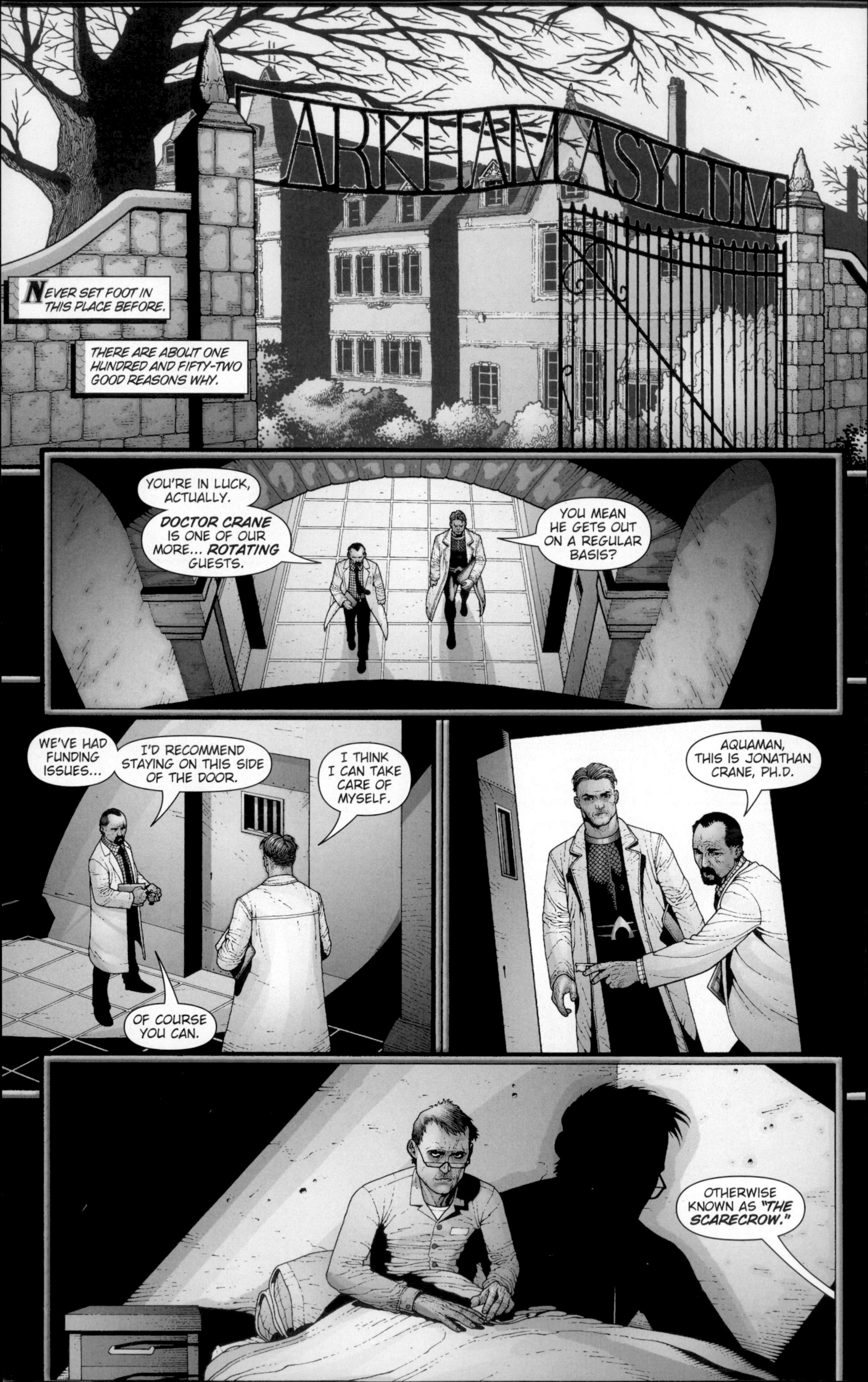
ARKHAM ASYLUM
NEVER SET FOOT IN THIS PLACE BEFORE.
THERE ARE ABOUT ONE HUNDRED AND FIFTY-TWO GOOD REASONS WHY.
YOU'RE IN LUCK, ACTUALLY. DOCTOR CRANE IS ONE OF OUR MORE... ROTATING GUESTS.
YOU MEAN HE GETS OUT ON A REGULAR BASIS?
WE'VE HAD FUNDING ISSUES...
I'D RECOMMEND STAYING ON THIS SIDE OF THE DOOR.
I THINK I CAN TAKE CARE OF MYSELF.
OF COURSE YOU CAN.
AQUAMAN, THIS IS JONATHAN CRANE, PH.D.
OTHERWISE KNOWN AS "THE SCARECROW."

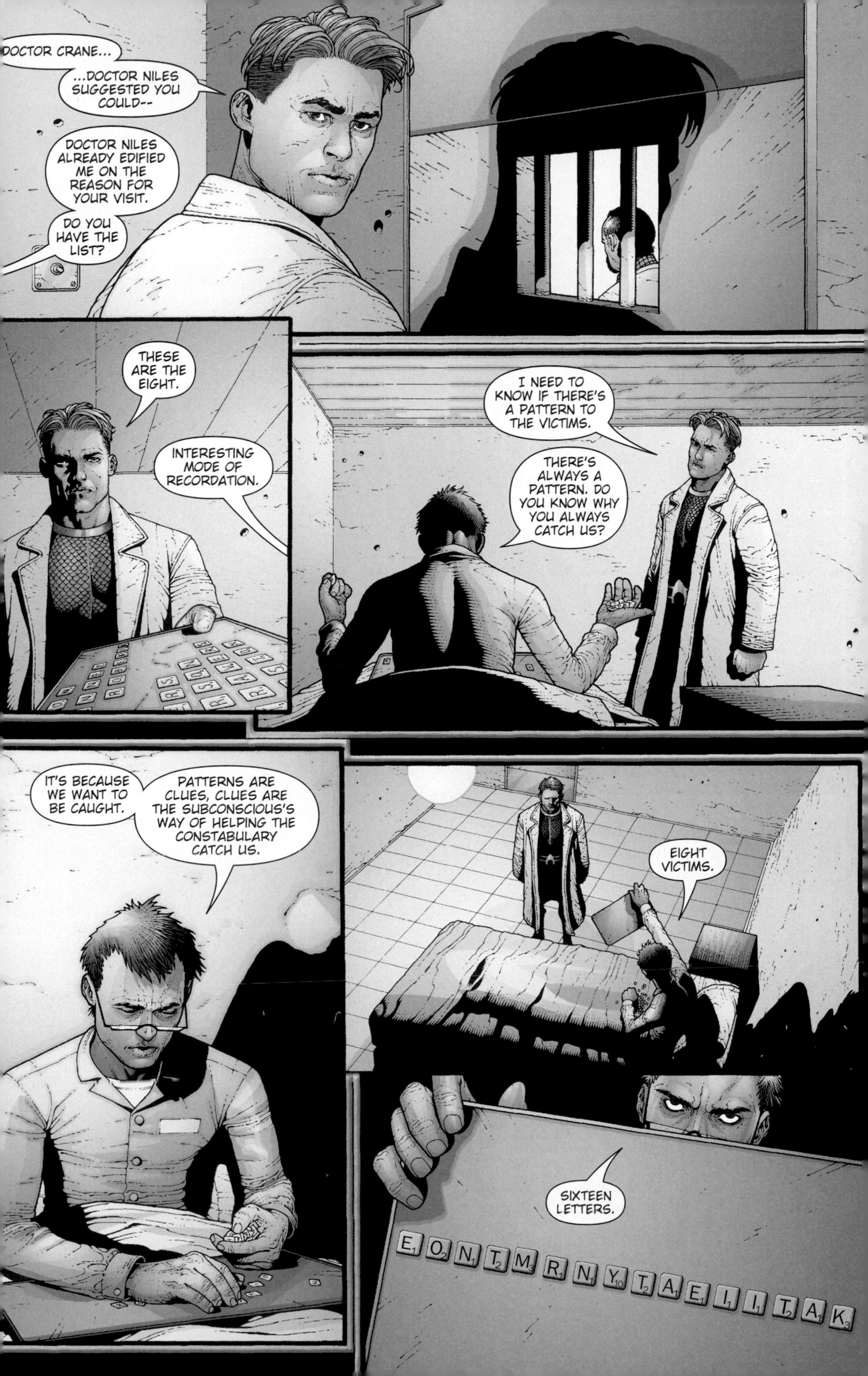

DOCTOR CRANE...
...DOCTOR NILES SUGGESTED YOU COULD--
DOCTOR NILES ALREADY EDIFIED ME ON THE REASON FOR YOUR VISIT.
DO YOU HAVE THE LIST?
THESE ARE THE EIGHT.
INTERESTING MODE OF RECORDATION.
I NEED TO KNOW IF THERE'S A PATTERN TO THE VICTIMS.
THERE'S ALWAYS A PATTERN. DO YOU KNOW WHY YOU ALWAYS CATCH US?
IT'S BECAUSE WE WANT TO BE CAUGHT.
PATTERNS ARE CLUES, CLUES ARE THE SUBCONSCIOUS'S WAY OF HELPING THE CONSTABULARY CATCH US.
EIGHT VICTIMS.
SIXTEEN LETTERS.
EONTMRNYTAEIIITAK

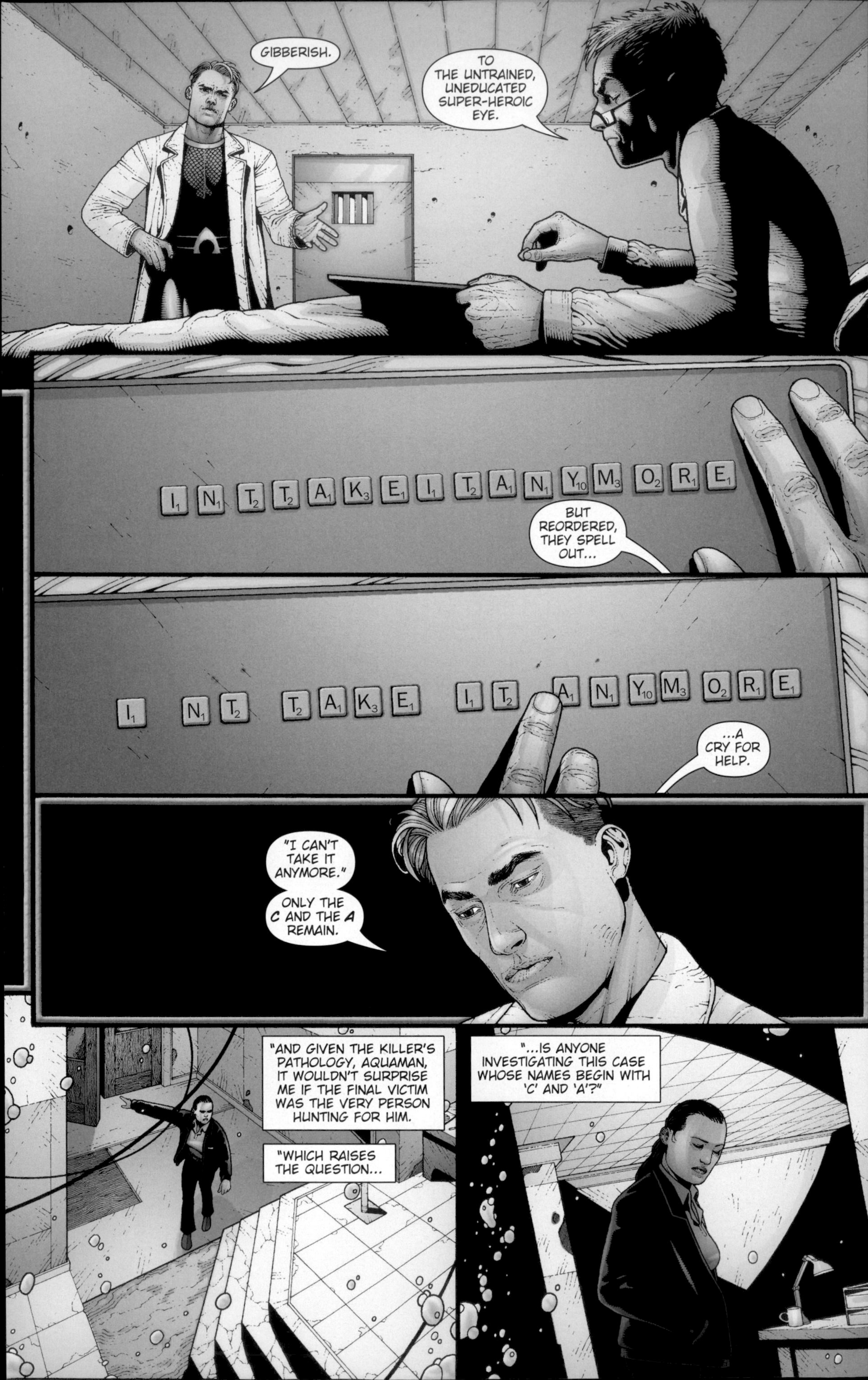
GIBBERISH.
TO THE UNTRAINED, UNEDUCATED SUPER-HEROIC EYE.
INTTAKEITANYMORE
BUT REORDERED, THEY SPELL OUT...
I NT TAKE IT ANYMORE
...A CRY FOR HELP.
"I CAN'T TAKE IT ANYMORE."
ONLY THE C AND THE A REMAIN.
"AND GIVEN THE KILLER'S PATHOLOGY, AQUAMAN, IT WOULDN'T SURPRISE ME IF THE FINAL VICTIM WAS THE VERY PERSON HUNTING FOR HIM.
"WHICH RAISES THE QUESTION...
"...IS ANYONE INVESTIGATING THIS CASE WHOSE NAMES BEGIN WITH 'C' AND 'A'?"

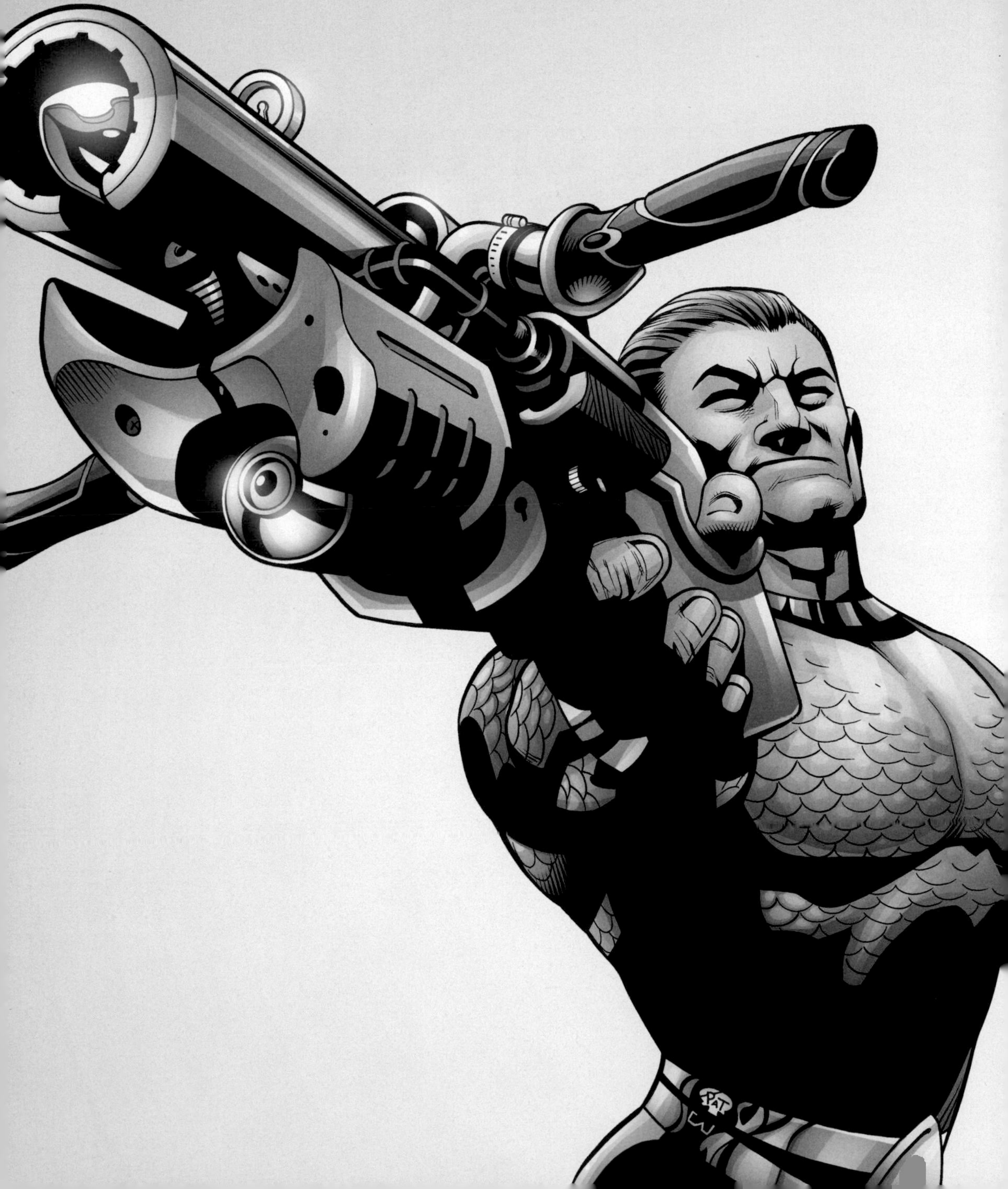

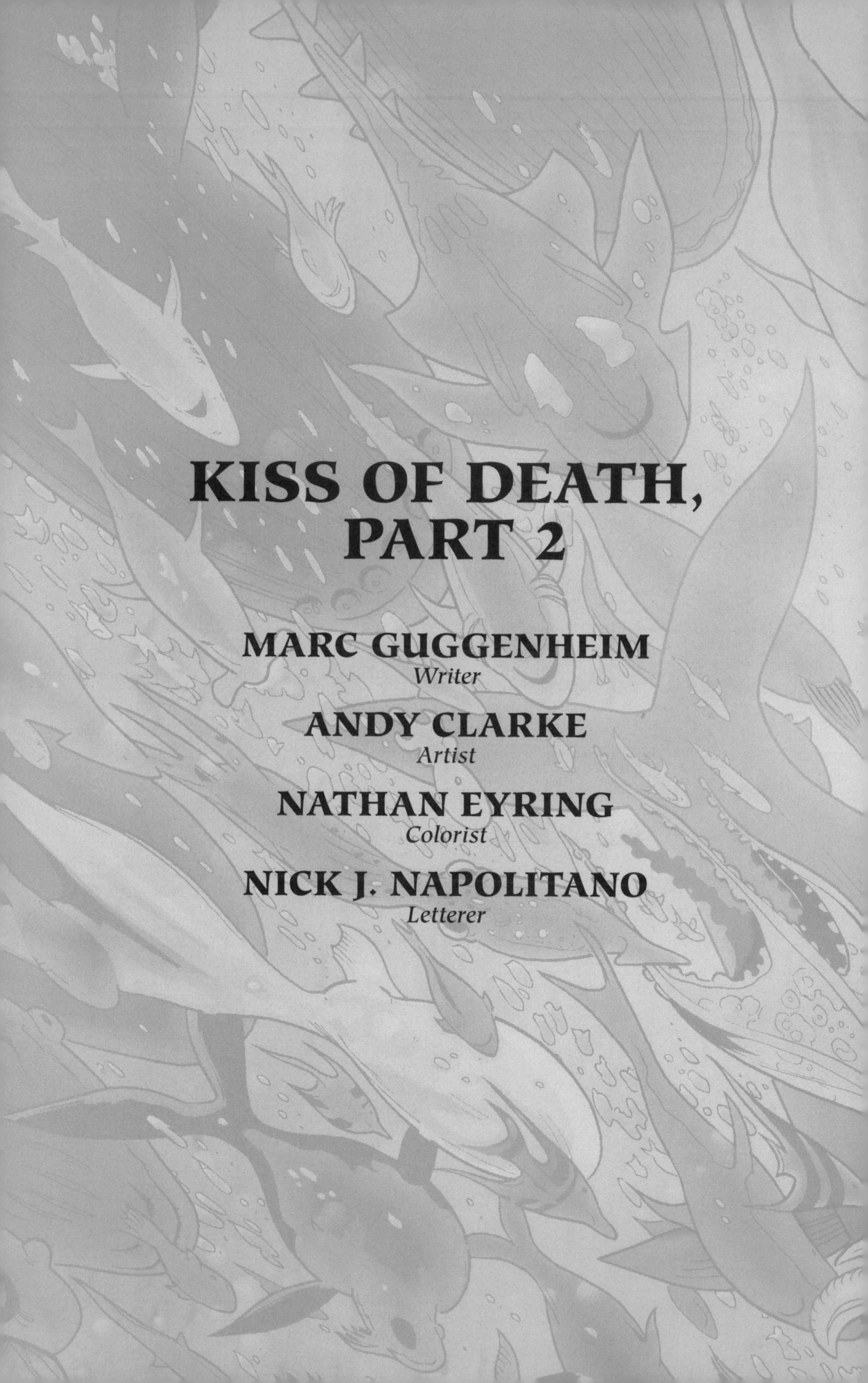

KISS OF DEATH, PART 2

MARC GUGGENHEIM
Writer

ANDY CLARKE
Artist

NATHAN EYRING
Colorist

NICK J. NAPOLITANO
Letterer

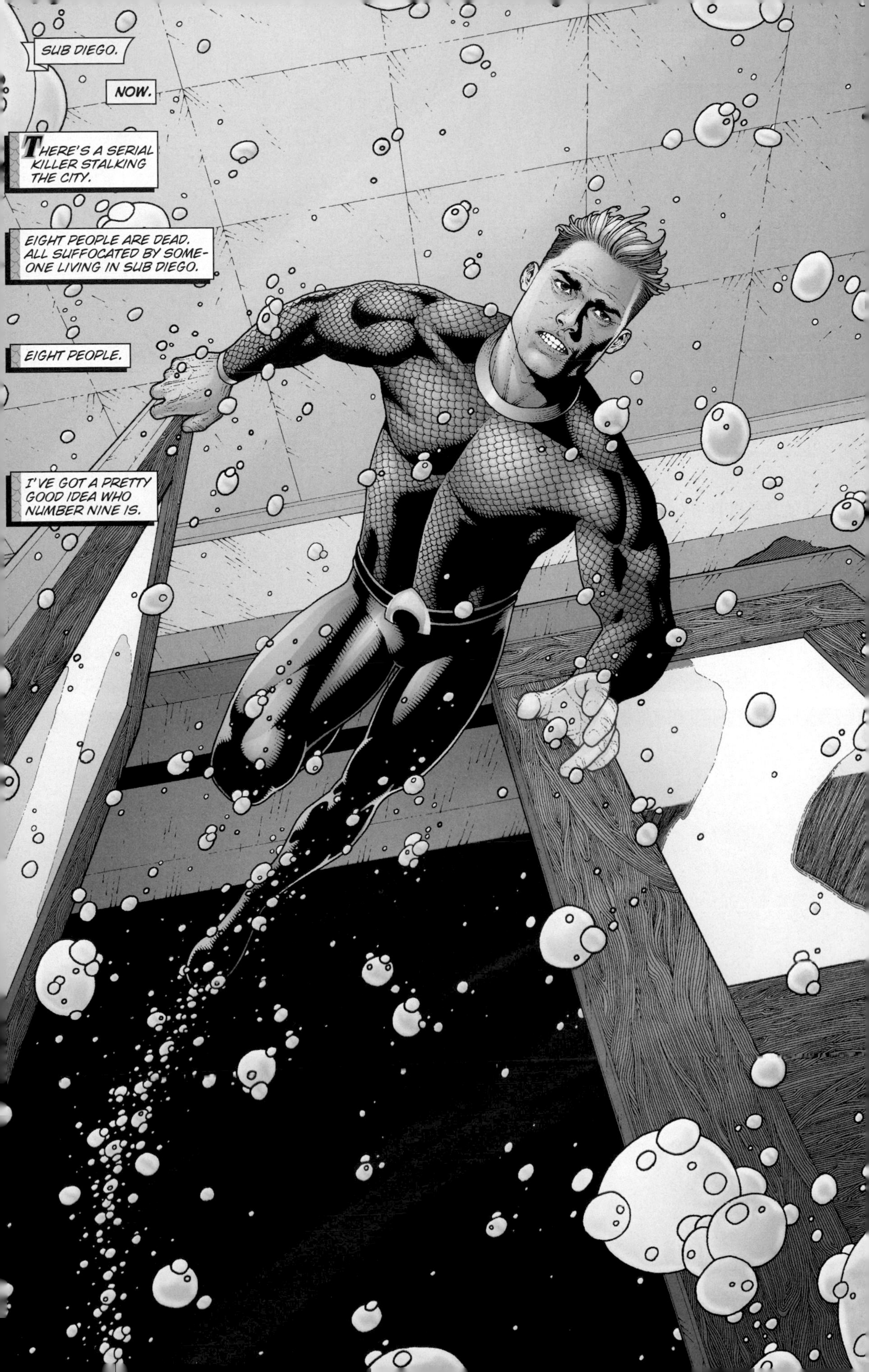
SUB DIEGO.
NOW.
THERE'S A SERIAL KILLER STALKING THE CITY.
EIGHT PEOPLE ARE DEAD. ALL SUFFOCATED BY SOME-ONE LIVING IN SUB DIEGO.
EIGHT PEOPLE.
I'VE GOT A PRETTY GOOD IDEA WHO NUMBER NINE IS.

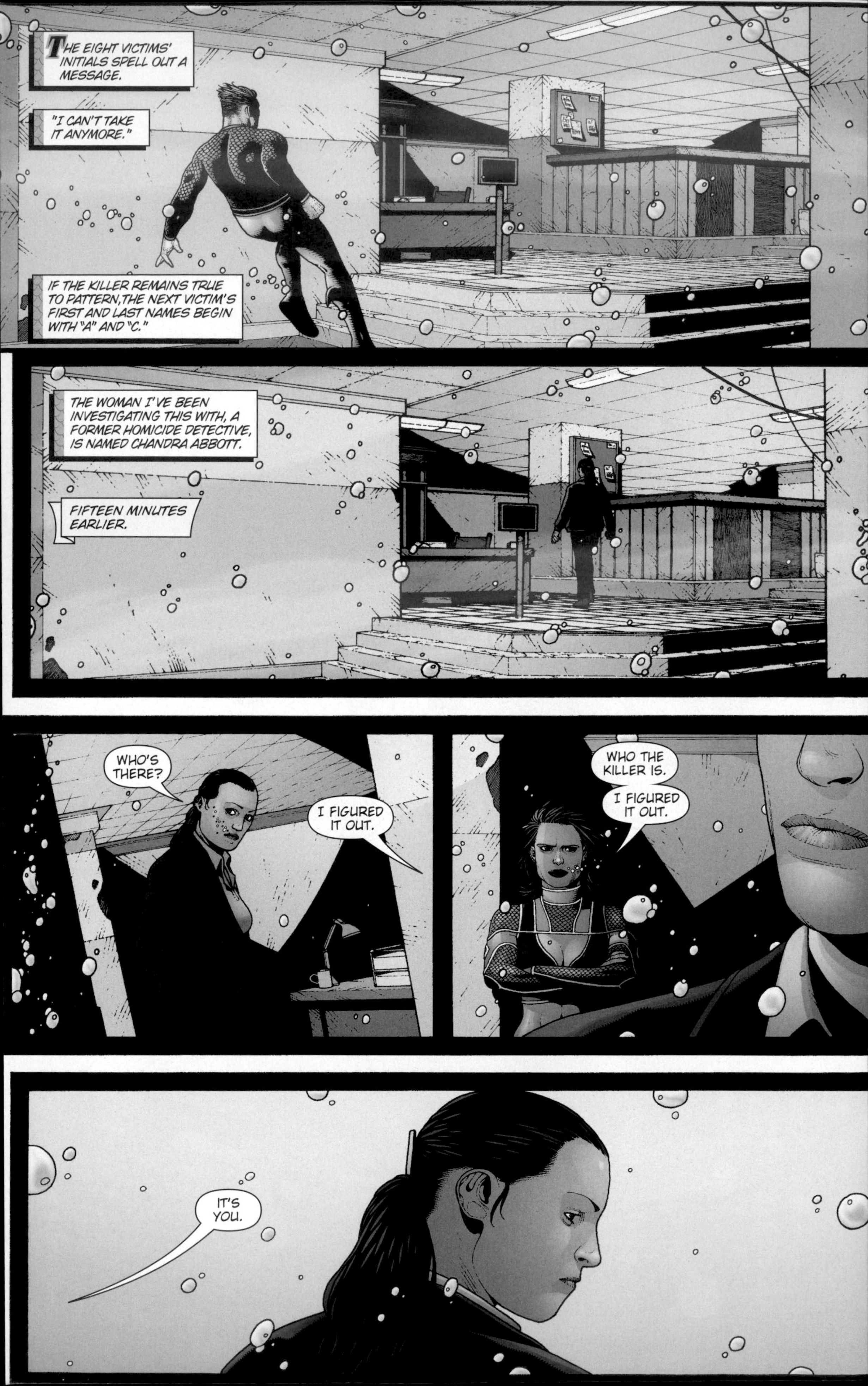
THE EIGHT VICTIMS' INITIALS SPELL OUT A MESSAGE.
"I CAN'T TAKE IT ANYMORE."
IF THE KILLER REMAINS TRUE TO PATTERN, THE NEXT VICTIM'S FIRST AND LAST NAMES BEGIN WITH "A" AND "C."
THE WOMAN I'VE BEEN INVESTIGATING THIS WITH, A FORMER HOMICIDE DETECTIVE, IS NAMED CHANDRA ABBOTT.
FIFTEEN MINUTES EARLIER.
WHO'S THERE?
I FIGURED IT OUT.
WHO THE KILLER IS.
I FIGURED IT OUT.
IT'S YOU.

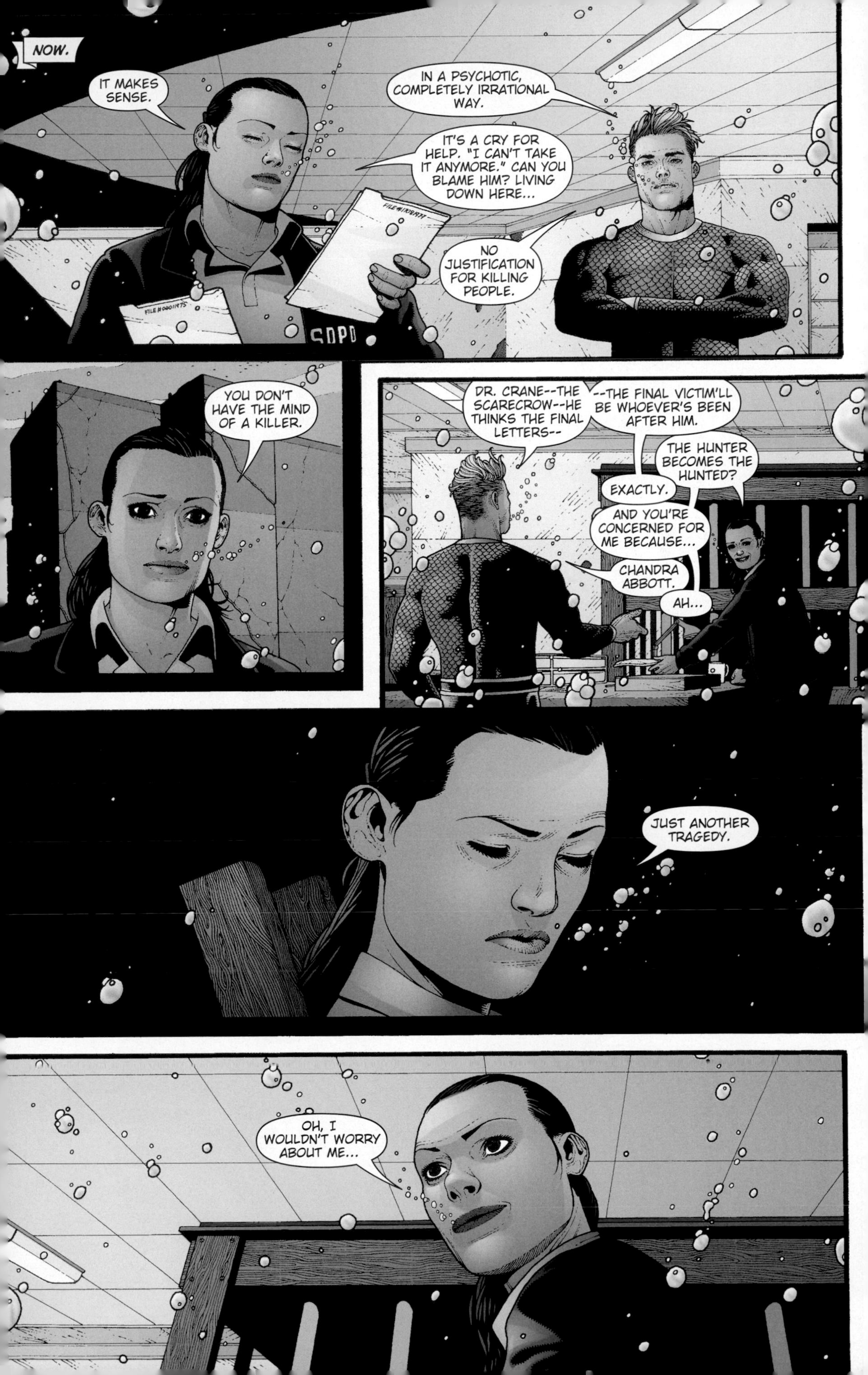
NOW.
IT MAKES SENSE.
IN A PSYCHOTIC, COMPLETELY IRRATIONAL WAY.
IT'S A CRY FOR HELP. "I CAN'T TAKE IT ANYMORE." CAN YOU BLAME HIM? LIVING DOWN HERE...
NO JUSTIFICATION FOR KILLING PEOPLE.
SDPD
YOU DON'T HAVE THE MIND OF A KILLER.
DR. CRANE--THE SCARECROW--HE THINKS THE FINAL LETTERS--
--THE FINAL VICTIM'LL BE WHOEVER'S BEEN AFTER HIM.
THE HUNTER BECOMES THE HUNTED?
EXACTLY.
AND YOU'RE CONCERNED FOR ME BECAUSE...
CHANDRA ABBOTT.
AH...
JUST ANOTHER TRAGEDY.
OH, I WOULDN'T WORRY ABOUT ME...

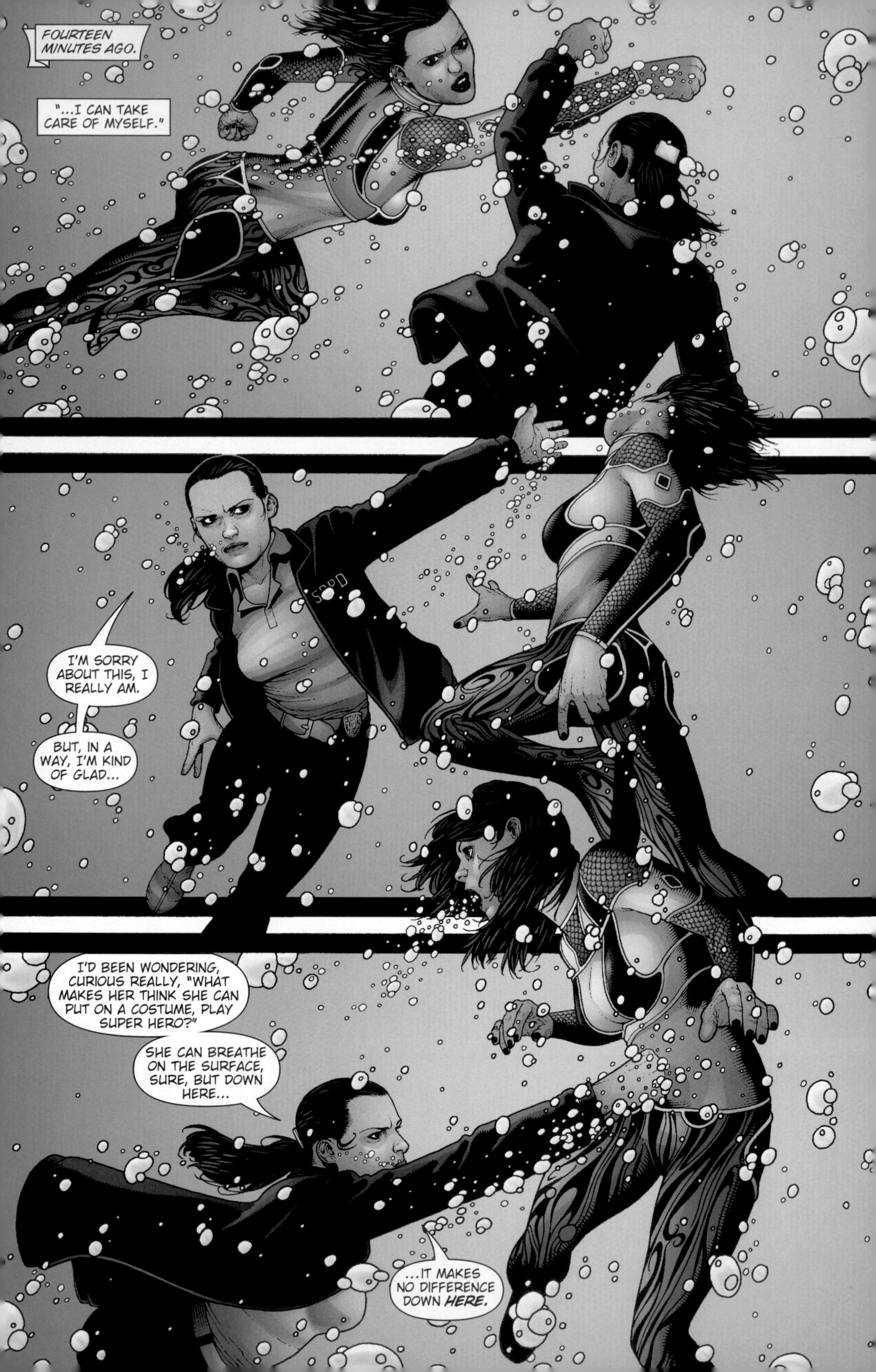
FOURTEEN MINUTES AGO.
"...I CAN TAKE CARE OF MYSELF."
I'M SORRY ABOUT THIS, I REALLY AM.
BUT, IN A WAY, I'M KIND OF GLAD...
I'D BEEN WONDERING, CURIOUS REALLY, "WHAT MAKES HER THINK SHE CAN PUT ON A COSTUME, PLAY SUPER HERO?"
SHE CAN BREATHE ON THE SURFACE, SURE, BUT DOWN HERE...
...IT MAKES NO DIFFERENCE DOWN *HERE.*

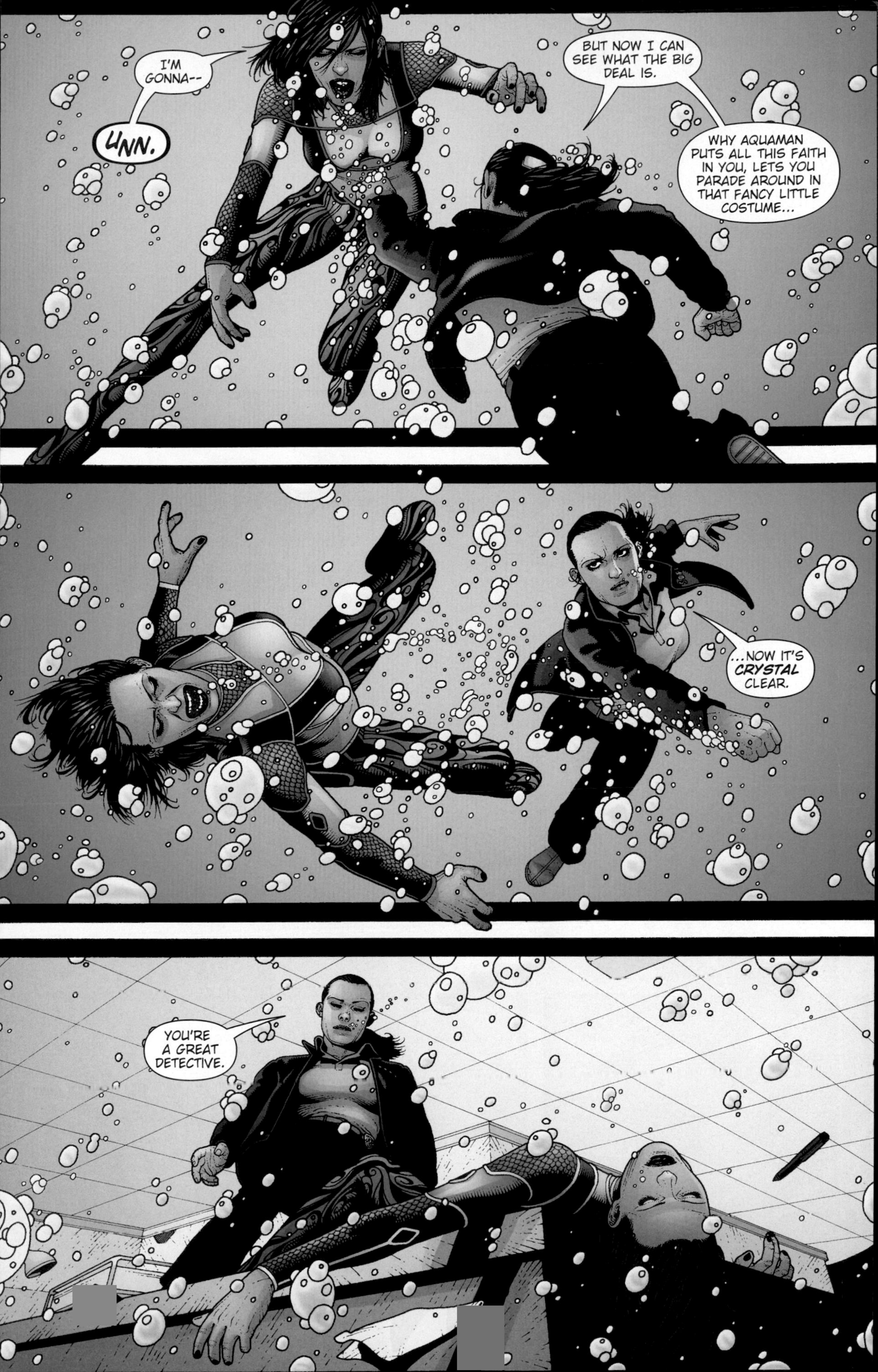
I'M GONNA--
UNN.
BUT NOW I CAN SEE WHAT THE BIG DEAL IS.
WHY AQUAMAN PUTS ALL THIS FAITH IN YOU, LETS YOU PARADE AROUND IN THAT FANCY LITTLE COSTUME...
...NOW IT'S CRYSTAL CLEAR.
YOU'RE A GREAT DETECTIVE.

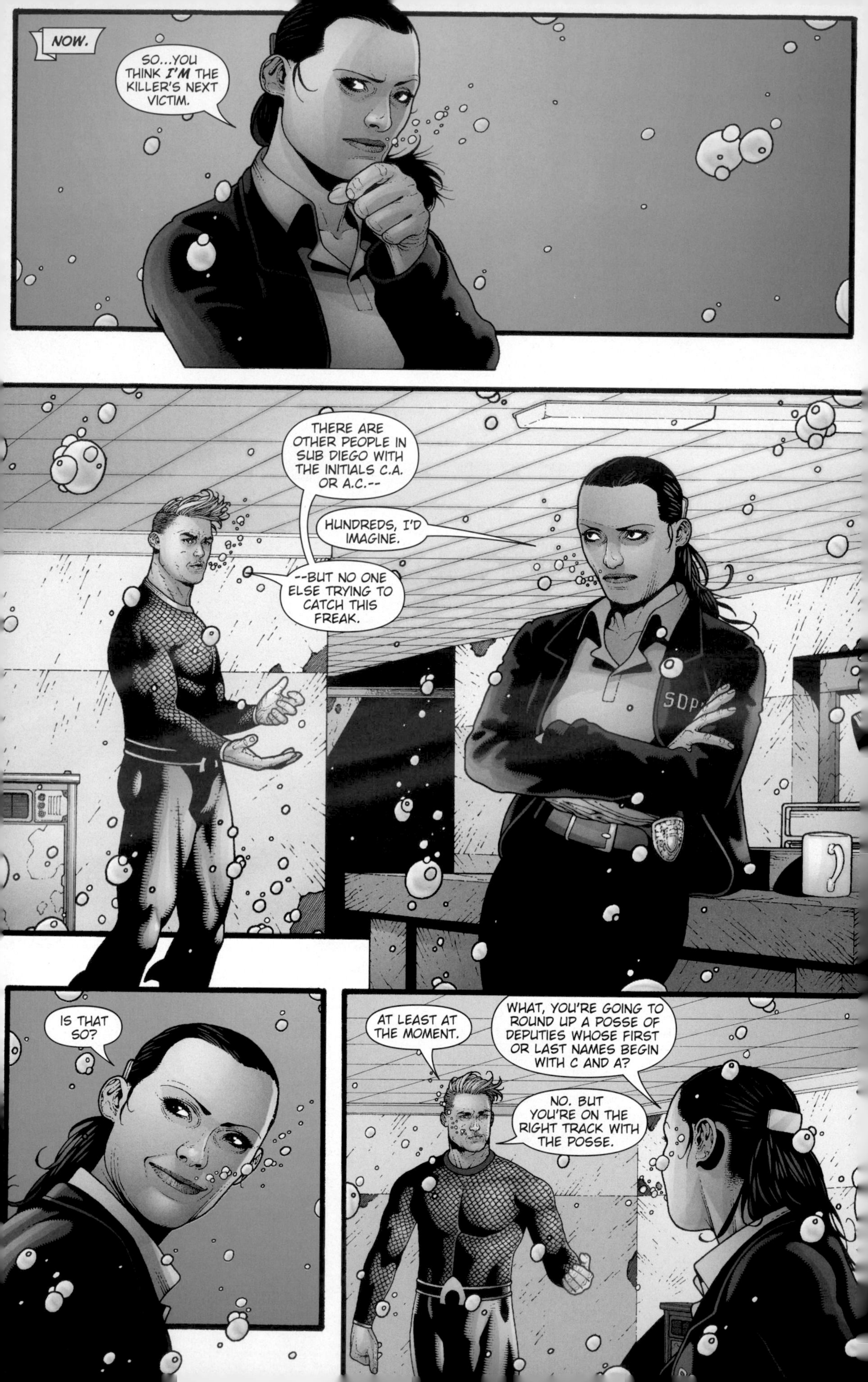
NOW.
SO...YOU THINK I'M THE KILLER'S NEXT VICTIM.
THERE ARE OTHER PEOPLE IN SUB DIEGO WITH THE INITIALS C.A. OR A.C.--
HUNDREDS, I'D IMAGINE.
--BUT NO ONE ELSE TRYING TO CATCH THIS FREAK.
SDP
IS THAT SO?
AT LEAST AT THE MOMENT.
WHAT, YOU'RE GOING TO ROUND UP A POSSE OF DEPUTIES WHOSE FIRST OR LAST NAMES BEGIN WITH C AND A?
NO. BUT YOU'RE ON THE RIGHT TRACK WITH THE POSSE.

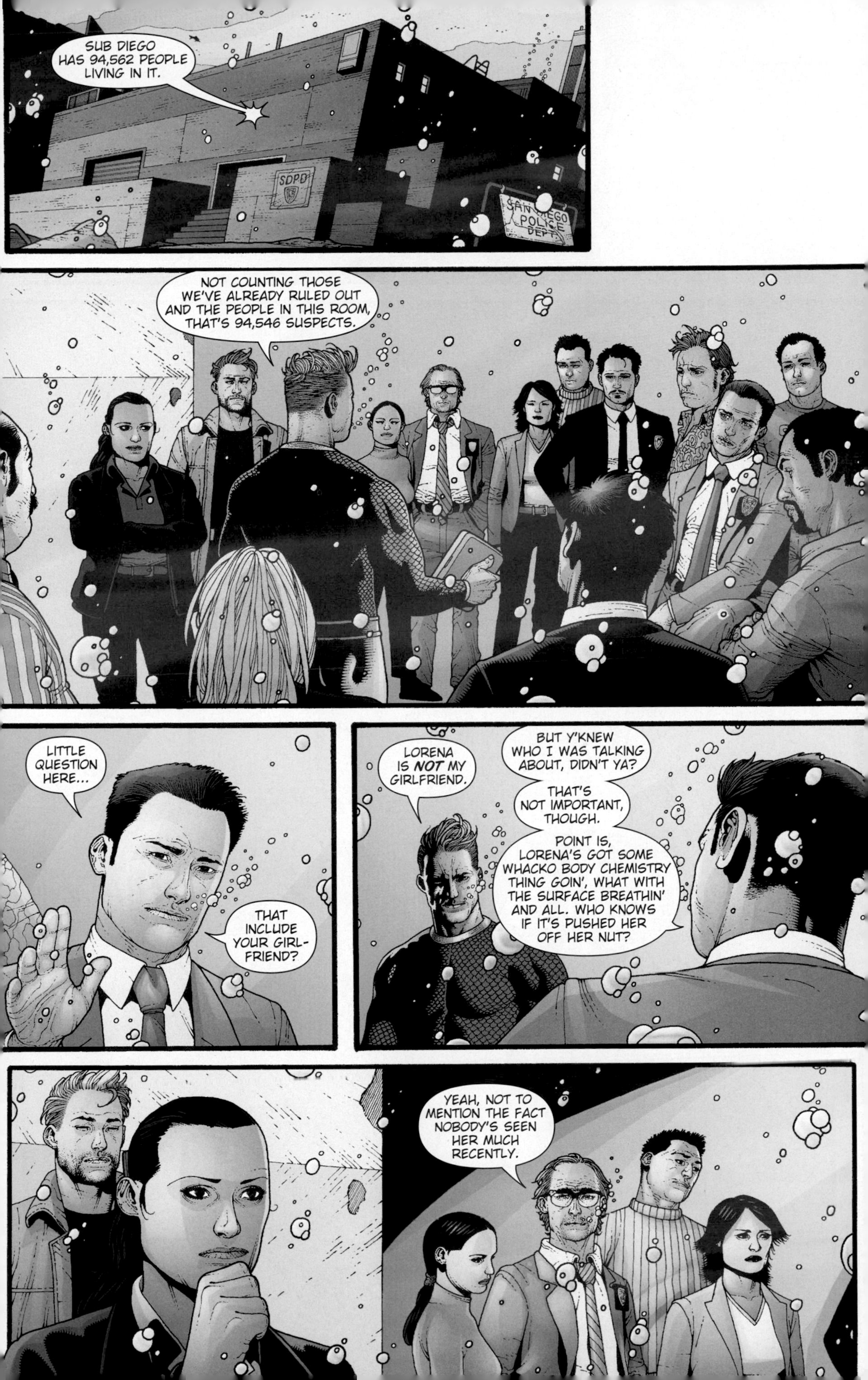
SUB DIEGO HAS 94,562 PEOPLE LIVING IN IT.
SDPD
SAN DIEGO POLICE DEPT.
NOT COUNTING THOSE WE'VE ALREADY RULED OUT AND THE PEOPLE IN THIS ROOM, THAT'S 94,546 SUSPECTS.
LITTLE QUESTION HERE...
THAT INCLUDE YOUR GIRL-FRIEND?
LORENA IS NOT MY GIRLFRIEND.
BUT Y'KNEW WHO I WAS TALKING ABOUT, DIDN'T YA?
THAT'S NOT IMPORTANT, THOUGH.
POINT IS, LORENA'S GOT SOME WHACKO BODY CHEMISTRY THING GOIN', WHAT WITH THE SURFACE BREATHIN' AND ALL. WHO KNOWS IF IT'S PUSHED HER OFF HER NUT?
YEAH, NOT TO MENTION THE FACT NOBODY'S SEEN HER MUCH RECENTLY.

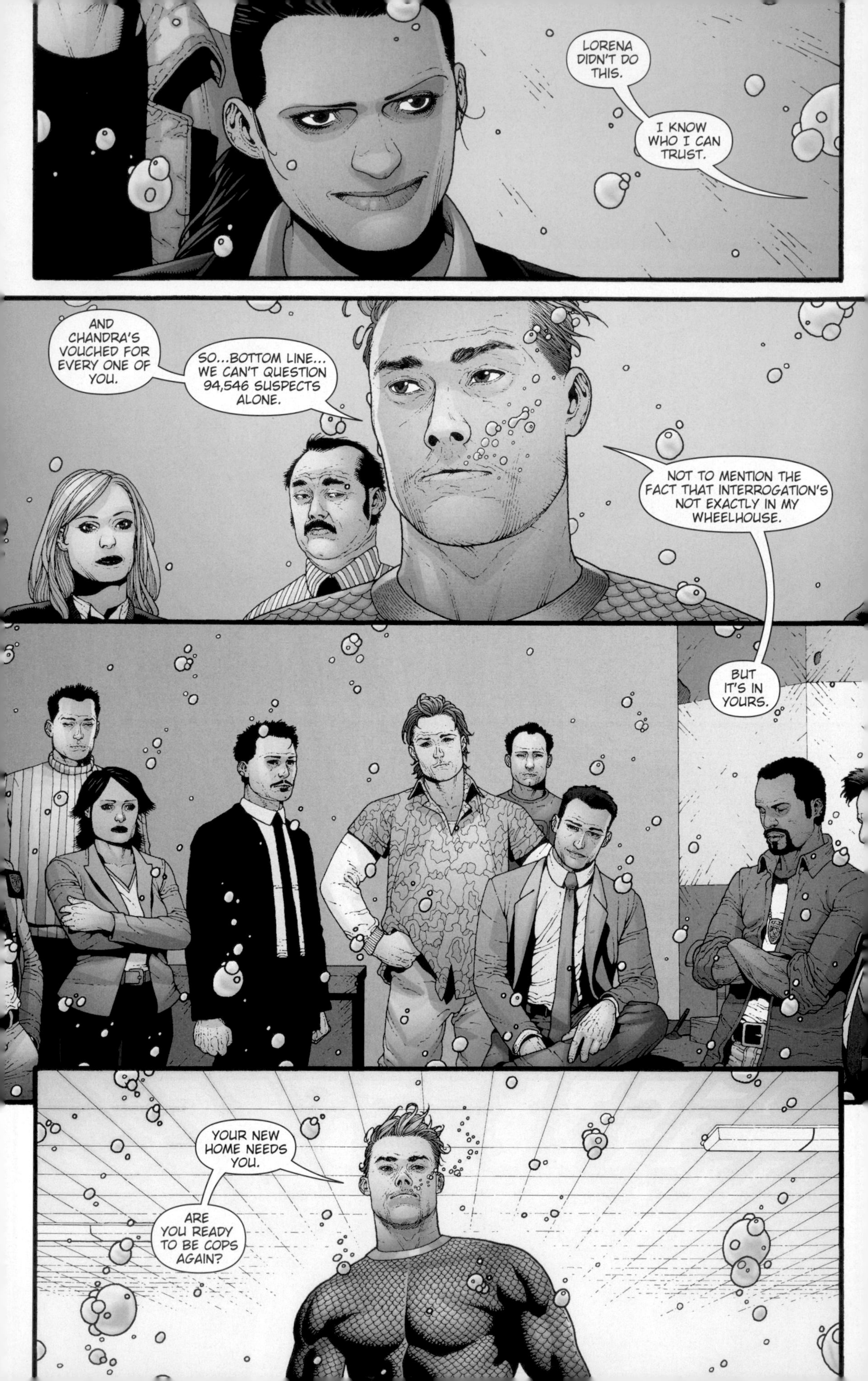
LORENA DIDN'T DO THIS.
I KNOW WHO I CAN TRUST.
AND CHANDRA'S VOUCHED FOR EVERY ONE OF YOU.
SO...BOTTOM LINE... WE CAN'T QUESTION 94,546 SUSPECTS ALONE.
NOT TO MENTION THE FACT THAT INTERROGATION'S NOT EXACTLY IN MY WHEELHOUSE.
BUT IT'S IN YOURS.
YOUR NEW HOME NEEDS YOU.
ARE YOU READY TO BE COPS AGAIN?

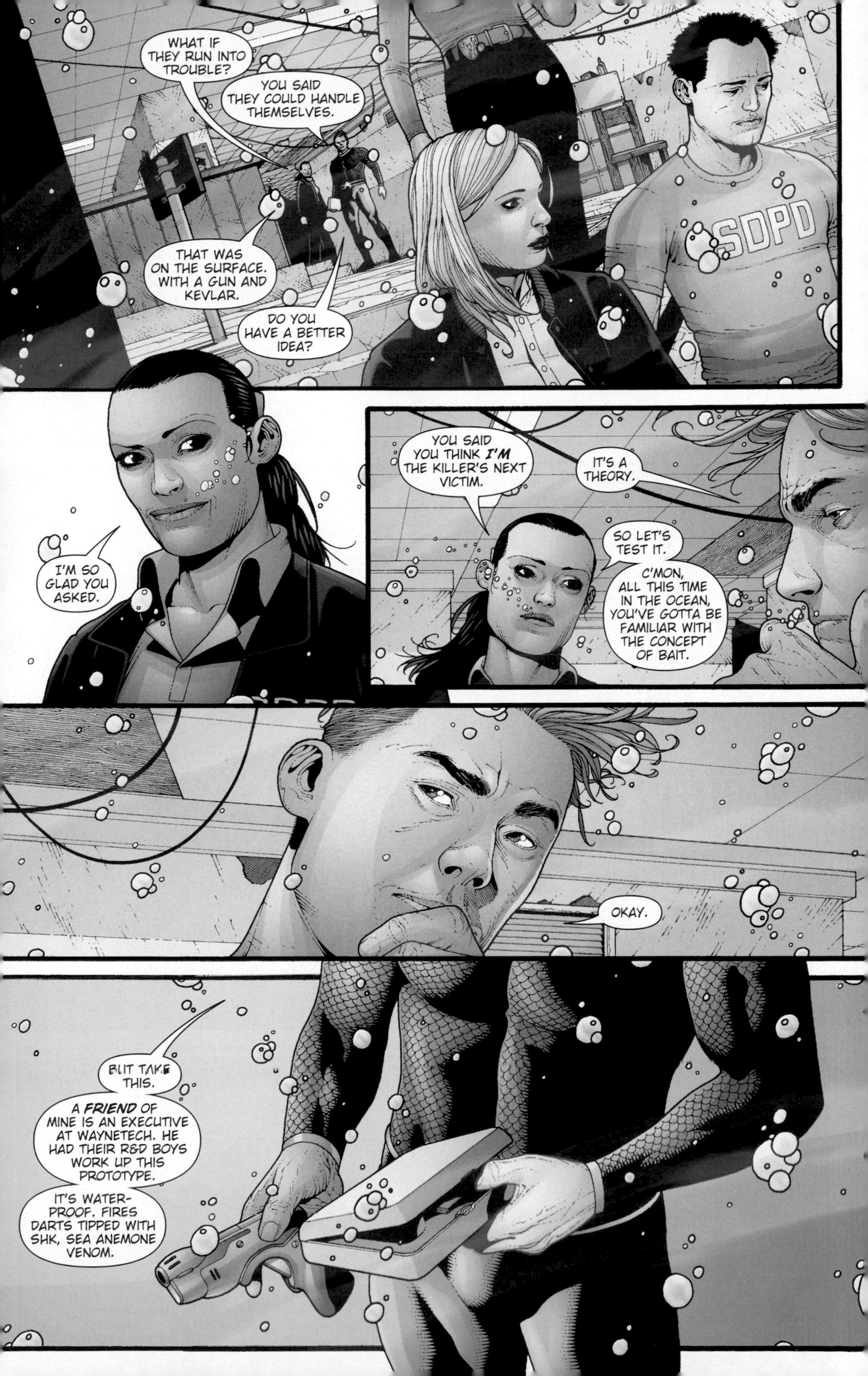
WHAT IF THEY RUN INTO TROUBLE?
YOU SAID THEY COULD HANDLE THEMSELVES.
THAT WAS ON THE SURFACE. WITH A GUN AND KEVLAR.
DO YOU HAVE A BETTER IDEA?
I'M SO GLAD YOU ASKED.
YOU SAID YOU THINK ***I'M*** THE KILLER'S NEXT VICTIM.
IT'S A THEORY.
SO LET'S TEST IT.
C'MON, ALL THIS TIME IN THE OCEAN, YOU'VE GOTTA BE FAMILIAR WITH THE CONCEPT OF BAIT.
OKAY.
BUT TAKE THIS.
A ***FRIEND*** OF MINE IS AN EXECUTIVE AT WAYNETECH. HE HAD THEIR R&D BOYS WORK UP THIS PROTOTYPE.
IT'S WATER-PROOF. FIRES DARTS TIPPED WITH SHK, SEA ANEMONE VENOM.

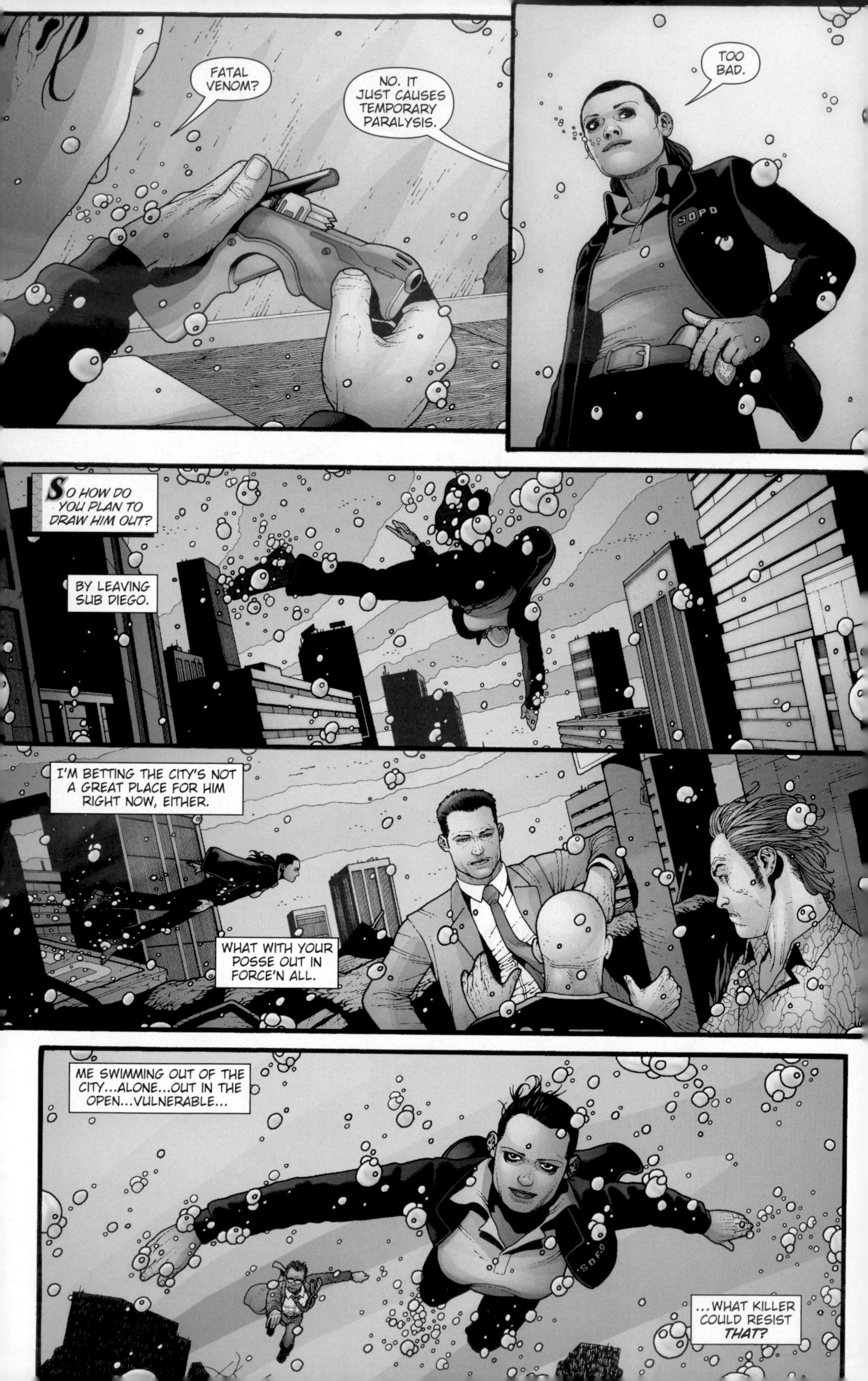
FATAL VENOM?
NO. IT JUST CAUSES TEMPORARY PARALYSIS.
TOO BAD.
SO HOW DO YOU PLAN TO DRAW HIM OUT?
BY LEAVING SUB DIEGO.
I'M BETTING THE CITY'S NOT A GREAT PLACE FOR HIM RIGHT NOW, EITHER.
WHAT WITH YOUR POSSE OUT IN FORCE'N ALL.
ME SWIMMING OUT OF THE CITY...ALONE...OUT IN THE OPEN...VULNERABLE...
...WHAT KILLER COULD RESIST *THAT?*

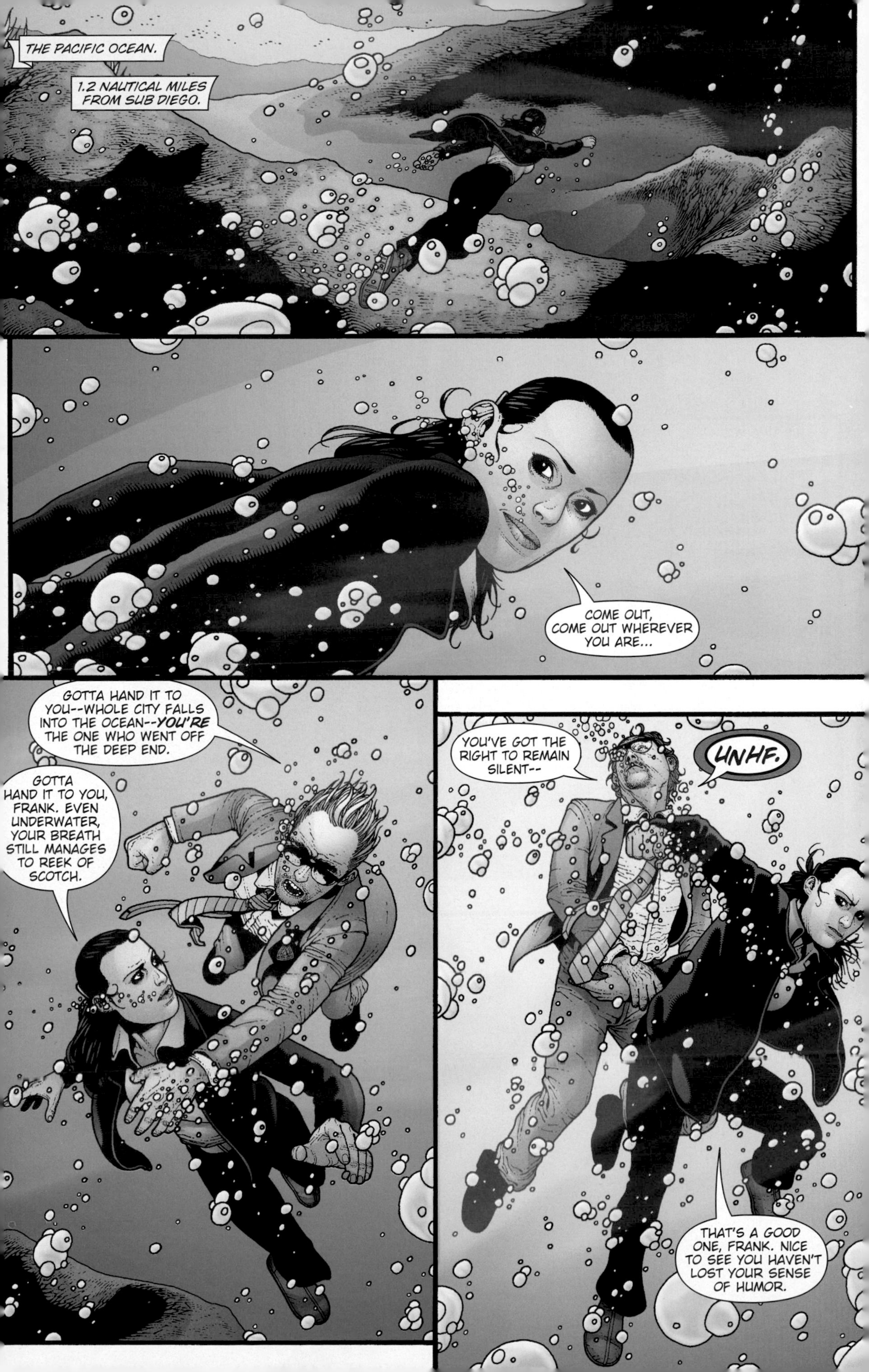
THE PACIFIC OCEAN.
1.2 NAUTICAL MILES FROM SUB DIEGO.
COME OUT, COME OUT WHEREVER YOU ARE...
GOTTA HAND IT TO YOU--WHOLE CITY FALLS INTO THE OCEAN--YOU'RE THE ONE WHO WENT OFF THE DEEP END.
GOTTA HAND IT TO YOU, FRANK. EVEN UNDERWATER, YOUR BREATH STILL MANAGES TO REEK OF SCOTCH.
YOU'VE GOT THE RIGHT TO REMAIN SILENT--
UNHF.
THAT'S A GOOD ONE, FRANK. NICE TO SEE YOU HAVEN'T LOST YOUR SENSE OF HUMOR.

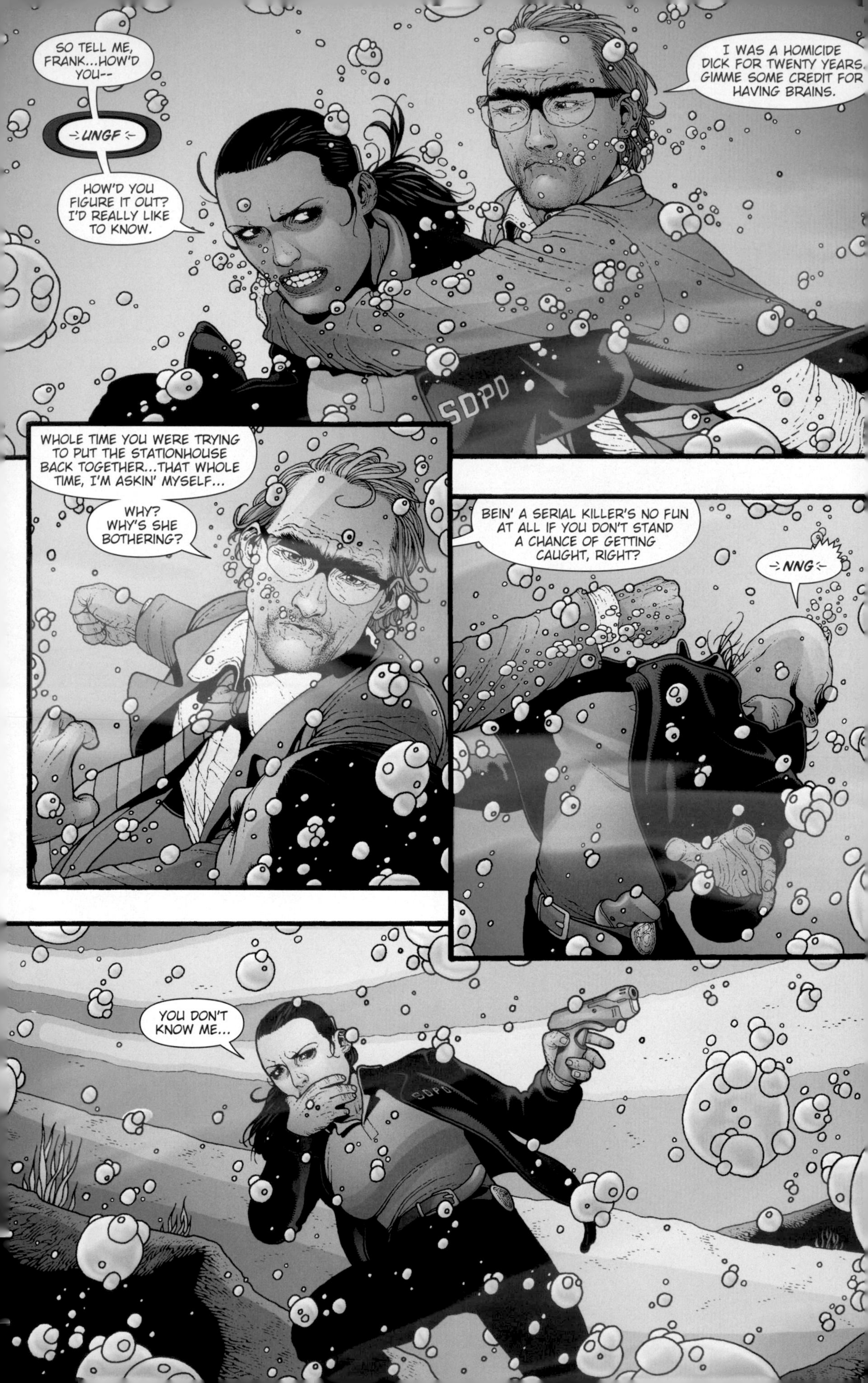
SO TELL ME, FRANK...HOW'D YOU--
UNGF
HOW'D YOU FIGURE IT OUT? I'D REALLY LIKE TO KNOW.
I WAS A HOMICIDE DICK FOR TWENTY YEARS. GIMME SOME CREDIT FOR HAVING BRAINS.
SDPD
WHOLE TIME YOU WERE TRYING TO PUT THE STATIONHOUSE BACK TOGETHER...THAT WHOLE TIME, I'M ASKIN' MYSELF...
WHY? WHY'S SHE BOTHERING?
BEIN' A SERIAL KILLER'S NO FUN AT ALL IF YOU DON'T STAND A CHANCE OF GETTING CAUGHT, RIGHT?
NNG
YOU DON'T KNOW ME...
SDPD

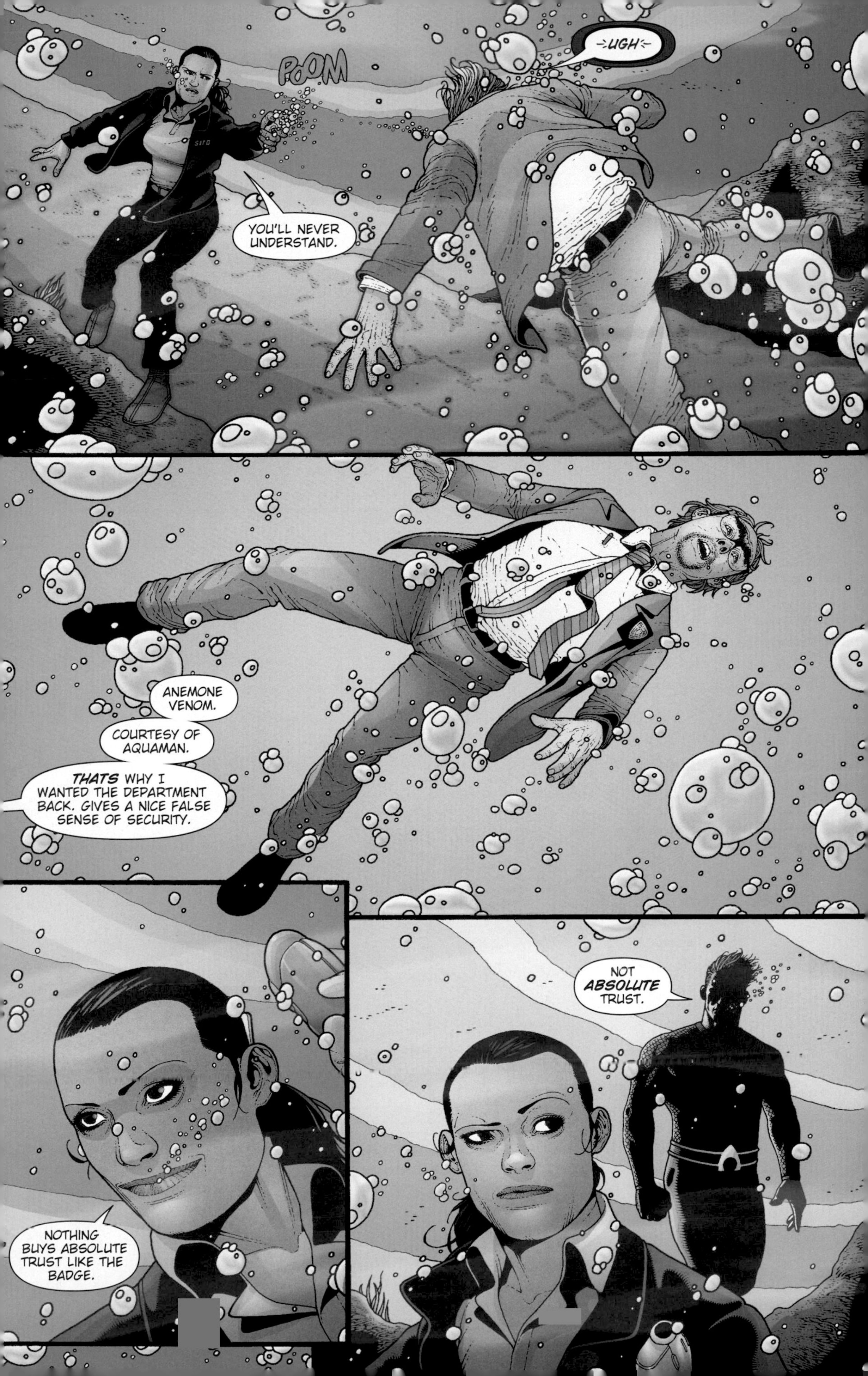
POOM
–UGH–
YOU'LL NEVER UNDERSTAND.
ANEMONE VENOM.
COURTESY OF AQUAMAN.
THATS WHY I WANTED THE DEPARTMENT BACK. GIVES A NICE FALSE SENSE OF SECURITY.
NOTHING BUYS ABSOLUTE TRUST LIKE THE BADGE.
NOT *ABSOLUTE* TRUST.

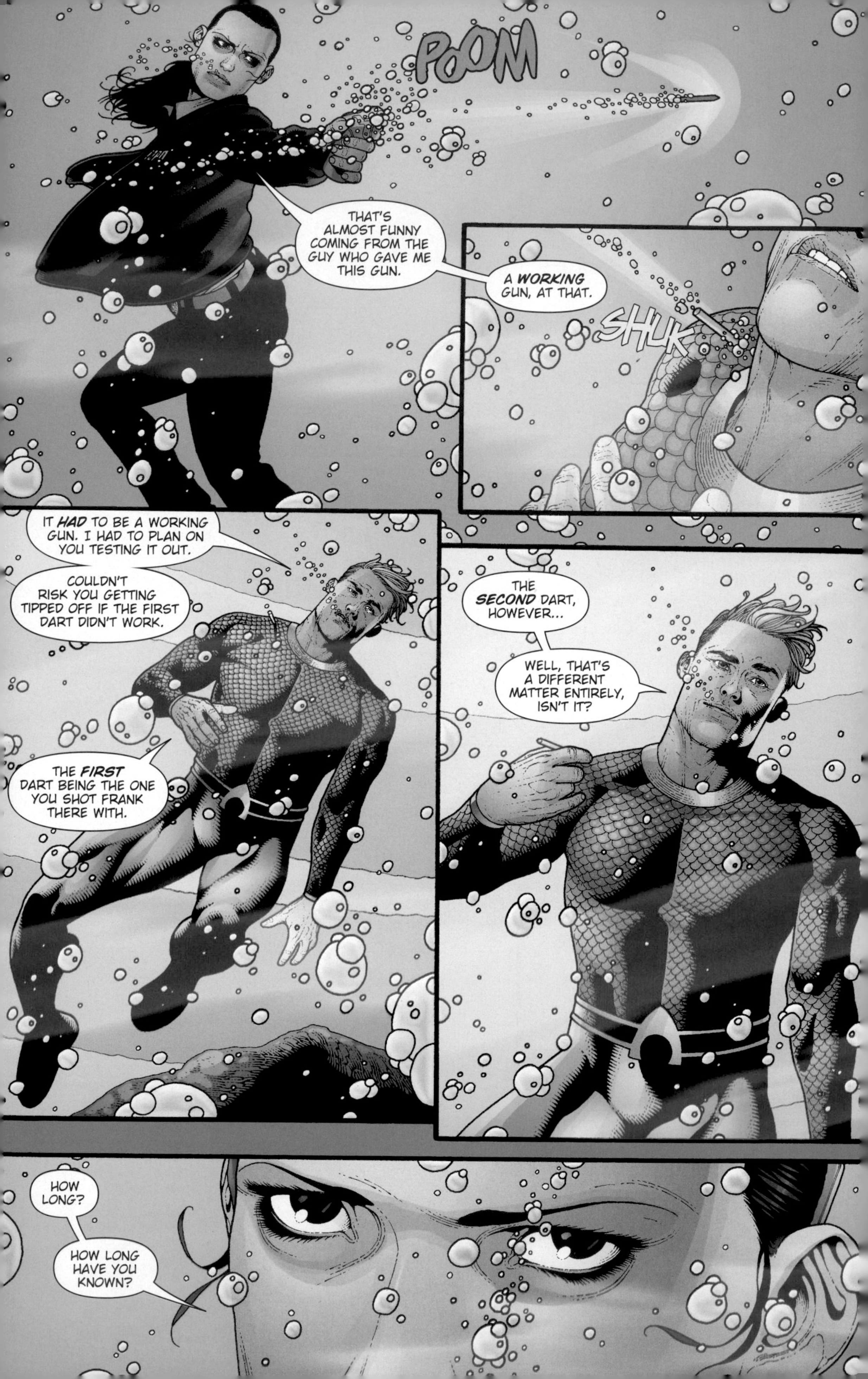
POOM
THAT'S ALMOST FUNNY COMING FROM THE GUY WHO GAVE ME THIS GUN.
A WORKING GUN, AT THAT.
SHUK
IT HAD TO BE A WORKING GUN. I HAD TO PLAN ON YOU TESTING IT OUT.
COULDN'T RISK YOU GETTING TIPPED OFF IF THE FIRST DART DIDN'T WORK.
THE FIRST DART BEING THE ONE YOU SHOT FRANK THERE WITH.
THE SECOND DART, HOWEVER...
WELL, THAT'S A DIFFERENT MATTER ENTIRELY, ISN'T IT?
HOW LONG?
HOW LONG HAVE YOU KNOWN?

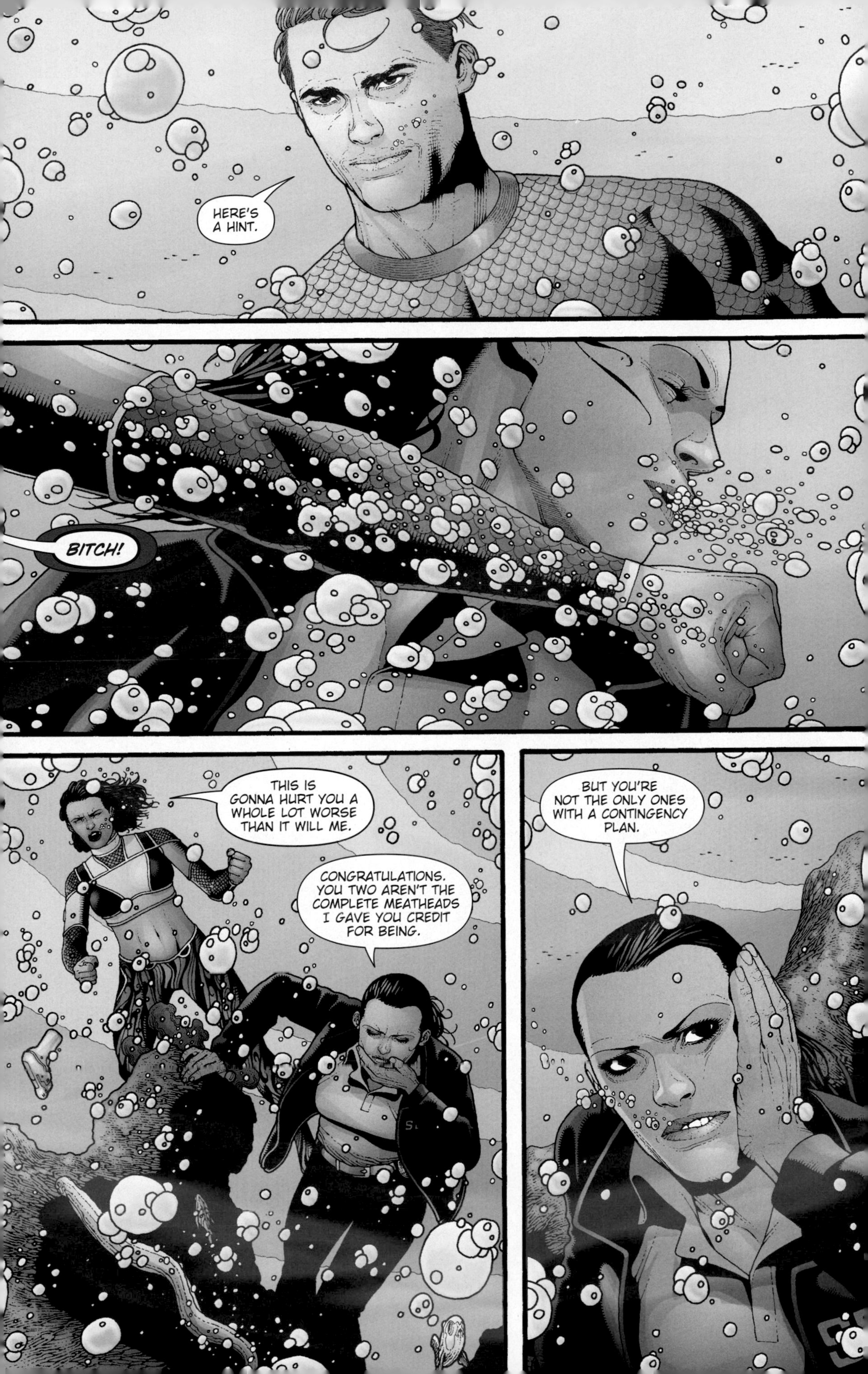
HERE'S A HINT.
BITCH!
THIS IS GONNA HURT YOU A WHOLE LOT WORSE THAN IT WILL ME.
CONGRATULATIONS. YOU TWO AREN'T THE COMPLETE MEATHEADS I GAVE YOU CREDIT FOR BEING.
BUT YOU'RE NOT THE ONLY ONES WITH A CONTINGENCY PLAN.

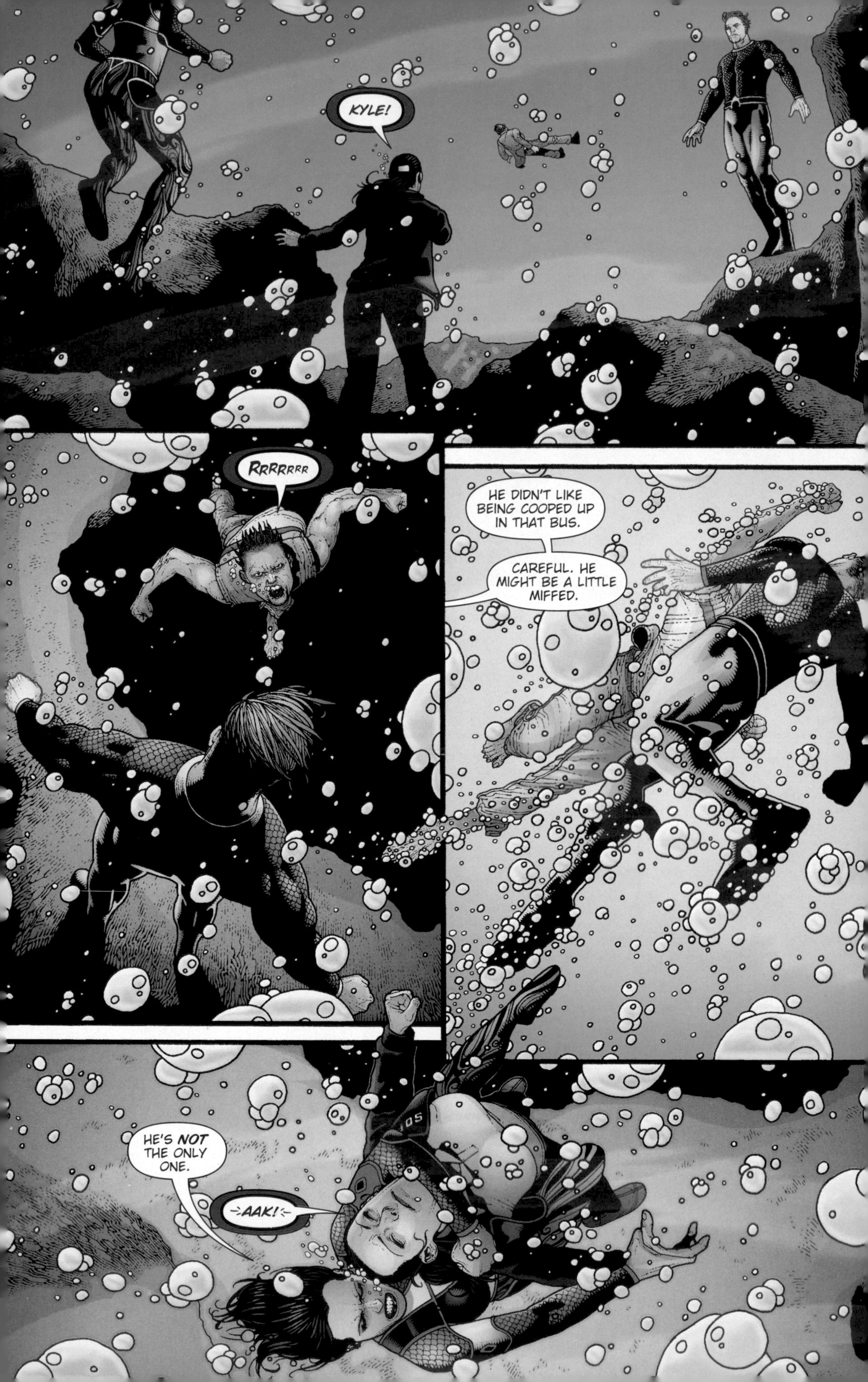
KYLE!
RRRRRRR
HE DIDN'T LIKE BEING COOPED UP IN THAT BUS.
CAREFUL. HE MIGHT BE A LITTLE MIFFED.
HE'S **NOT** THE ONLY ONE.
-AAK!-

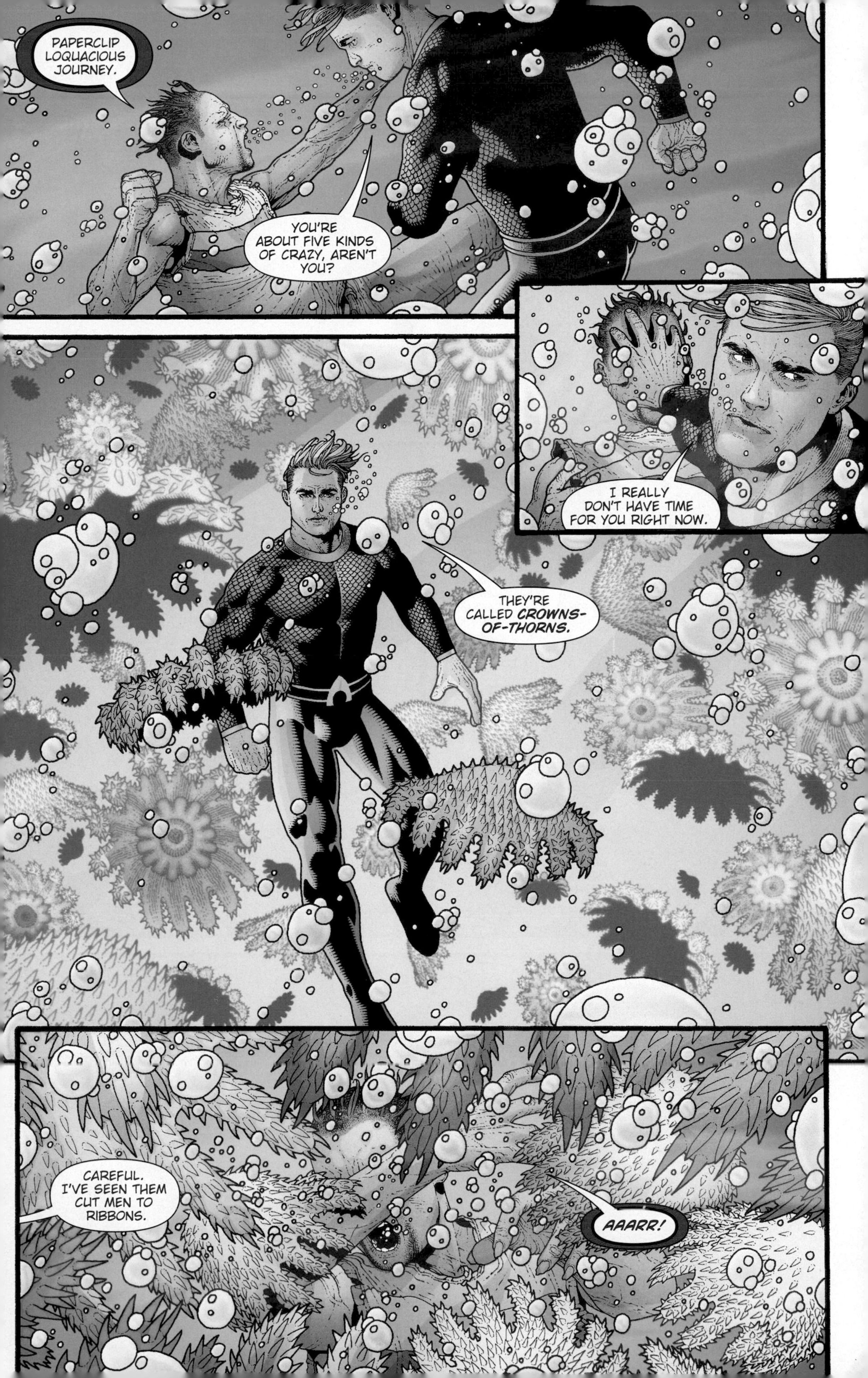
PAPERCLIP LOQUACIOUS JOURNEY.
YOU'RE ABOUT FIVE KINDS OF CRAZY, AREN'T YOU?
I REALLY DON'T HAVE TIME FOR YOU RIGHT NOW.
THEY'RE CALLED CROWNS-OF-THORNS.
CAREFUL. I'VE SEEN THEM CUT MEN TO RIBBONS.
AAARR!

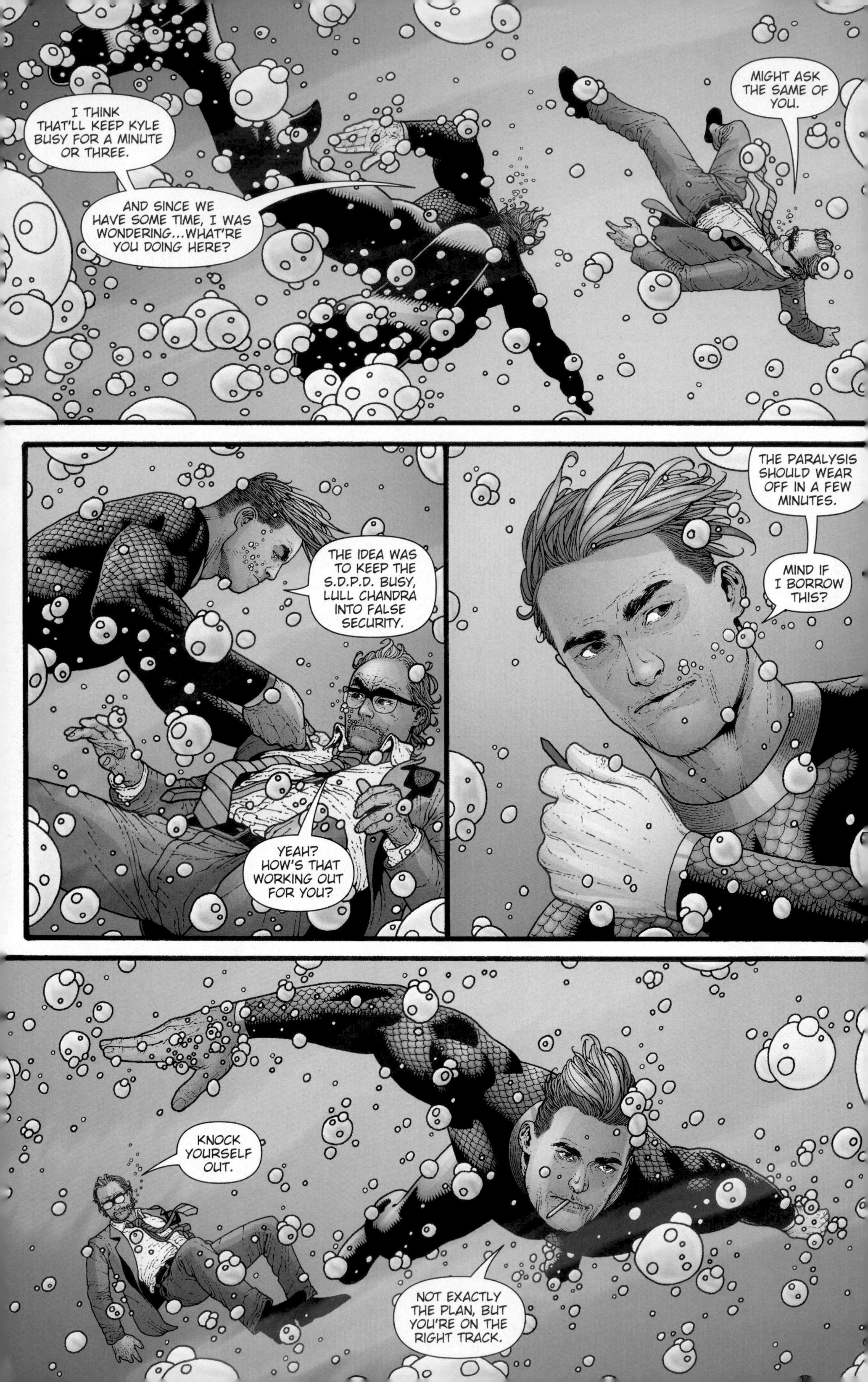
I THINK THAT'LL KEEP KYLE BUSY FOR A MINUTE OR THREE.
AND SINCE WE HAVE SOME TIME, I WAS WONDERING...WHAT'RE YOU DOING HERE?
MIGHT ASK THE SAME OF YOU.
THE IDEA WAS TO KEEP THE S.D.P.D. BUSY, LULL CHANDRA INTO FALSE SECURITY.
YEAH? HOW'S THAT WORKING OUT FOR YOU?
THE PARALYSIS SHOULD WEAR OFF IN A FEW MINUTES.
MIND IF I BORROW THIS?
KNOCK YOURSELF OUT.
NOT EXACTLY THE PLAN, BUT YOU'RE ON THE RIGHT TRACK.

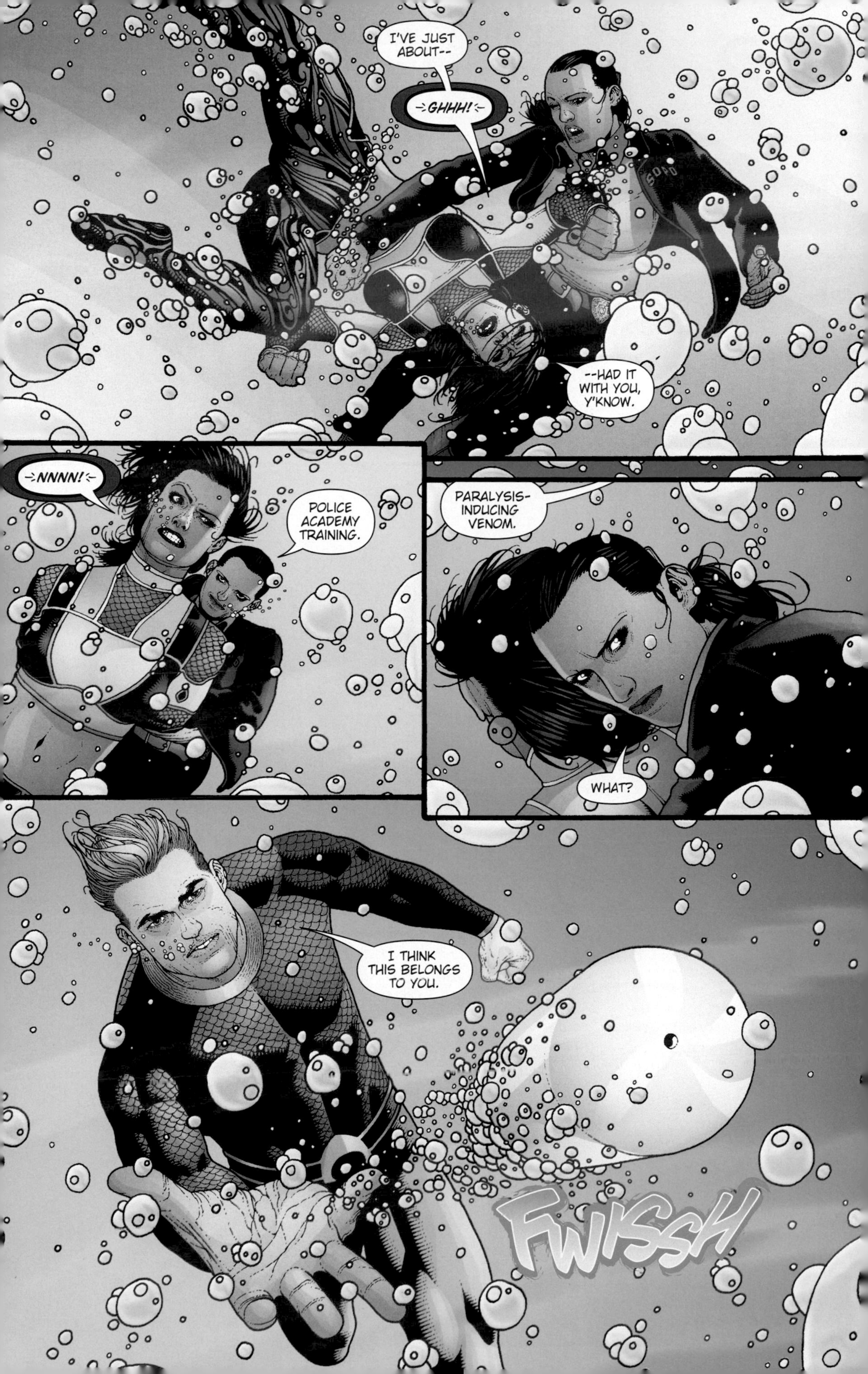

I'VE JUST ABOUT--
-GHHH!-
--HAD IT WITH YOU, Y'KNOW.
-NNNN!-
POLICE ACADEMY TRAINING.
PARALYSIS-INDUCING VENOM.
WHAT?
I THINK THIS BELONGS TO YOU.
FWISSH

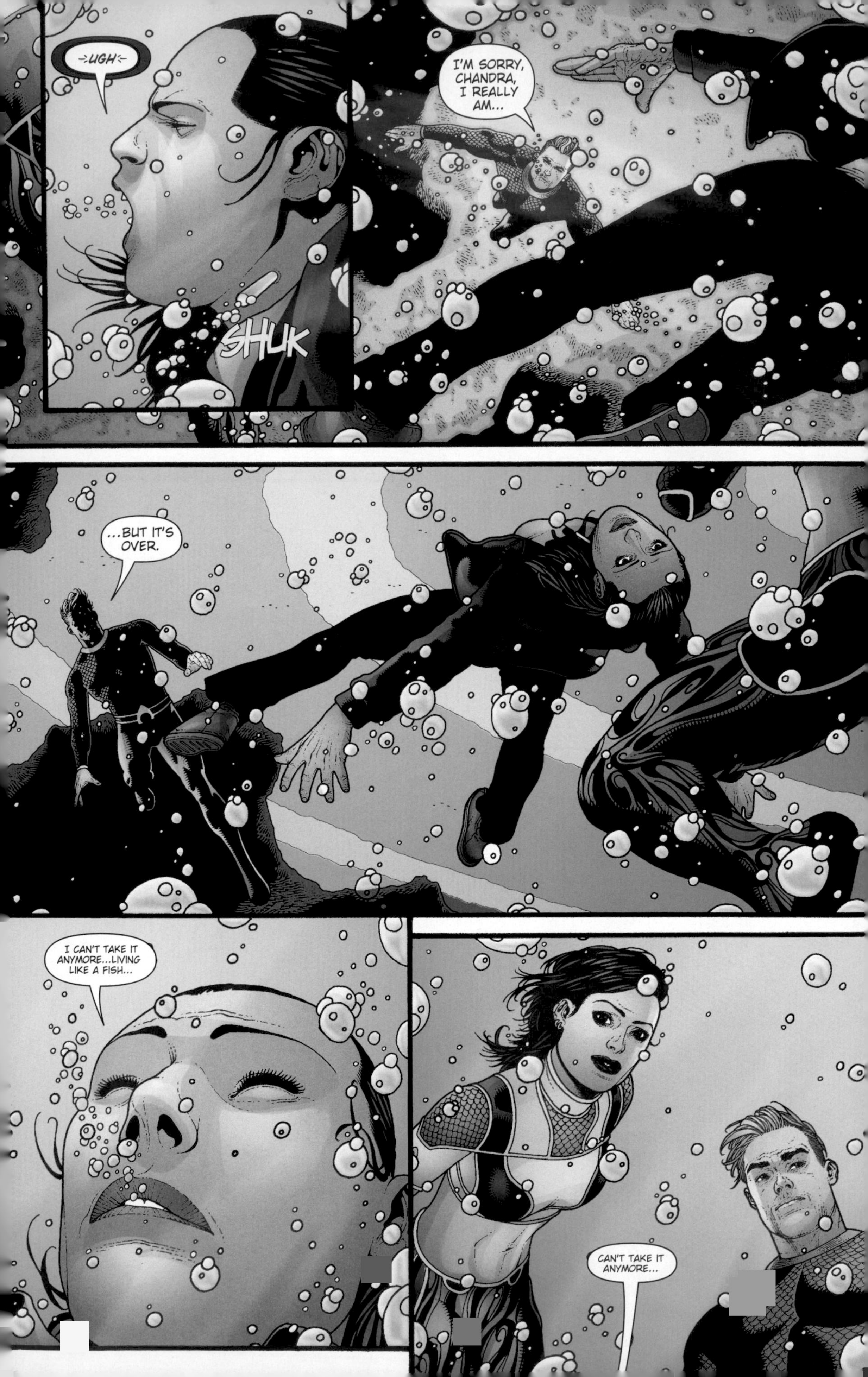
UGH
SHUK
I'M SORRY, CHANDRA, I REALLY AM...
...BUT IT'S OVER.
I CAN'T TAKE IT ANYMORE...LIVING LIKE A FISH...
CAN'T TAKE IT ANYMORE...

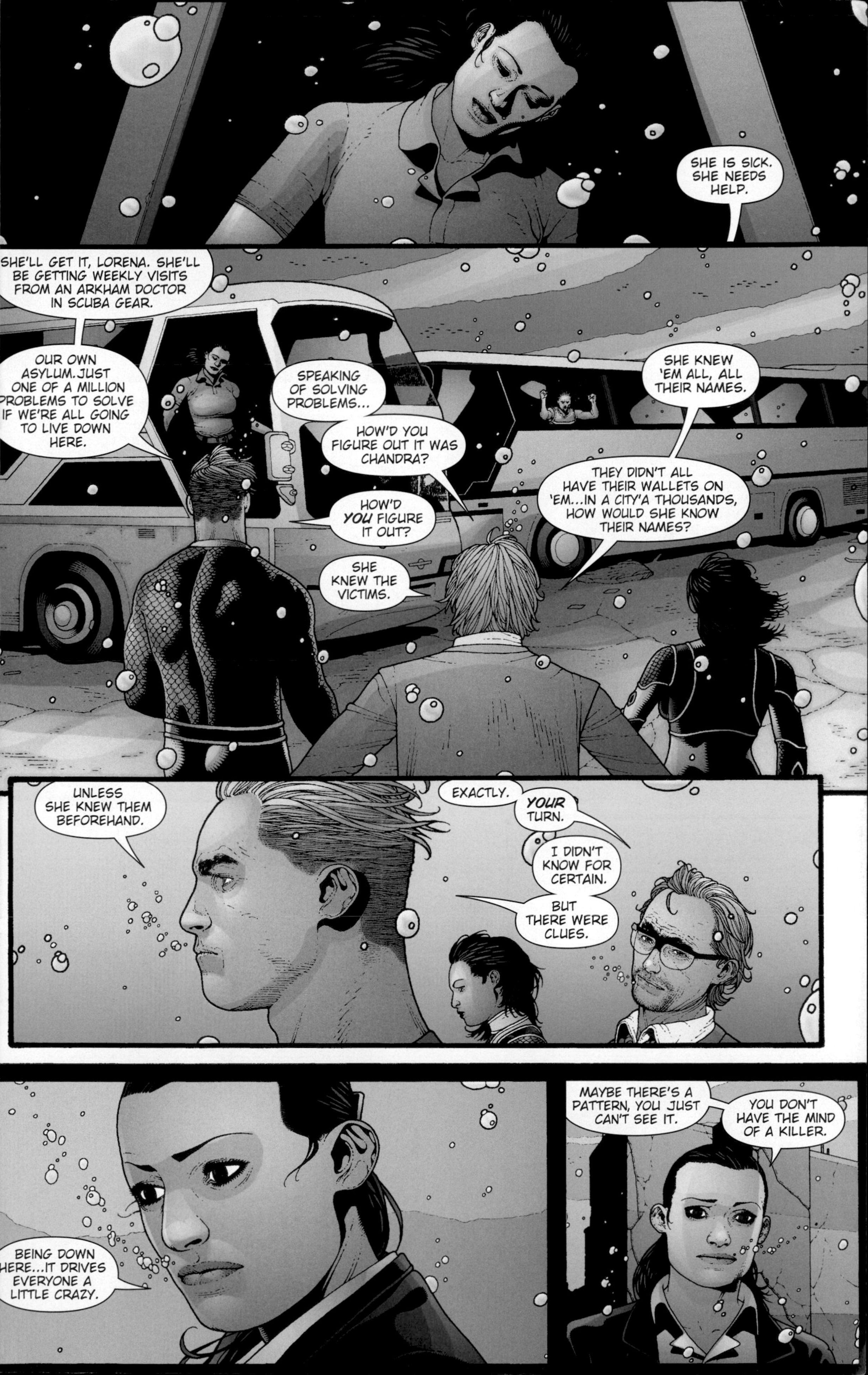
SHE IS SICK. SHE NEEDS HELP.
SHE'LL GET IT, LORENA. SHE'LL BE GETTING WEEKLY VISITS FROM AN ARKHAM DOCTOR IN SCUBA GEAR.
OUR OWN ASYLUM. JUST ONE OF A MILLION PROBLEMS TO SOLVE IF WE'RE ALL GOING TO LIVE DOWN HERE.
SPEAKING OF SOLVING PROBLEMS...
HOW'D YOU FIGURE OUT IT WAS CHANDRA?
HOW'D *YOU* FIGURE IT OUT?
SHE KNEW THE VICTIMS.
SHE KNEW 'EM ALL, ALL THEIR NAMES.
THEY DIDN'T ALL HAVE THEIR WALLETS ON 'EM...IN A CITY'A THOUSANDS, HOW WOULD SHE KNOW THEIR NAMES?
UNLESS SHE KNEW THEM BEFOREHAND.
EXACTLY.
YOUR TURN.
I DIDN'T KNOW FOR CERTAIN.
BUT THERE WERE CLUES.
BEING DOWN HERE...IT DRIVES EVERYONE A LITTLE CRAZY.
MAYBE THERE'S A PATTERN, YOU JUST CAN'T SEE IT.
YOU DON'T HAVE THE MIND OF A KILLER.

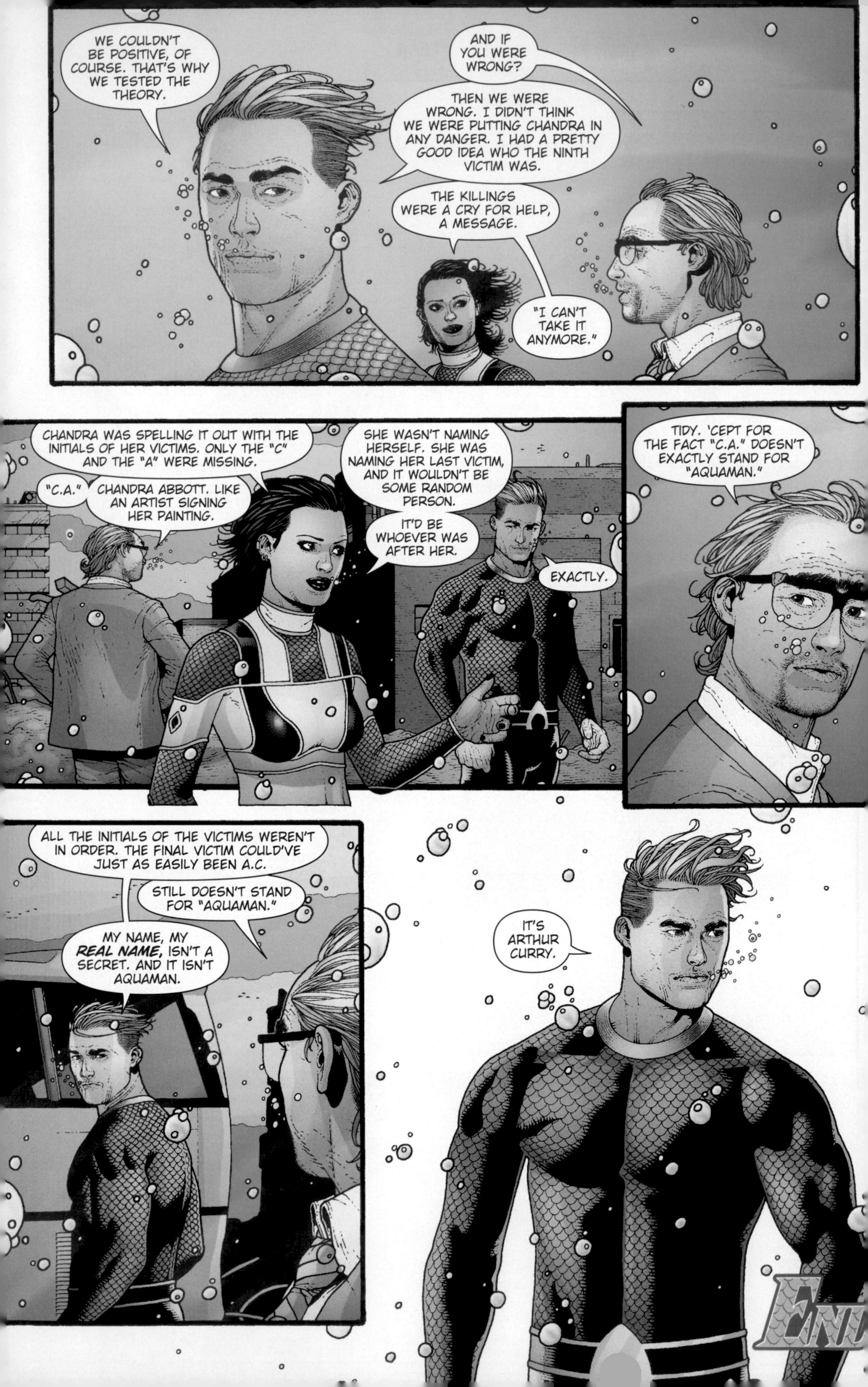
WE COULDN'T BE POSITIVE, OF COURSE. THAT'S WHY WE TESTED THE THEORY.
AND IF YOU WERE WRONG?
THEN WE WERE WRONG. I DIDN'T THINK WE WERE PUTTING CHANDRA IN ANY DANGER. I HAD A PRETTY GOOD IDEA WHO THE NINTH VICTIM WAS.
THE KILLINGS WERE A CRY FOR HELP, A MESSAGE.
"I CAN'T TAKE IT ANYMORE."
CHANDRA WAS SPELLING IT OUT WITH THE INITIALS OF HER VICTIMS. ONLY THE "C" AND THE "A" WERE MISSING.
"C.A."
CHANDRA ABBOTT. LIKE AN ARTIST SIGNING HER PAINTING.
SHE WASN'T NAMING HERSELF. SHE WAS NAMING HER LAST VICTIM, AND IT WOULDN'T BE SOME RANDOM PERSON.
IT'D BE WHOEVER WAS AFTER HER.
EXACTLY.
TIDY. 'CEPT FOR THE FACT "C.A." DOESN'T EXACTLY STAND FOR "AQUAMAN."
ALL THE INITIALS OF THE VICTIMS WEREN'T IN ORDER. THE FINAL VICTIM COULD'VE JUST AS EASILY BEEN A.C.
STILL DOESN'T STAND FOR "AQUAMAN."
MY NAME, MY REAL NAME, ISN'T A SECRET. AND IT ISN'T AQUAMAN.
IT'S ARTHUR CURRY.

AQUAGIRL *character sketches by* **PATRICK GLEASON**

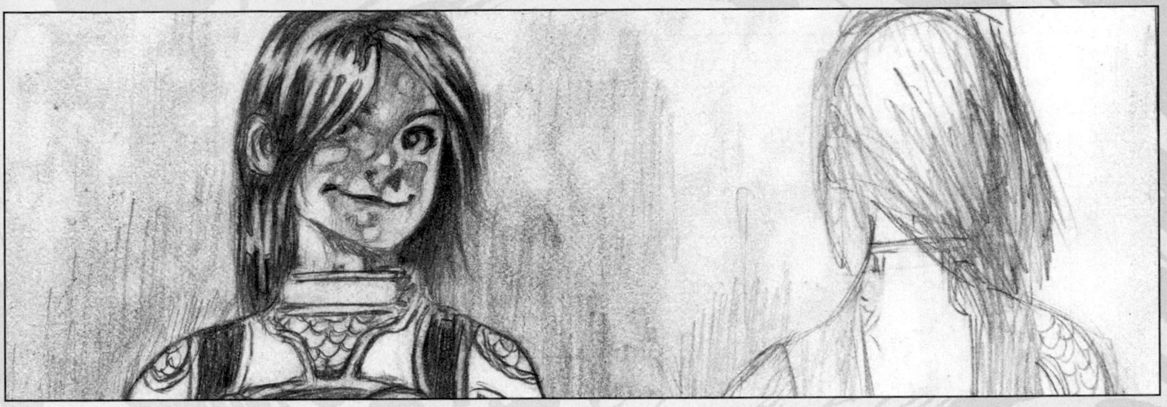

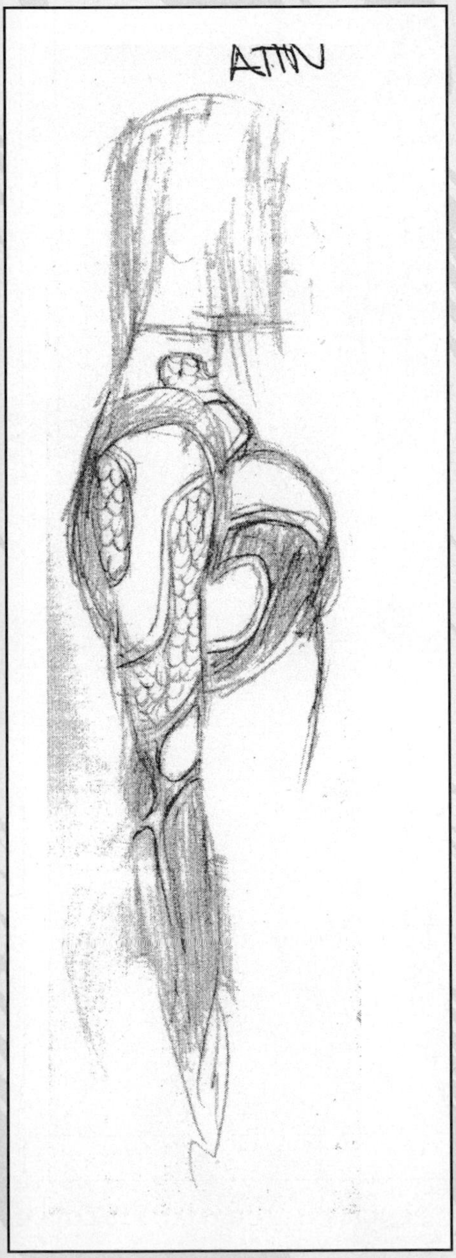
ATTN

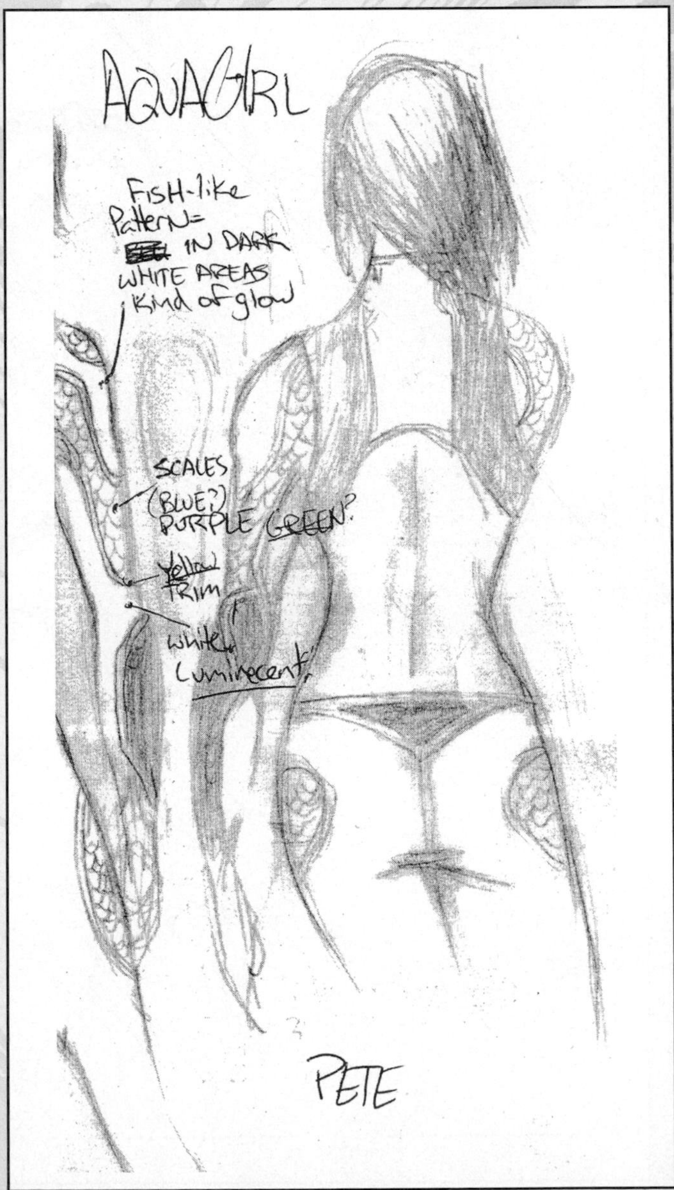
AQUAGIRL
FISH-like Pattern= IN DARK WHITE AREAS kind of glow
SCALES (BLUE?) PURPLE GREEN?
Yellow TRIM
white Luminecent
PETE

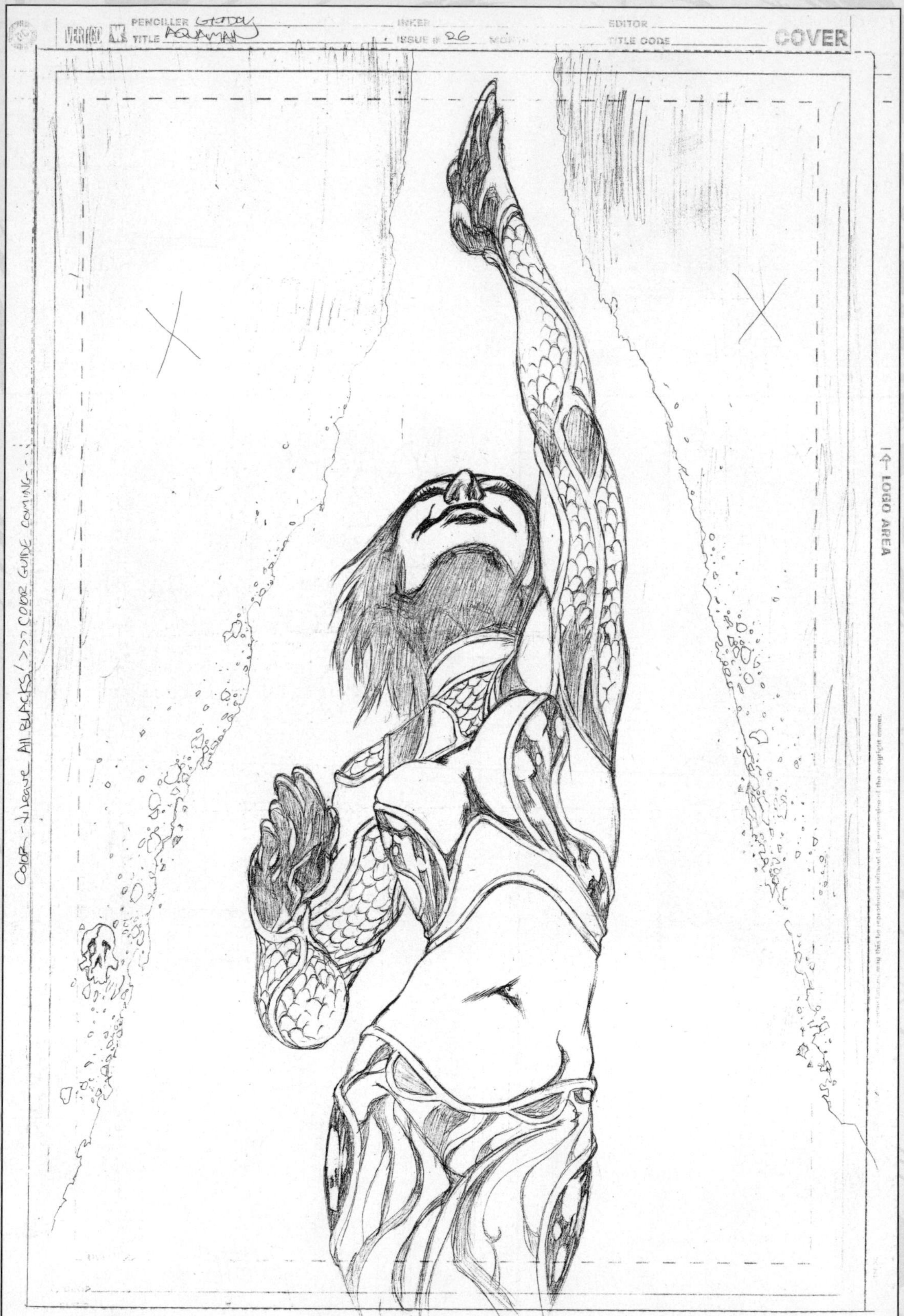
PENCILLER
TITLE AQUAMAN
INKER
ISSUE # 26
EDITOR
TITLE CODE
COVER
LOGO AREA

PENCILS TO AQUAMAN #26 COVER